VIEWS OF THE
SALISH SEA

One Hundred and Fifty Years of Change
around the Strait of Georgia

HOWARD MACDONALD STEWART

HARBOUR
PUBLISHING

INTRODUCTION

What is the Strait of Georgia?

THE STRAIT OF GEORGIA, together with the Strait of Juan de Fuca to the west of it and Puget Sound to the south, are now known collectively as the Salish Sea, in recognition of the Indigenous culture that developed over millenniums on the shores of these linked bodies of water. The focus of this book is the Strait of Georgia, what we can term the North Salish Sea, a discrete inland sea that is some 300 kilometres long and, on average, about 40 kilometres wide. It is delineated from Puget Sound and the Strait of Juan de Fuca by a string of small islands that straddles today's Canada–US border. It can be reached by ship from the open Pacific Ocean only through narrow passages between these islands or others along the northern edge of the sea.

Many more islands line its periphery and the mouths of deep fjords along its northeastern shore.

Oral historian Imbert Orchard noted that the Strait's coastline is "complicated… [with] so many island and mountain peaks—to say nothing of bays, narrows, inlets, sounds and channels—it's not at all easy to grasp."[1] Two centuries before, British navigator Peter Puget, sailing with George Vancouver in the 1790s, had remarked: "High snowy mountains, unfathomable inlets…steep rocky shores… The change in so small a distance is truly wonderful, even at the termination of these inlets high snowy mountains rise immediately at their back."[2] The sudden changes in elevation from coastal mountain peaks to the adjacent sea floor in places like Desolation Sound are the greatest in North America. In many places, cliffs, steep promontories, rocky islands and treacherous reefs punctuate forbidding shorelines. Elsewhere, flat stretches, known as the Nanaimo Lowland on Vancouver Island and the Georgia Lowland on the Mainland, spread up to 25 kilometres back from the sea. The rich delta of the Fraser River is an extension of this Georgia Lowland.

Geologically speaking, the Strait of Georgia and Puget Sound lie within a coastal trough that extends from southeastern Alaska to the Gulf of California, formed more than 150 million years ago when converging continental plates caused a downfolding of the Earth's crust. Over time, the remains of countless marine organisms and sediments eroded from the surrounding mountainous land

Pages 10–11: Sea lions on Mitlenatch Island in the northern Strait, with a backdrop of Mainland mountains. Mitlenatch Island is now a marine park.

Boomer Jerritt photo

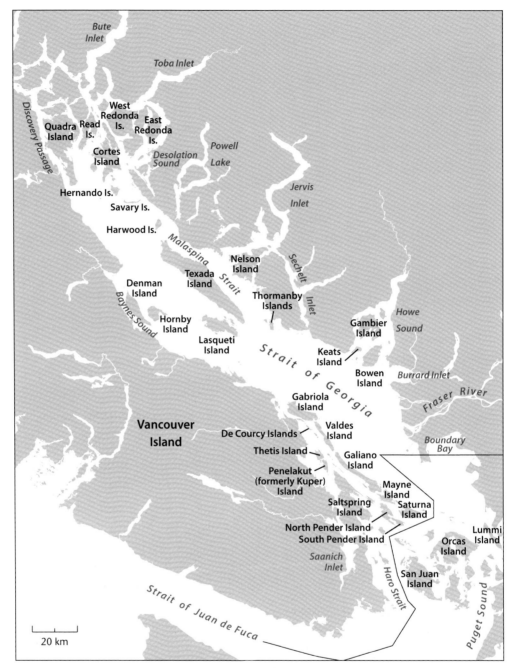

Figure 1: The Strait of Georgia, or North Salish Sea

accumulated in this depression and were formed under pressure into sedimentary rocks. The plates continued to collide and fold until a few million years ago, sometimes exerting such pressure that the rocks melted and then cooled to form igneous intrusions. The depression that forms the Strait assumed its present form about a million years ago.

The Strait today is surrounded by uplifted sedimentary and igneous rock that forms the Vancouver Island Mountain Range to the west and the Coast Range to the east. Vast lobes of ice from the Cordilleran ice sheet have advanced and retreated at least four times in the last million years, and the repeated combination of rivers of ice and melting glaciers has left deep U-shaped coastal valleys, interrupted drainage patterns

14

and unconsolidated deposits of material. Through the more recent glacial period, even as ice covered all but the highest peaks, extensive volcanic activity continued in the Coast Mountains. Other geological processes—including down-warping, glacial scouring and erosion—have continually modified the landscape. Savary, Harwood and James islands, for example, were all created when moraine material from melting glaciers was swept down the valleys onto outwash plains. Fjords along the Mainland coast continued to be deeply scoured by glaciers, while the main channel of the Strait remained relatively stable. The Strait is deepest—430 metres—off the east coast of Gabriola Island, but is only 55 metres deep on average. More recently, as the climate warmed and the glaciers retreated, the rising sea flooded coastal lowlands, and land depressed by ice slowly rebounded. The current equilibrium between land and sea was established around eleven thousand years ago.

These geological changes all affected the local climate on the Strait, though its cool dry summers, mild wet winters and relatively long growing seasons result mostly from its mid-latitude location and the warm currents sweeping across the Pacific. The mountains of Vancouver Island and on Washington state's Olympic Peninsula, across the Strait of Juan de Fuca, protect the region from most Pacific storms: the winds in the Strait normally range from 7 to 25 kilometres per hour, though storms occasionally bring gusts in excess of 90 kilometres per hour. The waves rarely reach over 2 metres high. More hazardous to navigation is fog, which can roll in over the

Looking across Howe Sound at the Mainland mountains from Hopkins Landing, near Gibsons. The drops from mountaintop to sea floor along the Strait's Mainland shore are some of the greatest in North America.

Dean van't Schip photo

northern Strait especially in winter, and over the southern islands in late summer.

Unlike this relatively uniform and temperate climate, the sea itself is highly changeable around the Strait. Twice a day it is swept by tides that rise and fall up to 6 metres. In some places, these tides gently expose and then flood flat beaches; in others, they drive roaring tidal rapids through narrow channels. Local currents shift endlessly around the Strait, though they tend overall to circulate counter-clockwise; they can run at over 15 kilometres per hour through southern channels, while those in the north can exceed 25 kilometres per hour. Seeing these narrow passages change quickly from millponds into raging torrents is an experience not soon forgotten, particularly if witnessed from a small boat. Yet water flushes far less through the Strait than in the open Pacific Ocean because the island barriers at the northern and southern ends restrict how much the water can move and mix.

Water temperatures in the Strait can range from 0°C in winter around the estuaries, where fresh water from the rivers meets salt water from the ocean, up to 24°C in summer in parts of Desolation Sound, where the tides circulate far less. Generally the water in the Strait is clearest and saltiest at its northern and southern ends, but rising and falling water levels in surrounding streams—especially the Fraser River, which contributes 80 percent of the fresh water that flows into the Strait—can cause these values to fluctuate. This is especially true when high waters on the Fraser in spring and early summer affect the clarity, salinity and temperature of the Strait's waters far to the north and south of the river mouth.

Given the great range of marine and shoreline habitats, it's no surprise that the Strait supports over 200 species of fish, some 300 species of invertebrates, more

Strollers enjoy the sun over the Strait at White Rock, south of Vancouver.

David Nunuk photo

than 130 species of marine birds and 16 kinds of marine mammals. Similarly, the region's roughly 500 species of marine vegetation range from tiny phytoplankton to giant kelp forests. A key element of the Strait's great biological productivity is its river estuaries, particularly the Fraser's, which contribute many of the nutrients necessary to support the Strait's diverse food chains. From zooplankton to salmon, seabirds to whales, the salt marshes and other wetlands around the estuaries act as nurseries for the young of a wide range of sea life, including critical intermediate feeders such as herring and other forage fish.

A short modern history of the Strait

Humans are inextricably linked with the other species living in and around the Strait. First settled after the retreat of the Wisconsin ice sheets about 10,000 years ago, the region long supported a large human population that depended upon the Strait's copious and diverse marine life to survive. Archaeologists cannot agree whether the first migrants came by land or sea, but they do concur that by about 3,000 years ago a highly developed culture had evolved in the area. As many as 50,000 or more Indigenous people lived around the Strait of Georgia in the mid-eighteenth century.

European navigators, mostly Spanish, British and Russian, first visited the northeast Pacific coast seeking trade routes, but they also found abundant sea otter, whose pelts could fetch a fortune in China. Late in the eighteenth century, following land and sea trade routes from Mexico and Alaska, the smallpox virus also arrived. Captain Vancouver's crews witnessed the devastating impact of this frightening disease on the Strait's Indigenous settlements in the 1790s. The coming decades brought

Table 1: Demographic change on the settlers' Strait: local populations, 1881–1981[3]

1881 Population of BC: 49,459 (~ 2/3 on or near the Strait)
Victoria area: Victoria: 5,925; North and South Saanich: 488
Vancouver Island, north of Victoria: Cowichan (and Saltspring Island): 848; Nanaimo & "Noonas" (Nanoose) Bay: 2,803; Comox/Alberni: 271
Vancouver area: New Westminster: 1,500

1901 Population of BC: 178,657 (~ 60% on or near the Strait)
Victoria area: Victoria: 20,919
VI, north of Victoria: Cowichan area: 3,613; Nanaimo area: 12,715; Comox area: 3,493
Vancouver area: Vancouver: 27,010; New Westminster: 6,499; Richmond: 4,802; Delta: 5,074
Islands (1891 figures): Gabriola: 125; Mayne: 197; Saltspring: 436

1921 Population of BC: 524,528 (~ 2/3 on or near the Strait)
Victoria area: Victoria: 38,727; Saanich: 14,693
VI, north of Victoria: Duncan area: 7,445; Ladysmith: 1,967; Nanaimo area: 9,068; Comox area: 14,018
Vancouver area: Vancouver: 117,217; New Westminster: 14,495; North Vancouver city & district: 10,602; West Vancouver: 2,434; Port Moody: 1,030
Mainland, north of Vancouver: Howe Sound: 3,844; Powell River area: 3,599
Islands: "The Islands" (southern): 3,804

1941 Population of BC: 817,861 (~ 2/3 on or near the Strait)
Victoria area: Victoria: 44,068
VI, north of Victoria: Duncan area: 13,835; Ladysmith: 1,706; Nanaimo (city only): 6,635; Courtenay: 1,737; Cumberland: 885
Vancouver area: "Greater Vancouver": 351,491, of which Vancouver: 275,353; New Westminster: 21,967; North Vancouver city & district: 14,845; West Vancouver: 8,362
Mainland, north of Vancouver: Powell River area: 7,624

1961 Population of BC: 1,629,082 (~ 2/3 on or near the Strait)
Victoria area: Victoria: 54,941; Saanich and Central Saanich: 51,828; Sidney: 1,558
VI, north of Victoria: Duncan town: 3,726; Lake Cowichan: 2,149; Ladysmith: 2,173; Nanaimo: 14,135; Parksville: 1,183; Qualicum Beach: 759; Courtenay: 3,485; Cumberland: 1,303; Comox: 1,756; Campbell River: 3,737
Vancouver area: Vancouver metropolitan area: 790,165, of which Vancouver: 384,522; Richmond: 43,323; New Westminster: 33,654; North Vancouver city & district: 64,627; White Rock: 6,453; Surrey: 70,838; West Vancouver: 25,454; Port Moody: 4,789
Mainland, north of Vancouver: Squamish: 1,557; Gibsons Landing: 1,091; Sechelt: 488; Powell River area: 13,368

1981 Population of BC: 2,744,467 (~ 2/3 on or near the Strait)
Victoria area: Capital Regional District: 249,473
VI, north of Victoria: Cowichan Valley Regional District: 52,701; Nanaimo Regional District: 77,101, of which Nanaimo: 47,060; Parksville: 5,216; and Qualicum Beach: 2,844
Vancouver area: Vancouver metropolitan area: 1,268,183, of which Vancouver: 414,281; Burnaby: 136,494; North Vancouver city & district: 99,319; Delta: 74,692; West Vancouver: 35,728; New Westminster: 38,550; White Rock: 13,550; and Port Moody: 14,917
Mainland, north of Vancouver: Squamish Regional District: 18,928; Sunshine Coast Regional District: 15,503, of which Gibsons: 2,594 and Sechelt: 1,096; and Powell River Regional District: 19,364
Islands (mid-1970s): all "Islands Trust" islands: ~ 10,000[4]

---

more waves of smallpox and new endemic diseases such as measles and influenza. Salish speakers of the Strait appear to have been particularly hard hit, suffering the effects of disease combined with aggression from neighbouring tribes.

Early in the nineteenth century, as Indigenous populations reeled from the onslaught of exotic diseases for which they had neither immunity nor treatment, a few outsiders began to live in the area. The Hudson's Bay Company built trading forts at Victoria and Nanaimo, and on the Fraser River. These would have been exciting and lucrative places for Indigenous people to visit. In 1849, when the British established a Crown colony on Vancouver Island, the Strait was still a very long voyage from Europe or the eastern coast of North America. The men in the forts, however, could see that a protected sea, a mild climate, abundant resources and available land made for a very pleasant place to live. They could also see the masses of fish that swarmed the river mouths and beaches, the timber that surpassed even the most spectacular forests east of the mountains and the promise of wealth from coal and valuable minerals. They knew that railways and steamships were transforming other places and that Anglo-American expansion had just leaped across the continent to California. Two tiny steamships already plied the Strait of Georgia, and it would not be long before steam locomotives reached the Pacific and opened up a new market for Vancouver Island coal. Ocean-going steamships would also soon reach the northeast Pacific Ocean, and they too would need coal. A symbiotic relationship soon emerged between the Royal Navy's growing need for coal and the settlers' need for naval guns to secure their claims to their new land.

Although the Indigenous people along the coast had always thrived on food from the sea, European settlers were expected to deforest the land and then plow it to plant food crops. The absence of deforested and plowed land around the Strait provided a plausible rationale—at least in settler law—to take over virtually all this land in a few short decades. Once the British Empire had declared its domain over the land, local representatives of the Crown could then sell it, and the British settlers who bought it would legitimise the Crown's claim by transforming this land into tidy British farms. That was the theory at least, and a hardy few invested decades of almost unimaginably hard labour trying to make it come true. Although most of the soil, except around a few rivers, turned out to be very poor, the timber was rich, the mining lucrative, the climate gentle, the landscape breathtaking and the fishing and hunting exceptional.

By the end of the nineteenth century, the Strait of Georgia had become a significant new outpost of Eurasian settlement in the Americas. An "all-Canadian" transcontinental railway linked markets in California and around the Pacific to new ones in eastern North America, and a growing fleet of steamers plied the inland sea. Both means of transportation helped transform the Strait, introducing the order and predictability of the industrial age. Lighthouses, buoys and publications predicting marine weather and tides all made marine travel safer, cheaper and more convenient. Such changes helped usher in a virtual resource rush around the inland sea.

Great expansion in economic activity went hand in hand with rapid growth in the settler population (see Table 1, page 18) and gave rise to a network of new settlements around the Strait. By the 1890s Indigenous people were a minority in their traditional homeland, and they were almost fully dispossessed and marginalised by the time World War I started. The Strait's many arms helped keep Indigenous communities apart, as did the government's Indian reserve system with its allotment of small tracts of land where Indigenous people were now expected to live. Never did the Indigenous people here rise up en masse to protest their dispossession as they did elsewhere, but they never stopped resisting it. And they remained a critical component of the local labour force well into the next century, working in settlers' mines, canneries, mills and fields.

The bloom on the rose had begun to fade by 1914, however, as the Strait's settlers sent thousands of boys to the greatest of Europe's wars. Until then, settlers on the inland sea had gone from strength to strength for decades. The naval base near Victoria still guarded the entrance to the Strait, but Vancouver had become its heart. After the arrival of the railway, that smoky mill town between Burrard Inlet and the mouth of the Fraser River grew rapidly, as Victoria's city fathers had feared it would. By the time the Panama Canal opened in 1914, Vancouver was drawing resources from all over the Strait and beyond, transforming them a little and shipping them out alongside Canadian grain and minerals from the rest of BC.

Signs of settlers' overexploitation of the Strait's resource wealth were already apparent to some before the Great War. A railway-building accident on the Fraser in 1913 had catastrophic effects on salmon runs that were already being overfished. A few vocal critics had begun to denounce the profligate harvesting of coastal forests, and their criticisms gradually appeared in government documents. But a sharp economic downturn, also in 1913, followed by the savage European war, then a global economic meltdown and another truly global war all impeded progress in resource conservation or righting historic injustices on the Strait. The rich resources of the inland sea still sustained many people between the two world wars. The sea also continued to absorb all waste consigned to it, including vast streams of organic and chemical waste from newly built pulp and paper plants on Howe Sound and Malaspina Strait, and copious quantities of sewage from rapidly growing towns all around the Strait. Just as urban sewers were seen as an efficient way to keep toxic human waste away from people and streams, pulp and paper plants could be seen as a profitable way to reduce the dangerously heavy fogs created by the burning of waste wood left over from the forest industry. And the sea appeared to have an infinite absorptive capacity.

Meanwhile, the Strait matured as a place for recreation and restoration during these years. Harried urbanites could find temporary relief relaxing by its shores, a short steamer or train ride from the city. People could savour the joys of the Strait's dry, mild summers by swimming in the sea or riding excursion boats to shoreline hotels. Summer camps opened for city children, while those who could built summer cottages for the whole family. Others from farther afield also found solace and places to recreate and re-create themselves in creative ways. Broken men from both wars restored themselves on its quieter shores. Growing numbers of people shared the joys of sport fishing.

After World War II, a new world order emerged with Anglo-America at the centre of the global economy. The Strait became an appendage of this North American imperial power, as it had been of the British Empire, and the region experienced another period of unprecedented economic growth and prosperity during the thirty years after the war. A growing network of roads and ferries offered car drivers access to peninsulas and islands that could previously be approached only by sea. Seaplanes reached remoter places, hastening the demise of the coastal steamers in the 1950s but increasing opportunities for settlement, resource extraction and recreation. As leisure activities assumed a larger role in many people's lives and livelihoods, beaches, seaside parks, summer camps and cottages, and small boats around the Strait all became more important than they had been. With them came growing alarm about the increasing pollution and the real-estate developers who threatened people's enjoyment of these pleasures. Indigenous people neared the bottom of their abyss as their jobs in fishing, farming and forestry gradually disappeared.

A new generation of anthropologists, archaeologists, writers and artists brought forward new narratives about Indigenous people in this post-war era. This helped make new space for Indigenous people to tell their own stories, while more people in settler society began to reflect on the Strait's First Nations experience. Writers such as Rachel Carson and local converts such as Roderick Haig-Brown challenged unbridled resource exploitation, calling on governments and citizens to adopt "environmentalism." And they gained support from growing numbers of town dwellers fed up with pollution. Organisations such as the Scientific Pollution and Environmental Control Society (SPEC) became influential for a while and warned of threats posed to the inland sea by mill effluent, sewage, oil spills and "superports."

The five interwoven histories of the Strait that follow flesh out the details of this tapestry. Threading their way through these chapters is a large and colourful cast of characters: navigators and other travellers, Indigenous people and their leaders, workers and entrepreneurs, politicians and civil servants, scientists and engineers, writers and artists, conservationists and environmentalists. And among them all is a recurrent theme: the fear of loss. British colonisers early on feared that Americans might seize control of their rich new Strait, for example, whereas Indigenous people feared the loss of access to their traditional lands and resources. Many later worried about overharvesting of fish and wood, while others grew increasingly alarmed about pollution in the waters around them. Pollution and various other influences were increasingly viewed as threats to citizens' enjoyment of the vast recreational values of the Strait.

Despite these many changing fears, the stories that follow are not traditional gloomy environmental histories about relentless decline and looming threats. Instead, they highlight the diverse and forever-shifting ways in which the Strait has affected the people who live around it, and how they have affected the Strait. The stories will hopefully help to make the Strait a richer place for readers—a more real and multi-dimensional place. They may contribute to building the kind of nuanced understanding that we, as a community of shoreline people, need if we are to effectively manage and care for this complex and precious sea and its shores, now and into the future.

THE SEA AS BARRIER, THE SEA AS HIGHWAY | 1

A PROTECTED LITTLE SEA like the Strait of Georgia doesn't present the same challenges to human movement as the vast expanses of an ocean. Yet whether any body of water is a barrier or an opportunity for human travel has much to do with the skills, knowledge and technology of those who navigate it. For the Indigenous people who lived along the Strait's many hundreds of kilometres of coastline for millenniums before 1849, the sea presented a ready route of travel, a nearly endless supply of food and a means of purification, but it also brought life-threatening storms and tidal rapids. By the early nineteenth century, Indigenous people had adapted to life by the sea in myriad ways and were moving themselves and their goods around it with ease in canoes wrought from giant cedars.

The arrival of seafarers from distant places initiated a period in which relations between the inland sea and human movement would begin to change frequently. Although the Strait always acted as both a barrier and a highway, rapidly shifting technologies redefined the role of the sea and people's narratives about it.

The late-eighteenth-century ocean voyages of British navigators James Cook and George Vancouver helped transform the outside world's understanding of the northeastern shore of the Pacific Ocean and speeded the region's integration into trans-Pacific and global trading networks. The Hudson's Bay Company (HBC), a British fur-trading company with a history dating back to 1670, began moving west into the region during the first half of the nineteenth century when it incorporated the Strait of Georgia into its broader "Columbia" region. The sea links with Britain, Hawaii and California established by the HBC would underpin the export-based economy that emerged on the inland sea later in the century. In the process, the HBC initiated now familiar patterns of movement among its establishments on the Lower Fraser River and in Victoria and Nanaimo. It moved goods and people, overcoming some of the Strait's navigational challenges with the inland sea's first steam-powered vessels.

Colonisation by a seafaring people, 1849–1880s

British colonisers of the land around the Strait who came after the HBC were confident in their ability to seize opportunities the global seas offered to those with the knowledge and courage to master them. The British were enamoured

Pages 22–23: BC Ferries vessel approaching the busy terminal at Horseshoe Bay. By the final decades of the twentieth century, such large car ferries had become essential for overcoming the marine barrier.

Murray Foubister/Flickr photo

with the sea, not just as a highway to success but as a key determinant of their national character. In the 1870s, novelist Robert Louis Stevenson suggested Britons felt possessive towards the sea, which symbolised their nation even more than the imperial lion. The sea, he said, was their bulwark, "the scene of…[our] greatest triumphs and dangers, and…[we] claim it as our own."[1] A decade later, an article on the "origins of the English" described the British as "folk of the sea, to whom the sea is a true home."[2] Similarly, a turn-of-the-century children's history extolled the British boy's "racial love for the sea" and his "especial birthright to the blue waters."[3]

The British love affair with the sea was transcendent but also practical. Long before John Masefield became Britain's poet laureate, his poem "Sea Fever" exclaimed he had to "go down to the sea again" to respond to a "wild and clear call [that]… could not be denied." This sea, woven into their character, they believed, stood for much that was admirable in that character: beauty, power, conquest, redemption, questing, life, healing and soothing. The British also recognised the practical value of this love match. Young Britons learned that their global dominance of commerce resulted from British command of the seas. These were people who could believe destiny had prepared them to control a small sea on the far side of the world. Britain was one of the few imperial powers that—like Spain and the United States—could exercise real power on such a distant sea. The colonies of Vancouver Island and later British Columbia were among the most remote places of mid-nineteenth century Europeans' "known world."

Virtually all colonists at mid-century came to the Strait by sea, and most ocean travel to the Strait would continue to be in sailing ships until the end of the nineteenth century. Getting there was considerably more challenging than sailing within it. Sea travel times between the east and west coasts of the US had already fallen considerably by the early 1850s, thanks to rapid improvements in maritime services stimulated by the gold rush in California. However, the usual trip from London to Victoria—around Cape Horn and usually via the Hawaiian Islands to take advantage of winds and trade opportunities—meant five or six months in a closely confined space, if all went well. The British Colonial Office considered the option of transporting emigrants via the Isthmus of Panama instead of around Cape Horn to reduce the length of the journey. It eventually decided it wouldn't be worth the risks associated with Panama's steamy climate and its sometimes troublesome residents.

William Lomas, who would later become an Indian agent in the Cowichan Valley on Vancouver Island, left behind an account of his passage from Liverpool via Cape Horn in 1862. If Lomas felt any "racial love of the sea" at the outset of his voyage, it was likely much diminished by the time he reached Victoria. He was prosperous enough to travel in relative comfort, but it was still a daunting voyage:

> July 11: The feelings of an emigrant on leaving the shores of his native land must be felt to be understood…dear ones whom you have seen, perhaps for the last time, will flash across your mind and do not tend to make the day a happy one.

The endless days of seasickness:

> July 13: You can have no idea of feeling sick for three or four days together without the slightest relief.
>
> July 15: So sick.

Months of sharing close and uncomfortable quarters with unpleasant travelling companions:

> July 22: [T]he most disgraceful fellows I have ever been amongst. Most…cannot speak ten words without two or three oaths, and they are all a drunken lot…cabin is very close.

Bad food and services:

> July 26: [T]he mustard and pepper have been sent unground and no mill to grind with. The cooks are disgusting fellows, very dirty, and scarcely ever sober since we started. The doctor…always drinking.

Uneasiness about the new country:

> August 20: Saw some Columbian [i.e., British Columbian] papers from April which gave very black accounts of the hardships of persons arriving without at least £100. Many of our passengers are wishing themselves back in England, but…by God's help, I must succeed.

Then, after a month and a half at sea, except for the terrifying prospect of sailing through the mountainous waves, snowstorms and icebergs of Cape Horn that still lay ahead, things began to look up:

> August 25: If I were starting again I could pay my passage by taking out articles to sell on board…onions sell at 3d each…2/ [2 shillings] is refused for cheese per lb. Wilson and I have bought two hams, nearly 50 lbs weight. We can sell for 1/6 [1 shilling, 6 pence] but are waiting until it is 2/.

> October 28: Sold my champagne at 50% profit.

Otherwise, conditions did not improve as they approached Victoria:

> November 4: Several rats are found, dead, in the water casks. This adds considerably to the flavour. The biscuits, too, are all alive and…the maggots are of a very large breed.

His boat, the *Silistria*, didn't stop at Honolulu and therefore made Victoria after only 128 days at sea, "the shortest passage of any sailing vessel that has been here yet."[4]

As ocean-going steam vessels gradually replaced sailing ships and transcontinental railways reached the Pacific in California, the average time it took to get to the Strait from Britain declined steadily. A dozen years after Lomas's journey, a future trader and politician on the Strait named Michael Manson made his trip out in barely thirty days. He had crossed the Atlantic by steamship to New York, travelled by train to San Francisco and then headed north by coastal steamer to Victoria.

Steam was also gradually replacing sail on the Strait itself, yet well into the twentieth century sailboats were still widely used for moving people and goods. Sailing vessels equipped with compass, lead, sextant and chronometer were not well adapted to navigating the inland sea. Although the Strait was calm much of the time, winter winds could be fierce and currents poured in and out, endlessly changing among the countless islands and reefs. The long, narrow fjords of the northeast shore were especially challenging for navigators, and sweeping the sea's north and south entrances were tides that could run like a mountain river in spring.

The Strait could be dangerous for navigators of any vessel in the 1850s and '60s, but particularly for gold miners eager to reach the Fraser River gold fields. Determined to get from Victoria to the river mouth, they would cross the sea in any craft they could find. A colonial official at the time reported that many miners perished on "hazardous voyages" through a "maze of archipelagos" then across a "stormy and dangerous gulf" that was challenging even for boats far larger and sounder than theirs.[5] And judging from the many reports of wrecks and salvage operations published in the *Colonist,* the following decades—the 1860s and '70s—were good years to be a salvager on the Strait. After the gold rush abated, coal ships in and out of Nanaimo figured in many navigational mishaps. So did vessels going through Plumper Pass (now Active Pass) and Seymour Narrows.

Homeric accounts of trips around the inland sea in those years describe unpredictable adventures in the face of currents, wind, fog and uncharted reefs and rocks. Writer Frederick Marsh recounted the story of a very old man from North Pender Island sailing to Nanaimo for the first time in the 1870s. Travelling through calms, fogs and rapids, he met Indigenous people boiling dogfish oil on the beach and Portuguese Joe Silvey and his First Nations family in their beach home. He spent four days waiting out a fog before finally completing the 80-kilometre journey. In 1881, the *Colonist* newspaper described a similar odyssey by vacationers sailing for days from Saanich to Cortes Island through a gauntlet of riptides and gales.[6]

Ottawa assumed responsibility for marine space after BC's entry into Confederation in 1871 and soon began to address the Strait's navigational challenges. The Department of Marine and Fisheries' (DMF) local agent in this "distant colony" was named "Inspector of Lights" and "Inspector of Steamboats," as lighthouses (see photograph page 29) and other navigational aids were early federal priorities on the Strait. Having inherited a single lightship at the mouth of the Fraser from the colonial authority, the federal government built a lighthouse at the entrance to Burrard Inlet in 1875 and one on Nanaimo's Entrance Island in 1877. Buoys were installed or upgraded on Burrard Inlet, English Bay, Gabriola Reef and Trincomali Channel.

An informal and poorly organised pilot service also helped tame the Strait's hazards, though its pilots were often drunk and it didn't appear to be a popular job. An 1869 regulation stipulated: "Pilots taken to sea on any vessel against their will shall be entitled to claim from the master or owner of such vessel the sum of five dollars per diem until the date of their arrival at the Port of Victoria."[7] After an 1873 shipwreck on Plumper Pass, Ottawa began to organise a more formal system.

The federal government was also prepared to invest in BC's ports, which would clearly become important assets once the railway reached the coast and would make the Strait a vital part of the chain linking the new dominion's resource industries with Asian markets. Although Burrard Inlet was recognised early on as one of the best locations for the rail terminal, it had no sizable non-Indigenous settlements until the 1860s. To facilitate navigation, the British Admiralty published marine charts using the hydrographic survey carried out by Captain George Richards between 1860 and 1862, and soon sawmills on Burrard Inlet were exporting lumber across the Pacific. From the mid-1860s to the late 1870s, more than forty ocean-going ships loaded lumber on the inlet each year.

Although Burrard Inlet's good entrance and protected anchorage were generally recognised, Victoria's newspapers were given to enumerating the Mainland port's drawbacks. Journalists in the capital reported that the approach to Burrard Inlet

The Georgina Point Lighthouse on Mayne Island around 1880. Ottawa's growing network of lights and buoys helped ships navigate the Strait's dangerous currents, reefs and rocks.
Image A-04588 courtesy of the Royal BC Museum and Archives.

suffered from the treacherous weather of the Strait and that Plumper Pass was often dangerous. The inlet's First and Second Narrows, they noted with disapproval, were barely 270 metres wide and subject to tides running over 16 kilometres per hour in full flood. Furthermore, they warned, American guns placed on the San Juan Islands could easily close the Strait to navigation entirely. Given that Victoria had a keen interest in touting its own local Esquimalt harbour, "the best port on the Pacific," such denunciations were hardly surprising.

While the *Colonist* stoked fears of losing ships on the Strait, two tiny HBC steamers, the *Beaver* (see photograph page 30) and the *Otter,* were serving as towboats there by the late 1850s. These boats were gluttons for wood but independent of capricious winds. They had proven their worth to HBC trading posts in Victoria and Langley and had shipped salt fish, lumber and coal to San Francisco. Now, as towboats, they helped guide ocean-going sailboats safely through tricky inland waters; a growing fleet of such tugs was soon towing these vessels through the Strait's many narrows.

The number of steam vessels on the Strait grew through the 1860s and early 1870s. Although early steamers could be as unreliable as the pilots and few stayed in business long, these boats became more regular and more predictable over time. They also became larger. Soon coastal steamships carrying ever more passengers and freight rendered the inland sea more familiar to settlers and began to transform life in the growing shoreline communities. Settlers could receive goods and even mail, and could ship what they produced to the world.

As the Strait became a highway for people and goods coming to the Pacific coast and for goods flowing from North America to markets abroad, it also posed a growing barrier to Victoria's aspirations of being the dominant port in BC. When the colonies of Vancouver Island and British Columbia came together in 1866, the *Colonist* heralded the "bringing together of people from the two sides of the Gulf of Georgia."[8]

Early reports had spoken glowingly of the abundance of good harbours around the South Coast; however, it became clear there were two principal contenders: Victoria–Esquimalt and Burrard Inlet. Competition between them intensified as merchants and speculators on both sides of the Strait vied for dominance. In the end, however, the outcome was decided by the location of the terminus for the "all-Canadian" transcontinental railway.

The age of rail was well under way elsewhere, and the railway's relatively late arrival on the inland sea was the object of much anticipation and speculation. Victoria's merchants, led by Amor de Cosmos and what historian Martin Robin called Victoria's "shopocracy,"[9] were determined that a transcontinental railroad should extend to the southern tip of Vancouver Island and that their city should be its terminus. They even suggested that BC's entry into Confederation ought to be made contingent on Victoria being named the terminus. Seldom missing an opportunity to stress the dangers facing ships bound for Burrard Inlet, Victoria's boosters declared that their city was "much closer to Europe and Asia" (about 120 kilometres closer by sea) and their proposed Bute Inlet route (see Figure 2, page 31) would be much better than the treacherous Fraser Canyon leading to Burrard Inlet.

Victoria's lobbyists did not seriously consider the challenge of laying rail along the steep shore of Bute Inlet, then across furious tidal rapids, but they aimed to demonstrate that the Strait represented no insurmountable barrier to a transcontinental railway. To prove that the northern Strait could be easily spanned, proponents of the Victoria terminus used charts prepared by George Vancouver in the 1790s. And like their "best port on the Pacific" arguments in support of the harbour at Esquimalt, they proclaimed that a railway on Bute Inlet would avoid the impassable Fraser Canyon and Burrard Inlet's treacherous currents. The *Colonist* also maintained: "To suppose that the time will never come again that Great Britain will be at war with the United

After decades helping others navigate the Strait's hazards, the SS *Beaver* fell victim to them. An inebriated crew wrecked her on Prospect Point in 1888, the same year a lighthouse was erected nearby.

Image A-00014 courtesy of the Royal BC Museum and Archives.

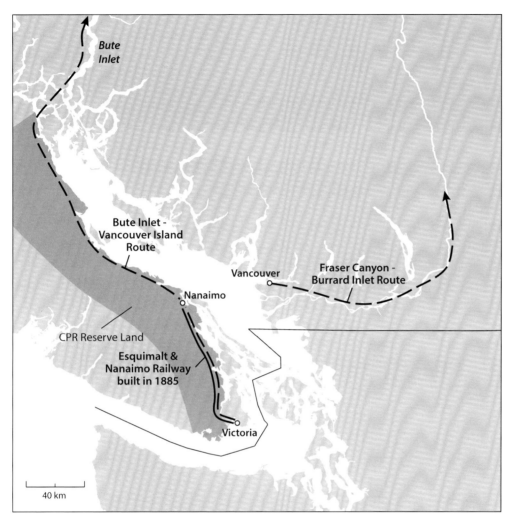

Figure 2: Those who believed the transcontinental railway's terminus should be Victoria favoured the Bute Inlet route from the interior over the Fraser Canyon-to-Burrard Inlet one.

States is to believe that the Millennium is close at hand. Twice during the past fifteen years has a war been imminent."[10] The British navy, they claimed, could readily secure the Bute Inlet route from American aggression, which would be impossible for a railroad following the Lower Fraser. After short hops onto and off of what was then still known as Valdes Island, they said, the railway could follow the flat, sheltered coast of Vancouver Island to Victoria. This route had the added advantage of easing access to Vancouver Island's rich natural resources.

Fear of losing the Strait's bounty to American expansionism was not unfounded, in part because railway building was more advanced south of the border. By the 1870s, most settlers on the Strait had reached the West Coast on American railways. Had there been hostilities, American forces travelling by rail would have been able to move more easily than Canadians or British soldiers, who would have been denied travel on American rails. Historian Richard White noted in the book *Railroaded* that an American engineer conducting a preliminary survey for the Northern Pacific Railway sought information about the Bute Inlet route, in case Vancouver Island became part of the United States.

With the arrival of the transcontinental railway in 1886, the quiet backwater known as Gastown, seen here in 1884, became Vancouver.

Image A-01009 courtesy of the Royal BC Museum and Archives.

Ultimately, Victoria's railway proposal suffered because of gaps in George Vancouver's mapping. He had failed to mark the narrow channels that separate Quadra, Read, Maurelle and Sonora Islands, labelling these four islands "Valdes Island" on his map. Considering the fierce tidal rapids running through some of these passages, one can understand why his crews neglected to investigate them. When more detailed surveys in the 1860s and '70s revealed the complexity of the Strait's northern perimeter, however, the Bute Inlet route looked less appealing.

Backers in Victoria were devastated when the Burrard Inlet terminus (see photograph page 32 and see Figure 2, page 31) was chosen in 1877. For the Canadian Pacific Railway (CPR), the challenges of the Fraser Canyon looked less daunting than the Strait's marine barrier. In fact, the transcontinental railway never reached Victoria, and Victoria has never dominated the economy of the Strait as Vancouver has. Victoria had prevailed over New Westminster to become the capital of the new colony when Vancouver Island and British Columbia were joined in 1866. And it had won the first round of competition between ports, being chosen over Burrard Inlet, Nanaimo and Alberni as the site for the British navy's main base on the northeast Pacific. In hindsight, these earlier victories must have bolstered Victoria's confidence to unreasonable heights, because its bid for the railway terminus does not seem plausible—140 years later, the Strait still has not been bridged. But for Victoria's settler elite in the 1870s, Burrard Inlet's bid for the railhead was akin to Surrey proposing today to become the urban core of the Lower Mainland. Both sides understood that in the age of rail, the terminus city would dominate the west coast of Canada. The success of Burrard Inlet's bid was never really in serious doubt, and its success helped ensure a rapidly growing settler economy focused on the Strait.

During these first decades of colonisation, the region was a maritime community similar, for example, to one that had grown up around Chesapeake Bay on the east coast of North America many years earlier. Both were places where most people travelled by water, often paddling or rowing, because roads were mostly bad or nonexistent. What roads there were, such as between Burrard Inlet and New Westminster, were rough trails and stayed that way for decades. The Vancouver

Island shore offered more manageable terrain, but even the Nanaimo to Comox road was a never-ending project in those years, often close to completion but never quite finished. The Nanaimo to Victoria road was similar, and it was eclipsed by the Esquimalt & Nanaimo (E&N) Railway after 1885. As long as most movement between settlements was via the marine highway, places on islands and peninsulas were not at a disadvantage. The Strait's infant settlements strove to open local post offices where passing steamers could deliver mail. Telegraph services and passenger ferries on Burrard Inlet also began in this period.

Both as a practical highway and a dangerous barrier, the Strait was a pervasive presence in settlers' lives. While sailing ships and steamers carried the heavy loads, some settlers bought dugout canoes and some added outriggers to make them more stable. Others hired Indigenous people to paddle for them. Mike Manson, later a prominent trader and politician on the northern Strait, hired an Indigenous canoe and crew to take him and his new bride from Nanaimo to Victoria in 1878. But most settlers, especially those living on the islands in the Strait, preferred rowboats. A few settlers lost their lives while rowing on the Strait each year, from bad luck, ignorance, too much drink or other miscalculations. But they rowed miles to hunt and fish, fetch groceries or visit neighbours. By the early 1880s, they could even row to collect telegrams with news from abroad, as telegraph cables now linked towns on both sides of the inland sea with the world beyond. Such startling technological change was destined to become the norm in the coming decades.

The acceleration of technological change, 1880s–World War I

Technological change—from telephones, wireless telegraphs, railways, universal time and cinema to bicycles, automobiles and airplanes—swept through the Strait during the three decades before World War I. This ever-changing world seemingly stuck on fast-forward made the Strait seem smaller and more easily organised. New technologies diminished or removed some of the barriers posed by the inland sea and facilitated an industrial onslaught on the region's resources, the Strait's "resource rush." Yet these same rapid changes also led many people to see the Strait as a calm and secluded refuge where they might escape the relentless pace of this industrial era.

The inland sea had been the natural focal point for early development in British Columbia, and steamships began to transform it at an accelerating rate as they linked the shores of the Strait more rapidly than sailboats, rowboats, canoes, horses and oxen could. Even while these other forms of transportation remained in use, steamers on the Terminal Steam Navigation Company's Howe Sound Route, for example, had begun to leave the Vancouver dock every morning of the week by 1908, stopping at West Vancouver's Great Northern Cannery, Caulfeild, Eagle Harbour Cannery, Bowen Island, Brunswick Beach (three days a week), Anvil Island, South Valley, Britannia, Potlatch (Thursdays only), Glacier Bay and Squamish. Steamer routes carried passengers to scores of other towns, villages and industrial sites around the Strait. Similarly, though the railway's arrival was not as transformative here as it was on the Prairies, it did accelerate the West Coast's integration with distant continental markets and made the Strait a conduit for evacuating natural resources from hundreds of thousands of square kilometres of Canadian hinterland. Railways also enabled mass immigration into the Strait in a way that ships did not. The speed and scale of this influx of land-hungry settlers and resource-hungry investors contributed greatly to what Richard White called a perpetual winter for Indigenous people, who were increasingly cut off from their traditional lands and resources.

Railroads had been transforming the geography of colonial domains since the mid-nineteenth century, and some have suggested that by 1900 they were "tightening their hold" on political, military, economic and private life as the rail networks became more dense.[11] New rail lines linked with modern port facilities were stimulating the growth of "primate cities" that quickly overshadowed the surrounding communities. And the idea of an all-Canadian transcontinental railway consummated old British dreams of pan-Pacific trade links from resource-rich North America to the ocean's prosperous and heavily populated western shore. Premier Amor de Cosmos had lost his petition in the 1870s to have Victoria declared the port terminus of a transcontinental railway. The Imperial Privy Council in London had declared that Vancouver Island did not need a railway because it already had "sheltered water communication" via the Strait and year-round ports that were "quite adequate to the needs of the population of the Island."[12] Vancouver Islanders, however, would not be denied their railway.

Once it became clear that no railroad would be built along Bute Inlet, Victoria's merchants began to stress the simplicity of ferrying trains across the Strait to Nanaimo. From there, they could complete a transcontinental route into Victoria. Despite bitter complaints from colonists, most of the southeast coast of the Island became out of reach for years after the province transferred a vast tract of "railway reserve" to the federal government in 1883. Almost a quarter of Vancouver Island was offered to whoever could build a railway from Victoria to Seymour Narrows (north of Campbell River). The prize went to coal magnate Robert Dunsmuir, who, with financial backing from American partners and $750,000 in federal cash, laid 125 kilometres of track between Victoria and Nanaimo to complete the Esquimalt & Nanaimo (E&N) Railway. Prime Minister John A. Macdonald drove in its last spike a year before the first transcontinental train pulled into Vancouver.

The E&N Railway eventually transformed communities from Victoria to Comox and helped spread settlers along the Strait's western shore, drawing them inland to places such as Duncan's Crossing and away from steamer stops at Cowichan Bay and Maple Bay. Steamship services suffered as a result and had disappeared from the Island's ports south of Nanaimo by 1905, when the CPR purchased the E&N. Two years later, in 1907, the railway company added two "mountain observation cars," the first in Western Canada. In 1912, at the peak of the resource rush, the E&N carried 300,000 passengers a year, a growing number of them tourists. By 1914, the line had reached up the Island to Qualicum and Courtenay, with a spur line west out to Port Alberni. But it never did reach Seymour Narrows.

Railways transformed the western shore of the Strait in other ways as well. The E&N carried farm produce from the Cowichan Valley, lumber from Chemainus and coal from Nanaimo. A spur line delivered copper from Mount Sicker, near Duncan, to tidewater at Crofton. An electric tram, unconnected to the E&N, opened new opportunities for Saanich farmers to sell to customers in Victoria. Short logging railways climbing the eastern slopes of Vancouver Island and larger islands in the Strait brought some of the biggest changes. The *Colonist* newspaper exclaimed that only the "fringe" forests had been touched: "Lumber interests…are only awaiting railway communication before the hum of the sawmill will echo through the virgin woods and trainloads of lumber will roll down grade to salt water."[13]

The transcontinental railway brought similar changes to the Strait's southeast shore, already the scene of a brisk sawmilling industry. The *Colonist* described busy mills, boat builders and local railways on the Lower Fraser in 1873. Granville, a collection of mills, bars and brothels that had grown up on Burrard Inlet starting in the early 1860s, was "making very rapid strides in the way of improvement."[14] The Lower Mainland was then utterly transformed by the arrival of the transcontinental railroad. The new City of Vancouver was founded the year the railway arrived, in 1886. Vancouver's combined role as rail terminus and deep-sea port ensured its future dominance of the inland sea. Land speculation was woven indelibly into the fabric of the new city, and every other place on the inland sea. Campbell River settler Frederick Lloyd Nunns confided in 1912 that he hoped the CPR might approach his land then find coal nearby, thereby elevating the market value of his pre-empted land. Tiny Savary Island, at the northern end of the Strait, was subdivided into thousands of fifty-foot lots the same year, in anticipation of soaring demand for recreational properties, buoyed by the opening of the new Powell River mill and the Panama Canal.

As on Vancouver Island, the railroad's arrival on Burrard Inlet (see photograph page 35) stimulated further railway construction. Interurban railways connected Vancouver with New Westminster and Lulu Island (Richmond) by the mid-1890s. Other lines extended into the farmlands of the lower Fraser Valley. There would, however, be no equivalent of the E&N running north along the rugged eastern shore of the Strait. The Howe Sound, Pemberton Valley and Northern Railway,

The arrival of the transcontinental railroad on the West Coast and construction of the CPR station in Vancouver, seen here in 1888, was the beginning of the city's rapid ascendance to "primate settlement" on the inland sea.

Image A-03232 courtesy of the Royal BC Museum and Archives.

incorporated in 1907 and started in 1912, extended south to Squamish. Taken over by the province and renamed the Pacific Great Eastern (PGE), it took another forty years to reach Burrard Inlet. The only other railways northwest of Howe Sound were for logging: short, steep-grade lines that would transform logging on the Mainland. Talk of railway-building engendered speculative frenzies, as people could see the power of railroads to seal the fate of towns and whole districts.

By the end of the nineteenth century, the growing feasibility of moving railway cars across the Strait by ferry kindled new hope in Vancouver Island's business community. One proposed option was a line to English Bluff (in today's Tsawwassen) from which railcars could be ferried across the Strait to a railway on the Saanich Peninsula, then south to Victoria. Another proposed rail–ferry connection would have run from Burrard Inlet to Gabriola Island, then by bridge to Nanaimo and on to Victoria. Even the challenging Bute Inlet route was briefly resurrected during discussions about additional transcontinental railways. Its proponents finally recognised, though, that bridging the narrow passages dividing what they now called the "Valdes group of islands" was probably less feasible than a "[railway] car ferry."

As the age of railroads swept the Strait, timetables began to structure people's movements and their lives. By the late 1880s, people could board a train in Victoria at a precise hour and get off at any of ten scheduled stops en route to Nanaimo, only four hours and forty minutes away. On the Mainland shore, similarly precise railway schedules proposed travel anywhere between Vancouver and the Atlantic coast. It was this reliable transportation connection to vast markets that made Vancouver an important hub, and its ascendance on the Strait grew as other new towns around the sea struggled to improve their own access to each other and to the world. Trains didn't always stick to their schedules, but they were vastly more punctual than steamers. This fact put growing pressure on steamships to become more reliable. They remained fundamentally important for many communities around the Strait. Much local politicking involved attempts to secure government support for communities' marine highway connection to the outside world, by building or improving local wharves, lighthouses and post offices. Every town strove to be on a coastal steamer route (see photograph page 37).

Earlier known for their capricious timetables, steamships on the Strait began to publish fixed departure times from major towns. The People's Steam Navigation Company advertised the steamer *Amelia*'s runs between Victoria, Nanaimo and Comox a couple of times a week in the summer of 1888, "stopping at all the way ports," including Denman Island, Nanaimo, Gabriola Island, Chemainus, Vesuvius and Burgoyne Bays on Saltspring Island, and Saanich. A decade later the SS *Comox* sailed out of Vancouver every Tuesday at nine a.m. and Thursdays and Saturdays at eleven a.m., headed for Texada, Lund, Shoal Bay and other places along the way. The SS *Coquitlam* left Burrard Inlet on Tuesdays at nine for Port Neville and Fridays at three for Texada and Lasqueti Islands, "calling at all intermediate ports" each trip. The schedules announced what time a ship left Victoria or Vancouver and its departure time from the northernmost port on the return trip. Arrival times along the way remained notoriously flexible.[15]

A rapid transition in the 1880s saw a few larger companies with more rigorous service and schedules replace the many small, independent, often unreliable shipping

services that had previously plied the Strait. By 1900, Canadian Pacific (CP), the Union Steamship Company (USC) and Canadian National were the key players. The first two serviced everywhere from Vancouver and Victoria to island and peninsular towns, and a long, shifting list of logging and fishing camps, canneries, sawmills and mines throughout the Strait and beyond. The CP Navigation Company, which ran between ten and twenty distinctive black, white and yellow Princess ships around the inside coast, became the dominant player in coastal shipping into the middle of the next century.

Larger settlements such as Vananda (on Texada Island), Comox and Nanaimo could count on service from more than one company, whereas smaller places had to be content with a single option. Of course, the steamship companies competed for the most promising new markets on the Strait. The *Colonist* reported in 1902, for example, that Vancouver interests were "putting on a steamer" to secure new business in the southern islands, as well as Ladysmith and Crofton.[16] If CP boats did not stop there, a settlement needed to attract USC boats. The latter company, spawned from a Burrard Inlet ferry service in the late 1880s, filled a niche left by the larger CP company. It eventually grew to sixty ships and serviced a large number of smaller ports, especially out-of-the-way logging, fishing, canning and mining operations; isolated communities on islands of the northern Strait; and eventually even the Queen Charlotte Islands (Haida Gwaii) and southeast Alaska. Becoming a USC stop was a life-and-death issue for many of these smaller places with no other links to the world. A steamship opened up new options; suspension of service had the opposite effect.

The *SS Joan* and *SS City of Nanaimo*, steamers that sailed between the Mainland and Nanaimo. Arrival times were flexible, and though steamships weren't always faster than sailing ships, they were more reliable because they were less constrained by winds and tides.
Image B-04718 courtesy of the Royal BC Museum and Archives.

A place could transcend the marine barrier if a steamship could be counted on to stop in there even once or twice a month. For those dwelling on islands and peninsulas or in fjords, this was especially important. If they had to, settlers on the southern Strait could go back to using small boats to move themselves and their produce to the larger towns on the Mainland or Vancouver Island. It happened when service to Gabriola Island was cut in the 1890s. Settlers farther up the Strait, however, faced bleaker prospects. The bottom line was that a person could only easily get off the remoter shorelines if they were on a steamer route. Looking for land as a new arrival on the coast at the beginning of the twentieth century, Francis John Barrow rejected an otherwise attractive Pender Island property because it was too far off the regular steamer route. Meanwhile, fishers, loggers or miners and their families living on Read Island, or in Desolation Sound or Pender Harbour, could find themselves in the heart of urban civilisation in a matter of hours by steamer. They could then return home with greater ease because scheduled departures from the largest towns were far more reliable. More important for many coastal dwellers, coastal steamers enabled reliable shipment of whatever one needed to obtain from the outside world or send to it. Mail and new faces could be expected with every arriving boat. Even if one had to row out to meet the steamer—as one did in the smallest places—steamships were a lifeline.

All of this rapid growth in steam-powered shipping stimulated ship building on the Strait, especially along Burrard Inlet and False Creek. Larger vessels were still brought in from Britain—sometimes in pieces to be assembled on the Strait—but smaller ones were built locally. A number of ships, such as the *Princess Mary*, the *Comox*, the *Chelhosin* and others, achieved almost legendary status, evoking what writer Roderick Haig-Brown in Campbell River remembered as a universal "sense of friendliness and gratitude." Publisher Howard White compared travelling on the Sunshine Coast's steamships to the stimulating and festive atmosphere of the Mardi Gras in New Orleans.

Steamships also catered to the growing number of people who sought recreation on the Strait after the 1880s. CP boats connected with the CPR's transcontinental trains at the beginning of the twentieth century. The *Colonist* reported in 1907 that the CPR steamer *Princess Victoria*, "the most palatial craft in the coasting business," landed its transcontinental tourists in Victoria "in time for dinner."[17] Settlements like Bowen Island and Sechelt that started as logging sites became destinations for urbanites riding the steamships to weekend retreats or longer holidays spent in seaside hotels and cottages. With Vancouver consolidating its role as the Strait's dominant settlement, Burrard Inlet soon became the one place a person could depart from to reach any corner of the Strait, as long as it was on a steamer route. It also became the place that people from those corners turned to, more than any other, to relax, shop, drink, socialise, escape from work or look for it.

Beyond the Strait, steamers were slowly replacing sailing ships on ocean routes. Australian historian Geoffrey Blainey estimated in *The Tyranny of Distance* that the ocean-going steamships of 1914 were twice as fast as the average sailing ship of the 1850s and considerably more reliable. Long-distance shipping costs declined substantially, and with the opening of the Panama Canal, the Strait's mines, mills and canneries could competitively ship their goods by steamship to virtually any port in the world.

With the rail link established, Canadian Pacific launched trans-Pacific mail, passenger and freight services, and its *Empress* ships went on to dominate the trans-Pacific passenger trade until the mid-twentieth century. Many other transoceanic lines also put into Vancouver by World War I, among them the Canadian-Australian Royal Mail Steamships, the Hamburg America Line, the East Asiatic Company and the Royal Mail Steam Packet Company. Ocean-going steamers arrived in the Strait's other ports in larger numbers as well, in order to load the rapidly growing output of its primary industries (see Figure 3, page 40).

Increases in marine traffic stimulated demand for more navigational support, including lighthouses, pilots, port authorities, navigation rules, and charts of tides and currents. Sailing ships were in slow decline but were still widely used and continued to run aground or sink regularly, particularly in winter. By the mid-1880s, sternwheelers, which had crossed the Strait for twenty-five years, had been declared dangerously insecure and banned from navigation on the sea, much to the consternation of local merchants who depended on them. Around the same time, the *Colonist* newspaper—which had earlier reported so many marine tragedies on the Strait and had worked hard to paint the inland sea as too dangerous for international shipping—wrote: "[Since 1858] the waters have been traversed at all seasons and by all description of craft…[and] not a single mishap has occurred."[18] This was not the first or last time that depictions of navigational risks on the Strait would be subject to considerable licence, depending on who was writing and to what end.

Whatever the shifting hyperbole of local journalists, both steamers and sailboats continued to face considerable navigational hazards on the Strait. American coal boats were frequent visitors and victims. The coal ship *Thrasher* from San Francisco ran aground on rocks near Gabriola Reef on a calm, clear night in July 1880 while being towed by two tugs. Two years were spent trying to get the ship off the rocks before it finally sank, leading to legal wrangling that ended up at the Privy Council in London in 1884. Two years later, the American ship *John Rosenfeld*, with all its fittings and 3,900 tons of Vancouver Island coal aboard, was sold at public auction as it lay wrecked off Saturna Island. Pleasure boats also fell victim to the Strait's hazards. The *Colonist* reprinted stories from Seattle papers late in the summer of 1884 about the pleasure yacht *Lotus*, which had left Port Moody to cruise the Strait two weeks earlier, then disappeared.[19]

Some notoriously dangerous places claimed growing lists of victims: Quadra Island, Gabriola Reef, the First and Second Narrows of Burrard Inlet and the shifting sandbars at the mouth of the Fraser River. Historian Jeanette Taylor recounted in *The Quadra Story* that Billy Assu and other young men from the Cape Mudge reserve on Quadra Island risked their lives often in those years to rescue

The Comox Wagon Road in 1911: Note the old-growth Douglas fir. The E&N Railway had not yet reached the Comox Valley, and travel by sea was still more comfortable and reliable than road.

Image G-02423 courtesy of the Royal BC Museum and Archives.

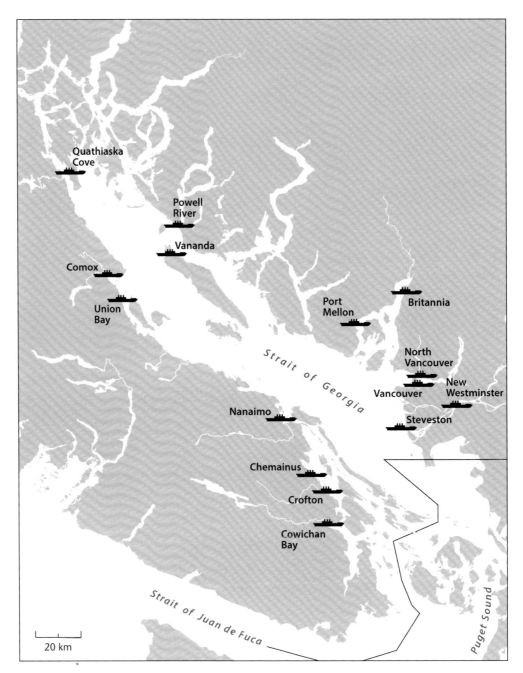

Figure 3: Major ports on the Strait, 1914. These were critical for moving the Strait's resources onto the ocean highways.

shipwreck victims. Most of the Strait's hundreds of kilometres of shoreline remained uncharted and most of the hazardous reefs, rocks and shallows went unmarked throughout the 1880s. Only in the early 1890s would the steamship *Quadra* under Captain John Walbran begin systematically mapping and marking such dangerous stretches around the Strait. He concentrated on sites that had already claimed victims and routes that were followed by ships exporting natural resources.

In addition to fixed hazards, fog was a worry, especially in autumn, because it increased the risks of running aground and of collisions between vessels. Foghorns were erected at the entrance to Burrard Inlet in the late 1880s and the entrance

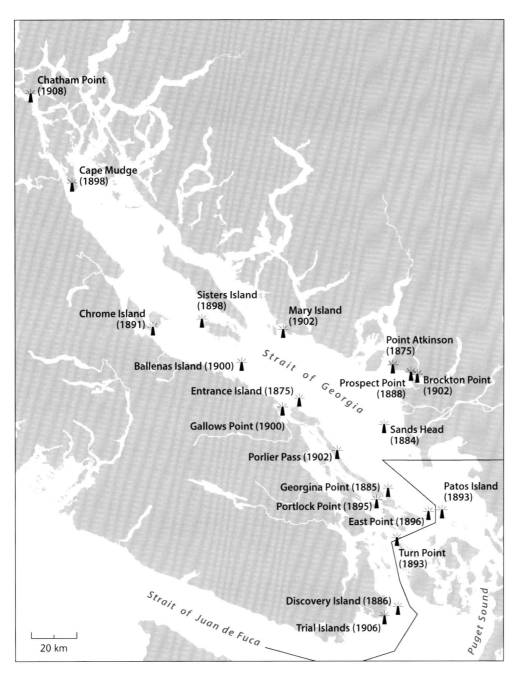

Figure 4: Lighthouses on the Strait and at its entrances by 1908 (with dates of establishment): these helped settlers transcend the marine barrier.

to Nanaimo harbour soon after. A decade later, Ottawa's DMF announced it was installing a foghorn on the Ballenas Islands off Parksville that would blast every fifteen seconds. The fogs were getting heavier, at least partly due to the increased burning of sawmill waste and logging slash in hills around the Strait.

More than any other aid to navigation, though, lighthouses transformed the Strait. New lights were erected on the Strait's southern approaches, the southern islands, the entrance to Baynes Sound (see photograph page 42) and the First Narrows early in the resource rush to ensure the safe passage of passengers and cargo. Miners streaming north to the Klondike in the late 1890s stimulated another

The Yellow Rock Light on Chrome Island, off Denman Island. The south entrance to Baynes Sound became heavily travelled by ships loading coal at Union Bay. Ten died when the steamer *Alpha* wrecked here in 1900.

Image I-55237 courtesy of the Royal BC Museum and Archives.

flush of lighthouse construction at places along the way: Sisters and Ballenas Islands and Cape Mudge on the southern tip of Quadra (see Figure 4, page 41). These lights, often 30 metres or more above sea level, occupied sites that had been of strategic importance for Indigenous people long before the settlers' arrival. Projecting their beacons across the sea, they became local landmarks and powerful symbols of the Strait's new industrial age. Some became important social institutions and their keepers, local celebrities.

New systems of governance—regulations, reporting structures and the bureaucracies to implement them—were needed for the administration of these new technologies. The DMF was required to report regularly on its achievements and related expenditures to Parliament; local papers followed these reports carefully and stimulated demand for further reductions in navigational hazards. The safer the Strait became, the more inexperienced navigators ventured onto it, even in winter, and the more government help they needed. The waves of people pouring north to the Klondike at end of the century were reminiscent of those who had come for the Cariboo gold rush forty years earlier, and this increase in vessel traffic through the Strait led to a further surge in marine accidents and yet another long list of demands for Ottawa to make the sea safer. One result was that by 1900, local papers were publishing weather forecasts. Then they began to report on actual weather conditions around the sea throughout the day. The DMF oversaw tidal surveys soon after and started to publish reliable estimates of the timing and scale of daily tides, as well as the direction and velocity of currents at various locations around the sea. The value of this new information for local trade and commerce, said the *Colonist*, could "hardly be overestimated." It proudly declared the new Canadian tidal survey results so "absolutely dependable" that they could be incorporated into the charts of the British Admiralty.[20]

The settlers' new ports around the Strait (see photographs page 44 and page 45) were the portals through which the fruits of the resource rush could be shipped to world markets. By 1890, Nanaimo harbour was shipping 400,000 tons of coal a year. A newer coal port at Union Bay in the Comox Valley also moved hundreds of thousands of tons annually by 1900. But Burrard Inlet had rapidly become the inland sea's most significant port. Lumber exports out of Hastings Mill and Moodyville had reached over 25 million board feet a year by the mid-1880s, then doubled over the next decade. Coastal and ocean-going traffic continued to grow throughout the resource rush, and wood remained Burrard Inlet's main export. More and more wood and tinned salmon were being shipped from the mouth of the Fraser as well.

Modern communications technology also helped bind coastal communities into tighter networks. The Dominion government introduced wireless technology to the inland sea in 1907, linking wireless stations at Shotbolt Hill in Victoria and Point Grey outside Vancouver. Telegraph was the dominant form of modern communication for a while, but as early as 1890 Vancouver Island also had a telephone link to the Mainland. By 1911, the province as a whole had 20,000 telephones, most of them in Vancouver. By 1914 some of the larger islands in the Strait, and even a few of the smaller ones, had telephones.

While communication links improved, Burrard Inlet and the Lower Fraser remained the Lower Mainland's principal ports, though other options were considered. The CPR briefly thought about developing docks at Kitsilano Point in the 1880s and revisited this option, with plans being drawn up for massive piers, railyards and warehouses there three decades later. These plans were eventually shelved, at least partly on account of potential difficulties securing Kitsilano Indian Reserve land. As well, a more grandiose scheme had emerged a couple of years earlier for a new harbour facility between the north and south arms of the Fraser, where Vancouver Airport is now located. It called for two-and-a-half kilometres of piers, a new industrial zone and a railway through Point Grey to Burrard Inlet. This plan was also eventually set aside.

Bold optimism prevailed in the final years before World War I, and the prospect of increased ship traffic through the Lower Mainland after the opening of the Panama Canal animated local dreams. Although no major new ports were actually built in those years, private interests and the federal government invested heavily in expanding and upgrading existing facilities. Ottawa then incorporated the Vancouver Harbour Commission in 1913 to protect its claim to the Strait as Canada's western sea highway to global markets. A similar body was created for the north and middle arms of the Fraser. And federally appointed harbour commissioners were empowered to establish rules governing harbour navigation, construction and maintenance. They administered waterfront property, policed the harbours and guided development of the ports.

The global economic downturn in 1913 followed by the onset of World War I muted the expected growth in port activity, however. Initially the only big increase in traffic was in grain exports, mostly wheat from the new Prairie provinces. Once it was proven that grain would not spoil when passing through the tropical climate of Panama, grain exports through Vancouver increased a hundredfold in the first few years after the canal opened..

Steam-powered tugs proliferated on the Strait after 1890 to guide the sailing ships that transported this grain and other resources across the ocean. Slow but powerful, these small vessels drew little water and were highly manoeuvrable. They were well suited to the inland sea, where they were indispensable for moving larger

Right: Coal docks at Union Bay in the Comox Valley were moving hundreds of thousands of tons annually by 1900.

Image A-04577 courtesy of the Royal BC Museum and Archives.

Below: A sheltered harbour and proximity to Cumberland's mines ensured a steady stream of deep-sea vessels, as well as sailors in Comox taverns.

Image E-00409 courtesy of the Royal BC Museum and Archives.

Bottom: Ships loading at Hastings Mill in Vancouver in the 1880s. Note the absence of steam-powered vessels.

Image D-04081 courtesy of the Royal BC Museum and Archives.

vessels through difficult stretches and raw materials around the Strait. The business of moving log booms with tugs from remote sites to sawmills around Vancouver grew rapidly after 1900, dominated by a handful of companies. Tugs also began pulling scows loaded with sand and gravel from the Strait's beaches and quarries to Vancouver building sites.

Although steam was the most important power source for transportation on land and sea at the time, gasoline-powered engines were beginning to appear. Reginald Pidcock, an early Indian agent on the northern Strait, had always travelled by canoe through his large "Agency." When he died in 1902, his successor was soon using a gas-powered launch. Similarly, by this time the BC Provincial Police had already begun using their own gas launch to patrol the Strait.

Some observers began to claim that modern technology had tamed the Strait. An article published in Nanaimo in 1910 reported that CPR steamers had been crossing the inland sea for twenty years in all kinds of weather and had never had an accident. The *Colonist* suggested that the Strait (and Puget Sound) had become "full of safe harbours" and there was no longer any "rock or shoal that is a menace to navigation."[21] Yet, with more and more people living and working on and around the Strait, other stories suggested it was premature to banish lingering fears. Ten people perished at the end of 1900 when the *Alpha*, carrying a cargo of tinned salmon to Japan, foundered by the Chrome Island lighthouse off the southern tip of Denman Island. A few months later the *Princess Louise*, with a full cargo and twenty-five passengers, ran aground off the Thormanby Islands north of Sechelt. Later in 1901 the steamer *Hattie*, carrying 175 passengers and a small fortune in gold from Skagway, ran aground between Lasqueti and Texada islands. A couple of years after that, the *Vadso* was lost on a reef north of Comox Harbour. In 1911, the *Iroquois* foundered off the north end of the Saanich Peninsula, drowning twenty-five passengers.

Travel by boat remained the most expedient way to get to and from many places on the Strait, and the sea remained an essential highway linking settler communities. Yet in this age of steam, many people were still moving around the Strait under human power or sail. Canoes and rowboats (see photograph page 46, top) were still being built and were widely used in virtually every community. Indigenous people were still making cedar dugouts for their own use and for trade with settlers

Salmon ships like these on the Fraser River in the 1890s would have needed help from steam tugs to navigate the Strait.

Image C-00471 courtesy of the Royal BC Museum and Archives.

Dinghies such as these seen on the beach beside Alexander Street in Vancouver in 1899 used both oars and sail.

Image B-04128 courtesy of the Royal BC Museum and Archives.

(see photograph page 46, left). These could be huge: a Comox elder interviewed in the 1950s recalled her father and uncle launching a 21-metre canoe on the Comox estuary in the mid-1880s. The *Colonist* reported that a 9-metre dugout canoe had been mysteriously abandoned on the southern Strait in 1896.[22]

Geologist George Dawson carried out his extensive geological survey of the Strait in the mid-1880s entirely under sail, and Michael Manson conducted his lucrative business supplying Texada Island mines and various reserves in the northern Strait the same way. As in earlier decades, sailing the Strait remained an adventure. An old Saltspring Island settler recounted his father's stories to Frederick Marsh—possibly embellished over time—of moving the family's livestock across the Strait by schooner when he was a boy. On one memorable trip, the aging captain called the boy to the tiller in a gale off Point Grey and then promptly dropped dead, leaving him to run aground in False Creek, where he discovered rats had eaten the skipper's nose as he lay dead on the deck.

Well-crafted and seaworthy canoes, like this one in Vancouver Harbour in the 1890s, would be widely used on the Strait by both Indigenous people and settlers for decades to come.

Image H-04742 courtesy of the Royal BC Museum and Archives.

Sailing, paddling or rowing could be treacherous, especially if one didn't pay enough attention to weather or tides, but they offered a fallback in places where isolated settlers could not count on a steamship to pull in at the right time, if at all. Denman Island's farmers relied entirely on oars and sail to move their produce to markets as far away as Nanaimo until they built a wharf and attracted a steamship in the 1880s. Even after steamers started calling in, some continued to row their produce across to the big island. Farmers on the southern islands and Howe Sound regularly braved winds and currents to row their goods to the Lower Mainland. The Thulin brothers at Lund got their supplies delivered from Burrard Inlet every few weeks, but when they needed extra supplies, they had to row almost 200 kilometres to Vancouver. Charles Groth, an early settler on Galiano Island, pulled on his oars to get everywhere—especially across Plumper Pass to pick up mail and groceries on Mayne Island. Groth also pulled to overcome the intense isolation of his new life, as did many others.

So, for those people connected by steamship the Strait was a highway, whereas for others on the most isolated reaches of the sea who weren't connected by steamship, the Strait became even more of a barrier in a world increasingly dependent on national and international trade. But the rapid spread of gas-powered technologies would soon drive further change in relations between humans and the rest of nature around the inland sea.

Boats, trains and automobiles in the interwar years

Trends visible on the Strait before World War I became far more important in the interwar years. As gasoline-powered technology became cheaper, automobile use expanded significantly, though the Strait's road network, like its railways, developed unevenly. Gasoline-powered logging trucks (see photograph page 47) and fishing boats allowed resources to be extracted across a wider area even as the processing of this harvested wood and fish became more centralised around fewer major centres. Port activity grew rapidly through the 1920s, particularly in Vancouver. This was a time, too, when steamships and smaller boats did brisk business moving people to a growing collection of pavilions, hotels, cottages and camps at recreational sites all around the sea (chapter 6). The companies expanded their fleets in the 1920s to accommodate this growth. Yet the ports stagnated along with the rest of the economy during the Great Depression of the 1930s, and the steamships that had figured so prominently on the Strait in the first half of the century would barely survive the 1940s. Throughout, the Strait remained an important actor in people's lives, even as its roles continued to change.

Isolated towns on the Strait, if they were big and prosperous places like Powell River, could attract regular steamship service and thereby overcome the marine barrier. More marginal places such as Lasqueti or Read Islands expanded and contracted with

Gasoline-powered trucks like this one at Rock Bay were replacing trains in the woods by the 1930s, allowing logging to extend farther up slopes and do more damage to spawning streams.

Image F-08875 courtesy of the Royal BC Museum and Archives.

the ebb and flow of local logging and fishing, and their steamship services came and went with them. By World War II, it was only these communities on islands or cut off by the Mainland fjords that remained fully dependent on steamships to link them with the rest of the Strait community and the world beyond. Indigenous people, now mostly marginalised on small reserves around the Strait, were encouraged by Ottawa to congregate into larger settlements to ease government's burden in providing services to them.

The marine highway remained critically important for the Strait's resource industries. Vancouver Island mines continued to ship coal to distant markets, though their shipments started to decline in the 1920s (chapter 3). Coal deposits on Texada Island and the Malaspina Peninsula had also attracted investors' attention for a while, largely because their coal could be moved cheaply by sea. On the Mainland, mills still depended on the sea to transport logs and to export their lumber, pulp and paper. Many loggers living around the sea depended on steamers, especially Union Steamships, to get them in and out of isolated logging operations, most of which by this time were north of the Strait. Powerful tugs, many diesel- or gasoline-powered by the 1920s, were indispensable on the inland sea, particularly for moving log booms and chip barges. Booms had become familiar features on the open Strait and in protected bays and inlets, where they rode out storms (see Figure 5, page 49). Gathering logs escaped from booms became a new line of business. Commercial fishing on the Strait remained an important industry (chapter 4), especially for salmon, herring and groundfish borne by sturdy wooden fish boats built in communities on the shores of the sea.

The number of ocean-going ships visiting the Strait soared after 1914, and port activity became an important part of the local economy on Burrard Inlet. Deep-sea vessels putting into the Port of Vancouver grew by ten times, from 130 ships in 1913 to 330 in 1919 to over 1,300 in 1928. Roughly 40 percent of these boats were of British registration, 25 percent American and 15 percent Japanese. By 1930, close to 25,000 smaller vessels working the coast also put into Burrard Inlet annually. The tonnage of freight shipped through Vancouver expanded from around 350,000 tons in 1913 to about 5 million tons in 1928. Exports were mainly a mix of raw materials, with grain being the most important by volume and value. By 1929, Vancouver was exporting more grain than any other port on the Pacific coast of the Americas. By far the most valuable import was Asian silk for the North American clothing industry.

More passengers also moved through Vancouver's port in the 1920s (see photograph page 50). Between 1924 and 1926 alone, that number rose from 800,000 to over 1.2 million. The *Railway and Harbour Report*, a paper prepared for Vancouver's Town Planning Commission in 1927, confirmed that such robust growth in passenger numbers was important not only for the revenue it brought but also for its advertising value: "Few cities," claimed the report's authors, "have so great an opportunity of securing a personal contact with citizens from every corner of the world."[24] However, the report also noted the pressure all this activity was putting on port facilities in Burrard Inlet.

Now controlled by the federal government's newly established Port Authority, the Port of Vancouver extended along the southern shore for nearly 10 kilometres between the First and Second Narrows. Canadian Pacific Railway yards occupied

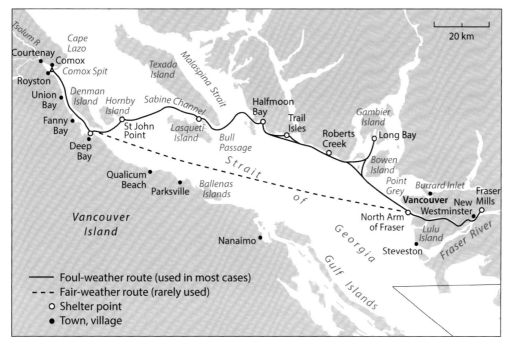

Figure 5: Routes for moving logs from Comox to Fraser Mills in the interwar years (from Mackie 2000).[23]

almost a quarter of this area. Other rail interests and the Harbour Commission accounted for another quarter, various industries for a further quarter, leaving a final quarter as "undeveloped waterfront." Most of the 9 kilometres of the northern shore of the inlet designated for the port were also "undeveloped." But even there, sawmills, creosoting plants, booming grounds, docks, boat builders and other industries already occupied thousands of metres of shoreline. The authors of the report noted that the port "belongs to the Dominion more than to Vancouver. It is an essential national asset (see photograph page 51, top) and should be recognised as such." And they underlined the need to "[conserve] for strictly harbour purposes the entire water frontage of Burrard Inlet."[25] As other stakeholders' demands for access to the shore grew, so did the federal government's fear of losing its access.

Other ports and harbours around the Strait developed during this period as well. The North Arm of the Fraser River was an important booming ground, storing logs especially for the massive Fraser Mills complex at New Westminster. Across the Strait in Nanaimo, an agreement made in 1924 divided jurisdiction for shoreline development beyond its old port between the federal and provincial governments. Smaller places struggled to build or maintain their own wharves with as much support as their local MPs could cajole from the federal government. Others meanwhile prospered greatly from moving high-value illegal alcohol into the US during their Prohibition years, and preferred to keep the federal government at arm's length.

Everyone seemed to be on the move in the years just after World War I. The steamship companies increased their business with excursion boats and shoreline recreational properties. The Union Steamship Company, for example, built up a valuable excursion trade along the Mainland shore, linked with its properties on Bowen Island and around Sechelt. Canadian Pacific developed a rival excursion-

The SS *Empress of Canada* is seen entering Vancouver Harbour in 1925. Burrard Inlet was now Canada's Pacific portal, the port a valuable asset for the local and national economies.

Image I-31453 courtesy of the Royal BC Museum and Archives.

boat destination on Nanaimo's Newcastle Island. Writer Francis Dickie on Quadra Island tried hard to convince the USC to give him free passage on its ships. He sent autographed copies of his magazine articles, claiming they were developing tourism on the BC coast. "[Y]ou will have particular interest in seeing this valuable tribute I have paid to the fishing attractions of one point on this coast served solely by the Union Steamers," he wrote before noting "the large outlay" that USC made annually for advertising. "Knowing as you so fully do the immense value of articles of this nature in attracting travellers," he continued, "a few paragraphs in…a magazine or newspaper or book outweigh in reader attention value thousands of dollars of paid advertising."[26] Dickie kept no record of the company's response.

The links between the ports and the railways grew even stronger after World War I, as the rail companies became key investors in Vancouver's wharves and warehouses. Across the Strait on Vancouver Island, despite construction of better highways and a rapidly growing automobile fleet, passengers were still making tens of thousands of trips annually on E&N trains (see photograph page 51, bottom) between Victoria and Courtenay, which had become the centre of a vibrant logging, mining and farming economy in the Comox Valley. The railways were also carrying more recreational passengers around the Strait. Incorporated in 1912 with the goal of linking Vancouver to Prince George, the PGE initially reached from North Vancouver to the new communities of Whytecliff and Horseshoe Bay. Describing the latter, the West Vancouver government boasted in 1918 that it had "natural grandeur…rippling waters…[and a] fringe of enticing beach."[27] A couple of years later, ferry service began between Horseshoe Bay and Bowen Island, and by 1926 the Union Steamship Company and the PGE were jointly offering excursions to the head of Howe Sound by ship and then on to Alta Lake by rail.

Ships and trains remained important means of transportation around the Strait, but increasingly, as in most other parts of North America, the ability to own and operate a car was rapidly becoming a key determinant of self-respect and "middle class decency."[28] The automobile fleet on US roads multiplied a hundredfold between 1908 and 1927, from 200,000 to 20 million. British Columbia's own motor vehicle fleet increased five times faster between 1906 and 1930, from 200 to 100,000. So it's hardly surprising that the Strait, like so many places, was to be transformed by highways and cars (see photograph page 52). People began moving around the sea more and more by road, but most of their destinations remained beside the Strait.

Seen from the Marine Building in 1938, Vancouver Harbour—now classed as an "essential national asset"—was recovering from the effects of the Great Depression.

Image I-30079 courtesy of the Royal BC Museum and Archives.

Rail had become indispensable for transporting people and goods along the Strait's Vancouver Island shore by the 1920s, displacing much seaborne traffic, but highways had already begun to displace rail.

Image F-06559 courtesy of the Royal BC Museum and Archives.

Members of the Pidcock family, from Courtenay and Quadra Island, earlier remarked in their journals mostly about the weather, fishing and lumbering; after World War I, when the family opened a garage in Courtenay, their focus shifted to automobiles. Although still mindful of the weather, they became increasingly preoccupied with the state of various cars, family road trips and beach picnics up and down the highway that now stretched along the entire western shore of the Strait. On most of the other side of the sea, highways were slower to come. Horseshoe Bay was accessible only by water or rail until the late 1920s, when the seaside road that finally linked it with Burrard Inlet towns was considered an engineering marvel. Unemployed men earned ten cents an hour in the 1930s working along Howe Sound on the Squamish Highway; it would not be completed until the 1950s. Summer cruiser and amateur filmmaker Francis John Barrow described the "celebrated [new] road which joins Gibson's Landing and Pender Harbour" during the summer of 1939. He was impressed by the "rock work" and the highway's exorbitant cost but met only one car on the road during hours of walking. Two years later, he reported driving for

Improved roads changed patterns of movement and offered new opportunities for tourism. Here, a car pauses at a viewpoint on Malahat Drive in 1920.

Image D-09356 courtesy of the Royal BC Museum and Archives.

the first time on another new highway that linked the wharf at Lund to Powell River, then continued a few more miles south in the direction of Jervis Inlet.[29]

Some of the larger islands developed their own road networks. Denman Islanders declared theirs the Island of Roads in the 1940s and took great pride in their 40 kilometres of "very good roads" and their fleet of forty cars.[30] The arrival of cars on relatively big islands, such as Denman and Quadra, enhanced the islanders' sense of community. Previously connected only by boat or rough tracks, they had often found it more difficult to reach other parts of their own islands than to reach other shores. This growing sense of "island consciousness" might also be strengthened by isolation from the expanding highway network linking communities on Vancouver Island and the Mainland. Smaller islands that had earlier worked hard to attract steamships now had to get car ferries. Discussions about ferry services, run more or less well by local entrepreneurs, figure prominently in regional histories of the interwar years. As with steamships, securing a car ferry service could open up new opportunities, whereas losing a ferry greatly complicated people's lives. Islands close to the Vancouver Island or Mainland shores, such as Denman and Bowen, had car ferries by the 1920s, as did the larger southern islands, though their service was not always reliable.

Other technologies contributed to the breaking down of the marine barrier. The first dial telephones in the province were installed in the modern little industrial town of Powell River in 1921, and even Lasqueti Island, far out in the Strait, had telephone service by the 1930s. Airmail sent from major towns like Vancouver and Victoria to Britain took only four days by 1939, but service wasn't of the same quality everywhere around the Strait: Francis Dickie complained mightily that same year about his deteriorating mail service at Heriot Bay on the east side of Quadra Island. Steady improvements in navigational technology and infrastructure meant that vessels in the Strait faced fewer daunting hazards, yet these remained significant. A new hazard appeared in Vancouver Harbour, where a low bridge was built across the Second Narrows in 1925. Sixteen vessels collided with the bridge during its first five years of operation, and it was closed for much of the early 1930s.

Towns around the Strait were as hard hit as other parts of Western Canada by the ferocious economic downturn that lasted for a decade after 1929. Rapid growth in transportation infrastructure and activities on and around the Strait—like the general optimism and economic prosperity of the 1920s—did not continue into the 1930s. The bottom had fallen out of coal markets by then, with a predictable effect on ship traffic and with fewer passengers embarking on recreational excursions. Yet steamships, trains, ferries and automobiles continued to move people across and around the inland sea in familiar ways through the 1930s and the war years. More changes would come not long after the war was over.

The Strait in the era of the automobile, 1945–1980s

The ways that people and goods moved around the inland sea continued to change after 1945, though not as dramatically as in earlier years. An effervescent post-war economy stimulated spending on transportation infrastructure in general. The federally administered Port of Vancouver continued its inexorable rise as import and export trade through the Strait's ports grew rapidly. New roads and ferries made it possible for more vehicles to cross the Strait and reach the communities expanding quickly along its shores by the 1960s (see photograph page 53). Cars came to dominate everywhere except along a few steep-sided Mainland fjords and on the smaller or more isolated islands. With steamships' days of supremacy now over, replaced by cars for most people, perceptions of the Strait's role as both a barrier and a highway once again evolved.

In the first years after 1945, CP and USC steamships still carried goods and

Growing car ownership, better highways and ferries, and rising incomes all stimulated demand for waterfront recreation in places like Qualicum Beach, seen here in 1949.

Image I-28490 courtesy of the Royal BC Museum and Archives.

passengers more or less regularly to Williamsons Landing, Hopkins Landing, Gibsons Landing, Roberts Creek, Sechelt and so on up the Mainland coast and on to many of the northern islands. On the largest southern islands, "boat day" was still an event— an opportunity to meet friends and gossip at the dock while waiting for the *Princess Mary*. Many vessels were fitted out to take a few cars or trucks on board, though they were not well suited to this task. In fact, the steamships' decline was not just a result of the automobile's rise. Many smaller communities had been shrinking for decades due to the centralisation of canning and sawmilling (chapter 3), so fewer places needed steamship service. With logging camps moving farther inland and farther north as accessible stands around the inland sea were cut, companies often used their own boats or flew their workers into camps on float planes.

The USC lost its federal government subsidy in 1958 and, unable to make a profit without it, sold its last ships a year later. By the 1960s, only a few small coastal freighters still serviced ports of call on the Strait's northeast shore. Denman Islanders mourned their CP ship service, lost in 1954, but at least they had a car ferry. Hornby Island lost its steamer service around the same time, and its resort owners went through difficult years before getting their own ferry. After thirty years of lobbying, in the mid-1950s, a ferry service across Jervis Inlet finally linked Powell River with the outside world by highway. Similar changes happened around the Strait, with new ferry runs starting and established ones growing, and by the late 1950s most of the Strait's larger islands had reliable car ferry services.

Two car ferries a day linked Vancouver on the Mainland with Nanaimo on Vancouver Island most of the year in the 1940s, five times a day in summer. By the early 1950s, Puget Sound's Black Ball Lines had begun providing service that stimulated coastal ferry development and shook up the industry. Its boats could load and discharge vehicles at both ends, making it easier to meet ambitious timetables, and it could offer a prompter and more reliable service than Canadian Pacific's Princess ships. CP's car ferry service to Nanaimo was comfortable but its procedures for ticketing, feeding passengers and loading and unloading vehicles in particular remained slow and cumbersome. The arrival of the innovative Black Ball also shook up sleepy beachside towns like Horseshoe Bay and Gibsons Landing. In 1953, over the protests of Horseshoe Bay's alarmed residents, the company launched its Nanaimo service. By the mid-1950s, a total of twenty ferries a day were plying this run, carrying more than 350,000 vehicles and 1.25 million passengers a year.

Lasqueti Island, most islands in Howe Sound and all of the islands in Jervis Inlet remained without ferry service, but not for lack of trying. In the 1950s, an enterprising Lasqueti resident corresponded with the provincial attorney general, Robert Bonner, and with the Sons of Freedom sect of Doukhobors, many of whose members were serving time in provincial prisons in the Fraser Valley after participating in violent protests in their Kootenay communities. The Lasqueti businessman worked to convince both sides that Lasqueti's tranquil beauty, sunrises and sunsets over the water could calm these troubled people—the only thing needed was a car ferry. The Doukhobors returned to their homes in the Kootenays, however, and Lasqueti never did get car ferry service.

By the end of the 1950s, the ferries were headed for a crisis. Black Ball, by then the main ferry service to Vancouver Island and the only one servicing the Sechelt and Malaspina peninsulas, was repeatedly shut down by strikes in the summer of 1958. The province announced the same year that it would establish its own ferry service between Tsawwassen and the Saanich Peninsula. After unsuccessful attempts to improve the reliability of the Black Ball and CP services, the province decided to greatly expand its own presence in the business. W.A.C. Bennett, the energetic leader of the province's free-enterprise government, declared that ferry connections between Vancouver Island and the Mainland "shall not be subject either to the whim of union policy nor to the indifference of federal agencies."[31] His government bought all of the Black Ball ferries and docks around the Strait for $6.7 million in 1961.

Victoria's new British Columbia Ferry Authority was meant to help ensure that Vancouver Island shared in the province's economic growth during those years. By the mid-1960s, ferry traffic was increasing at over 10 percent a year and Premier Bennett often boasted that his province now owned "the largest ferry fleet in the world." The fleet was growing especially to accommodate tourist traffic during the summer, when close to three-quarters of all vehicles carried were for recreational travel and nearly 40 percent were from outside the province. Long delays were common at that time of year, yet expanding the fleet to remedy the situation led to excess carrying capacity in the winter.

Rapid growth in ferry services (see photograph page 56, top) pleased most people around the sea, at least initially, as more car drivers wanted to get to more places and spend less time getting there. The stubborn reality was that for drivers, the Strait was a barrier. In the late 1960s, Patrick McGeer, leader of a small Liberal caucus in the provincial legislature, proposed a new time-saving route across the Strait from Point Grey to Gabriola Island by ferry, and then on to Nanaimo by bridge. Many Gabriola Islanders vigorously opposed this "improvement," but McGeer's plan had supporters elsewhere. Improved ferry service to Bowen Island stimulated a steep rise in real-estate values as that island became more tightly bound to Vancouver. When USC sold its recreational property at Snug Cove on Bowen Island for development, most buyers were not cottagers but permanent residents, including commuters to Vancouver.

Not everyone wanted to see ever more, ever larger ferries, however. The southern islands' location between the province's two largest cities made them especially susceptible to rapid development after World War II, and improved ferry service fuelled this growth. Ambitious planners from the newly formed Islands Trust, a planning authority created in the mid-1970s to preserve the unique nature of the Strait's islands (chapter 6), aimed to reduce private vehicle traffic, not just because of congested ferries but out of concern that the growing number of cars were transforming the bucolic rural character of the islands that the Trust was mandated to protect. A ministerial brief in 1975 stated: "Trust policy states that ever increasing car ferry traffic is contributing to the destruction of the islands."[32] Bowen Island, Gibsons and similar places seemed destined to become car-infested playgrounds or suburbs of the growing metropolis on Burrard Inlet, and the Trust was determined to prevent the spread of this trend on "its" islands. Horseshoe Bay (see photograph page 56, bottom) had become chronically congested on land and sea, with growing evidence of the danger of recreational boats and ferries sharing the same small harbour. Its value as recreational space was greatly reduced within a few years of the construction

At Swartz Bay, the ferry MV *Cy Peck* loads for Saltspring Island in 1947. Islands needed car ferries to ensure their economic survival but by the early 1970s, some wondered if the ferries had succeeded too well.

Image I-20713 courtesy of the Royal BC Museum and Archives.

Horseshoe Bay, seen here in 1955, was transformed from a quiet beach resort into the Strait's busiest ferry terminal. The Upper Levels Highway opened in 1960, easing access from Vancouver.

Image I-27993 courtesy of the Royal BC Museum and Archives.

of the ferry terminal. Elsewhere, the new and expanding terminals were consuming tidal flats and foreshore, destroying prime fish and seabird habitat in the process.

Highway development around the sea was closely linked with the ferry network and followed a similar rhythm: a slow-moving late 1940s followed by rapid acceleration through the 1950s and into the 1960s and the beginning of pushback in the 1970s. Many of the islands still had charming rural roads and trails after World War II and functional but inefficient road networks. Writer Frederick Marsh noted that many southern islands had no road linking the whole island, just a collection of tracks starting in one place and ending in another. Each track he found on Galiano had its own character and moods, by turns "stimulating, subdued, warmly colourful, aloof and austere."[33] In contrast, Saltspring—which was bigger and more populous—had 200 kilometres of roads by the late forties. Texada Islanders vigorously lobbied the province for improvements to their road system after 1945 and got them. A bridge restored the overland road link between North and South Pender Islands, which had been dredged early in the century for a steamship canal. Lasqueti's roads improved and its tiny vehicle fleet grew, even without a car ferry.

On the heavily populated Lower Mainland and Vancouver Island shores, highways became busier and much more developed. Similarly, traffic increased tremendously along highways built earlier on the Sechelt and Malaspina peninsulas after ferries linked them to the outside world in the 1950s. In *Sunshine Coast*, Howard White described the change in 1950s Sechelt, where traffic moving through town between the new ferry terminals at Gibsons Landing and Earls Cove began to overshadow the older axis of movement between the Strait and Sechelt Inlet. The province finally opened the beautiful, treacherous highway up the east shore of Howe Sound in 1958. By the 1960s some had begun to question whether all the new highway spending was appropriate. A controversial proposal in 1966 to build a highway through Stanley Park to a second bridge across the First Narrows evoked a ferocious reaction from citizens and city officials determined to protect the splendour of their seaside park. The Islands Trust a decade later tangled with the provincial Department of Highways, insisting it was "extremely important" for highway engineers to relax the "urban" standards that were leading to "excessive tree clearing and unsightly cuts and fills" on Trust islands' rustic roads.[34]

Highways eclipsed passenger railways along the sea as decisively as ferries had displaced steamships. The E&N still ran an average of twenty trains a day between Victoria and Courtenay in 1946, but by 1955 just one train a day went in each direction. In the late 1960s, CP Rail began applying for permission to discontinue the E&N passenger service, pleading that it was "uneconomical." Recalling the 800,000 hectares of rich forest land originally granted to the railway from Saanich to Seymour Narrows, the government repeatedly demurred. In the 1970s, CP Rail reasoned that the line's trestles were unsafe but was again obliged to respect the original commitment to provide rail service despite the tiny passenger numbers.

Like the steamships, most overseas passenger liners ceased operating in the first few years after World War II as air travel became cheaper, safer and more widely available. But Vancouver was by then firmly established as Western Canada's major rail terminus, and Vancouver Harbour had become one of the world's major ports (see photograph page 58).

By 1960, the Port of Vancouver consisted of seventeen deep-sea ship berths and three berths for coastal vessels that together handled 12 million tons of freight a year. Traffic grew rapidly, and Vancouver was soon moving more tonnage than any other Canadian port, mostly bulk exports such as potash, coal, sulphur, copper concentrate, pulp and paper, lumber, grains and vegetable oil. Ports on the Fraser River also expanded and by the 1970s were handling the entire, rapidly growing flow of Canadian automobile imports from Japan.

The North Fraser Harbour Commissioners were proud of having converted their once hazardous waterway into "a modern well planned harbour serving the many

Ports, including Vancouver Harbour (seen here in 1966), remained key elements of the Strait's economy, but conflicts with other stakeholders along the shore increased steadily.

Image I-21769 courtesy of the Royal BC Museum and Archives.

requirements of navigation, industry and the public."[35] However, in a letter to the new provincial environment ministry in 1976, the port's manager noted that port authorities were feeling increasingly constrained by the demands of other users of the river mouth. Federal fisheries officers frequently questioned the dredging operations that were being carried out regularly to keep the river navigable. Conflicts were growing as well between commercial navigation and a massively expanded fleet of pleasure boats. Recreational users threatened to reduce the space available for log booms and other industrial users. Rumours were circulating that the province might build a new ferry terminal at the mouth of the North Arm, which would greatly complicate harbour management. Overall, the port managers felt other government agencies and the public did not understand the complexity and gravity of the situation on the North Fraser, the conflicts between the port and other users, or the threats to navigation that might ensue from poorly planned port development. The Harbour Commission proclaimed its determination to ensure that the port could be shared by public and industrial users, but its bias was clearly in favour of the latter. These conflicts among an increasingly diverse set of users underlined the fact that the Lower Mainland's ship traffic was rapidly surpassing the capacities of Burrard Inlet and the Fraser mouth to meet its needs.

The solution, proposed by the Vancouver Port Authority and sanctioned by the federal government in 1966, was to build a "bulk terminal" at an isolated site to handle very large volumes of raw material. In this case that meant a massive port expansion south of the Fraser at Roberts Bank, where a new "superport" would be developed to ship coal to Japan. The idea, which reflected changes in international maritime technologies, was to separate port activities from the port city. By 1970, the Port of Vancouver, which now extended far south of the Fraser, was shipping almost 27 million tons of freight annually—more than double the amount of the previous decade—and more than 80 percent of Western Canada's exports were moving through Lower Mainland ports. A study in the mid-seventies claimed that 10 percent of jobs in the Vancouver area were "port related," and the port generated more than $600 million in wages and salaries annually, or 12 percent of the metropolitan area's total payroll.

Port activities started to come under scrutiny for their adverse effects on the environment, from Environment Canada and the province's own fledgling environmental authority, as well as an emerging community of environmental non-governmental organisations (NGOs). Among the criticisms given substantial coverage in local newspapers through the 1970s were claims by NGOs that industry was encroaching on sensitive marine habitat. In 1974, an umbrella group known as the BC Environmental Council stated in a submission to Victoria: "[I]ndustry should not be allowed to sprawl along our waterfront." The group was outraged that *Freightway to the Pacific,* a promotional bilingual English-Japanese film produced by the Fraser River Harbour Commission, encouraged foreign (in particular, Japanese) industry to locate at low-cost industrial sites near the Fraser mouth. Already, it claimed, a Japanese automaker was blacktopping acres of riverside for car storage, in "most wanton disregard for both waterfront and agricultural lands." The port authorities worked hard to promote their case in the court of public opinion, and the environmentalists concluded that industry, agriculture, fishing, waterfowl and recreation could coexist on the shore, but only with "careful and coordinated planning by all levels of government."[36] Such "integrated planning" had become a panacea for some in those years when it was perceived as a universal solution for increasingly complex, intractable conflicts and challenges related to resource and environmental management.

The most intense criticism was directed at bulk-loading facilities expanding in the deltaic plains and tidal flats south of the Fraser. Productive marine habitat, critics feared, would be disrupted in the areas to be dredged, and permanently lost in those to be filled. These changes would set in motion others, including coastal erosion and deposition, and changes to the marine habitat in general that would be more difficult to predict. Although government and business analysts still used the economists' language of "cost-benefit analysis," they began to embrace a new language of "environmental impact assessment." At least in theory, they began to transcend pure resource and transport economics to include new considerations about environmental costs and benefits. Their discussions pondered, for the first time, things like "significant impacts," "cumulative effects" and "indirect effects" of proposed port projects on "valued elements of the marine ecosystem" such as tidal flats, eelgrass, plankton, herring, salmon and waterfowl.

At the end of the 1970s, federal environmental authorities recommended that the National Harbours Board scale back its latest plans for expansion of the Roberts Bank bulk-loading port and smaller facilities at nearby Delta Port. Federal Minister of Environment Len Marchand supported recommendations from his Environmental Assessment Panel, which concluded that the Fraser estuary, including Roberts Bank,

After engineers used explosives to blast away the notorious Ripple Rock in 1958, Seymour Narrows no longer contained the Strait's greatest navigational hazard. It was bad for business east of Quadra Island, however, as most ships could now pass through Discovery Passage on their way to and from the North Coast.

Image D-05548 courtesy of the Royal BC Museum and Archives.

was "a unique ecological area of great importance [because] Fraser River salmon are dependent upon its preservation, as are many thousands of migratory birds." The full proposed expansion of the port, in the opinion of the federal environmental authority, would present "an unacceptable threat to the Roberts Bank ecosystem." Instead, it recommended a more limited expansion in an area judged to be of "minimal ecological value."[37]

Not surprisingly, this cacophony of conflicting demands from diverse users stimulated fears of impending loss among many people around the Strait. Some feared loss of opportunities to use the seashore for port activities or for industries that needed to be by the sea. Other towns around the sea outside the Lower Mainland were also engaging in their own lively export trade, albeit on a more modest scale, mostly involving lumber, pulp and paper.

To make marine travel safer out of the northern Strait, an underwater mountain called Ripple Rock in Seymour Narrows near Campbell River was blasted into oblivion. It had claimed twenty large ships and more than 100 lives since the 1870s. The *Vancouver Sun* described Ripple Rock's destruction on April 5, 1958, as the "biggest non-nuclear peace time detonation ever" when almost 1,400 tons of explosives sent a wave 2.5 metres high onto the shores of Vancouver and Quadra Islands. Nurses and ambulances had been posted in the streets of Campbell River, 15 kilometres away, ready to help possible victims, but they couldn't even hear the blast.[38] Removing the treacherous submerged rock eliminated the risk of colliding with it or getting caught in the dangerous tidal currents that had swirled around it for thousands of years.

The neutralising of Ripple Rock made Discovery Passage the preferred route for

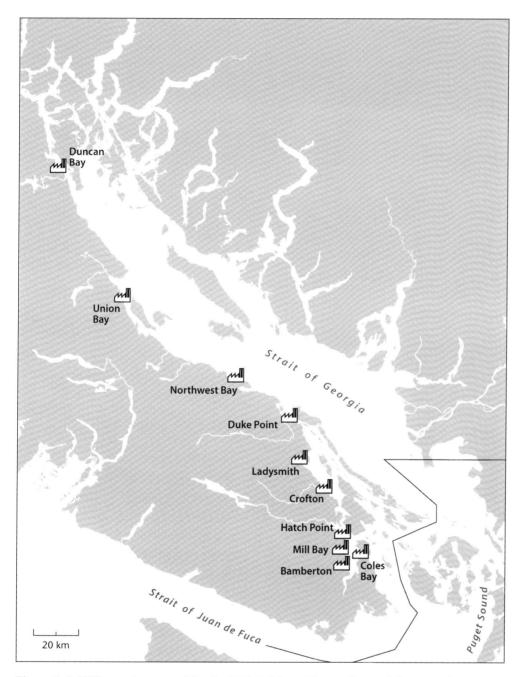

Figure 6: A 1977 report prepared for the BC Ministry of Recreation and Conservation proposed a number of industrial sites on the Strait where such development would result in "minimal" ecological loss, according to the report's authors.

most coastal vessels heading north. Although smaller shoreline communities farther east suffered, opening Seymour Narrows stimulated growth in Campbell River. In 1971, that city exported almost 3 million tons of forest products in 300 ships; for Powell River, these exports were a little over half a million tons in 200 ships. Copper was still being shipped from Britannia on Howe Sound and Hatch Point on the Saanich Peninsula, iron from Texada Island, and limestone from Texada and Bamberton on Saanich Inlet. All of the Strait's ports shipped almost entirely raw and semi-processed natural resources and were doing a booming trade.

So while Vancouver had first felt the fear of losing industrial opportunities around its port, this fear began to spread around the Strait. A confidential consultants' report prepared for the province's Ministry of Recreation and Conservation in 1977 identified eleven sites outside established ports that had good potential for industrial development on eastern Vancouver Island and where, the report suggested, "ecological loss in terms of community, habitat, and resource value will be minimal" (see Figure 6, page 61). The authors stressed that these areas should promptly be reserved for industrial use to prevent "further intrusion" of residential or other non-industrial uses. Stretches of shore suitable for industry were becoming increasingly rare around the sea, they said, and were therefore valuable and should "not be squandered." They discounted the negative impacts such zoning could have on other users of these areas but suggested their report be confidential "to prevent the price of land in these areas going up." Four of the eleven recommended sites were partially or wholly located on Indian reserves, where inflated land values were unlikely to be a problem.[39]

Meanwhile, on the water, the sheer number of pleasure boaters and their lack of maritime navigation experience was creating growing problems. Ottawa had amended the Canada Shipping Act in 1962 to improve its governance of small recreational vessels, and ten years later it initiated a small-craft rescue service on the Strait with 5.5-metre launches based at English Bay and Active Pass and in Victoria. People living in isolated corners of the Strait might be familiar with the sea's dangers, but most summer boaters had little experience with its capricious power, in particular tidal rapids. The Skookumchuck Rapids at the entrance to Sechelt Inlet, for example, drowned dozens of inattentive casual boaters and even a few experienced ones. People might view the Strait's water as having mostly been "tamed," but such tragedies were a reminder that it could still be dangerous.

By the 1980s, the Strait was becoming a busy place where residents, businesses and pleasure seekers competed for space while boats, trains, cars and, increasingly, airplanes competed for access. The many surplus military aircraft available after World War II were used to increase access to the most isolated corners of the Strait. Entrepreneurs, resource companies and residents of small communities around the sea found it increasingly convenient to fly where earlier they had travelled by ship. Frederick Marsh met a logger and resort developer in the southern islands in the late 1940s who told him he could "fly to the Mainland in a few minutes anytime we phone for a plane. Every other week we close the mill on Friday and hire a seven passenger plane for the boys to enjoy a change in the city."[40] Mines and forestry camps began to rely on these fast and convenient, though not always safe, small aircraft to move their staff in and out of isolated operations. The Texada iron mine, for example, opened its own airstrip in the early 1960s.

Rapidly growing Campbell River emerged as the hub for small aircraft serving isolated communities and resource extraction operations on the northern Strait and beyond. By the end of the 1960s, Campbell River was Canada's largest seaplane base. However, like other modes of transport around the sea, aviation also began to face pushback from other stakeholders. Vancouver's shoreline airport on Sea Island was redeveloped in the 1970s with relatively little outcry but an earlier attempt to construct a runway at Spanish Banks was vigorously rebuffed, especially by the Vancouver Parks Board. And in Comox, environmental activist Melda Buchanan led a successful struggle against plans to infill part of the Comox estuary for airport construction.

The inland sea as barrier and highway

The 1986 World Exposition on Transportation and Communication (Expo 86) drew over 20 million visitors to Vancouver, and its organisers credited the event, justifiably, with "introducing Vancouver to the world." Vancouver and other settler communities around the sea had been shipping the Strait's resources out to that world for over a century by then. People had also been moving across and around the inland sea in ways that changed constantly as the Strait's relationship with human movement was redefined by each new technology: canoe, ship, railway, car, airplane. Settlers were initially as dependent on the marine highway as Indigenous people were, as the sea linked their tiny communities with one another and with the outside world. The railway that brought an unprecedented tide of immigrants to the shores of the Strait also began to reduce dependence on travel by sea. As highways and automobiles replaced steamships around the Strait, the sea became as much of a barrier as it had ever been in historical times. For most people, car ferries became the critical technology for transcending this barrier; for a few, airplanes served the same function. But the era when most people moved around the Strait by sea was over.

While the sea became a barrier for most people living on it in the automobile era, it remained an increasingly important highway for international trade. After all, ocean transport was still a cheap and efficient way to move the Strait's, and the rest of Western Canada's, resource wealth to the world (chapters 3 and 4). Governments and industries were inclined to exploit this natural-resource wealth and maximise the economic potential of the Strait's ports. However, using the inland sea to supply the global marketplace stirred fears of loss among local residents who wanted the Strait to stay their quiet refuge, their healthy recreation space, their backyard wilderness (chapter 6). And they were not alone. Increasingly, local Indigenous communities were beginning to reassert their traditional rights to the Strait, its resources and its shorelines.

EMPTY LAND OR STOLEN LAND? THE COLONIAL STRAIT | 2

AS MANY AS 50,000 people, perhaps more, lived around the North Salish Sea (Strait of Georgia) before the onset of epidemics in the late eighteenth century. Sustained by an abundance of food from the sea, this was a relatively dense population compared with those in other parts of pre-contact North America. Salmon spawning in streams around the Strait, in particular the immense Sockeye salmon runs of the Fraser River, were the basis for sophisticated fishing technologies that had given rise to a culture and an economy constructed around these fish. Herring appears to have been as fundamentally important for Indigenous people farther north on the Strait as salmon were to those living near the mouth of the Fraser.

Most Indigenous communities around the inland sea were located on beaches at the mouths of streams. These locations reflected the importance of marine food sources as well as considerations about ancestors and other social, political and defensive concerns. Many seasonal settlements—especially on islands—were in places well situated for harvesting shellfish and camas root, hunting marine mammals and birds, and fishing. Autumn camps were at river mouths for the return of the salmon. In the coldest, wettest months, most people congregated in larger settlements, often in sheltered coves and inlets beside beaches that were protected from winter storms and could be more readily defended against marauders for whom the Strait's protected waters were a convenient highway. Marine harvests were usually plentiful, which brought wealth and gave people time for recreation and artistic expression.

Pre-colonial society on the Strait was tied together in various ways. Most people around the sea spoke languages of the Coast Salish group, which extended south into Puget Sound (the South Salish Sea) and west onto the shores of the Strait of Juan de Fuca (the West Salish Sea). They were also linked by networks of marriage and elaborate systems of economic cooperation and ceremony. Virtually all resources of the sea and adjacent shore were controlled by a particular community, family or individual. And in a preliterate society, tying these natural resources to cultural property such as names, songs and roles in traditional ceremonies helped people to remember and communicate the elaborate webs of ownership and culture. These were ways to pass along knowledge about marine resources and harvesting technologies such as the shellfish gardens and tidal weirs in places such as the Comox estuary, and Cortes and Quadra Islands.

Society around the sea was hierarchical and knowledge based, but much of this complex traditional knowledge was not shared common property; instead, it was what we would call "intellectual property" vested in individuals, families and kinship groups. High- and low-status people and slaves knew their places and roles in society. High-status people had detailed knowledge of their genealogical history; low-status and slave people were deemed to have forgotten theirs. When waves of epidemic disease ravaged the Strait's population, they diminished people's capacities to pass on orally transmitted knowledge that belonged to them.

The seeds of change for the Strait's Indigenous people and the onset of their catastrophic losses were sown prior to European colonisation. Their sea was on the margins of the eighteenth-century geopolitical struggles that played out on the northeastern Pacific Ocean once other countries learned of Russia's secretive, and extremely lucrative, sales of sea otter furs in China. The Strait's Indigenous people did not participate in this brisk trade though it affected them indirectly, as their traditional rivals to the north and west grew stronger by participating in it. Nor were the Strait's people directly affected when Britain's Hudson's Bay Company (HBC) lost control of the Lower Columbia River basin to American immigrants before 1850. But they began to feel the impact of these power struggles when the HBC reinforced its claim to Vancouver Island and a stretch of Mainland shore tucked between the expansive American and Russian empires. Outsiders arriving on the inland sea before mid-century were almost all employees of the HBC, which moved its centres of operation north from the Lower Columbia to the Lower Fraser and the southern tip of Vancouver Island.

The HBC was not keen on uncontrolled European settlement around the inland sea. The company aimed instead to maximise its profits by trading with Indigenous people. So when Britain began discussing settlement of Vancouver Island in the 1840s, the HBC occupied an ambiguous position. It had unique knowledge of the local Indigenous people and their rich resources, but the company's relations with these people and their place might not match the needs of the Empire's colonisation plans. Royal Navy lieutenant Adam Dundas reported to the British Colonial Office that the HBC was interested only in promoting its own interests and did not need colonists; instead, it needed to trade with the "Savages."[1] The well-established company found itself in limbo between the Indigenous people's old world and the settlers' new one, and its dominant role would not continue long into the settlement era. Its efficient trading system, on the other hand, was instrumental in ushering in much change on the Strait.

Although the HBC did not control the Strait before the mid-nineteenth century, it had established discrete centres of power inside the walls of its forts there. More importantly, the company had introduced a system of exchange that linked the Strait to distant markets hungry for its minerals, fish and wood. In the decades before colonisation, the HBC depended almost wholly on Indigenous labour. Between 1800 and 1850, a few hundred Canadians, Brits, Hawaiians, Métis and Chinese people— almost all men—lived among thousands of Indigenous people around the inland sea. Salish-speaking people worked to control access to the HBC's forts, excluding whomever they could and exercising their own forms of control over these valuable power objects. So the local Lekwungen people welcomed the arrival of European traders in Victoria because they saw these well-heeled newcomers as proof of their own spiritual power. The traders enabled the Lekwungen to convert readily available local resources into precious blanket currency.

As settlers replaced traders after 1850, they encountered Indigenous communities traumatised by a gauntlet of epidemics that had started decades earlier. Looking at anomalies in the archaeological record, some researchers suspect that periodic scourges of exotic disease may have begun on the Strait as early as the sixteenth century. Smallpox probably spread along trading routes from central Mexico, reaching the Strait in the 1780s. In the 1790s, British navigator George Vancouver found the shores of the inland sea lined with deserted villages and human skeletons. Such epidemics may have recurred along the coast up to eight more times between 1800 and the 1860s. By 1850, previously isolated populations with little inherited resistance had suffered a lethal mix of chronic and epidemic diseases, including tuberculosis, smallpox and measles. Similar epidemics had already transformed most of the western hemisphere. The early nineteenth-century Strait of Georgia might be described, as historian Shawn Miller depicted sixteenth-century Latin America, as a place where "disease conquered the human species."[2]

Evidence of demographic collapse around the Strait is still being uncovered. Archaeologists Nancy Greene and David McGhee have spent a decade examining and documenting tens of thousands of Douglas fir stakes 15 centimetres in diameter, spread over several kilometres of tidal flats in the Comox estuary. The stakes outline a large number of sophisticated fish traps capable of catching vast quantities of groundfish, salmon and other species. Carbon dating suggests that many large traps operated simultaneously, the oldest dating back almost 1,400 years, the most recent to the 1840s. Infrastructure of this scale would have fed—and required collaboration by—Indigenous populations far larger than those in the Comox area at the time of European settlement.

Geographer Cole Harris estimated in *Resettlement of BC* that populations on the Strait fell 90 to 95 percent in the century after the 1780s, which is similar to the decline estimated for Mexico's Indigenous population during its first century of contact with the Spanish. Without reliable statistics on death rates for specific epidemics in individual communities, there is no consensus on the numbers and there likely never will be. However, disease appears to have reduced the Indigenous population on the inland sea to a far greater extent than the infamous plagues that killed between a quarter and a third of Europe's population in the fourteenth century. Unlike Europeans after the Black Death, the Strait's Indigenous people, caught up in a tide of change beyond their control, had no opportunity to rebuild their own shattered societies. By 1850, travellers around the Strait reported streams and shorelines bursting with fish. Their stories helped make the place an attractive candidate for integration into global trade networks and a destination for Victorian settlers and sportsmen. The bounty they described was at least in part the result of the rapid decline in Indigenous fisher populations.

Declining Indigenous populations coincided with Britain's growing interest in colonisation and the Royal Navy's desire for a strategic foothold in the northeastern Pacific. London was responding not just to the American takeover of the Oregon Territory but to a global list of alarming developments, from starvation in Ireland and rebellion in Upper and Lower Canada to ongoing Russian and American expansion. As one rationale for the colonial project, British officials cited the need to impose the civilising rule of the British Empire to protect settlers from Indigenous groups and Indigenous groups from each other. Archaeological evidence suggests that the inland sea, like the Mediterranean and Baltic regions in earlier times, had been a relatively stable place where coastal communities engaged in endemic warfare of different kinds. Most of this conflict was local, more often involving seizure of property rather than conquest of territory. Yet the Strait has clearly been contested space for a long time.

Many signs of conflict and defensive alignment among shoreline communities appear in the archaeological record. Quadra Island historian Jeanette Taylor and other writers have described the elaborate defensive fortifications, escape tunnels and trenches the Salish-speaking Comox people developed around the northern Strait to defend themselves from Kwakwaka'wakw and Haida speakers arriving from the north. This inter-regional level of conflict may have intensified as European contact in the nineteenth century tilted the balance of power away from the Salish speakers of the inland sea; Salish speakers' military strength was clearly waning during the decades after first contact.

In the 1790s, the northern boundary of the Salish-speaking region probably extended beyond Kelsey Bay, well past the north end of the Salish Sea. The Kwakwaka'wakw-speaking people may have lived beyond the reach of the first epidemics sweeping the Strait in the late eighteenth century. These northern people also benefited more from the rich sea-otter trade and the advanced weapons it financed. By the mid-nineteenth century, the Kwakwaka'wakw speakers had moved much farther south and were established on Quadra Island and mixing with dwindling Salish-speaking communities as far south as Comox and Qualicum. Violent confrontations between the two language groups continued in the first century after European contact and were cited to help justify colonial rule.

Land hunger was a more important impetus for British colonialism than local peacemaking. This was an era in which Europeans were rushing into "unoccupied" lands in many parts of the world. As they had been doing elsewhere since the sixteenth century, the settlers applied "colonial assumptions of progress, superiority and civilisation"[3] to the Strait's Indigenous societies and then imposed their own new order, rules and laws. This process had evolved and increased in efficiency for over three centuries before it reached the northwest coast of North America. It was particularly robust in the final decades of the nineteenth century, when it coincided with the growth of laissez-faire economic policy and the final wave of European colonial expansion.

The Strait's Indigenous communities had highly developed systems of control over space and, in particular, over marine resources. But individual ownership of land—a dominant preoccupation among arriving settlers—had no meaning for Indigenous people. Even in those few cases when early settler governments reimbursed them for land around the Strait, Indigenous people apparently understood they were accepting settlers' goods in exchange for the right to use particular resources, not granting the alien notion of "perpetual exclusive ownership" of land.

Colonisation on the Strait focused on gaining control over land and resources and imposing settlers' rules for governing these. With this process came a change in the perception of land and resources from things that could be used by certain clans or groups to things that could be permanently, legally owned by individuals. The European concept of "improvement" was a key element in this transformation. Land improvement as a basis for establishing ownership had deep roots in British common law. To improve land was to take idle land—land whose productive potential was being "wasted"—and render it fruitful. Used as a rationale for the English seizure of Irish lands in the seventeenth century, this process of "converting frontiers into assets" was applied in other regions colonised by Europeans.[4] This shift in perception was at the core of the Strait's dispossession process and, as in many other places, it was accompanied by dramatic changes in the way land and resources were used. The region could hardly have been said to be empty of settlement before European colonisation, though this was sometimes suggested. It was far easier to maintain that most of the land around the Strait was not bearing fruit in the way it could be under European tutelage.

An official declaration of sovereign control over all land and people inhabiting the Strait was a prerequisite for subsequently applying settlers' property laws. The British Empire made this claim first and then passed it on to the government of British Columbia when the colony joined Canada in 1871. And though the federal government was assigned control over Indigenous people, it would continue to haggle with the province for decades after Confederation over what lands BC's Indigenous people should have. In fact, the process of establishing settler control on the Strait was broadly similar to other nineteenth-century colonisation projects around the world, from Algeria to Australia. What they all had in common was an intense land hunger among white European settlers that was initially characterised by relatively fluid relations between colonisers and colonised in which land was acquired through formally negotiated purchases. This approach prevailed during the first decade of colonisation on the Strait. Later it shifted, as it had elsewhere, to "firm, unilateral, overpowering, subordinating and anger provoking applications of sovereign power."[5]

The Strait's transformation also involved dramatic ecological change. Experiences with colonial expansion elsewhere again offer useful insights. Spanish colonists introduced intensive pastoralism to the Mezquital Valley of Central Mexico in the sixteenth century, and it rapidly replaced an Indigenous system of irrigated agriculture that had supported dense populations. Just as this Spanish colonial technology marginalised the Mexican Indigenous population, rendering people unable to support themselves as they had in the past and greatly diminishing their future options, the industrial fishery controlled by British settlers rapidly displaced and marginalised the Strait's Indigenous people.

Although early European travellers in the western hemisphere often talked about having entered a "New World" in the Americas, it was in fact a very old one. It was only after Europeans arrived and complex relations evolved between them and the very old societies that were already established on these lands that a new world really began to emerge. In Latin America, this process took a century after European arrival. It took about as long on the Strait of Georgia. First came a trading relationship, then a few decades of colonisation followed by the arrival of the railway and the beginnings of mass immigration in the 1880s.

The establishment of imperial control of the Strait, 1849–1880s

Once the world's other empires recognised Britain's claim over a stretch of the northeast Pacific shore, settlers were needed to secure its control. James Fitzgerald, writing to the Colonial Office in 1849, was more optimistic than some about the prospects for settlement: "It seems difficult to overrate the rapidity with which trade might increase if an industrious and persevering race were to establish themselves on the Northern Shores of the Pacific Ocean."[6] This settlement would be part of the second great wave of European imperialism that gave rise to, among many other things, an energetic republican American empire and a less populous Canadian federation tied to Britain, with its own dreams of westward expansion.

Disease and disappearance

Settler society on the Strait was not destined to be a hybrid spawned from its old and new worlds. The settlers simply aimed to replace Indigenous societies with their own. Underestimates of the Indigenous population may have guided colonial policy from the beginning; a report to the Colonial Office in 1849, for example, suggested all of Vancouver Island contained 5,000 "Natives."[7] The actual number was probably higher at the time, yet disease would help low estimates like these become more accurate. A final smallpox epidemic in the early 1860s swept through Indigenous communities, killing an estimated 15,000 people, a very large proportion of the total population of the new colonies of Vancouver Island and British Columbia. By the late 1860s, many Europeans spoke of travelling through an almost empty Strait, with only the occasional Indigenous cooking fire, canoe or camp. A surveyor named George Drabble, who travelled widely around the northern Strait between the 1860s and the 1880s, reported seeing many deserted Indigenous houses and villages.[8] Meanwhile, arriving settlers were hungry for land and for the Strait's abundant and seemingly untouched resources. If the people who had once considered these places their own were no longer visible, then these traces of past occupation—abandoned houses, burial grounds and camas pastures—could be safely ignored. The Strait's settlers were more inclined to see themselves as building a new outpost of European civilisation on an empty landscape.

By the 1870s, settlers were concentrated around New Westminster and Victoria and still numbered less than 11,000, or about a third of the new province's overall population, with Indigenous people accounting for about two-thirds. Settler sawmills, mines and farms controlled considerable space and resources around the Strait, while the HBC had receded into the background. And by the early 1880s, when the transcontinental railway was a certainty though not yet completed, most of BC's population was concentrated on or near the Strait. Indigenous people remained the majority of the province's population into the mid-1880s but not around the inland sea. For example, the Cowichan people, who had numbered an estimated 5,000 in the early 1800s, had fallen to 500 a century later. It was a rapid and dramatic transformation (see painting page 73 and photographs page 73, page 74 and page 75) though a relatively peaceful one.

This decline of local Indigenous people did not arouse much sympathy among

From 1858, this painting depicts the houses and canoes of a village on Nanaimo Bay. Compare with the photo below, taken seven years later.
Image PDP02144 courtesy of the Royal BC Museum and Archives.

Nanaimo around 1865: One of the Strait's most important settler towns, Nanaimo shipped coal around the Pacific. The HBC's bastion (upper right) was already a relic.
Image B-01431 courtesy of the Royal BC Museum and Archives.

settlers. As settler communities grew and became more self-sufficient, the remains of Indigenous societies became more "strange" to them. When they were not working for settlers, Indigenous people now mostly lived on reserves, places that were beyond the pale for most settlers. Settlers increasingly looked upon the reserves' occupants with irritation or contempt, and "half-breeds" born of settler and Indigenous parents aroused particularly strong disapproval.

In the same way that settlers were given places around the Strait as though no one else had any claim to them, places were given new names as though they didn't

Compare this circa 1865 photo of a Cowichan village at Quamichan with Amblecote farmhouse (see photograph page 75), built on Quamichan Lake in the 1880s.

Image G-06605 courtesy of the Royal BC Museum and Archives.

have names already. The British sprinkled English renditions of Indigenous names—Sechelt, Comox, Qualicum, Nanaimo, Cowichan, and so on—across their maps, but a great many places were summarily renamed in honour of distant patrons, friends or mistresses. It wasn't just ancient Indigenous names tied to local people and stories that got erased. Whereas the Spanish had called the Strait "El Gran Canal de Nuestra Señora del Rosario la Marinera," Captain Vancouver rechristened it the Gulf of Georgia in honour of his monarch, King George III. Other places around the Strait were renamed for more immediate symbols of imperial power and authority: British sailors and their ships. Oral historian Imbert Orchard commented on the "nobility" imparted by the new names around Jervis Inlet, where Prince of Wales Reach extended into Princess Royal Reach, below Mount Victoria and Mount Albert, in the vicinity of Mount Wellington, Mount Churchill and Marlborough Heights.[9]

Pax Britannica

British military experts reported in 1849 that the Indigenous people of Vancouver Island were "numerous, well-armed, brave and warlike" and might pose a significant threat, and they called for British troops and ships to protect future settlers.[10] By 1859, settlers in Victoria often seemed less worried about Indigenous people than about their American neighbours, who officials feared might "wrench the keys to the Gulf of Georgia from our hands."[11]

During the early years of European settlement, Indigenous men around the sea did in fact pose a significant threat of violence but mostly to other Indigenous people. The record after 1850 abounds with settlers' stories of violence between First Nations, most often between locals and northern intruders. An alliance of Salish speakers attacked northern raiders at Maple Bay around 1850, killing most of them. The survivors wreaked havoc on Comox villages as they returned north. Two years later another murderous attack on northern interlopers, by Sechelt warriors this time, was reported north of Nanaimo. Several years later, settler Adam Horne reported "one of

Established not far from Quamichan village (outside present-day Duncan) in the 1880s, Amblecote farmhouse hosted guests attracted by boating and fishing. The owners also grew English holly and shipped it by rail across Canada at Christmas.

Image H-02712 courtesy of the Royal BC Museum and Archives.

the most gruesome massacres in our Island's history" at the mouth of the Qualicum River: Haida flaunted the severed heads and scalps of slaughtered Qualicum men as they paddled onto the Strait with the women and children taken as slaves. A handful of Bella Bellas were trapped and massacred by Cowichans in Ganges Harbour in 1860. Other Bella Bellas, ordered out of Victoria by Governor James Douglas in 1861, staged a surprise attack on the Penelakut people on their way north. Over 200 Penelakut were slaughtered in "one of the worst massacres recorded."[12] The British navy pursued the marauders north to Discovery Passage, where they fired a few volleys into the Bella Bella camp but couldn't arrest their leaders.

Such carnage witnessed, or more often heard or read about, helped confirm settlers' notions about the savage nature of Indigenous people. In their minds, it seemed clear these were uncivilised people who needed British law to protect them from one another. Or as local Indian Commissioner G.M. Sproat remarked to the Minister of the Interior in Ottawa in 1876: "The occupation of the country by the whites was attended by one great advantage to the Indians. It stopped the constant inter-tribal warfare, which every year caused the deaths of several hundred men in the prime of life."[13] While Indigenous people on the Strait suffered from ongoing intertribal violence after mid-century, the substantial threat to early settlers predicted by the British military didn't materialise, beyond a few incidents. The *Colonist* suggested in 1861 that, while the capital could probably take care of itself during an uprising, colonists on the Strait itself would need protection.[14] Yet the "Indian threat" to settlers on the inland sea was ambiguous at best, and much diminished by disease. Even intertribal warfare declined steeply with the last great epidemic.

Although many settlers saw Indigenous people as difficult to live with, they couldn't really live without them either. Rear Admiral Joseph Denman's gunboats were called out more than once to protect Comox Valley settlers who felt threatened by Lekwiltoks from Quadra Island who had come to fish on the Comox estuary. When Denman arrived to drive them off in 1865, however, settlers prevailed upon him to leave the Indigenous people alone, because their labour was sorely needed on settler farms. Settlers also depended on them for fish and venison.

By the mid-1870s, unrest was on the rise again among Indigenous people. It was being fanned largely by growing discontent over the new province of British Columbia's intransigence towards First Nations' demands for land. Stories of violence among Indigenous groups also reappeared. Sproat reported in 1876 that Indigenous people from Barclay Sound had crossed the Island and massacred "20 or 30 Punt-lahtch" people at Comox.[15] A year later the *Nanaimo Free Press* published a rumour about a canoeload of Queen Charlotte people murdered near Plumper (Active) Pass in revenge for a number of Cowichan murdered by northerners.[16] These stories about Indigenous warfare just added to the earlier ones and would reverberate around the Strait for generations to come.

Settlers were mostly concerned about "strange Indians" coming in search of work. Not surprisingly, given the tradition of intertribal enmity, Indigenous people from beyond the Strait were often not welcome on the new reserves, nor were they legally entitled to live there. Indian Reserve Commissioner Sproat suggested these "strange Indians" were more given to prostitution and drunkenness and needed a place of their own where they could be controlled by police. He concluded that a reserve for "strange Indians" might be useful in Nanaimo, but that it was "a purely Municipal concern." Later, on his way through Chemainus, Sproat reminded his Indigenous wards that they must keep their dogs under control, avoid damaging settlers' livestock and not jump fences or cross settlers' fields when "good public roads" were open to them.[17] In other words, by the late 1870s the Strait was firmly in settler hands and the earlier "Indian threat" had been downgraded to a public nuisance.

Land hunger

Concerns about Indigenous violence helped justify colonisation, but land acquisition was the settlers' abiding preoccupation. Early on, before the gold rush started in the late 1850s, the HBC had controlled Vancouver Island and the adjacent Mainland, "undisturbed by land seekers."[18] Compared with their successors, the HBC were generally attentive to Indigenous people's needs. But then the colonial government of James Douglas faced a lucrative crisis: a sudden influx of mostly American miners headed for goldfields up the Fraser. The unruly new arrivals set off a flurry of government activity aimed at securing British claims to land and resources. Governor Douglas's Land Proclamation of 1859 defined the Crown's right to all lands and minerals, as well as a process whereby land could be divided into different units, then sold. The two new colonies of Vancouver Island and British Columbia (created on the Mainland in 1858), then the unified colony of British Columbia, needed money to secure control over their vast territories. Douglas requested money from London to cover the costs of his government, particularly for land surveying and communications. London refused, and the result was a very liberal policy aimed at generating revenue from the sale of land and resources.

Victoria's chronically indebted government started selling farmland "wholesale" and granting resources to "anyone willing to pay a modest price."[19] Only about 800 hectares had been surveyed by 1858, mostly in the vicinity of Victoria. Over the next two years, 70,000 hectares more were mapped and divided into 40-hectare lots on southern Vancouver Island; 16,400 hectares were divided into 64-hectare blocks across the Strait on the Lower Fraser. Colonial Secretary Carnarvon in London, perhaps suspicious of Douglas's sympathies, warned him not to "give land to Natives" in a way that might impede future settlement. Lord Carnarvon knew the colony would need all possible revenues from land sales and taxes.[20]

As settlement began in earnest in the 1860s, settlers soon found Governor Douglas was too inclined to listen to Indigenous people's concerns. Douglas had tried, albeit incompletely, to respect British colonial policy, which recognised Aboriginal land rights. The Legislative Council that replaced Douglas refused to recognise any such title. The new settler government's position—at odds with British policy—was that Indigenous populations did not really own the land and therefore had no legal claim to compensation for it. Many settlers established their own claims, however. Over the next fifty years, "there was scarcely a public figure in BC who did not acquire large holdings."[21] They were the leaders of the new settlements growing up around the Strait—in the Cowichan, Comox and Fraser Valleys, Nanaimo and Oyster (Ladysmith) Harbours and Burrard Inlet. Many new places were built on middens metres deep, testimony to centuries of Indigenous occupation, now erased from the public record.

Settlers and their surveyors judged that Indigenous people had been unwilling or unable to "improve" their land. This land was therefore, by the settlers' rules, theirs for the taking—vacant, unused and waiting only for the hand of civilised folk to bring it to fruition. Settlers' laws explicitly prohibited pre-emption of "inhabited" land. By the early 1860s, a great deal of Indigenous territory may have looked "empty," if one didn't look too closely. Yet there often were signs of prior Indigenous presence. The famed anthropologist Franz Boas, studying the Cowichan people in the 1880s, had no doubt about Indigenous ownership of terrestrial space and of critical marine areas and resources. George Drabble noted much evidence of previous Indigenous occupation when he surveyed pre-emptions for farms, mills, mines and canneries across the valleys, bays and islands of the northern Strait in the 1860s and '70s. But Drabble understood these things as relics from a past age—as meaningless to new settlers as Roman ruins in the British countryside. Few settlers were inclined to challenge this assumption: they needed land and their government needed money. First they pre-empted land, then land taxes became payable. Land sales and taxes had become a vital source of government revenue.

Pre-emption was easy for white male British subjects, though land laws were frequently adjusted. Initially, settlers could obtain land with a short letter and a rough-drawn map showing where they had staked their claim, citing coordinates (range X, section Y) if they had them and noting the name of the district (Cowichan, Comox, etc.) in which it was located. A decade later there was a simple form to fill out: a Certificate of Pre-emption. This form confirmed that the pre-emptor had made "permanent improvements"—mostly forest clearing and fencing—worth at least $2.50 an acre. A sketch map of the land was added to the back of the form, but by the 1880s you could submit map coordinates without a map if the land was in a district that had been surveyed. In the 1860s and '70s, such elegant procedures facilitated much pre-emption around the Strait, where the Saanich Peninsula and nearby islands, and the Cowichan and Comox Valleys were all deemed to have good agricultural potential. Pre-emptions around Burrard Inlet started in the early 1860s as well. Few saw much potential for farming, but there were good prospects for lumbering and new towns. Hardy individuals began claiming land around Howe Sound in the 1870s. Pre-emption documents from this era occasionally mentioned deserted villages, but most land was simply described as "vacant" or "unused."

Stories of wondrous early land acquisitions abound on all shores of the Strait. Parksville settler John Hirst paddled ashore in 1870 to pre-empt at the mouth of Englishman River, though it's hard to imagine the mouth of that important salmon river as "unused space." Trader (and later politician) Michael Manson and his brothers made their claims on Cortes Island around the same time, near the landing that would bear their name. The founder of Gibsons Landing sailed from Vancouver to pre-empt land at the mouth of the Fraser in 1886 but a gale blew him across to Howe Sound, so he pre-empted there instead. Many local stories speak of settlers who were "the first landowner" in this or that valley, bay or island. "First landowners" often told of finding Indigenous people's tools, utensils and weapons on their new land, many in deep clamshell middens. These artifacts did not undermine the logic of pre-emption; they were not seen to be linked with any prior Indigenous "ownership" but simply added to the romance of the land. Arrowheads and axe heads that were found corroborated stories of Indigenous violence, reconfirming the settlers' civilising mission.

Other colonial instruments: reserves and religion

The network of mostly tiny reserves that appeared around the inland sea, as in the rest of BC, was established differently from reserves in many other parts of North America. There was no mass movement of Indigenous people away from their traditional places. Instead, space was reserved for them at or near locations where they had lived, fished and died for centuries. Governor Douglas was of mixed racial heritage, as was his wife, Amelia. He kept a careful watch on the chronic interracial violence in adjacent American territories and was determined to prevent it in his constituency. He largely succeeded, even during the challenging gold-rush years. Douglas had established the first reserve in the colony on Victoria harbour in the early 1850s and aimed to negotiate treaties with people around the Strait. A few treaties were signed on southern Vancouver Island, where Douglas helped these communities protect their treaty lands and allowed them the same rights as settlers to acquire lands beyond the reserves. Both of these policies ended after Douglas left colonial government in 1864. When Joseph Trutch became Victoria's Commissioner of Lands and Works, he promptly reduced the size of the "Douglas treaty reserves" and prohibited Natives from owning land outside reserves. Indigenous people around the Strait began demanding—but not receiving—payment for traditional territories being pre-empted by settlers.

Discontent among Indigenous people grew throughout the province in the years following BC's entry into Confederation in 1871, raising the spectre of "Indian war." They grew angry as the extent of their losses became clear, and they began to understand how little land they were being allotted by settler governments. At the same time, Victoria remained convinced they were "giving away" too much land to the "Indians." A federal-provincial Joint Indian Reserve Commission was established to find a solution. Neither Victoria nor Ottawa was under much pressure to favour Indigenous people, who had been stripped of the right to vote in 1872. Yet the commission's intervention helped prevent the kind of bloody interracial warfare then raging in the western US. This was largely due to G.M. Sproat, a member of the commission, who urged settler governments to avoid using bellicose tactics with First Nations people on the sea and who, like Governor Douglas, believed in the capacity and potential of Indigenous people. In letters to the Minister of the Interior in Ottawa, Sproat reported he was "much pleased with these Indians…They showed good sense and proper self-respect in all their dealings with us. They gave me the idea of a vigorous intelligent race, capable of considerable improvement if they are judiciously encouraged in the efforts which they seem willing to make to overcome their old habits. They already contribute largely to the revenue of Canada, and I see no reason why they should not, in a generation or two, become useful citizens."[22]

The Joint Indian Reserve Commission was a prickly federal-provincial partnership that travelled the Strait and other parts of the province laying out new reserves. Created in 1876, it was initially composed of three commissioners: one federal appointee, one provincial appointee and a joint appointee. The commissioners' tour of duty began at the mouth of the Fraser, where they visited newly established reserves. They continued on to Burrard and Jervis Inlets, then across to Comox, Nanaimo and the Cowichan Valley before returning to Victoria.

Before long, the commission was reduced to just Sproat, whose official job description said he was to "as little as possible interfere with any existing tribal arrangements" and particularly "not to disturb the Indians in the possession of any villages, fishing stations, fur trading posts, settlement or clearings which they might occupy."[23] Sproat generally interpreted his mandate as Indian commissioner in favour of his Indigenous charges. When choosing land to allocate for reserves, his primary criterion was to ensure Indigenous people's access to traditional fisheries. Sproat often accepted Indigenous people's arguments based on their various occupations, activities and attachments. And he responded favourably to Indigenous requests for more land when he felt he could.

As their "Indian Reserves" began to be laid out, Indigenous people around the Strait had another opportunity to register their opposition to settler encroachments. Sproat recorded their rising frustration, protests and complaints up and down both shores of the Strait. He believed violence could easily break out. The Minister of the Interior later reported to Parliament: "If there has not been an Indian war [on the coast], it is not because there has been no injustice to the Indians, but because the Indians have not been sufficiently united."[24] Sproat's letters to the Ministry of the Interior described a beleaguered people coming to terms with the new settler society and their progressive confinement to reserves. Sproat worried about the Squamish men on Burrard Inlet and Howe Sound and the Sechelt on Jervis Inlet. Many of them had never been assigned their own reserve and worked as itinerant loggers supplying Burrard Inlet sawmills. He expressed concern that many such young Indigenous men were so busy logging or working in mills that they neglected to learn traditional skills from their elders or to support them in negotiations over reserve land. The young labourers did not seem to share their elders' concern about securing control over traditional lands because they were making so much money working in the settler economy.

Noting that Indigenous people on Burrard Inlet had no chance of gaining more land on the North Shore, which was already filling up with sawmills and settlements, the commission awarded them reserves totalling about 1,295 hectares at the head of Howe Sound. Sproat wondered whether it might be better to concentrate First Nations on centralised reserves where they could receive better health care, education and Christian ministries, or to leave them on smaller reserves to which they were attached through traditional activities. As it turned out, they received some of each. Larger reserves were no longer an option in more heavily settled places like Burrard Inlet. Squamish people in what became Vancouver's Stanley Park wanted a reserve there but were refused because they were deemed to have no "old associations" with the spot. The Comox were more successful in securing a tiny reserve at their traditional burying grounds on Goose Spit, though they were advised that they should avoid dispersing their graves over such a large area in the future. In the Cowichan Valley, where the original Douglas reserves had already been reduced in size, survivors of the once powerful Cowichan people were warned they must not interfere with the white settlers.

"Traditional association" with a place was necessary to establish Indigenous claim to it, but that alone was far from sufficient. Coal mines could limit the extent of a reserve even in places of traditional association. Logging, likewise, intruded into many reserves, and settlers could also squat in places of traditional association and then claim them. Traditional association was seldom deemed to apply to places of "seasonal occupation," though many Indigenous people had practised seasonal movement between settlements. Most places along the shore that had been occupied for hundreds of seasons by people gathering clams and camas, or fishing, were not deemed to be places of traditional association.

By the late 1870s, Sproat was deeply concerned about the crisis facing Indigenous societies and was increasingly critical of the settler response. He reported to his minister that while some tribes on the Mainland shore might be growing slightly, they were also being devastated by alcohol, syphilis and prostitution. He was concerned that married Squamish and Musqueam couples now had barely one child on average; at this rate their numbers would drop quickly. While they were benefiting from wage labour and missionary support, he said, Indigenous people were facing a deepening crisis, and the government's response was unsatisfactory. As Sproat's criticisms became more strident, his boss, Indian Superintendent Israel Powell, took him to task over his expense accounts. Sproat described the frustration of Indigenous people hand-logging near traditional settlements on the Malaspina Peninsula. Their requests for forest lands—which Sproat deemed reasonable—were ignored. By 1880, after reporting that the conditions of the Strait's Indigenous people were the worst in the province, Sproat was fired. Friends of Superintendent Powell obtained rights to valuable timberland shortly afterwards, beside the small reserves established on the Malaspina Peninsula near the stream now named Powell River.

Sproat's replacement, Peter O'Reilly, returned the system to what would become the norm: governance of Indigenous people by settlers, for settlers. Settler governments ensured that as the Indigenous population fell, the land available to survivors was reduced too. By the late 1870s, the total area in the new "Indian Reserves" on the southeast side of Vancouver Island—an area of 7,500 square kilometres—amounted to about 75 square kilometres, or about 1 percent of the land.

As Indigenous people were confined to reserves, clergy were assigned growing responsibility for their pacification. It was a strategy whose repercussions are still being felt today. While government-appointed Indian agents sought to help Indigenous people understand and cope with their place in settler society, clergy were given the more challenging task of helping Indigenous people embrace their new life as part of a Christian god's scheme for them. After the last wave of smallpox devastated Indigenous communities, healthy and well-fed missionaries may have had less trouble convincing the survivors that their traditional spiritual advisers lacked power and that their traditional beliefs were fundamentally wrong. Missionaries such as Oblate Father Paul Durieu, working with the Sechelt and Sliammon people, required Indigenous people to abandon their traditional dancing and potlatching and to avoid alcohol and gambling. The Durieu System, established by the early 1870s and based on the premise that Indigenous people were "big children," was a series of rules enforced with physical punishments and fines. Its showplace was the town of Sechelt, where a number of Sechelt-speaking bands were congregated under Oblate supervision.

By 1880, almost every corner of the Strait had been occupied or claimed by settlers. New layers of government rapidly replaced traditional Indigenous authority. Generally speaking, the closer these new governments were located to Indigenous populations, the less sympathetic they were to Indigenous interests. The task was complicated: the Dominion was responsible for Indigenous *people*, but the province still controlled their *land*. The federal government was acutely aware of the potential dangers of unrest among Indigenous people in its newly colonised territories and was anxious that nothing upset plans for an "all-Canadian" railway to the Pacific. The politicians in Ottawa insisted that BC was giving First Nations on the Strait far too little land. For provincial leaders in Victoria, this was another example of Ottawa's failure to understand the Pacific province: coastal peoples would continue to fish and hunt rather than farm, so obviously they didn't need as much land as Indigenous people did east of the mountains.

Victoria suggested that Ottawa was sowing disharmony in the province's relationship with Indigenous people by creating unrealistic expectations about how much land they should expect to receive. The province's policy, BC's politicians said, was to encourage "their Indians" to "mingle" within settler society and soon become part of it. Contradictions between this and other provincial policies, such as denying Indigenous people the right to vote and keeping their children out of settler schools, were not addressed. The province further maintained that First Nations could pre-empt land if they could demonstrate their capacity to "intelligently cultivate it." But they would do better, Victoria insisted, by supplying fish and lumber to settler merchants. In this mutually beneficial arrangement, they argued, Indigenous people would supply the merchants with export goods and the merchants would relieve them of the need to find new markets for their goods.

The Dominion had indeed failed to comprehend BC's unique situation, but only because of BC's unique legal strategy. Ottawa assumed that the province had respected the Royal Proclamation of 1763, which called for recognition of Aboriginal title and required that Indigenous lands be formally ceded to the Crown in exchange for "suitable compensation." Victoria's policies dated from the time of the first colonial government after Douglas, which had refused both measures.

A new British shore

Some early settlers aimed to establish a "new British shore" around the Strait by renaming places and building farms in order to transform the damp wilderness into something resembling the British seaside. Today, these ambitions might seem like the fantasies of isolated people looking for something familiar in a strange land, but there *were* important parallels: the South Coast of BC sits on the northeast Pacific shore in the same position as the south coast of Britain on the northeast Atlantic and has a similar climate. Colonists noted how certain places around the Strait seemed like home—South Pender Island a bit of England, Denman Island like the Orkneys, and so on. Although the Mainland shore was far more rugged than Britain's, it might be seen as a surrogate Scottish Highlands. With the discovery of coal and then iron on the Strait, some imagined it becoming a coastal version of Britain's industrial Midlands.

A key step in making the settlers' new land seem more like home was creating something that was less panoramic wilderness and more pastoral agricultural landscape by the sea. The agricultural potential of most of the land surrounding the Strait was extremely limited, but successive settler governments insisted that agriculture should play a central role on the Strait, even if mining, fishing and forestry were obviously going to be important as well. The alluvial soils of the Lower Fraser and much of the east coast of Vancouver Island from Seymour Narrows to Saanich were deemed especially suitable for agriculture. Farming began in earnest on the Saanich Peninsula and nearby Saltspring Island in the 1850s. As the Douglas government gained better knowledge of the agricultural potential of the Strait's western shore, it tried to focus agricultural settlement on the Cowichan and Comox Valleys.

Men from Victoria—mostly disillusioned miners back from the Cariboo gold rush—began to claim pre-emptions in these valleys in the early 1860s. Many farms were then pre-empted on the islands, especially in the southern Strait and on Denman Island. Clearing this land was tremendously hard work, and settler farmers depended heavily on Indigenous labour. Settlers also quickly pre-empted most of the "natural meadows" along the shore of the Strait, land where Indigenous people had earlier used fire to keep down the forests and encourage the growth of the camas lily, whose roots they harvested in early summer. When BC entered Confederation in 1871, a little over 5,200 hectares were being cultivated, almost entirely in the districts of New Westminster and Victoria. This amounted to roughly 0.4 hectares of cropland per non-Indigenous inhabitant—hardly an agricultural settler movement.

A new Indigenous proletariat

Indian Commissioner Sproat reported that many of the Indigenous people he met in the 1870s were broken people. They had lost confidence in their traditional ways and were not able to embrace the new culture sweeping them aside; they had trouble seeing a place for themselves in settler society. New relationships defined by the settler economy were rapidly replacing the spiritual ties with animals and the Strait's landscape and the traditional trade relations that had sustained their ancestors. The settler economy focused on extracting and exporting resources at ever faster rates, and the most obvious role for Indigenous people in this new arrangement was as labourers. Even before settlement began, it was Indigenous labour that had enabled rapid growth in exports of cedar shingles and provided thousands of logs for the HBC's Nanaimo sawmill. They were the core of the workforce in that town's early coal mines and continued to work there even after British miners arrived. In an 1859 survey of the Nanaimo and Cowichan districts, the Great Britain Emigration Commission had noted the quality of Indigenous labour: "The Indians, though numerous, are perfectly peaceful and are made use of by the whites as ploughmen, servants, voyagers, in fact, labourers of all kinds of work. Their pay and rations amount to little, and, if kindly treated and properly superintended, the results of their labour are profitable."[25]

Sproat commented on the mutually advantageous relationship between Indigenous labourers and settlers. A new Qualicum reserve, he suggested, would be "useful to white settlers and to employers of labour generally" because it would mean "Indians within reach…somewhere outside of the settlements."[26] By the late 1870s and early 1880s, opportunities for Indigenous workers had expanded further. Historian John Lutz observed in *Makuk* that "if any Aboriginal Peoples in the country were interested in working for the settlers, it was the Straits Salish, and if any had access to employment, it was them." In fact, this full-time or seasonal work in settlers' canneries, farms and mills became central to Indigenous people's survival strategies in a system otherwise increasingly closed to them after the first few decades of European resettlement. And this abundance of labouring opportunities for the Strait's Indigenous people helps explain the remarkably peaceful nature of the colonial transition around the inland sea.

Many newcomers in these early days of resettlement may have perceived that they were occupying essentially empty land. Legally speaking, settler governments declared that their populations were "improving" land left idle by Indigenous people, who had become available as workers in the budding settler economy.

The consolidation of colonial dispossession, 1880s–World War I

Already disoriented by dramatic changes prior to the 1880s, the Strait's Indigenous people saw their losses mount further and their traditional world turned upside down over the next thirty years. First, the arrival of the transcontinental railway consolidated the settlers' domination of the Strait as they rapidly overcame the barriers posed by the inland sea, using it as a highway to ship North America's resources to the world outside. Second, Indigenous people were consigned to mostly tiny shoreline reserves where no one could own land, only the "improvements" on it. Places where their families had fished, hunted and harvested camas and where they had buried their dead for many generations had been "legally" pre empted by settlers. Those who could read the work of contemporary writer Lewis Carroll might have recognised their new life as an experience similar to Alice in Wonderland's tumble down the Rabbit Hole.

Disappearance and collapse

By 1891, the number of Indigenous people in BC had fallen to 23,620, which was barely a quarter of the young province's overall population. As Indigenous numbers declined, the settler population mushroomed and the province's total number of inhabitants approached 400,000 by 1911. In the final years before World War I, the number of settlers increased more rapidly still so that by 1914, Indigenous people made up barely 5 percent of BC's population, and less than that around the Strait. Tuberculosis was endemic on reserves and venereal diseases were reducing fertility. Some observers claimed that Indigenous people had been "going away to take up other occupations" and mixing with the settler population.[27] Alcohol was also taking its toll. This is the era in which one begins to see widespread reference to problems with "drunken Indians" in government files and newspaper articles. Government and missionary efforts to concentrate Indigenous populations, combined with their inclination to congregate in fewer settlements as their numbers declined, meant they *were* disappearing from growing stretches of the Strait's shoreline.

"Indians," no matter what their status within their own hierarchies, were seldom welcome in "respectable" settler society at this time. As younger settlers replaced older ones, ignorance of Indigenous culture increased and the gap between settlers and Indigenous people grew. By 1900 few whites other than missionaries, and anthropologists such as Franz Boas, had any acquaintance with Indigenous languages. Indigenous people and newcomers had previously shared a coastal lingua franca known as Chinook. Although it lingered longer on the western shore, Chinook progressively fell into disuse on most parts of the Strait. Cole Harris suggested in *Resettlement* that BC around this time had essentially no past, just a present and a future—and both belonged to the newcomers. It was reminiscent of George Orwell's *Nineteen Eighty-Four*: "Who controls the past controls the future: who controls the present controls the past." Along with many place names, the Indigenous past and its stories, so deeply rooted in local places (see photograph page 85), had been written out of the settler narrative.

The idea that the Strait's Indigenous people might be disappearing was widespread and reflected a growing belief in social Darwinism: that only the fittest survived. The corollary, in settlers' minds, was that if Indigenous people were in fact disappearing, then taking their land and resources before someone else did was a prudent move in those times of freewheeling speculation. This perception conveniently justified the settlers' voracious pre-emption of lands around the sea. It also revealed a lack of understanding about Indigenous people's mobility and the nature of the social ties that linked them to extended family groups more than to single places. As more and more Indigenous people died, many survivors moved to other settlements to be closer to their relatives. And individuals who moved frequently, as Indigenous people often did, might elude the records of federal Indian agents altogether, thereby losing their claim to membership in a recognised band or to land on a fixed reserve. This was another, accidental way of "disappearing."

The Strait's Indigenous people, however, would not fully disappear. By 1900, smallpox still broke out occasionally, but there was now widespread inoculation and growing resistance to the disease. Encouraged by progressive leaders such as Billy Assu at Cape Mudge and mission schools, more Indigenous children were learning

A graveyard in Comox around the 1890s: the Indigenous past was rapidly disappearing from the settlers' Strait, pre-empted by the settlers' present and future.

Image NA-39711 courtesy of the Royal BC Museum and Archives.

to read and write English. Authorities gave them Christian names that could be more easily pronounced by settlers.

Reserves, agents, potlatches & federal-provincial disputes

The Strait's beleaguered Indigenous population was subject to a growing web of government controls. The federal Indian Act of 1876 had aimed to, among other things, suppress Indigenous cultures. An 1885 amendment to this act outlawed their traditional spiritual ceremonies and dances. Yet another amendment before World War I required all "status Indians" to obtain permission before appearing in traditional costumes in any dance, exhibition or pageant. While colonial power was mostly applied peacefully, threats of violent sanction remained a potent tool of persuasion. Michael Manson, the settler trader and provincial politician on the northern Strait, told of exercising authority over the Cape Mudge people in the late nineteenth century. Manson had met with resistance when he visited their reserve in his capacity as the local Justice of the Peace to investigate a suspicious drowning. He told community leaders: "[I]f they did not obey me in everything very dire punishment would be dealt out to them, the war vessels would be sent to blow up and burn their villages, the leaders of the tribe would be hanged and the Chief and all his family would be forever barred from being elected or holding the position of Chief of the tribe."[28] Unsurprisingly, Manson's threat worked.

No single arm of settler government had full responsibility for Indigenous people, and no single perception of them prevailed within settler society. As a result, the settlers' new system for "governing Indians" was complicated and full of baffling contradictions from an Indigenous perspective. Victoria controlled their land, while Ottawa was responsible for their bodies and churches watched over their souls. Victoria ruled the forests while Ottawa controlled the Strait's sea life. The federal

Department of Indian Affairs was learning to take care of its new charges as the resource rush gathered steam. Federal Indian agents were responsible for keeping records of Indigenous people, though some felt the province ought to begin recording the births, deaths and marriages of "their Indians," as they did with settlers.

Indians came to be defined as "irresponsible children" under settler law (see photograph page 86), and the province was adamant that the kids should remain wards of the "federal crown." Federally administered Indian reserves, meanwhile, contributed to growing separation between the Strait's Indigenous and settler populations and seemed to be linked with Indigenous people's poverty. The Royal Commission on Indian Affairs, launched in 1913, recognised that the tiny size of the Strait's reserves might be contributing to the ongoing decline of Indigenous populations, while the province and many towns endeavoured to decrease their size still more.

Although James Douglas and G.M. Sproat had determined the boundaries of many early Indian reserves, Peter O'Reilly, who succeeded Sproat as Indian reserve commissioner, laid out the greatest number. He was not as preoccupied with Indigenous people's concerns as Sproat or Douglas had been, and the boundaries of the reserves O'Reilly laid out in the 1880s and 1890s often resembled the new borders being drawn across Africa in those years—straight lines that reflected very little understanding of the societies they affected. Historian Robin Fisher has suggested that O'Reilly may have been appointed *because* of his lack of concern for Indigenous people. Often travelling the Strait on a Department of Marine and Fisheries steamer, he was usually impervious to Indigenous people's complaints about his decisions. Whereas settlers around the Strait were excited by the prospect of the railway's arrival during O'Reilly's early years as commissioner because they felt it would boost land prices, Indigenous people increasingly feared losing what they had. They frequently sought clarification about their rights to traditional territories. Perhaps unsurprisingly, settlers could usually count on O'Reilly's sympathetic ear, while he often concluded that Indigenous people were failing to effectively "use" or "occupy" land sought by settlers.

Federally appointed Indian agents governed most aspects of reserve life, and they played a host of roles that had earlier been carried out by traditional Indigenous authorities. Agents dispensed justice, settled disputes and controlled public nuisances. They cooperated with clergy to suppress potlatches, alcohol abuse and prostitution, and they made sure that Indigenous labourers showed up when and where they were needed. Indian agents were also expected to help Indigenous people improve their farming and fishing and, in order to avoid the "unnecessary" cost of formal land surveys, they helped their charges decide how to informally subdivide their reserves among themselves. Furthermore, agents were expected to counsel their charges to avoid "intruding or trespassing upon the lands, fisheries, etc. of other people or Indians [note the distinction]." And agents "ensured law and order" and dealt with troublesome or drunken Indians by keeping them "on the reserve."

The potlatch—a traditional ceremony in which individuals made conspicuous displays of their wealth by giving much of it away to other community members— was a thorny issue. Churches longed to claim Indigenous souls, and the biggest barrier, they reasoned, was Indigenous people's traditional belief system. This belief

Peter Sitholatza, "a Kuper Island Indian of the Penelakut tribe" (circa the 1910s), was one of the Strait's disenfranchised Indigenous people, who were now classed by Ottawa as "irresponsible children."

Image A-07104 courtesy of the Royal BC Museum and Archives.

Circa the 1890s, these Sechelt musicians were part of the push to forget the potlatch and find more "respectable" ways to be happy in settler society, under the firm guidance of Christian clergy.

Image F-02405 courtesy of the Royal BC Museum and Archives.

system was most clearly manifested in the increasingly elaborate potlatch ceremonies that proliferated around the sea in these decades, despite their legal prohibition after 1885. Missionaries, and some Christianised Indigenous people, were determined that settler law must eliminate this "heathenish custom in vogue among the Indians." The potlatch, they said, made it impossible for these people to "acquire property or become industrious with any good results." Men were forcing "daughters and wives to go into prostitution to earn the money for it."[29] Like earlier violence between Indigenous groups, the excesses of the potlatch seemed to confirm the need for a corrective intervention by settler society. What many could not see—though the more observant missionaries certainly could—was that the potlatch was central to Indigenous people's traditional "prestige economy" (see photograph page 87). Government efforts to suppress the potlatch mounted after the 1880s, but it was not easily eradicated.

Land hunger, the province & local governments

Pre-emptions continued through the 1880s and into the 1890s, stimulated by the railroad's arrival, distant markets for the Strait's resources and growing local markets for farm produce and real estate. Settlers claimed land where it was still available early in the resource rush, mostly on the less hospitable Mainland shore. Small farms and orchards also appeared on the shores and islands of Howe Sound. For example, a decommissioned Royal Engineer had pre-empted over 100 hectares at Sechelt in 1869 and many followed him, claiming land from Howe Sound to Desolation Sound.

While Victoria was generally unsympathetic to Indigenous concerns, many local governments were openly hostile. Indigenous people and their reserves were usually a nuisance to rapidly growing settlements, to be gotten rid of or at least hidden away. Reserve land was unsightly, untaxable, unavailable and increasingly in the way of urban development. A growing list of towns and cities expressed their frustration with Indian neighbours who were occupying valuable land and thwarting the ambitions of new settlements to grow and prosper. The new Corporation of Surrey was incensed by federal government plans to establish a reserve at Semiahmoo Bay in the late 1880s. Even Peter O'Reilly—usually the settlers' ally—pointed out that Indigenous people had clearly been occupying this place for a long time. Captain Christian Mayers further confirmed seeing them at this site since 1858. However, Surrey countered that this was "about the best place in BC for a sea side summer resort," and these weren't even "BC Indians" but a crowd of "American Indians" who went there for "drunken orgies."

If granted this reserve, claimed officials in Surrey, the First Nations people would be "a source of danger and moral blight in our midst." In turn, Indian Affairs cited a number of "expert witnesses," including Bishop Durieu, who confirmed that these really were "BC Indians." But Surrey was not prepared to lose this valuable waterfront without a fight. Even if these weren't American Indians, they argued, they came to this shore for only a few weeks a year to fish. Presumably settlers would stay longer at their beachside cottages. Besides, these Indians had cultivated only eight of the 125 hectares they were claiming. Finally, once the reserve looked inevitable, Surrey tried to have it restricted to no more than 20 hectares. This was necessary, it said, to reduce harm to Surrey, which already had 117 applications to purchase two-acre (0.8 hectare) lots for summer residences on the bay. The Semiahmoo reserve was eventually established in 1887 on 130 hectares of land; much of it would eventually be leased to the Municipality of Surrey for recreational purposes.

Other reserve land in or near towns was becoming the target of vigorous efforts to wrest it from Indigenous owners. The towns of Comox, Qualicum, Ladysmith and Duncan all launched their own campaigns to remove or diminish local reserves with very similar arguments: Indigenous people were failing to "develop" land that had been "given" to them and so did not deserve to keep it. Most settlers felt that "Indians who did not use land set aside for them in ways consistent with newcomers' assumptions had no right to retain it."[30] Many towns saw their development as being handicapped by their inability to develop this valuable land, especially reserve land along the shore or riverbanks, which much of it was.

Early in the new century, Ottawa gave in to growing national pressure and amended the Indian Act to make it legal for towns with at least 8,000 inhabitants to seize adjacent reserve lands "in the interest" of the public and Indigenous people, even if the latter didn't consent. Municipalities and firms could also expropriate portions of reserves, without permission, where land was needed to build roads, railways or other infrastructure. By 1913, towns around the Strait were in a feeding frenzy, goaded on by a heady real-estate boom and inspired by the City of Victoria, which had managed to displace Indigenous people from the Songhees Reserve on its inner harbour.

Squamish people were similarly "unsettled" from their reserve at Kitsilano Point, or Snauq, where Indigenous people had been fishing nearby sandbars (later christened Granville Island) for many generations. For the new City of Vancouver, the reserve was an eyesore near the increasingly popular English Bay beach, and officials felt many more economically valuable things could be done with land at the entrance to what was becoming an important industrial area on False Creek. In its haste to consummate the "unsettling" of Snauq, the province overstepped its legal mandate and bypassed federal authorities. The ensuing legal quagmire lasted for decades, and the Squamish retained control of much of the land they had been persuaded to vacate. A local paper described Victoria's actions in the Snauq affair as "the greatest scandal in the history of the Provincial government of BC" and declared them "liable to a term in the penitentiary [if undertaken by]…an individual in the community."[31]

Other instruments of colonial government

With the Strait firmly under settler control by the late nineteenth century, the same sort of expropriation that had taken place on land was also conducted on the water. Settlers claimed the sea as their own to exploit on as large a scale as they could manage, and fish quickly became a key export commodity (chapter 4). Yet salmon, herring and clams also remained indispensable food resources for Indigenous people. The DMF in Ottawa began on the water what the Indian Reserve Commission had begun on land, progressively stripping Indigenous people of control over resources that had sustained them for centuries. Commercial fishermen even fished waters theoretically reserved for Indigenous people, as the Royal Commission on Indian Affairs reported in 1916:

> With respect to small reserves described and constituted as "fishing stations" and covering streams from which the Indians from earliest days have been accustomed to obtain their fish food supply, it has been in numerous instances declared in evidence by the interested Indians that the purpose and utility to them of these reserves has been wholly or in large measure destroyed by the subsequent allowance of cannery seining licences by which such "fishing stations" have been blanketed and rendered of no use to the Indians.[32]

Indian commissioners Sproat and O'Reilly had assumed Indigenous people would maintain control of the salmon fishery. The DMF, on the other hand, never intended for settler industry to be denied this valuable resource. The industrial fishery needed Indigenous labour but did not want Indigenous competition. Lobbying to curtail traditional Indigenous fishing activities began almost from the outset of the settler fishery and intensified with the arrival of the railway. By that time, more than 6,000 commercial fishers were active on the Fraser, many new canneries had been built and the first evidence of overfishing was already visible. A poor Sockeye run in 1916 was blamed on First Nations "food fishing" and two years later, the DMF brought in the first regulation to govern Indigenous people's fishing for food.

The new fishing rules were at least as hard on Indigenous people as the new land laws were. While settler fishers could set their nets at the mouths of salmon streams, Indigenous people might be arrested or fined for fishing in the wrong place or at the wrong time or using the wrong gear. The DMF placed limits on the types of fish Indigenous people might catch, requiring them to obtain permission to sell salmon, ostensibly because of a concern that First Nations fishers were the main cause of declining fish stocks. In many places, as concerns about fisheries depletion

Cowichan salmon weir: Weirs were a technology developed by trial and error over centuries but contested by federal authorities in the early 1900s. By 1900, the Cowichan Valley was home to the Strait's largest concentration of "remittance men," many attracted by its good fishing and hunting, which brought them into conflict with Indigenous fishers.

Image G-06604 courtesy of the Royal BC Museum and Archives.

began to appear in the public record, so did accusations that Indigenous people were important contributors to the problem. The Royal Commission on Indian Affairs, which was launched in 1913, heard repeated warnings from settlers about First Nations' "wasteful" use of salmon especially. But an Indian agent complained it was difficult to teach conservation to his wards in light of the "huge waste of salmon by the [settlers'] Fraser River canners."[33]

Indigenous people increasingly worried about their access to food fish.[34] When they were not fishing for the canneries, they could fish *only* for their families' food and they had to ask Ottawa's permission even for this "privilege." And successive settler governments began to see traditional fishing practices as unacceptable. The Cowichan people, for example, struggled with Ottawa for years over their right to use their traditional weirs on the Cowichan River (see photograph page 90), which authorities deemed "a distinct violation of the law." A deal was eventually struck limiting the Cowichan to three weirs. Then they were limited to using only dip nets, which they had not used much in the past. These regulations were put in place because settler sport fishermen, enamoured with the Strait's Chinook and Coho salmon and Steelhead trout in particular, were growing alarmed by the "depredations" of Indigenous fishers. Controversy over the Cowichan weirs, for example, was stimulated partly by sport fishers protecting their favourite angling stream. Ironically, when Indigenous people raised their own conservation concerns, particularly about the growing export of Chum salmon to Japan, federal officials dismissed their concerns about depletion out of hand. The government ignored the fact that Chum—a species mostly of interest to the Japanese Canadian commercial fleet at this time—was an important source of food for Indigenous people. It conceded, however, that such Indigenous complaints were a sign that local First Nations people were becoming "somewhat more progressive," less like "helpless children" and better able to "accept conditions as they exist today."[35]

Fish were not the only traditional food source under siege. By 1914, Indigenous people on the southern Strait needed permits to hunt deer too. These permits were issued by the provincial game wardens, but only on the recommendation of an Indian agent and after consideration of an applicant's age and family size. Even duly licensed, Indigenous hunters could take no more than four deer in total in a season and three of any single deer species, unless they obtained special permission from the game warden. The northern Strait was still classified as "unorganised districts" where First Nations hunters could kill more than four deer in a season, but only to feed their families. They were prohibited from selling the meat. Indigenous duck hunters were likewise circumscribed by new laws, though in 1914 the provincial game warden advised his agents to "be lenient" in enforcing the rules—except near the Strait's largest towns—when it came to those duck species that "are not esteemed edible by white people."[36]

Soon, the need for new transportation infrastructure was also used as a reason to remove land and resources from Indigenous hands. A federal government report summarised the "Indian land" around the sea that had been leased for other uses between 1871 and 1911. It was a long list: strips for moving logs to the shore or building railway and highway rights-of-way, land for developing urban and port infrastructure, marine space for storing log booms, and on and on. Indigenous communities were vulnerable to these demands because so many were located on shorelines (see photograph page 91), where the ports, railways and roads so critical for the growth of the settler economy all converged. The Dunsmuirs' E&N Railway cut a 30-metre swath across the Esquimalt reserve, removing all the timber and houses that were in the way. Citing the Railway Act of 1879 and its later amendments, the company aimed to expropriate the entire Songhees reserve for its Victoria terminal and it eventually received part of it.

The Indigenous village at Coal Harbour, seen here in 1886, would soon make way for the new port of Vancouver; compare this with the photo of the harbour in 1888 (see photograph page 35).

An 80-hectare Squamish reserve at the mouth of the Capilano River was reduced first by 1.4 hectares for a road right-of-way in 1912 and then by another 7.5 hectares for a railway in 1913. In 1917, the Harbour Commission had acquired rights to the reserve's foreshore. The smaller Squamish reserve at Kitsilano Point was reduced by 4 hectares in 1886 and 1902, first for a CPR bridge across False Creek and then for a railway through the reserve (it was never built). The federal government's Harbours Board also insisted, unsuccessfully, on its right to part of the reserve for new harbour and rail facilities. Then another 3.2 hectares of the Kitsilano Point reserve were taken to build the Burrard Street Bridge in 1930. Sometimes residents of these reserves received compensation; often they didn't.

Settler demands for recreational space also removed Indigenous people from traditional territories. Semiahmoo Bay, discussed above, was just one case. By 1900, Vancouver's new Parks Board had removed all Indigenous homes except one from a former village site, Whoi-Whoi, on Burrard Inlet in Stanley Park. Elsewhere around the sea, Indigenous people began to lease their reserve land on beaches so that settlers could build summer cottages. Perhaps they calculated that it was better to offer this land on long-term leases than to risk losing it because it was "not being used."

The success of a reserve, however, was often judged by how well people were farming it. The Royal Commission heard testimony praising Indigenous people in Saanich who "display evidence of considerable intelligent cultivation."[37] At Nanoose and Comox, the Indigenous people were criticised for leaving so much land uncultivated, suggesting that perhaps they had more land than they needed. Failure to farm more land or properly manage land they did farm was widely seen as an indictment of a dissolute lifestyle. Yet without an agricultural tradition to draw on and with limited lands of uneven quality, they required much technical advice to become "good farmers." And, as "Indians," they weren't able to get the technical support that Ottawa and Victoria provided to settler farmers.

A group of men at Warburton Pike's home on Saturna Island in 1887: Many people had come from Britain to be gentleman farmers, sport fishers and hunters on newly acquired land in the Strait.

Image B-07179 courtesy of the Royal BC Museum and Archives.

Indigenous people's only source of technical advice was their Indian agent, who had many other duties. Despite difficulties adapting to farming, Indigenous people on some reserves before World War I began to claim the right to 64 hectares each. An Indian agent in the Cowichan Agency explained to the Royal Commission that such demands were "purely political." Indigenous people, he said, had been coached by "dangerous radicals" and were "only asking this because white men are allowed to pre-empt a hundred and sixty acres [64 hectares] of land."[38] It seemed obvious to authorities that Indigenous people could never make good use of such large tracts of land for farming even if they were still available, which they weren't.

From Riel and railways to the McKenna-McBride Commission

Indigenous people were not the only ones dissatisfied with colonial dispossession around the Strait before World War I. Many settlers, backed by their provincial and municipal governments, felt First Nations still had too much land. As was common among colonial governments around the world at the time, the Royal Commission on Indian Affairs, or the McKenna-McBride Commission, was launched in 1913 to "settle the land question once and for all." Here, as in most other colonial territories, this commission was another opportunity to break earlier promises to Indigenous people. Premier James Dunsmuir, son of coal magnate Robert Dunsmuir, had approached Ottawa as early as 1901 calling for "better terms" for BC. Many BC reserves, he said, needed to be reduced because too much valuable agricultural land was held by too few Indigenous people. The Department of Indian Affairs, having spent many years negotiating these reserves, was slow to respond. When Premier Richard McBride pressed a more forceful claim in 1912, the federal government acquiesced and launched a joint federal-provincial commission the following year. The McKenna-McBride Commission was tasked with "equitably adjusting" reserve boundaries "one last time." Full and unfettered authority over reserves would then be handed to the federal government.

The Royal Commission allowed settlers and Indigenous people to plead their cases (see photographs page 93). Complaints from the Strait's rapidly growing towns have been described earlier. The commissioners also received eloquent testimony from Indigenous participants, though they seldom responded positively to them. Chief Julian from Cortes Island told them: "If we do not kill deer out of season we have nothing to eat."[39] In the Cowichan, Chief Que-Och-Qult complained: "The cost of living…has greatly increased while at the same time the Indian's facilities for earning his living had been greatly handicapped by the fishing and game laws of the whites and the reduction of the Indians' natural food by the demands of the white market." Indian Dick reported: "Everything has been taken from us and we have nothing. They have taken our grub and we have nothing at all. God gave us fish and animals so that we might live on the country and they have taken all these things away from us." Chief Joe Eukahalt remarked: "The white men are making laws that are getting our people into trouble…They cannot get their grub anywhere without being guilty of violating some law."[40]

Such moving statements from Indigenous leaders revealed the enormous changes to the lives of their people that had taken place since the onset of Eurasian resettlement of the Strait only a couple of generations earlier. From their perspective, the inland sea and its rich littoral had been theirs from time immemorial. Now this place and its resources were mostly off-limits to them and would be shared only very sparingly, according to the arcane rules and norms of the newcomers.

Stagnation but not disappearance during the interwar years

Indigenous people lived mostly outside settler society, though they remained a valuable industrial proletariat around BC's inland sea during the interwar years. The settlers' Strait was now well integrated into global socio-economic networks but its people were three times wounded between 1914 and 1945: by a savage war in Europe, a decade-long severe economic downturn after 1929, and a truly global conflagration. Not surprisingly, this turbulent period did not see much opening of settlers' minds to the oppressed Indigenous minority in their midst. It did, however, see an end to more than a century of declining Indigenous populations.

A vanishing culture

By 1921, Indigenous people had not disappeared, as a succession of provincial and municipal governments had hoped they might. They now accounted for only 4 percent of British Columbia's population, however, and probably about the same around the Strait, which remained the province's centre of gravity. The Indigenous population finally stopped shrinking in the 1920s, though physical traces of their culture (see photographs page 93, bottom, and page 94) were still vanishing

Headman of the Malahat Indians (top) and Musqueam chief and subchief (bottom) in 1913. They attended the McKenna-McBride Commission hearings, where they learned settlers needed more land.

Images H-07040 and II-07081 courtesy of the Royal BC Museum and Archives.

Right: House post at Cowichan in 1936: A relic of a fading cultural legacy.
Image F-02584 courtesy of the Royal BC Museum and Archives.

Far right: War canoe races at the Cowichan Bay Regatta in 1922: Other traces of the Indigenous past were fast disappearing, but people could still make canoes.
Image B-09426 courtesy of the Royal BC Museum and Archives.

Below: Chief Billy Assu of Cape Mudge, seen here with his family in the 1920s, recruited Indigenous labour for the settler fishing industry. Federal authorities confiscated his people's potlatching regalia in the same decade.
Image D-04578 courtesy of the Royal BC Museum and Archives.

from the landscape. In *Sunshine Coast*, publisher Howard White remembered the Pender Harbour settlement of his childhood, where "only a few traces remained of the teeming, robust Salish city." At nearby Sakinaw Lake, only vague traces remained of the Sechelt people's intricate fish traps, which early in the twentieth century were described as "a masterpiece of stone age engineering." By mid-century they had virtually disappeared, obliterated by loggers. Huge forest fires on the Malaspina Peninsula in 1918, and another twenty years later between Comox and Campbell River, destroyed many traces of the Indigenous presence in those areas. In Stanley Park, an iconic symbol of natural splendour on the doorstep of the Strait's dominant city, the final "Indian squatters" were evicted and their houses razed in the early 1940s. In 1943, the Vancouver Parks Board briefly considered constructing an "Indian Museum" on the site of the Indigenous settlement called Whoi-Whoi in Stanley Park. Instead, a memorial was erected to the lumber industry.

Summer cruiser Francis John Barrow and, a decade later, writer Frederick Marsh both noted a growing scarcity of Indian artifacts. Barrow was in the habit of searching Indigenous middens he found while looking for pictographs around the northern Strait and beyond. By the late 1930s, he complained regularly of finding promising midden sites already emptied of artifacts. Marsh reported a few years later that on the southern islands, "Indian relics" that were once common, such as "flint spearheads, chisels, pestles and stuff like that, all over,"[41] had become hard to find. Many of the clamshell middens, where artifacts could most easily be found, were disappearing under houses and streets.

Attempts to eradicate Indigenous culture paralleled the disappearance of its physical remains. Suppression of the potlatch escalated in the new century. The Cape Mudge people had to hand over their potlatching regalia in the 1920s. Masks and costumes, deemed sinful vestiges of a pagan past, were surrendered to federal authorities to be destroyed. Instead, they were transferred to the National Museum in Ottawa. Despite the ban and missionaries' pressure to enforce it, potlatch ceremonies continued around the Strait in the interwar years. Settlers who witnessed them were awed by the powerful rituals. In *Adventures in Solitude*, Grant Lawrence recounted the story of Alice Bloom, a settler on Okeover Inlet off Desolation Sound in the interwar years. Bloom "recalled with great fondness that on certain nights each winter, she and her family would secretly watch the Natives dance around a raging bonfire on the shores of Kahkaykay during their potlatch celebrations, their singing filling the night."

Frederick Marsh recounted a similar story from a Mrs. Forbes about a potlatch she witnessed in the same period at Penelakut village: "Around a fire built, Indian style, in the centre of a long community lodge with a hole in the roof to let out the smoke, thirty performers danced with increasing frenzy before several hundred Indian spectators. A handful of privileged whites...looked on from a high gallery... The rhythmic beating of tom-toms caused dancers and spectators to sway in unison. The atmosphere, blue with smoke and ruddy in the flickering firelight, seemed to pulse with highly charged emotion...Their men...danced almost to exhaustion."[42]

Indigenous people were expected to "assimilate" rather than pursue these traditional cultural practices (see photograph page 96), let alone pursue claims to traditional lands that Victoria and Ottawa now considered pointless. Duncan Campbell Scott, the head of Indian Affairs through much of this period, described a "sentiment for the extinguishment of the Legal Indian" and expressed his own goal of "getting rid of the Indian problem" by ensuring all Indigenous people were fully "absorbed into the body politic."[43] Concerned that Indigenous people were not shedding their traditional culture fast enough, successive governments began forcing Indigenous children into residential schools. Legislation passed in 1920 obliged parents, under threat of imprisonment, to send children who were between five and fifteen years of age to residential schools to learn "practical skills." Indian agents and RCMP officers began rounding up the children and sending them to schools in places like Sechelt, Mission and Kamloops. There, children were often abused and were forbidden to speak their parents' languages. Many Indigenous people are still experiencing trauma related to the residential school experience today.

Opening of a residential school in Sechelt in 1922: Indigenous students were brought in from communities around the sea and were expected to become good Catholics.

Image NA-41837 courtesy of the Royal BC Museum and Archives.

Continued land hunger

The intense land hunger that had consumed so much Indigenous traditional territory abated somewhat in the interwar period, but even if settlers no longer sought Indigenous land for farming, towns, railways and industries still did. The Squamish and Musqueam reserves, from the mouth of the Fraser to the head of Howe Sound, were frequent targets. At the dawn of World War I, the City of North Vancouver had joined forces with adjoining North and West Vancouver district governments in an unsuccessful effort to acquire 300 hectares of Squamish land adjacent to their settlements.

In the early 1920s, perhaps inspired by the Pacific Great Eastern Railway's (PGE) expropriation of a portion of the Squamish reserve at the north end of Howe Sound and anxious to expand industrial activities adjacent to its own new PGE terminal, the City of North Vancouver returned to its pursuit of the Squamish band's land. The municipal government suggested its Indigenous neighbours should be removed to the other Squamish lands at the head of Howe Sound. The Squamish leadership successfully resisted: "What would we do up Howe Sound?" they asked.[44] They were no longer fishers and had never farmed, and their work at the time took place mostly at Burrard Inlet's docks and mills. Railways could still expropriate with impunity, but Indigenous people were better at resisting municipal encroachments. The Squamish, by the mid-1920s, were organised and skilful in defending their interests, though the many resolutions they passed still had to be "subject to the approval of the Department of Indian Affairs." By the end of World War II, they were major owners of industrial land in North Vancouver.

Governance

The Royal Commission on Indian Affairs dragged on through the early years of World War I with the goal of reaching a final agreement on land allocation for Indian reserves throughout BC. The province contested the commissioners' recommendations, still finding the reserves too large, while Indigenous groups continued to see them as too small. This wrangling went on through most of the interwar period. Victoria and Ottawa finally agreed on reserve boundaries, and the official transfer of reserve land to the federal government, in 1938. In the province as a whole, they added about twice as much land (350 square kilometres) to reserves as they removed (190 square kilometres). The overall *value* of the land they removed from reserves, however, was roughly six times greater than the value of the land that was added.

Around the Strait, slight reductions were made to already small reserves. Along the western shore, total reserve land was reduced from 4.05 to 4.04 acres per person and on the Mainland shore from 6.66 to 6.60 acres per person. Ottawa and Victoria shared the money generated by the sale of these expropriated lands, with the federal share going, as usual, into Indian Affairs trust funds. Both governments expected this would be the final word on Indigenous land allocation. After hearing a land claims presentation by the Allied Tribes of BC, the federal government had again amended the Indian Act in 1927. From then until 1952, it was simply illegal for Indigenous people to raise funds to pursue land claims, except in the unlikely event that they obtained permission to do so from the Department of Indian Affairs.

By the 1920s, the federal fisheries department had become the resource manager for the industrial fishery. The canneries had secured exclusive control over almost all commercial salmon fishing by this time, and fisheries regulations enhanced Indigenous people's opportunities for work in the industry. Boats owned by Salish and Kwakwaka'wakw speakers became a substantial component of the commercial fleet on the Strait, while Indigenous women remained an important part of the canneries' labour force. Indigenous people's right to fish for their own food, on the other hand, came under further assault. Beleaguered Fraser River Sockeye runs, though much reduced by the landslide at Hells Gate in the Fraser Canyon in 1913, were showing modest signs of recovery by the late 1920s. As in earlier years, however, Indigenous people continued to be singled out as a threat to fishery conservation efforts. The chief federal fisheries inspector for BC declared in 1929 that Indigenous people no longer needed a food fishery. And early in the 1930s canners tried, in vain, to demonstrate that the food fishery was superfluous by supplying reserves with crates of canned pilchard and Chum salmon.

The damage being done to sport fishing by Indigenous fisheries was a public concern. Saanich Inlet had become a popular sport fishing site, with a growing collection of summer cottages on its shores. Indigenous people on the inlet, earlier guaranteed the right to fish there under their Douglas treaties, were first prohibited from using nets at that site, then banned from fishing on the inlet altogether. A similar proscription of First Nations food fishing in favour of the sport fishery eliminated their right to take fish from North Vancouver's Capilano River with anything other than an angler's hook and line.

Indigenous communities around the Strait also struggled to retain access to traditional clam beds. For example, when the Comox lost control over rich clam beds surrounding Tree (Sandy) Island, a tiny archipelago at the head of Baynes Sound, they appealed to the government to get them back. Clams were an important traditional food source for the Comox, and the islands had been pre-empted by a settler and then sold to the British Lords of the Admiralty at the end of the nineteenth century.

They were later transferred to the Canadian navy, which used them for target practice in the 1930s. Denman Island settlers had also begun digging clams on Tree Island, while the fish-canning conglomerate BC Packers claimed the beds too, though it had stopped working them by the late 1930s. The Comox tried to broker a complex bargain in which they guaranteed the navy access to nearby Goose Spit in perpetuity in exchange for renewed Indigenous control over Tree Island's shellfish-rich foreshore. Negotiations ensued between Ottawa and Victoria, and while Indian Affairs was able to secure the barren islets, it could not convince the province to surrender the foreshore around them—which was all the Comox people really wanted.

The removal of Japanese Canadians from the West Coast in 1942, and the seizure of their fishing boats, some seen here at Annieville dike on the Fraser River, meant new opportunities for Indigenous fishers.
Image C-07293 courtesy of the Royal BC Museum and Archives.

As they had with their claims to land—until such actions became illegal—Indigenous people also protested the erosion of their fishing rights. And associations of Indigenous fishers became surrogate political organisations in this period, since the Indian Act had otherwise muffled all resistance. The Native Brotherhood of BC, founded in the early 1930s, became the principal voice for Indigenous fishermen on the coast, but its members' efforts to secure control over fishing grounds adjacent to their reserves—as had been envisioned when these reserves were originally demarcated—were unsuccessful. In the late 1930s, Andrew Paull, Secretary of the Progressive Native Tribes of BC, wrote to the Superintendent General of Indian Affairs in Ottawa to ask for exclusive use of the waters off Cape Mudge for the people of that reserve. He explained:

> Waters in front of the Cape Mudge reserve are the spawning grounds of the Codfish but it will soon be depleted as Japanese fish in front of this reserve for ten months of the year…The opposite waters in this channel is reserved for sporting fishermen and the Indians cannot fish there commercially. On their side of the channel in front of their reserve, it is overrun with Japs fishing for Codfish, and during the salmon fishing season…gradually and by degrees the native Indian is squeezed out of the only means he has in these parts of earning a livelihood.[45]

The Minister of Fisheries refused Paull's request, however, citing his ministry's need to protect the "public right to fisheries," even those adjacent to reserves. The minister declared, "The granting of fishing rights or privileges to one class of fishermen that would not be available to others would not be feasible."[46] It was a bold argument in light of the long list of other rights and privileges that Indigenous people were denied at the time.

Paull's claim of Japanese Canadian fishermen's depredations at Cape Mudge was a familiar refrain by the 1930s. Decades earlier, such complaints had figured prominently in testimony to the McKenna-McBride Commission. Indigenous people's perception of the "Japanese threat" to the Strait's natural bounty was widely shared in the white fishing community, and these fishers may have been an easier target for Indigenous discontent than the white bosses of the industrial fisheries. The sudden removal of Japanese Canadians from the West Coast in 1942 (see photograph page 98) helped make World War II a time of "unprecedented gains" for Indigenous commercial fishers. Many boats were suddenly available, the war effort needed fish, and it needed labour in the boats and canneries.

Impacts of farming, forestry & transportation

By the interwar years, the idea of the Strait being converted into a version of the British seaside had receded, and much of the land that had been cleared for farming or logging was returning to forest. Meanwhile, smaller tracts of (often the best) forest land disappeared under new towns and cities, so that BC was the least agricultural province in the Dominion by the 1920s. Writing in *Maclean's* magazine in the mid-1930s, Comox Valley naturalist Hamilton Mack Laing noted the dwindling popularity of "stump ranching" around the sea. He predicted that much of the land that settlers had worked so hard to clear was destined to become golf courses and drive-in movie areas within a generation. Agriculture on the southern islands began to stagnate due to their growing isolation from the ever more highway-based economy on the Mainland and Vancouver Island. The thriving market gardens of Japanese Canadians on these southern islands were an important exception, but these did not survive World War II.

Ultimately, the myth of the yeoman farmer by the sea had helped legitimise the rapid dispossession of the Strait's Indigenous people, yet much of that land had never been farmed at all, only logged and then abandoned. This story of "improvement" survived at Indian Affairs, however, as the department's forestry directives stipulated: "Lumbering operations on a Reserve must, as far as possible, be co-ordinated with the clearing and preparation of the land for cultivation, and the principal aim to bear in mind should be to restrict such lumbering to certain prescribed areas, so that the cutting of timber under permit shall constitute the initial step toward agricultural improvement."[47]

Ottawa clearly had little understanding of either farming or lumbering around the Strait. Yet, as the directive suggests, the department carefully governed logging by Indigenous people on their reserves. All timber was deemed common property, and any timber sold to interests off the reserve had to be approved by a majority of adult male members of the band. Any band member who wanted to harvest timber had to first obtain a recommendation from the band's governing council and then permission from the Department of Indian Affairs. He or she could then cut and sell reserve timber under the local Indian agent's supervision, but "in no instance should timber be removed from a reserve before the dues [payable to the Department of Indian Affairs] have been collected."[48] Finally, Indian agents were to warn their wards "of the fallacy of regarding their timber as a perpetual source of income. It is far easier to exercise a judicious conservation of timber resources *today* than to face the expensive alternative of re-forestation in the *future*."[49] Once again, federal pronouncements were remarkably out of touch with the realities of the settlers' Strait, where systematic overharvesting of timber had become the norm (chapter 3).

Just as they had before the war, a number of reserves, perhaps making virtue of necessity, continued to earn significant income from leasing their foreshore to industrial users, especially for log booms. Although the foreshore in front of reserves had often been contested in the past, with First Nations repeatedly claiming control over the beaches in front of their allotted land, Indigenous authority was increasingly questioned during the interwar years, especially by owners of houseboats and log booms. Eventually the province gained control over beaches in front of reserves, except where Indigenous right to these beaches had been explicitly mentioned when the reserve was established, which it seldom had. In some cases, the province required Indian Affairs to repay rent it had previously charged forestry companies to store their booms off reserves. Reserves lost their foreshore rights to Ottawa in harbours that were under its control. The newly constituted "public harbour" on Burrard Inlet, for example, asserted its own control over the foreshore and considerable stretches of shoreline previously controlled by the Squamish people.

Expropriation of reserve lands for transportation infrastructure also continued through the interwar period. After World War I, the new highway system that rapidly developed around the Strait diminished a number of reserves. Provincial highway engineers were confident of their rights and eager to get on with their projects, as the Malahat people discovered in the mid-1920s. They were given no advance warning before piledrivers and carpenters showed up to construct a ferry terminal on their Mill Bay reserve. A few days earlier, the provincial engineer had sent a letter to the Department of Indian Affairs stating simply that the province was about to build a landing for a ferry service that would traverse Saanich Inlet (see photograph page 100) and that the chosen site lay within the boundaries of the reserve. "It is necessary," he wrote, "that construction commence immediately which does not allow time for formal notification but proper plans and descriptions will be filed in due course."[50]

It turned out that people on the Malahat reserve were "bitterly opposed" to this ferry terminal. The bureaucrats of Indian Affairs had no choice but to acquiesce, however, because except for a few federally controlled harbours, the province was now deemed to "possess the foreshore." Indigenous people's only rights were to "access and ingress"—to come and go across the beach in front of their reserve. Indian

The Brentwood–Mill Bay ferry at Mill Bay in 1967: Built over an Indigenous cemetery in the 1920s, the Mill Bay ferry terminal's compressed construction schedule apparently prevented them from consulting with the local First Nations community before work began.

Image I-21464 courtesy of the Royal BC Museum and Archives.

By 1945, the Cowichan (here performing the Whale Dance) were without their traditional masks.
Image I-27569 courtesy of the Royal BC Museum and Archives.

Affairs officials did point out that it was, nonetheless, unfortunate that the ferry slip had been located over their cemetery, from which remains should be exhumed and reinterred elsewhere at the expense of the province. Unfortunate as well that the new road leading to the ferry dock had been built "through practically the only good piece of land on the reserve where the Indian village is situated and will disturb a considerable amount of Indian improvements." It also threatened to foul the reserve's water supply.[51]

The same, but different

Settler assaults on Indigenous people's claims to space and resources around the Strait continued through the interwar period, but the ability of Indigenous communities to resist was growing. They salvaged vestiges of their cultural heritage (see photograph page 101). They learned the intricacies of settler laws and governance and how to work within them. The people at Cape Mudge had asserted themselves in negotiations with local cannery owners and loggers, and Chief Billy Assu had ensured that his people received more equitable working conditions. He encouraged them not to assimilate but to adapt in order to benefit from the settlers' ways without losing their identity. At Cape Mudge and elsewhere around the sea, Indigenous leaders now knew that their dispossession had contravened the settlers' own laws.

Some settlers, too, began to recognise that the colonial adventure may not have claimed just "idle lands" and "unused resources" but also the birthrights of others. Among the men returning from war in Europe and Asia were those who could see the injustice faced by their Indigenous comrades, who had also fought and died for Canada but still could not vote in their own country.

The beginnings of decolonisation after World War II

The decades after 1945 were a period of decolonisation around the world. World War II had demonstrated some possible outcomes of theories of racial superiority. The horrors of this war, and then independence movements across Asia and Africa, stirred growing consciousness of settler societies' unjust treatment of Indigenous peoples. Many Indigenous communities around the Strait had become deeply dysfunctional after more than a century of disease, dispossession, marginalisation, racism and attempted cultural genocide. Yet they were also remarkably resilient: they had refused to meet settler society's expectation of their disappearance and remained determined to reclaim their heritage.

Reappearance

W.A.C. Bennett, the provincial leader through the 1950s and '60s, reflected the attitudes that still prevailed when in 1958 he celebrated the history of BC's first century as "the story of development, of the building of a…*homogeneous* [emphasis added] province; of a God fearing pioneer people dedicated to progress, strengthened by their contest with a great land at first reluctant to yield its full resources."[52] Before the era of federally financed multiculturalism, which began in the 1970s, there was no obvious place for Indigenous people in Bennett's vision of a homogeneous settler society hewing resources from a reluctant land. Even naturalists on the inland sea, such as Hamilton Mack Laing, whose perspectives were often trenchantly at odds with Bennett's and who had some appreciation of Indigenous heritage, still tended to celebrate mostly the resplendent nature of the place rather than Indigenous people's ties to this nature. Early in the post-war era, many people around the inland sea were more likely to associate Indigenous people with beer parlours than with nature.

Although Indigenous people were still often disregarded—particularly by the provincial government and industry—a growing number of writers, scientists and academics were stimulating greater public awareness of Indigenous culture and concerns. James Matthews, the first archivist at the Vancouver Museum, interviewed Squamish people through the 1930s, and in 1948 the museum issued the result: a quirky collection of hand-typed pages and original photographs listing and discussing Indigenous place names on Burrard Inlet and Howe Sound that had been "certified correct" by the Squamish Indian Council. It was a remarkable act of recognition in a city that until then had mostly erased traces of Indigenous occupation. Matthews's work with the Squamish revealed deeper human bonds with places now overlaid with recently acquired settler names.

West Point Grey, which was filling with settler homes and seaside parks, had been called Ulksen. Lumberman's Arch, on the Burrard Inlet shore of Stanley Park, had been erected on the site of the large village called Whoi-Whoi (or Xway xway), named for the traditional masked dances that had been performed there. Caulfeild in West Vancouver had been Stuck-Ale, a name describing the foul smell of gas that rises naturally to the surface there. Horseshoe Bay had been called Cha-Hay, a name evoking the sound made by millions of herring moving across the water as they spawned on the bay. Homer Barnett, Wayne Suttles and other anthropologists devoted their careers to studying Coast Salish–speaking people. Their work began to seep into the public discourse and inspired a new generation of researchers. Like Matthews's work and a growing body of archaeological evidence, these studies raised awareness among the settler population of complex, long-standing human relationships with the rest of nature on the Strait.

By the 1960s, writers and journalists such as Roderick Haig-Brown and Imbert Orchard were presenting the public with positive images of Indigenous people and their struggles. Haig-Brown was effusive in his praise for the Cape Mudge people's "very great chief" Billy Assu. Haig-Brown, who lived in nearby Campbell River, had known Assu for decades and their families would later be linked by marriage. Orchard, in his extensive oral history of the Strait, explained to CBC listeners in the early 1960s: "Often the Indian child in a residential school was forbidden to use his native language or sing his own songs. As a result, a culture was destroyed, and an alien culture superimposed, without any regard to the psychological effects."[53] This story of Indigenous people's trauma had seldom been heard in settler society at the time.

The threats that local writers and artists depicted around the sea were now likely to be loggers, developers and others promoting rampant urban growth. Poet Earle Birney and Haig-Brown were more inclined to portray past Indigenous cultures on the sea as "ecological Indians"[54] who had achieved a harmony between humans and nature and whose secret had been lost to industrial society. Literary critic Allan Pritchard suggested that Haig-Brown and others may have tried to establish a tie with Indigenous people out of a desire for a more legitimate claim to belonging in their adopted land. What their work did was highlight the reality of Indigenous people's dispossession, a theme explored in books such as Jack Hodgins's *Resurrection of Joseph Bourne*.

By the 1970s, the province's interpretation of "local heritage" that needed preserving around the sea was a hodgepodge of familiar settler vestiges—early post offices, churches, stores and cemeteries—mixed with mysterious petroglyphs (rock carvings) from the Strait's Indigenous world (see photograph page 107). A brochure celebrating the Diamond Jubilee of Saanich District in 1965 declared that South Saanich had been purchased on February 6, 1852, through an agreement signed by local Indigenous people and that North Saanich was purchased from them five days later. Few other settler communities on the Strait could hark back to such agreements with Indigenous people, and many would begin to regret such deficiencies. Around this time, Indigenous people began to reappear in official representations of the sea's past.

By the late 1970s BC's roadside information panels, which were erected at scenic lookout spots along the highways, described "Indian woodworking tools of the Northwest Coast" and "Food and cooking of the Northwest Coast Indians."[55] The provincial archaeologist expressed concern about the degradation of "archaeological resources" on many of the islands in the Strait. Less than 10 percent of 800 archaeological sites on the islands were still intact, he reported, and many had been disturbed during the century of resettlement. "The worst offender" had been "construction of permanent and summer residences…[while] marine facilities such as ferry landings, wharves, marinas and the like have also taken a great toll."[56]

Indigenous people themselves were increasingly involved in efforts to salvage their cultural heritage. The Cape Mudge people lobbied Ottawa for decades to return their potlatching regalia, which had been confiscated in the 1920s. Anxious to improve relations with Indigenous people, Ottawa agreed. In 1979, the band opened its own museum to house these precious vestiges of its past. Other bands such as the Sechelt carved magnificent replicas of traditional dugout canoes and staged high-profile canoeing events to emphasise their maritime heritage. Some reimagined a past that was more harmonious than it may have been. In 1986, for example, the Sechelt and Sliammon people welcomed a traditional Haida canoe, though they had seldom been as welcoming in earlier centuries.

Recognition of rights

After World War II, Victoria and Ottawa began to return to Indigenous people some of the fundamental rights and inheritance that had been taken from them, though the federal "Indian Affairs" administration remained in place. The right to vote in provincial elections, withdrawn in 1872, was restored in 1949. The federal government did the same in 1960. The right to hold potlatches was reinstated in 1951, although confiscated regalia mostly remained in museums and private collections. Amendments to the Indian Act the same year called for Indian agents to be replaced by band chiefs and for bands to begin taking control of local administration. The residential school system was progressively shut down in the 1960s and '70s.

Devolution of control over budgets and financial management to Indigenous governments contributed to considerable development on many reserves. New schools and infrastructure were built and land development projects were initiated, mostly leasing land to non-Indigenous people. Ambitious plans by the Cowichan to develop hundreds of residential lots on Kuper (today Penelakut) Island in the mid-1970s did not get off the ground. But ten years later, the We Wai Kai people at Cape Mudge successfully opened a tourist hotel and restaurant on Quadra Island. The Sliammon, north of Powell River, describe the 1970s as the time of "the most development activity" in their history: they built fifty new homes, a fire hall, a band office, a kindergarten, a sewage treatment plant, a health clinic, a soccer field and a community centre. They also invested in an oyster farm and a salmon hatchery. The following decade, the Sechelt became the first Indigenous community in Canada to be granted "self-government" status. However, the most significant change in Indigenous governance, one that affected the future of all people in the Strait's broader community, was the passage of Canada's Constitution Act of 1982. By clearly recognising and affirming "aboriginal title," it opened the door to a long and still ongoing series of negotiations over Indigenous claims to land and resources.

Indigenous land hunger

While Indigenous people may have been more visible than before, settler society continued to absorb their traditional territories on the Strait even after World War II. The Powell River Company dammed the Theodosia River in the early 1950s to generate hydroelectricity for its ten paper machines, destroying another salmon stream that local people had fished for countless generations. Nanaimo's Duke Point industrial park and ferry terminal were built on top of Indigenous settlements and burial sites two decades later. By the 1980s, however, the most visible land hunger on the Strait belonged to Indigenous people, who were attempting to reclaim traditional territories with renewed vigour. Ottawa had virtually outlawed such claims in the 1920s, curtailing their pursuit for half a century. When the federal government formally considered Indigenous land claims again in the 1970s, the door was opened to the possible existence of "unextinguished aboriginal rights" in Canada. A torrent of litigation ensued, supported by the growing body of literature on Indigenous history, economy and culture discussed earlier. Today, while most First Nations around the Strait are involved in complicated land-claim negotiations with the provincial and federal governments, few claims have been settled (chapter 7).

Renewed fisheries rights

Despite the fact that Ottawa began to recognise certain Indigenous rights after World War II, federal fisheries managers continued to favour the commercial fishery over First Nations fishers. Many Indigenous people still lived near traditional food-gathering sites by the mouth of the Fraser, Cowichan, Qualicum, Courtenay, Squamish, Capilano and other rivers. But for many, their connection with the once-sustaining fishery had become tenuous. The fishing fleet that had grown dramatically in the interwar years was in decline again by the 1960s in many Indigenous communities. Fewer Indigenous people were working in the canneries and their communities were finding it harder to secure enough salmon to feed themselves. The Indigenous fishing fleet shrank further in the 1970s as the federal government used licensing restrictions to force "less efficient" boats out of the commercial fleet (chapter 4). Many of these were owned by Indigenous fishers, and one immediate result of Ottawa's move to "improve the economic performance" of the modern fishing sector was to halve the number of Indigenous people employed in it.

A few years later, the federal government was heralding its efforts to "make the fisheries work" for Indigenous people through its ambitious Salmonid Enhancement Program (SEP, chapter 4). A "Native Programme" within the SEP announced that it was going to contribute to Indigenous people's well-being through training and job creation, an enhanced food fishery and community development. By the 1970s, ten bands living on the shores of the Strait had become completely removed from the commercial fishery, while another thirteen remained involved, but mostly with "minimal participation." The total Indigenous fishing fleet around the sea amounted to fewer than forty boats: five seiners, twenty gillnetters and thirteen trollers. These were, noted an SEP report, a mere "remnant of a much larger fleet once active in Georgia Strait." Per capita return from fisheries in those communities was estimated at $125, lower than in any other region on the BC coast. The only Indigenous communities where fishing was playing a significant economic role were in Comox, Qualicum and Sechelt.[57]

Barriers to entry in the fisheries were increasingly prohibitive in most Indigenous communities on the Strait and the Lower Fraser. The same SEP report explained that even if there might be a "widespread desire to return to commercial fishing" among reserve residents, it wasn't possible in most cases. Few young people had fishing experience, and the commercial fishery was no longer important on many reserves. Of the estimated 1,500 Indigenous commercial fishermen working on the entire BC coast in the mid-1970s, only seventy-one lived on the Strait and another seventy-five on the Lower Fraser. Indigenous people on the inland sea, noted the report, were losing the fishing tradition; fathers were not fishing and therefore were not passing on fishing skills to their offspring. Young people in bands without members who were already active in the commercial fishery found entry into the industry virtually impossible. The increasingly competitive, capital- and technology-intensive nature of the fishery was blocking their entry.

The issue of Indigenous access to a food fishery remained contentious. It was linked to the evolving commercial fishery and was still marked by conflict between Indigenous people and federal authorities. The conflict escalated in the late 1960s, especially on the Fraser. As historian Dianne Newell explained in *Pacific Salmon Canning*, "Indians were no longer content simply to pay a fine or go to jail silently." A federally consecrated food fishery took place mostly near the mouths of the Strait's major salmon rivers. It represented barely 2 percent of the total salmon caught by the commercial fleets in the 1970s, but it was certain to be a far more significant component of the planned "escapement," that portion of the salmon runs that remained to enter spawning rivers after eluding the commercial fleet and sport fishers at sea. In order for the federally prescribed escapement to remain large enough for a sufficient number of fish to make it to the spawning beds, it needed to accommodate fish taken in the rivers by the Indigenous food fishery. A larger escapement would mean fewer fish for commercial and sport fishers but more for the food fishery. A smaller escapement would mean more fish for commercial and sport fishers but either a smaller Indigenous food fishery or fewer fish making it to the spawning beds, which could severely threaten future catches.

Like their claims to land, Indigenous people's claims to salmon for food were becoming an increasingly sensitive political issue, arousing strong feelings in both those for and against. By 1978, federal policy gave the food fishery "priority over all other salmon fisheries," with only the requirements of escapement having higher priority. Theoretically at least, the food fishery would proceed even if commercial or sport fisheries had to be closed. But this policy assumed levels of knowledge, understanding and political will that seldom existed in reality. Indigenous people harboured an understandable concern that, whatever Ottawa's rhetoric about the food fishery, federal authorities would be tempted to further undermine access to the salmon that Indigenous people looked upon as their natural entitlement.

It *was* maddeningly difficult for federal fisheries officers to gain reliable information about the food fishery. They knew that Indigenous people's demand for subsistence salmon around the sea remained significant and that this food fishery would likely continue to grow. Its estimated catch had surpassed half a million fish by 1974. They also knew that some Indigenous communities, such as those on the Cowichan and Lower Fraser Rivers, were unable to meet their needs due to fishing restrictions and that they were being supplied with food fish by other bands. But federal authorities couldn't gauge the scale of this problem, and fisheries agents had lingering and sometimes justified suspicions that Indigenous people were occasionally selling their food fish to non-Indigenous people. Across the border in Washington state, Indigenous fishers had secured the right to take up to half the state's allowable catch of salmon by the mid-1970s. Ottawa, however, still refused to recognise any unique Indigenous rights beyond a food fishery.

The Pearse Commission in the early 1980s offered convincing recommendations for change in federal policy. The latest in a series of more than twenty such commissions of inquiry into the state of Canada's Pacific fisheries, the commission paid far more attention than its predecessors to the Indigenous fishery. Led by economist Peter Pearse, it blamed the sorry state of Indigenous fisheries on a century of ill-conceived federal and provincial policy. It recommended that the federal government recognise Indigenous claim to the salmon catch and called for sweeping changes that would give Indigenous communities a far more active role in managing both their food fishery and the commercial fishery. It would take the federal government almost ten years to begin responding to these suggestions, but it was another sign that perceptions of long-standing Indigenous grievances on the Strait and beyond were changing in settler society.

Indigenous people in the Strait's new world

The colonial dispossession that had taken place on the Strait was broadly similar to what occurred in other parts of the province and country. It was mostly complete by the end of the nineteenth century as a veritable resource rush took hold there. The collapse of Indigenous populations due to disease, the incoming settlers' profound hunger for land and resources, a diverse collection of legal and technological instruments of colonisation, and evolving transportation technologies all contributed to profound and very rapid changes in the relationship between humans and the rest of nature on the Strait.

Indigenous resistance to this dispossession had been ongoing, but by the 1980s Indigenous people were once again becoming important players on at least some stretches of the Strait. In many ways, they had internalised settler ways of interacting with the inland sea and its resources but were increasingly reluctant to submit to the will of settler governments. In many places, they had strong legal claims to far more of the Strait's shoreline and resources than parsimonious settler governments had given them in the past. As a result, it was settlers who now began to worry about losing access to the rich shorelines and natural resources of the Strait.

RESOURCE MINING BY THE SEA: MINING AND FORESTRY

3

An introduction to the Strait's resource mine, 1849–1980s

WHEREAS THE STRAIT'S Indigenous people had found practical uses for a great many elements of their natural environment, the settlers who arrived after 1850 were mostly interested in a few raw materials with rapidly growing global markets. Indigenous people with long-standing ties to the place were inclined to look upon its natural resources as an inheritance requiring careful stewardship. In contrast, settlers arriving from afar and looking to make their fortune in a strange land were more inclined to see a veritable resource mine: unlimited quantities of minerals, wood and fish, there for the taking.

The Hudson's Bay Company's (HBC) ocean-going ships and global trade networks had allowed it to access markets around the Pacific for the Strait's resources, including Nanaimo coal, Burrard Inlet timber and Fraser River Sockeye. Further advances in transportation and the rapid dispossession of the Strait's Indigenous people then helped set the scene for a frenetic "resource rush" that ensued around the inland sea between the mid-1880s and World War I. A global downturn in 1913 depressed markets for all of the Strait's export commodities, yet mining, and especially forestry and fishing, remained fundamentally important to the Strait's settler economy between the wars and contributed to another boom after World War II.

Having derived much sustenance from the Strait's natural bounty, many settlers believed its "unlimited resources" would continue to bring prosperity in the long term. The reality of mines, however, is that they always get worked out, and fish and wood were being harvested faster than they could be replenished. As resources diminished and human populations grew around the Strait, each industry experienced growing tensions. Foresters who were devastating salmon spawning streams came into conflict with fisheries advocates. Commercial fishers catching salmon met with increasing resistance from sport fishers and Indigenous people seeking fish for food. Mines poisoning coastal waters with acid drainage were brought to task, haltingly, by provincial authorities. Other kinds of resource industry pollution, and the impacts of these industries on recreation, went from being marginal issues to critical ones and again the province responded, slowly (chapter 5). Advocates of sustainability and environmental stewardship continued to challenge the perception of the Strait's resources as unlimited commodities for export.

Pages 108–109: Lumber being loaded on a ship at Chemainus Sawmill in the 1890s.

Image E-08040 courtesy of the Royal BC Museum and Archives.

Early mining by the shore, 1849–World War I

Mining, mostly of coal and copper, was the Strait's biggest industry in the first decades of colonisation, and it played a decisive role in the early settler economy. These early mines, and the many quarries that opened in the following decades, were successful in large part because the water highway made them economically viable, easing exports to both nearby and distant markets.

Global coal production increased a hundredfold between 1800 and 1900, and coal quickly became the Strait's most important export after mid-century. Nanaimo's coal, first mined using Indigenous labourers, was being shipped to Honolulu and San Francisco Bay by the early 1850s. Discovery of more extensive coal beds stimulated rapid growth in production, and Nanaimo was soon one of the Strait's largest towns, shipping 25,000 tons of coal a year by the late 1850s. Coal wharves dominated the waterfront, and the town centre was built on tidal lagoons and flats filled with mining waste.

Robert Dunsmuir's Vancouver Coal Mining and Land Company bought the HBC mines at Nanaimo in 1861, and within a couple of years Nanaimo was loading almost 33,000 tons a year for California alone. Completion of the Central Pacific Railway in 1868 further boosted the American market for Nanaimo's high-quality bituminous coal. Production grew to 80,000 tons a year by the 1870s, by which time Nanaimo's settler population had reached a thousand. A decade later, Nanaimo's population was nearing 5,000. The British navy's ability to dominate the oceans now depended on its access to coal supplies around the world, and its ships patrolling the North Pacific depended on the Strait's coal.

The Dunsmuirs lived at the head of Departure Bay in Nanaimo, where they could oversee the loading of their coal. They were shipping over half a million tons a year, by 1893, to California, Oregon, Alaska, China and the Russian Far East (see photographs page 112 and page 113). Between the mid-1880s and 1900, Nanaimo's population doubled to 10,000, about half the size of Vancouver at the time. Coal mining had also begun at Union (later called Cumberland), near Baynes Sound, in the late 1860s. That operation struggled until Dunsmuir acquired the mine in 1884, the same year he received the vast Esquimalt & Nanaimo Railway land grant. By the late 1880s, the Dunsmuirs' Union Mine was linked by a new railway to a deep-sea port on Baynes Sound, where the instant town of Union Bay grew up around the coal wharves. The mine transformed the local economy, and Cumberland's coal became a driving force in the Comox Valley.

Departure Bay coaling facilities in the 1880s: Nanaimo coal fuelled trains in the western US. A BC Ferries terminal would later be built on the same site.

Image E-06769 courtesy of the Royal BC Museum and Archives.

A geological survey led by Dr. G.M. Dawson combed the BC coast in the 1880s, searching mainly for coal deposits around the Strait. Dawson didn't find any exciting new prospects, but others were undeterred. Over the next twenty-five years, miners searched for coal in many places around the inland sea, from Tumbo and Saturna

Islands to Campbell River and Quadra Island and many places in between. Gabriola Island was the scene of much excitement over prospective coal mines in the late 1880s and '90s. Local papers regularly announced promising deposits on Gabriola, which were just as regularly followed by disclaimers. Coal output on the western shore of the Strait, meanwhile, went on climbing through the first decade of the twentieth century. The Dunsmuirs developed another port town from which to export their coal, produced by new mines south of Nanaimo. They named it Ladysmith in honour of a rare British victory in the Boer War. By 1908, $66 million worth of coal had been extracted from Vancouver Island and remaining reserves were judged inexhaustible. Yet barely two years later, perhaps sensing coming changes, the Dunsmuirs sold their coal mines along with vast tracts of their railway lands.

Coal stimulated the economy, but metals seemed to offer the best prospects for getting rich quickly. A short-lived gold rush had erupted on the lower Squamish River valley in 1858. A little copper was mined there too, and on Saltspring and Lasqueti Islands. Other sites on the Strait were thought to be rich in copper, but prices were low and Chile's giant mines were closer to Atlantic markets. Initially, iron was felt to be the better prospect and even generated a scandal in Victoria in the early 1870s. Amor de Cosmos, BC's second premier, was accused by political opponents of using his position to gain access to rich iron claims on Texada Island and then launching the company's stock on the London Stock Exchange while he was in that city on provincial business. The affair brought down the de Cosmos government, but it launched an iron-mining industry on Texada that continued off and on for a century and even attracted the interest of New York's powerful Rockefeller family for a while. Iron was also mined, very briefly, on Redonda Island in the early 1890s.

It was soon clear, however, that copper was the most interesting metal on the Strait (see Figure 7, page 115). New opportunities had emerged for copper producers by the 1880s, as Montana's vast Anaconda copper mine began shipping its ore to Puget Sound on the new Northern Pacific Railway. Anaconda had successfully challenged Chilean dominance of global markets and demonstrated the viability of western North America's copper producers. Technological developments, particularly the

Bessemer conversion process and electrolytic refining, stimulated copper demand. Growth in electricity generation and distribution, and growing numbers of electric motors, all required the pure copper wire that these new processes produced.

Low-grade copper extracted near the shore could be cheaply transported by sea. A mine was opened at Mount Sicker in the 1890s and almost 250,000 tons of ore was extracted from it by 1908. Smelters were built to render its ore, first at Crofton and then at Ladysmith (see photograph page 116, top). More exciting copper finds were made farther north. High-grade copper mixed with gold was found near Vananda (see photograph page 116, bottom), on the other side of Texada Island from the iron mine. By 1900 Texada had been declared "Canada's most precious rock," and its northeastern corner along Malaspina Strait "the richest twenty five square miles in BC." Vananda became the focal point of a heady wave of mining-based excess that generated an exuberant social life. At the peak of its short boom, seven mines operated around the town, which boasted a small but memorable opera house.

Copper also transformed Howe Sound. Two prospects on Bowen Island aroused much interest in the late 1880s and early '90s, leading to predictions that the island would become the province's next big mining centre. A mine operated there for one morning but things didn't work out as planned; it closed for good by noon, and Bowen's copper boom was over. Copper was mined far longer at nearby Britannia Beach, south of Squamish. Discovered in 1888, the Britannia property sold at the turn of the century for $2 million. The mine was soon shipping 200 tons of rock a day to the Crofton smelter and went on to extract immense volumes of low-grade ore for seven more decades. Prospectors staked claims to many more copper and gold deposits around the Strait in these boom decades, from the Capilano River to Quadra Island. These claims were usually said to contain "copper mixed with gold," a description that was sure to boost their market value, but few mines actually opened. The ones that did open—notably on Lasqueti and Quadra Islands early in the twentieth century—didn't live up to expectations and soon closed.

A seemingly endless supply of coal and minerals fit perfectly with the settlers' tendency towards materialism and short-term goals. They seemed obsessed with getting ahead, which meant exploiting resources, accumulating wealth and enjoying their newfound prosperity, and they had little time to notice or contemplate such things as the toxic chemicals flowing into the Strait. Mining would continue around the Strait after World War I, though coal mining declined and then ended. The early importance of the industry on the inland sea, and the role Indigenous people had played in it, would not be seen again.

Mining on the Strait after World War I

Mining declined around the inland sea after World War I, though the provincial government mostly continued to back the industry enthusiastically and regulate it reluctantly. Coal production peaked in the early 1920s and then went into a tailspin. Long the most important market for Vancouver Island coal (see photograph page 117, top), California had discovered oil and stopped importing the Strait's coal completely by the mid-1920s. However, the war had stimulated demand for copper, which was used to make electrical wiring and armaments, and ore was shipped from Mount Sicker and Texada Island until the reserves were depleted in the

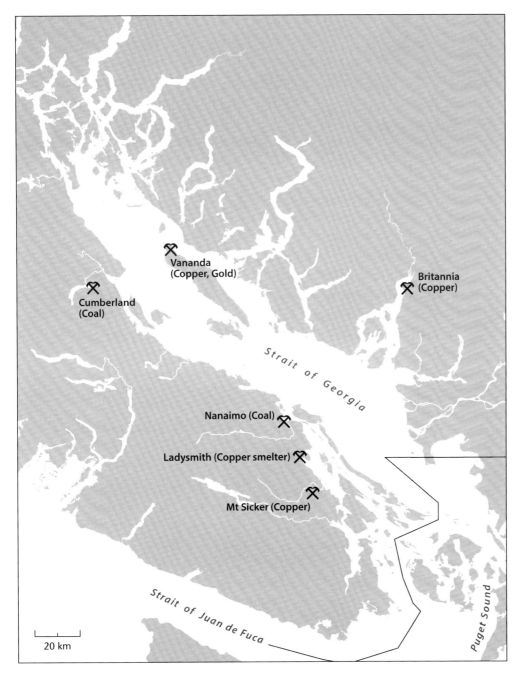

Figure 7: Major mining and smelting activities on the Strait in 1914.

1920s. Much ore remained at the Britannia Mine on the steep shore of Howe Sound, though. Accessible only by boat, the Britannia settlement was almost wiped out by an avalanche in 1915, and a flood killed nearly a hundred people at the new townsite in 1921. But copper production climbed, and by the 1930s Britannia had become the largest copper mine in the British Empire.

Despite rapid growth in mining globally after World War II, the industry continued to slow down on most parts of the Strait as the most accessible mineral reserves declined, though there were exceptions. A popular summer resort and retirement community had developed in Gillies Bay on Texada Island to replace mining in the

The Tyee Copper Smelter in Ladysmith around 1900.

Image G-02211 courtesy of the Royal BC Museum and Archives.

interwar years. But an upsurge in the demand for iron to produce steel saw the island's rustic charm evaporate overnight when a new iron mine began operating near Gillies Bay in 1952. It exported almost 1.5 million tons of ore, mostly to Japan, before the mine closed in the 1970s. The Britannia Mine continued to thrive past World War II, remaining Western Canada's largest copper producer. However, it closed for good in 1974, after the ore ran out.

Although mining had been the dominant economic driver in the early settler years, it soon ceded its place to fish packing and then to forestry as the primary industry around the Strait. And as it lost its economic value, its true costs started to come to light. The effects of decades of dumping mining pollutants into the Strait slowly came to public awareness. The province opened the Britannia Mine Museum in 1975 depicting the industry in a favourable light, but by 1980 the site was also recognised as one of North America's largest sources of heavy metal pollution. More than 40 million metric tons of tailings had been dumped directly into Howe Sound or used as fill around Britannia Beach, and the site continued to leach toxic copper

Smelter at a mine at Vananda, on Texada Island, in 1899: Vananda's mines responded to soaring worldwide demand for copper.

Image I-55309 courtesy of the Royal BC Museum and Archives.

Waste rock from the Union Bay coal washer (seen here in the 1920s, near the end of Vancouver Island's coal boom) is perhaps still affecting water quality in Baynes Sound in the twenty-first century.

Image D-07220 courtesy of the Royal BC Museum and Archives.

and zinc into Britannia Creek and Howe Sound long after the mine had closed.

In an overview of coastal BC prepared in the early 1960s, Roderick Haig-Brown suggested it was "by no means unlikely that another major [copper] producer [like Britannia] remains to be found somewhere in the unexplored immensity of the Coast Range."[1] And he was right. In the late 1970s, a mining company with rights to rich copper and molybdenum deposits underlying much of Gambier Island in Howe Sound announced that it planned to extract 250 million tons of ore from the island property. The perception of the Strait as a limitless natural resource had shifted, however, and locals, mostly cottagers from Vancouver, considered the proposed mine a grave threat to their island.

Projected to cover two-thirds of Gambier Island, the development was to include an open-pit mine 300 metres deep, several dams and tailing ponds, ore storage and transport facilities, and a bulk-loading port. The operation was expected to blast 90,000 tons of rock a day, which would generate vast storage piles and create a fine cloud of dust over the island. The mine, said its proponents, would be floodlit at

Granite Bay at the north end of Quadra Island, once the site of both a gold mine and a large railway logging operation.

Boomer Jerritt photo

night so it could operate around the clock. And it was in line with BC's Mineral Act, which permitted this sort of development on Crown land. It was drastically at odds, however, with the island's own land-use plan. It also clashed with the recently created Islands Trust (chapter 6), which encompassed Gambier Island. After a bitter five-year struggle, the company eventually abandoned the proposal. In this instance at least, the Strait's role as recreation space prevailed over its role as a resource mine. The forests would remain more of a battleground.

Mining the forests of the Strait, 1849–World War I

Britain had become a key player in global timber markets by the late eighteenth century. Lumber, especially for ship construction, had become an indispensable commodity, moved by sea across ever greater distances in the early nineteenth century as both demand and local deforestation increased in many locations around the world. Demand

A stand of old-growth Douglas fir on Vancouver Island. As colonial planners in London noted in the mid-19th century, such gigantic, high-quality timber was a treasure waiting to be exploited.

lightphoto/Thinkstock/iStock photo

from boat builders declined later in the century, but other uses for wood—especially for the construction of houses and railways—ensured that it continued to soar. By the latter half of the nineteenth century, the Strait's wood had become a valuable commodity in this rapidly growing global market. The forests of the inland sea remained the heart of BC's forest industry well into the twentieth century. This was partly because of the great value of the giant trees that grew in the temperate coastal forests; partly because of the ease with which this timber could be moved to shoreline mills, then lumber, pulp and paper exported from them; and partly because of the Strait's ability to absorb vast volumes of untreated waste with few apparent ill effects.

The HBC built a sawmill in Victoria in 1848 and one in Nanaimo a few years later. These small mills employed Indigenous workers and made few inroads into Vancouver Island's forests. However, HBC dispatches alerted the British Colonial Office to the immense untapped forest resources of this place. According to Governor James Douglas, it was a land of "*inexhaustible* [emphasis added] forests of the finest fir timber in the world…which [together with its rich fisheries] will become a source of boundless wealth to its inhabitants at some future time."[2] A decade later, colonial planners in London noted, "The principal timber…grow to a gigantic size."[3] Yet for early settlers intent on farming, these enormous trees were often more a nuisance than an asset and commercial logging initially remained very small-scale.

In 1865 the Crown began to grant timber leases. Previously timber could legally be cut only on the logger's own land, but under the new system commercial lumbering on land leased from the government spread quickly around the Strait. To ensure that local lumber needs were being met, the province virtually gave away the coastal forests to lumbermen. For example, the Moody Sawmill paid 2½ cents per hectare for more than 40 square kilometres of timberlands around Burrard Inlet. The inlet had the advantage of combining heavily timbered slopes with a sheltered deep-water port, and its mills were already shipping hundreds of thousands of board feet of lumber every month to the San Francisco Bay area by the early 1860s. By 1863 the Moodyville mill on the northern shore of Burrard Inlet, near the present-day foot of Lonsdale Avenue in North Vancouver, was sawing 40,000 board feet of lumber a day. Hastings Mill soon opened on the south side of the inlet, and by 1868 the two were producing close to 10 million board feet of lumber a year, as well as a million shingles and 2,000 spars for sailing ships. Victoria's *Colonist* newspaper was often critical of

Mainland competitors, but in 1868 it crowed that Burrard Inlet lumber was "already so highly esteemed at San Francisco as to bring $2.50 more per thousand feet than Puget Sound lumber."[4]

Until the 1880s, most of the trees for the Strait's timber exports came from Burrard Inlet, though the mills were already drawing from other places along the Mainland shore as early as the 1870s. The Moodyville mill leased timberland on the lower Squamish River in 1870. Others began logging in Howe Sound, where all nine settlers on the 1875 voters list were "lumbermen." Indigenous communities at Sechelt, Sliammon and Cortes Island were all logging and assembling booms for towing to mills in the southern Strait by the mid-1870s. And by the time settlers arrived at Gibsons Landing in the mid-1880s, loggers had already cleared the trees. Small logging operations appeared on the steep shores of Jervis Inlet and Desolation Sound at the northern end of the Strait as well. By the early 1880s, Burrard Inlet and New Westminster sawmills were transforming timber from almost every shore of the Strait and shipping it around the Pacific.

Vancouver Island developed its own lumber industry, as mills opened at Chemainus in 1862 and near Comox in 1877, and soon settlers clearing land for farming along the Vancouver Island shoreline were selling their timber to a number of local sawmills. By the mid-1880s, many small sawmills on the east coast of the Island were supplying local demand, while more logs were dispatched to mills farther down the shore. Logging had become a major part of Vancouver Island's economy, and the historical record abounds with stories of early loggers who came ashore and made their fortunes.

In these early decades of lumbering on the Strait, the only practical way to move giant logs any distance was by water. The region lacked the broad, flat rivers that eased log extraction in eastern North America, so the Strait itself played this role. Yet even with copious amounts of dogfish oil applied to skid roads and a team of stout

Logging at Jericho near Vancouver; the area later became one of the city's most popular shoreline parks.

Image I-66029 courtesy of the Royal BC Museum and Archives.

oxen (see photograph page 119), it was not easy to pull immense, rough-barked logs, so logging was usually restricted to the first few hundred metres in from the shore. Still, harvesting these trees with axes or large handsaws and then hauling the timber to the shoreline was extremely laborious and dangerous. At tidewater they were bucked into shorter logs and stored until there were enough to make a boom that could be towed to a sawmill.

When the Canadian Pacific Railway reached Burrard Inlet, the Strait's already expanding forest industry grew even more rapidly. Between 1871 and 1911, the number of sawmills in the province increased almost tenfold, from 27 to 224; the workforce in forestry grew from fewer than 400 people to more than 15,000. Most of these jobs were around the inland sea, with the majority of them concentrated around Burrard Inlet, which had nine large mills operating by 1890. The Moodyville and Hastings mills alone were producing more than 40 million board feet a year, or a third of the province's overall production.

Most forests around the inland sea had not been touched by industrial forestry in 1880, and some contemporary observers even bemoaned the fact that these very large trees were limiting the Strait's agricultural potential. The province had assumed responsibility for forests when BC joined Confederation in 1871. In 1884 it introduced a new timber licensing system with looser regulations, while the forest industry moved to increase its harvest with investments in new technologies. Under the new system, the intent to farm was no longer a prerequisite for obtaining land.

In 1889, for example, the logger John Glover gave notice of intent to apply for licences on about 40 square kilometres of land "for timbering purposes" on Sechelt's North West Bay, Thormanby Island, the shore of Malaspina Strait by the Sliammon Reserve, by Squirrel Cove Reserve and other parts of Cortes Island, and on Valdes (i.e., Quadra Island) near the Cape Mudge and Drew Harbour reserves. The locations of Glover's claims suggest he may have aimed to use a lot of Indigenous labour. Perhaps such large tracts of timber had become available beside new reserves after uncertainties about reserve boundaries were resolved. In any case, this was just one of many signs that logging was gathering momentum. It has been said that "the majestic timber stands of Vancouver Island and the coast of the Mainland were… disposed of in large tracts on easy terms to all comers for over thirty years."[5]

Timber licensing continued as harvesting technologies evolved. A dozen years later a Mr. Emerson leased around 35 square kilometres of timber on the waterfront of Nelson and Hardy Islands at the mouth of Jervis Inlet, on Howe Sound and elsewhere around the Strait. Emerson announced his intention to start logging immediately with more than a hundred men and four big donkey engines (steam-powered winches). The rapid dispossession of the Strait's Indigenous people had been based on the premise that they were not "using the land"—not making it bear fruit the way European farmers could. Yet now the settlers were building much of their economy on logging, which was difficult to construe as "adding value" to land unless the land was going to be farmed or built upon after it was logged, which it seldom was. Instead, most forest land was essentially being mined—logged and abandoned—leaving behind mostly infertile, eroded land that would be worthless for decades to come.

Interest in West Coast forests grew as eastern North America's timber supplies diminished. Between 1890 and 1910, American lumbermen carefully assessed virtually every accessible forest around the Strait and elsewhere in the province. Early in the 1900s, with distant investors buying up many timber licences, Victoria took greater notice of the value of its timber. A provincial Royal Commission on Timber and Forestry in 1907—by which time 3.6 million hectares of forest land had been leased—spoke warily of the "insatiable nature of the continental demand for standing timber." By 1912, the province had established what historian Robert Cail would praise forty years later as "the best method yet devised": timber sales by public auction with control of the land retained by the provincial government.

Eastern industrialists invested heavily. Sales soared from barely $2 million at the turn of the century to $150 million by 1913—well over half of this capital from American investors. Richard Rajala, in *Clearcutting the Pacific Rain Forest*, described this transformation in the forest sectors of coastal BC, Washington and Oregon as an "industrial revolution." This revolution was largely financed by eastern capital and comprised, among other things, much larger-scale logging and milling with improved technologies, as well as greater integration of the regional industry into continental networks.

The government in Victoria promoted the development of exports, rebating royalties paid for lumber shipped outside BC. Exports to the rest of North America grew rapidly after the arrival of the railway, and new North American markets led to new opportunities. Cedar shingles, mostly from the shores of the Strait, became a key export to eastern markets: BC was supplying half of Canada's shingles by 1908 and 80 percent by 1921. Exports outside North America became relatively less important than before the railway, but they remained significant. The *Colonist* reported in 1898 that mills around the southern Strait were still exporting to South Africa, Australia, East Asia and Europe.

Growing dependence on these eastern markets resulted in greater instability in the demand for wood products. As the continental economy rose and fell, so too did the eastern markets, which led to cyclical overproduction problems in the forestry industry. In the 1880s, almost all logging was being done close to shore, and oxen or horses hauled the logs over skid roads to points where they could be gathered into booms and then towed by sea to a sawmill. This logging was necessarily selective, taking only the most valuable trees, though many others were damaged in the process. By 1900, however, larger operations on the Strait had begun using steam-powered donkey engines to extract logs, though many smaller operators still logged with animals. The donkey engines greatly boosted productivity and allowed logging operations to move farther inland. The "revolution" in the forest then gathered steam as the larger companies built numerous railways to move timber from the hillsides down to the shore. These technologies helped ensure that BC's forest industry remained concentrated on the Strait longer than it would have otherwise, as they made it easier to harvest higher-altitude stands when wood supplies along the shore were exhausted.

Periodically Victoria faced pressure from loggers who had cut more logs than they could sell to local mills and who then sought permission to export their surplus to American sawmills across the border. The province refused, sternly enforcing its prohibition on raw log exports and launching patrol boats on the Strait in search of miscreants. In fact, small sawmills proliferated around the Strait, though overall milling capacity became concentrated at a few sites on the southern Strait. The large mill at Chemainus was cutting half a million board feet a day by 1890. The owner, John Humbird, was a lumberman from the American Great Lakes region. Like other entrepreneurs moving into the rich forests of the Strait's western shore, Humbird had made a deal with the Dunsmuirs. He bought 400 square kilometres of their forest land close to Chemainus and in the Comox Valley, agreeing to build a sawmill for the export market at Chemainus (see photographs pages 108–109 and page 123). American entrepreneurs John Rockefeller and Andrew Carnegie also bought forest land from Dunsmuir, then eventually visited Chemainus to sell it to the Humbird mill. Around the turn of the century, with forests depleted in the Cowichan Valley, Chemainus became more dependent on Comox Valley timber. Humbird owned 200 square kilometres of forest there and began building railways to extract it. Small operations were already cutting timber along the seashore and up the riverbanks near Comox.

Logging expanded greatly when larger companies began to play a dominant role in the early 1900s, towing most of the harvest to southern mills. By World War I the Canadian Western Lumber Company was the largest in the province. It had assembled an impressive collection of forest resources, railways, tugboats and sawmills and controlled a vast expanse of high-quality, even-aged Douglas fir stands that stretched along the coastal plain between Comox and Campbell River. The company's wood supplied its Fraser Mills plant in New Westminster, which had become the second-largest sawmill in the world. Increasingly, logging was becoming capital-intensive, with railways following the receding timber up the hillsides.

As early as 1888, the *Colonist* reported that logging had ceased around Burrard Inlet for lack of suitable timber. All the large mills, it said, were bringing their timber

An early logging crew on the Tsolum River in the Comox Valley, standing in front of old-growth Douglas fir.

Courtney & District Museum, Walter Gage photograph. Photo: 990.24.289.

from 80 to 200 kilometres away. Logging had spread quickly along the Mainland shore north of Burrard Inlet starting in the 1880s. Unlike on Vancouver Island, where settler farmers turned to lumbering to increase their income, on the steep Mainland coast and northern islands many loggers were the first to settle, albeit briefly. Loggers in those years often lived transient, uncomfortable lives as they moved wherever the extremely dangerous work of felling and pulling massive trees off steep slopes took them. Others were able to combine logging with a relatively sedentary lifestyle. The reality was that many settlers around the Strait came to depend on logging for their well-being, often turning away from farming to find more lucrative work in logging or at sawmills.

In the final years before World War I, pulp and paper mills began to appear on the Strait. Leases for cutting hemlock trees—judged unsuitable for lumber—had first been granted as far back as 1891. In 1900 the province announced plans to encourage pulp manufacturing. The following year, twenty-one year-long leases finally became available for cutting pulp wood, at five cents per hectare and fifteen cents per cord. Four of these leases were let, covering a total of 140,000 hectares. Dr. G.M. Dawson's earlier geological survey of the Strait had noted the presence of several large lakes in the Powell River area, with a short river spilling from one of the lakes into the nearby sea. The place was ideal for a pulp and paper mill—copious water, enough head to generate electricity and hundreds of square kilometres of forest available near the shore. For a decade after the introduction of pulp wood leases, the Powell River area had remained like other parts of the coast—a place where hunters, fishermen, loggers, tourists and "stump ranchers" coexisted—but this changed suddenly with the construction of an "instant town."

Employees' houses, roads, a power plant, wharves and four papermaking machines

Chemainus Sawmill in 1895; John Rockefeller and Andrew Carnegie eventually sold their Vancouver Island timberland to the Chemainus sawmillers.

Image E-02574 courtesy of the Royal BC Museum and Archives.

replaced the Indigenous village on the river now named for the Sliammon people's nemesis, Israel Powell (chapter 2), all in less than two years. Taking advantage of numerous stands of hemlock on the Strait's wetter slopes that made excellent paper, the Powell River Company shipped its first 17,000 tons of newsprint by the end of 1912. By 1913, more than a thousand loggers were working in the woods around the town. The mill worked day and night, seven days a week, giving this stretch of shore a different feel from the rest. Many neighbours welcomed this industrial complex, as it was a good market for local farmers' produce and loggers' timber and offered urban amenities much closer than Vancouver. The pungent odour of sulphite pulp making was only *really* noticeable when one was downwind, and few settlers paid much attention to the mill's copious liquid waste. Smaller sulphite mills built in the same period had similar mixed effects on their neighbours in Howe Sound.

The Strait's early forest industry generated a great deal of waste. Especially before donkey engines began to facilitate log extraction, many millions of board feet of good timber were left in the woods and burned by the loggers in vast pyres that easily spread out of control. Diaries and newspapers at the end of the nineteenth century are full of reports of fires raging and smoke cloaking the Strait throughout the summer. Destructive and wasteful logging practices began to attract criticism. *Woodsmen of the West*, a novel of the period by Martin Grainger, described logging around the sea variously as "mining" and "butchery." Grainger went on to act as secretary for the province's first Royal Commission of Inquiry into Timber and Forestry, and its report gave rise to a provincial Forest Act in 1912 and a Forestry Service that was created to enforce it. The act mostly focused on fire control and on improving methods of log scaling (estimating the volume of lumber in harvested logs) but did little to address the industry's assault on the forests that had so upset Grainger. Damage to spawning streams used for skidding logs or buried under slash, and erosion of deforested soils by torrential winter rains, continued unabated.

The Strait's forest industry expanded most rapidly in the first decade of the twentieth century. Revenues from the forests and mills bolstered Victoria's finances, while sawmills or logging became the economic backbone of many settler communities, including Vancouver. The province's new Chief Forester, H.R. MacMillan, confirmed in 1914 that the industry was now the province's key sector. He declared the future bright because half the province was still covered in high-value first-growth forest, and less than 10 percent of it had been logged. Most of this logged land, however, was around the Strait and a few people, like Grainger, were beginning to suggest that the perception of the forest as an inexhaustible resource that could be harvested at will was an illusion. Yet the forests remained a lucrative place to work, for both settlers and Indigenous people. Calls for more careful stewardship were drowned out by the urgent demands of total war after 1914, as they would be again during World War II.

Forestry in the interwar years

Forests remained the Strait's most valuable resource after World War I as the business of liquidating old-growth forests around the inland sea developed its own culture. Early movie footage, such as that shot by Francis John Barrow during his many summer cruises on the Strait, captured the drama of logging on its shores. The sea was alive with log booms being towed to mills and ships loading lumber and paper.

The opening of the Panama Canal meant that ships from the west coast could now cross from the Pacific to the Atlantic Ocean without having to circumnavigate South America. This route significantly reduced shipping times and costs and made coastal lumber more competitive in eastern US markets.

Many of the Strait's communities depended heavily on the forest for their survival, but nowhere more than Powell River. By that time it had become one of the Strait's major centres of railway logging, with more than twenty locomotives pulling 300 cars over 160 kilometres of track. The town's population grew from around 2,000 in 1921 to 8,000 in 1941, though local timber supplies were approaching exhaustion by the 1940s. Across the Strait, the Comox Valley was almost as dependent on forestry in the interwar years. According to Richard Mackie's *Island Timber*, the valley was still "the Garden of Eden for loggers…almost solid fir, flat terrain, dense stands, five foot fir on the stump," while the main actor in the local industry, Canadian Western, was "hell bent on harvesting the low lying accessible old growth." Its subsidiary Comox Logging and Railway did the logging, and its towboat company moved the logs across the Strait to be milled at its giant plant in New Westminster.

Such rapid harvesting stimulated growing concerns about forest depletion. Before World War I, the Royal Commission on Forestry had focused mostly on the forests around the inland sea, where the industry was concentrated. The commission had recommended the province look upon its timber royalties not just as revenues but also as capital being depleted from the forests. The commissioners suggested public money earned from forestry should not pass into general revenues until enough funds were reinvested to ensure future forest productivity. They called for firm government control over harvesting methods. Looking back thirty years later, Haig-Brown reported: "These findings have been utterly disregarded."[6] Despite a Forest Act being passed in 1912, forest management remained a low priority for subsequent provincial governments.

The province's first tree nurseries were developed in the 1920s and some reforestation started in the 1930s. Yet Haig-Brown painted an alarming picture of the state of the forests in the early 1940s. "In the depression years the average man in British Columbia had time to think about his province," said Haig-Brown, and he had "good cause to think hard and searchingly" about his future. Looking at this future, he declared, "There was nothing to give him satisfaction. He saw a giant industry, using most powerful methods that were obviously wasteful not only of present but of future timber stocks" and "thousands upon thousands of acres…that had borne heavy timber [and were] now unproductive." Even in "the tremendous Douglas fir and cedar and hemlock stands of Vancouver Island and the Lower Mainland, there was no sure future."[7]

Haig-Brown reported that the public had begun to express widespread concern about degraded forests by the 1930s "through boards of trade, in the press, at community meetings…[and] social organizations." The province ignored these signs until the late 1930s, when its Department of Lands published an account of its forest resources. The report, wrote Haig-Brown, presented a "terrifyingly full confirmation of the worst nightmares of public opinion." He chastised the government for its disappointing response to this report. But the province's Chief Forester, E.C. Manning, was mobilised by it. Manning, wrote Haig-Brown, was "that very rare individual, an inspired civil servant…[He] saw that an industry so vast, wreaking such tremendous physical changes on the face of the land, must inevitably affect adversely other industries such as fishing, agriculture, the tourist trade and anything that depended upon a natural resource, whether that resource was soil, water, fish, game, fur or scenery."[8]

Manning perceived that there was little or no government control over logging. He estimated that something like 60 percent of the forests logged by the late 1930s would remain barren or understocked far into the future. Virtually all forests were being cut far beyond anything like their sustained yield capacity. Douglas fir stands around the inland sea were by far the province's most valuable resources (see photograph page 126), and they were going to be seriously depleted by the 1950s. Despite initial opposition from the forest industry, Manning succeeded in introducing a number of forest management improvements, particularly in the Douglas fir stands on the Vancouver Island shore of the Strait. He aimed to improve fire protection and logging methods, and enhance forest regeneration after logging. The industry soon came around to supporting this approach. Haig-Brown described it as "inadequate even in the [limited] areas to which it [was] applied…but still the greatest step towards forest conservation in the history of the province."[9]

When World War II broke out, forest harvesting increased. The cut levels, which were already judged to be far in excess of regeneration rates, increased significantly in the early 1940s to support the war effort. For Haig-Brown, despite a modicum of new regulation, logging methods remained "haphazard and extravagant and ill conceived."[10] E.C. Manning was killed in a plane crash in 1941. Two years later, another Royal Commission on Forestry—known as the Sloan Commission—was appointed to address growing fears of timber shortages and the large forestry companies' demands for improved security of tenure. The Sloan Commission recommended "sustained yield" forest management, wherein an "annual allowable cut" of timber would be established based on the estimated growth rate of the forest. Unlike many such commissions, the Sloan Commission was highly influential, though its recommendations failed to result in a "sustained yield."

Part of the problem was that forest-harvesting technologies had advanced much faster than forest management practices. Logging railways and the use of overhead logging, which involved suspending cables to move heavy logs over difficult terrain, had produced vast clear-cuts in valley bottoms. Immense expanses were denuded and left without nearby sources of seed. The result was extensive areas, particularly in the Strait's rich Douglas fir forests, where natural forest regeneration was failing by the 1920s. Bulldozers and logging trucks then moved logging farther up hillsides onto steeper, previously inaccessible slopes, which increased the damage to streams in unstable upper watersheds. Improved tree-harvesting technologies also left behind a lot more "waste wood" in the forest. Pulp and paper mills on the Mainland shore used some of this waste, but no mills were built on the Vancouver Island side of the Strait until after World War II.

The waste that most worried contemporary observers was the wood fuelling the

Logging operations at the Bluebird Mill in Qualicum, 1918: Part of the transition to more capital-intensive harvesting. Old-growth Douglas fir logs like these were the province's best timber.

Image B-07567 courtesy of the Royal BC Museum and Archives.

fires that raged through the summers around the sea. Some fires—on the Malaspina Peninsula in 1918 and in the Comox Valley in 1922 and 1938—were huge and became the stuff of local legend. But smaller blazes, often set by loggers and fuelled by their waste, burned out of control every year. People complained about the smoke, summer after summer. A terrifying blaze raged out of control for weeks between Campbell River and Courtenay in 1938, threatening both towns. It burned over 300 square kilometres of forest and destroyed millions of board feet of timber, and more than 2,000 firefighters struggled to keep it under control. On his summer cruise through the Strait that year, Francis John Barrow complained that the smoke was ruining his photography. Ash from the inferno spread as far as Victoria, "fog" all the way to Portland. Haig-Brown, more inclined than the forest industry to worry about other stakeholders, called for the prompt reforestation of the worst-affected areas, claiming that "taxes on tourist revenues of the future would far more than cover the costs of replanting."[11]

To many, pulp and paper production was the ideal solution to the forest industry's profligate waste. Canada had become the world's largest newsprint producer by 1939, and by late in World War II, Canada was producing half of the world's newsprint. Powell River had become the world's largest pulp and paper mill, loading 200,000 tons of product every year onto the freighters arriving at its wharf at a rate of one every two days. Powell River's wood supplies by then came from far beyond the Strait.

A public perception of the need to move towards more effective control of the forest industry and sounder stewardship of the Strait's forest resources had begun to emerge in the 1930s. But this idea was subsumed, as it had been a generation earlier, by the urgent demands of a world at war.

Forestry boom and bust after 1945

The economies of many places on the Strait continued to rely heavily on logging even after 1945. Forests such as those on Lasqueti Island that hadn't seen much logging earlier due to their lower-quality timber were logged more intensively as their wood became more marketable.[12] Previously inaccessible stands could be more easily exploited by truck loggers, and rugged Texada Island, for example, supported almost thirty truck-logging operations in the late 1940s. Though only half of the operations remained by the mid-1950s, they were still shipping 15 million board feet a year off the island. Writing around the same time, Frederick Marsh noted the central role of logging on some southern islands in the late 1940s, where newly arrived loggers occupied cabins built earlier by farmers, and descendants of settlers fell back on logging as their other sources of income dried up. Other island loggers, tired of being condemned by their neighbours for "ruining the beautiful islands,"[13] began planning subdivisions instead (chapter 6).

On the Mainland and Vancouver Island, large integrated firms increasingly began to dominate the forest industry. They expanded their control of wood supplies and invested heavily in new pulp and paper technology that could utilise everything from sawdust to trees. BC's largest mills remained concentrated around the inland sea into the 1960s (see Figure 8, page 129), even as local wood supplies continued to shrink. Raw wood and fibre could easily be shipped to these mills from coastal forests farther north, and their lumber, pulp and paper products easily shipped out. In the

1950s, the Powell River mill was taken over by forestry giant MacMillan Bloedel and remained the Strait's largest industrial complex. By then, its ten papermaking machines were producing over 250,000 tons of newsprint a year and the mill employed close to 2,000 workers. The town's population rose from around 8,000 in the late 1940s to a peak of 20,000 in 1980.

Pulp and paper plants transformed the economies and atmospheric conditions of the Cowichan Valley, Nanaimo and Campbell River as well. Haig-Brown, offended by the pollution from the new Campbell River pulp mill, wondered how much its emissions were affecting the health of local citizens and forests. Again these new mills had been located at sites where they could take in vast quantities of fresh water and then dispose of similar volumes of liquid waste into the sea. Producing a single ton of pulp required up to 250,000 litres of fresh water, mostly for debarking logs or cooling machines. And a mill producing 500 tons of pulp a day might consume over 90 million litres of fresh water in the process. Not surprisingly, the big mills were responsible for a considerable amount of local marine pollution (chapter 5).

The growing importance of these large mills was part of a broader trend towards corporate concentration in the Strait's forest industry. By the 1950s, smaller logging and milling operations were being pushed out of the industry by larger, integrated firms that could better build and operate large mills and manage the large tree farm licences (TFLs) being offered by the province. With Victoria relying on revenue from the profits of these large firms, the government often equated the interests of their leading companies with the public interest. This helps explain Victoria's timid response to growing evidence of forests being depleted, mills polluting marine environments and loggers damaging salmon streams.

Technological change paralleled structural transitions in the industry. Roads and trucks replaced logging railways, and the old logging locomotives—newly painted— began to grace seaside parks from Vancouver to Courtenay. Large plants that could transform wood into plywood and various types of pulp and paper took over from simpler but less economically viable sawmills. Waste wood and sawdust, which had previously been burned on site or sold as domestic fuel, were turned into fibre for making paper. And gone were the days of sleeping in crowded bunkhouses; by the 1950s, many loggers got a place in town and drove their highly mobile equipment from one logging site to the next.

Improved methods for artificially regenerating tree seedlings allowed the industry to go on neglecting the need for improved logging practices. Like the fishery, the forest industry valued efficient production but often ignored scientific misgivings about the real, longer-term inefficiencies and hidden costs associated with these approaches. Just as the fishery couldn't resist the allure of farmed fish as a panacea, the forest industry embraced planted forests and maintained that logged areas could be easily replanted. In both cases, the seemingly infinite capacity to artificially regenerate these valuable resources helped dismiss fears of losing them through systematic overharvesting. In the woods, this new vision meant transforming "static and wasting wilderness (i.e., old-growth forests)" into "ordered ranks of flourishing young trees...a succession of cultivated forest crops more abundant and gainful than Nature could ever produce."[14] This fig leaf effectively allowed logging to be profligate and destructive around the Strait throughout these decades.

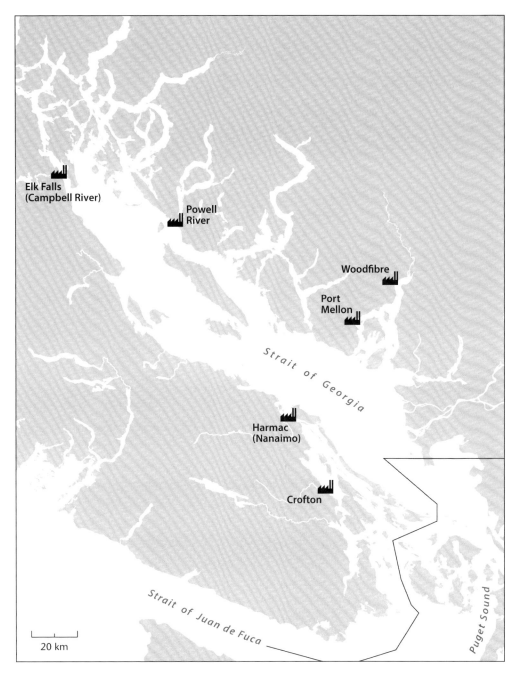

Figure 8: The pulp and paper mills on the Strait in 1960, which used waste wood and produced large quantities of liquid waste.

Technologies used on the Strait from the 1940s to the 1980s did little to mitigate the forest industry's impacts on other stakeholders or halt the decline of forest resources. Worries about forest depletion in the 1930s had been eclipsed by the war effort of the early 1940s. After 1945 these concerns were largely swept aside again, this time by the enthusiastic post-war boom. Haig-Brown reported in the 1960s that the "best of the sawmill timber" had been "stripped away" from the Strait, leaving the industry to earn revenues from plywood and fibre produced from second-rate timber. With the province's annual timber cut up to over 27 million cubic metres and having already "borne the burden of heavy cutting for over half a century," the more accessible forests around the inland sea were under "excessive strain." The sea's Douglas fir stands, which had been the great wealth of the industry, were "a thing of the past," though impressive stands of cedar, hemlock and true firs remained on some Mainland shores and, especially, beyond the northern limits of the Strait.[15] The deforestation was particularly thorough on the Vancouver Island shore, partly due to the railway lands that had been owned outright by forest companies and were therefore less constrained by Victoria's regulations. By the 1970s, these lands were the site of some of the world's largest clear-cuts.

The depletion of the Strait's forests continued more or less unabated through these years, with the harvesting rates diminished not by conservation but by occasional market downturns. Even a short-lived social democratic government in the 1970s did little to change the industry. Then, despite more rhetoric about sustained yields, the province's overall annual forest harvest increased from 150,000 hectares in the late 1970s to 225,000 a decade later. However, forests around the Strait contributed a steadily declining portion of this "cut" as the industry shifted to poorer stands in the interior of the province.

In her book *Green Gold*, Patricia Marchak alluded to the similarities between BC's forestry industry and a mining operation. As with resource exploitation in South America at the time, BC was consuming its renewable resources as fast as possible. The phenomenon, called *imediatismo* in Brazil (in contrast to *senso comum*, or common sense), described a tendency to seek immediate satisfaction without any thought for the future. In that country, runaway inflation spurred the resource rush, the idea being to spend whatever wealth you have today because it will be worth less tomorrow and virtually nothing next week. Latin American–style runaway inflation was not a problem on the Strait, yet the same pervasive lack of faith in the future existed. Some may have feared that the forest wealth so suddenly "inherited" by settlers might be lost just as quickly. Whatever the reason, Victoria's resource economists justified the exhaustion of resources by suggesting that the capital embodied in the forest could be converted into different kinds of capital to build the future post-resource economy. The reality for many forestry-dependent communities around the Strait was vastly different: well-paid jobs disappeared in the final decades of the twentieth century, only to be replaced by lower-paying service-sector jobs or unemployment.

UBC geographers Roger Hayter and Trevor Barnes characterised the Strait's post-war "mill towns"—places such as Crofton, Chemainus, Nanaimo, Powell River and Campbell River—as communities that had grown complacent due to a "Fordist wage bargain" struck between well-paid unionised workers and the forest industry. In other words, many communities had grown accustomed to the affluence assured by a rich supply of timber and fibre from coastal forests. But as this wood supply faltered in the 1970s and the deep economic downturn of the early 1980s hit the coastal forest industry particularly hard, the mills began to close and the belief in an inexhaustible resource came crashing down.

The government's policy of "sustained-yield forestry"—forest production that could be maintained indefinitely at some "sustainable" level—hadn't helped because harvesting had never in fact declined to sustainable levels. Victoria's decision to implement a forest tenure system—and cede control over public forests to long-term private-sector licence holders who could raise the capital needed to carry out "sustained-yield logging"—had not produced the desired effect. The province's head forester, C.D. Orchard, had earlier envisioned a merger of public and private interests, but others have suggested this idea was always fanciful and that "sustained yield" was mostly a rhetorical flourish to cover up profitable and unsustainable harvesting practices. Besides, critics have maintained, the province never had the staff it needed to properly control the pace or quality of logging.

Like many well-meaning conservation policies, sustained-yield forestry worked in theory but it seldom lived up to its aspirations in practice. There was confusion from the outset about how to implement it, how to calculate the volumes of mature timber used to set the "annual allowable cut," or how to accommodate the highly variable economic values of different forests. The complacency that prevailed in the post-war decades allowed provincial officials much latitude in their interpretation of this policy when faced with political pressure to maximise forest harvests. For example, the collaboration between Robert Sommers, the forest minister in BC's first Social Credit government, and the forest industry revealed the remarkably "flexible" way that sustained-yield forestry was applied in the 1950s. Sommers's party had come to power promising to eliminate the corruption of the province's 1940s coalition governments. Yet Sommers would be the first elected cabinet minister in the British Empire to go to prison when he was convicted of accepting bribes in exchange for generous forest licences.

After Haig-Brown's death in 1976, non-governmental critics of the province's forestry policy focused increasingly on the need to preserve "wilderness." Now an essentially urban movement, the new generation of forest preservationists was animated by the desire to protect nature, rather than to ensure the long-term future of the forest industry. By *wilderness* they meant old-growth forest, and this idea put them on a collision course with Victoria's strategy for progressively harvesting all remaining old-growth stands under the guise of sustained-yield forestry. Since very few old-growth stands were left around the Strait by the 1980s, when Victoria and the non-governmental organisations (NGOs) became locked in their "war in the woods," this struggle unfolded mostly around isolated old-growth forests beyond the inland sea, particularly on the west side of Vancouver Island.

Debate over how to manage second-growth forests on the Strait had a lower public profile but was still highly contentious. A key issue was that forestry companies owned large blocks of island forest that could turn huge profits if they were rezoned into residential lots for building cottages and retirement homes. Weldwood owned much of Gabriola and Denman Islands and MacMillan Bloedel much of Galiano, where 70 percent of the land was under forest company control. These large holdings help explain why the Islands Trust, which was created in 1974 to preserve the "unique character" of the islands in the Strait, cautiously embraced forestry (chapter 6) and made it as difficult as possible for forest companies to convert their forest lands into subdivisions that might threaten this character.

While they contemplated cashing in on a recreational land boom on the southern Strait, the forest companies also clashed with recreational activities farther north. Rather than a "war in the woods," it was a low-intensity "war on the water" that focused mostly on log booms (see photograph page 132). In the mid-1960s, one such battle was fought in Quadra Island's Gowlland Harbour, the only harbour in

The Canadian White Pine Company sawmill in New Westminster in 1947: The vast complex of sawmills around New West depended on logs towed in from around the Strait and beyond.

Image I-28018 courtesy of the Royal BC Museum and Archives.

Discovery Passage that was secure for boats in any wind. Local residents complained bitterly that the nearby pulp mill was taking more and more of their waterfront for log storage. A letter from a local citizen to the province's superintendent of lands summarised their concerns: "[Booms are] gradually making an incursion not only at the expense of the residents, but…operators of yachts and fishing vessels who use the Gowlland Harbour anchorage." The letter continued, "225 children receive swimming, boating and water skiing instruction in this area every summer…any further concessions for log storage…will destroy this recreational value." Finally, claimed the writer, "The roar of the high speed engines in the small tugs day and night, the destruction of the boat anchorage and booms of logs moored to the shore and in the channel will definitely reduce the value of waterfront property in the area."[16]

The mill's response reflected the self-assurance of the forest industry in those years. The population of Campbell River had increased from 2,500 to 7,500 since the mill opened, noted the mill's spokesperson. Close to 1,100 people, or about half the town's working population, were employed at the mill. Log storage areas needed to be close to the mill, protected from wind and tide, and the mill needed more log storage space. So, inevitably, the mill needed to use more of Gowlland Harbour. The superintendent of lands denied the company most of the new area it sought around Gowlland Bay but allowed it to keep the substantial area it was already using for booming. The province had begun to pay closer attention to these conflicts in the 1970s because it was interested in the possibility of establishing its own small marine parks on the same protected stretches of coastline. The fact that both parties needed these marine spaces primarily in the summer months only intensified the conflict. While still strongly supportive of the forest industry, the province had also come to recognise the critical importance of the Strait's "recreational values" (chapter 6).

From centre stage to senescence

By the 1980s, the forest industry was in steep decline: the warnings of conservationists had been ignored for decades and their long-abiding fear—of squandering one of the world's richest forest resources—had been realised. Signs of the industry's looming senescence had become evident ten years earlier when it began to be portrayed as a sort of aging cultural icon. In the 1970s, a new literary journal, *The Raincoast Chronicles* (published in Madeira Park on the Sunshine Coast), began documenting the rich social history of a century of settler logging (and other activities) on the Strait and beyond. In nearby Gibsons Landing, the Canadian Broadcasting Corporation (CBC) launched a television series in 1972 about log salvagers on Howe Sound. *The Beachcombers* played for twenty years to a global audience.

Vancouver had become rich on the profits of the Strait's forest industry. Yet the city aimed to make it clear through events such as Expo 86, with its focus on transportation and communications technologies, that it was transcending its early dependence on primary resources and becoming a "world-class city." The Strait had played a critical role in developing the forest industry, but increasingly the growing urban populations on its shores were valuing it more for its recreational assets than as a highway for logs or a waste dump for pulp mills. The industry would continue to operate around the inland sea, and it increased its efforts to replant forest land, but it was no longer the dominant force it had once been. Like mining and fishing, it was unmistakably in decline.

SMUGGLER CANADIAN SALMON

SMUGGLER BRAND

DISTRIBU...
M. D...

SALMON

SEA ISLAND CANNERY.

D. J. MUNN. MANAGER.

1 lb.

FRESH SALMON

BRITISH

DIRECTIONS.

Serve cold or hot. When required to be heated, put the can (before being opened) into boiling water for 30 minutes.

Peut etre servi froid ou chaud. Pour servir chaud, il faut mettre la boite (avant de l'ouvrir) l'eau bouillant 30 mi...

THE CONSUL'S BRAND

TRADE MARK.

FRESH

BRITISH

WILD BEAUTY BRAND

Wild Beauty

REGISTERED TRADE MARK

SALMON

1 LB. NET...

EMPTY CONTENTS AS SOON AS OPENED

SA...

The BRI... PACK...

RED

RESOURCE MINING IN THE SEA: FISH AND OYSTERS

4

THE FIRST EUROPEANS to visit the Strait of Georgia reported waters teeming with life, from herring to whales. Again it was the Hudson's Bay Company that started the international trade, shipping up to 2,000 barrels a year of salted Fraser River salmon to Hawaii, Tahiti and Australia in the 1840s. The company was exporting even more salmon around the Pacific and exploring new markets for herring in the late 1850s when it lost its monopoly control over the trade to non-HBC entrepreneurs. Many species of finfish and shellfish abounded in the Strait, but from the earliest days of the settlers' commercial fishery, salmon was by far the most important fish.

The settlers' early salmon fishery, 1849–1880s

The industrial fishery didn't develop much on the Strait through the 1860s, when it was still part of a British colony, though events in Britain influenced its future. A Royal Commission there asked whether British fish stocks were growing or diminishing, whether any modes of fishing were harming those stocks and whether any fishing regulations were harmful. Lacking reliable data, the commission saw no conclusive proof of declining stocks and declared that Britain's fisheries were being most harmed by the rules that governed them. The resulting Sea Fisheries Act of 1868 was a striking example of nineteenth-century liberalism: it abolished more than fifty laws that had been passed during the previous centuries. The result for Britain was that "Fishing became possible whenever, wherever and with whatever methods fishers pleased…[leading to] unbridled expansion of fisheries, and within a couple of decades it would have serious impacts on fish stocks and their habitats."[1]

Fifteen years later, amid growing worries about overfishing by North Atlantic fishers, British biologist Thomas Huxley informed the 1883 International Fisheries Exhibition that overfishing anywhere was "scientifically impossible" and, most likely, "all the great sea fisheries are inexhaustible."[2] His declaration informed the broad imperial context for the emerging settlers' fishery on the Strait.

Most visitors to Canada's new Pacific province in the 1870s were greatly impressed by the apparently limitless wealth of its seas. The *Colonist* exclaimed: "The real treasury of British Columbia is…the untold and immeasurable wealth of its fisheries. The waters of the Gulf of Georgia are alive with fish."[3] The same year, the annual report of Ottawa's new Department of Marine and Fisheries (DMF) included an essay describing these newly acquired "marine resources." It focused

Pages 134–135: Labels from a few of the early canneries around Vancouver. By 1900 there were over fifty at the mouth of the Fraser River alone, and many others around the Strait.

Harbour Publishing Archives

on the Strait, where salmon were "common…to every stream," herring spawned "in prodigious numbers" in its many bays and inlets, and oysters were "very abundant," especially around Comox. The report also suggested, "It may be desirable before long to bestow…closer attention" on these fisheries, especially as rapid developments in California fisheries were likely to stimulate others farther north. The authors saw no immediate need to extend federal fishery laws to the province, though they recognised their need to be better informed about the new Pacific fisheries. A certain diffidence among federal authorities was understandable in light of the very long time still needed to travel between Ottawa and the BC coast in the 1870s.

The settlers had arrived with their own highly evolved knowledge of fishing and fish processing. Like the Strait's Indigenous people, they prized its salmon above all else. The diversity of Pacific salmon species and their abundance, particularly at the mouth of the Fraser River, contributed to their value. Chum salmon (*Oncorhynchus keta*) spawned in the autumn and were the most plentiful species, though canneries considered their lean flesh the cheapest grade. Sockeye salmon (*O. nerka*) were smaller than Chum and travelled far up rivers to spawn in the summer, but their uniform size and the huge numbers of them spawning in the Fraser made them the most important fish commercially. Smaller Pink salmon (*O. gorbuscha*) spawned from early summer to early fall; like Sockeye, they had been a cornerstone of the vast Indigenous fishery in the Fraser basin and they quickly became another focus of the settlers' summer fishery at the mouth of this river. Coho salmon (*O. kisutch*) were larger than Pinks, though less numerous, and spawned in the autumn. Chinook salmon (*O. tshawytscha*) were the largest and least numerous species and spawned from early spring into the autumn. In the twentieth century, Coho and Chinook became the most prized sport fish on the Strait.

The Great Britain Emigration Commission's report on Vancouver Island described the Strait's "very rich and fat" salmon that could easily be "speared or shot or caught in nets" as they converged to ascend rivers, and settlers at the time did catch most of their salmon in nets of one kind or another. Within a couple of decades, fishermen working alone or in pairs in small boats were supplying fish to a rapidly growing collection of canneries. Experiments were made with salting, smoking and pickling salmon, but canning proved to be the best technology for transforming the abundant fish into a global commodity.

Modern fish-canning processes originated in late-eighteenth-century France, spread to Scotland and then to the lobster and salmon fisheries of North America's Atlantic coast in the early nineteenth century. Canning technology moved to California's Sacramento River salmon fishery in the 1860s, and from there it made its way north. Fraser River Sockeye were first canned in 1867, and by 1871 commercial canneries were operating at the mouth of the Fraser. In those early years, four canneries produced almost a million 450-gram tins of Sockeye a year. By 1880, a dozen canneries lined the Lower Fraser, shipping salmon to Britain to help meet growing demand for cheap protein from a hard-pressed urban working class. While the settlers around the Strait might savour fresh-caught fish, the vast majority of the salmon they caught were destined to be canned for this overseas market. The arrival of the railroad would open up other markets.

Federal law restricted the industrial salmon fishery to tidal areas. As Indigenous fishers had done before them, settlers established a network of seasonal fish-processing camps on sheltered shorelines. The Sockeye fishery at the Fraser mouth was tremendously valuable to the entrepreneurs controlling it, and masses of spawning salmon in those years *did* suggest an infinite resource. The *Colonist* reported that the Fraser above Yale in 1873 was "literally blocked with salmon."[4] In 1876, Indian Commissioner G.M. Sproat (chapter 2) described the salmon filling the Squamish River, so thick that he and his colleagues could have "killed by the scores" with their paddles alone.[5] Yet there was already talk of overfishing within a decade of the first canneries opening on the Fraser. The DMF introduced licensing for gillnetters and began to contemplate constructing salmon hatcheries to maintain stocks.

Salmon fishing at the centre of the resource rush, 1880s–World War I

The salmon fishery had overtaken mining as the Strait's most important industry by the mid-1880s, when canned salmon became BC's most valuable export. Most early commercial fishers on the Strait used gillnetters powered by oar or sail (see photograph page 139), but the new century saw growing use of purse seiners, motorised boats and gear, mechanised ice-packing equipment and more sophisticated harvesting techniques. These technologies allowed fishers to handle bigger nets more effectively, cover greater distances and fish for longer. As well, vast stationary fish traps were placed in the path of spawning salmon, mostly on the US side of the border.

The fish were so plentiful that even men using lines or nets from small boats could catch prodigious numbers of salmon. Charles Groth, an early settler on Galiano Island, rowed over to fish at the Fraser mouth in 1883. Before falling sick in early August, he had caught close to 7,000 salmon. Fishing with handlines out of his dugout canoe off Quadra Island, one of the Pidcock brothers caught more than 700 salmon in a single day in 1905.

Hundreds of small boats powered only by sail and oar fished at the mouth of the Fraser River around the turn of the twentieth century.

Image A-03941 courtesy of the Royal BC Museum and Archives.

With so many fish being caught, the canning industry grew rapidly and by the late 1880s the Strait's canned salmon was moving by ship around the world and by rail to eastern North America. New cold-storage technology also meant that higher-value fresh fish could be shipped to eastern markets starting in the 1890s, but canned salmon remained the most important commodity. The number of canneries at the Fraser mouth increased from twelve in 1880 to over fifty by 1900. New canneries were built on the east coast of Vancouver Island as well, on Burrard Inlet and at more isolated outposts around the Strait (see Figure 9, page 141). But Fraser River Sockeye (see photograph page 142) remained the heart of the industry. By the beginning of the twentieth century, the size of the Strait Sockeye run determined global salmon prices. Table 2 (page 140) illustrates the industry's development in those years.

An exceptionally large cohort of Sockeye typically returns to the Fraser every four years, and 1893, 1897, 1905 and 1913 were four such "big years." In 1892 (a small year), the canneries' pack of tinned salmon was ten times what it had been in the mid-1870s. The following year, the big year of 1893, the pack was 150 percent bigger. Although more modest than 1893, the packs in 1894 and 1895 were a large increase from 1892. And the pack of 1896, which was *not* a big year, exceeded even 1893's big-year catch. During the summer of 1896, the DMF steamer *Quadra* described "an immense number of fishing boats on the Fraser River, the Gulf of Georgia being completely covered with them for miles."[6] Then came 1897, another big year, and the biggest pack yet recorded. The big years of 1905 and 1913 continued to show substantial increases. But by 1913, the Fraser River Sockeye's share in the overall pack had already diminished.

By the early 1900s, prices were falling as BC's canneries faced growing competition around the Pacific from Russian, Japanese and US canners. In response they increased mechanisation, further augmenting their production capacities. As in lumbering, such technological advances contributed to periodic wasteful "overproduction" in the fisheries.

Table 2: Salmon canning in coastal BC, selected years, 1892–1913[7]

Year	Total BC salmon pack (48-pound cases)	Of which, cases from Fraser River canneries
1892	228,000	not available
1893	590,000	not available
1894	494,000	not available
1895	566,000	not available
1896	602,000	357,000
1897	1,024,000	877,000
1903	473,674	204,809*
1905	1,167,450	837,489*
1913	1,353,900	684,600*

*Only Fraser River Sockeye (i.e., Pink and other salmon not included)

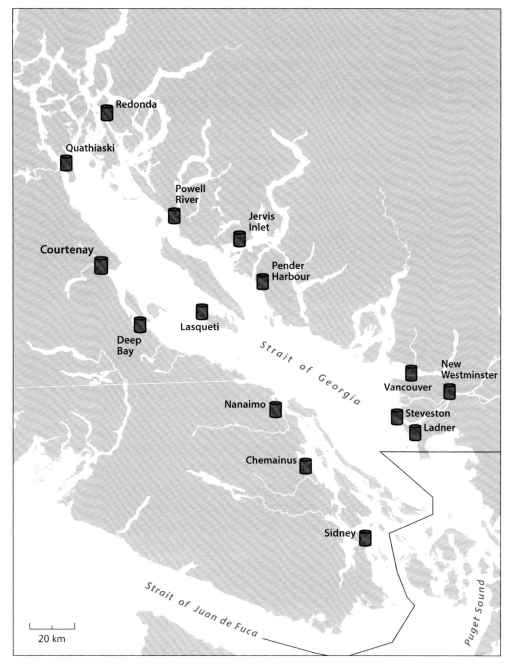

Figure 9: Sites on the Strait with one or more canneries in 1914. These canneries were transforming the inland sea's seemingly inexhaustible fish populations into commodities.

Federal fishery authorities established complex relationships with the Strait's fishers and canners during the resource rush, and with the governments in Victoria, Washington state and Washington, DC. The intensity of intergovernmental struggle reflected the great value of this fishery. After 1900, even as fishing was eclipsed by the Strait's rapidly growing forest industry, it also became the most valuable fishery in the Dominion. Ottawa led negotiations with the US and Washington state over rights and responsibilities related to the Fraser Sockeye. Some estimated that the stationary fish traps on the US side of the border were catching most of the fish, which led to growing complaints that Americans were taking all "our" salmon. When the Fraser

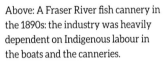

Above: A Fraser River fish cannery in the 1890s: the industry was heavily dependent on Indigenous labour in the boats and the canneries.

Image B-02522 courtesy of the Royal BC Museum and Archives.

Above right: This 1913 photo is entitled "Richmond; BC Canneries; 35,000 Sockeye Salmon." The landslide at Hells Gate on the Fraser River that year would prevent Sockeye from swimming upriver to spawn, and catches of Fraser Sockeye would not reach 1913 levels again in the twentieth century.

Image E-05031 courtesy of the Royal BC Museum and Archives.

Sockeye runs were big, hundreds of thousands of fish caught in those traps were simply thrown away because the canneries they were feeding lacked the capacity to process them. Canners at the Fraser mouth responded by launching hundreds more small boats to catch the fish that had eluded the traps. In Victoria, fishers set their own traps on the Strait of Juan de Fuca to gather the salmon before they reached US waters. Both sides recognised that the existing situation was unsustainable and continued to negotiate "fish sharing," but it took several more decades to reach a formal agreement.

The great value of salmon also contributed to smaller-scale conflicts. There was ongoing intimidation and "net theft" among competing fishers at the Fraser mouth, especially in small years when fish were scarcer and prices higher. Ottawa, though concerned, insisted that policing the fishers was a provincial responsibility, while the province had little or no presence on the sea. In reality, the fishing industry on the Strait in the late nineteenth century was remarkably unfettered by regulation. The federal Fisheries Act, which came into force in BC in 1878, governed the West Coast fisheries. Ten years later, fishing licences were required. By the 1890s, Canada's fishery authorities placed more regulations on fishing gear and the times and places different types of fishermen might fish. Ottawa still had little capacity to enforce such regulations, however. During the 1890s, the DMF had just two "fishery guardians" on the Strait, both at the Fraser mouth. Yet disputes with American fishers through this period often focused on the even weaker controls south of the border. As a result, Ottawa began to loosen controls on Canadian fishers and canners after 1900 in an attempt to ensure they were not disadvantaged in their competition with the Americans.

Ottawa also struggled with Victoria about jurisdiction over the fishery. The province and the local board of trade complained that Ottawa was earning far more from the West Coast fishery than it invested in it. Shortly before World War I, after two Royal Commissions on the fishery, Victoria and Ottawa still had a list of disputes awaiting resolution by the Imperial Privy Council in London. They had agreed that both levels of government could require fishers to purchase licences for gillnetting ($5 each) and setting salmon trap nets ($75), purse seines ($50) and drag seines ($25). Canneries (see photograph page 144) had to pay Ottawa $50 and Victoria $100 for their annual licences. The province also taxed the canneries for their land, and the fishers for every fish they caught in traps.

Over the long run, probably the most damaging outcome of federal-provincial discord over fisheries was Victoria's consistent failure to control the damage done to the fishery by the forest industry. Roderick Haig-Brown later suggested that logging damage to spawning beds and rivers had already contributed to reducing the size of three of the four cyclical big-year spawns of Fraser Sockeye between 1901 and 1913. Similar damage occurred in many other watersheds around (and beyond) the sea during the decades of intensive logging that followed. Federal fisheries authorities were unable to convince the province to control it.

As early as 1888, the *Colonist* newspaper reported the local board of trade's concern that salmon needed protection from overfishing. When catches rose in the big years, canneries worked day and night, and prices fell, sometimes to a few cents per fish. The only way for fishers to maintain their income was to increase their catch. Sometimes canneries then stopped buying fish altogether, leading to an appalling waste of fish as the surplus catch was dumped. During the small years, canneries slowed down their production but salmon prices rose and fishers might earn as much as thirty or forty cents per fish—which encouraged them to catch as many as possible. The naturally erratic nature of salmon runs combined with growing fishing pressure and signs of declining catches all stimulated demand for conservation measures.

A Royal Commission on the salmon fishery and ongoing negotiations with the Americans both provided a forum for debate and negotiations among industry stakeholders in the early years of the new century. There was disagreement within the commission, however, on how best to deal with overfishing and declining fish stocks. A "minority report" issued by

"Seeding the beds": stripping salmon of their eggs at an early Fraser River fish hatchery.

Image A-03957 courtesy of the Royal BC Museum and Archives.

dissident members of the 1908 Royal Commission complained that the commission's official report had ignored declining catches, especially on the Fraser. The dissenters maintained that more efficient equipment, combined with bigger nets and wider-ranging fleets, was causing stocks to decline, and they called for complete bans on fishing at certain times during the spawning season and for more effort to "seed the beds," in which young salmon would be raised in nurseries and then released into spawning streams. These ideas reflected the emerging views of federal fisheries managers, who had also begun to consider establishing some maximum level of sustained yield.

The Deep Bay Cannery (seen here in the 1910s), at the south end of Baynes Sound on Vancouver Island, had been the site of a whaling operation in the 1860s. A dogfish-rendering plant there sickened neighbours in the 1940s. Today, it is the site of a provincially funded shellfish industry research centre.

Image E-06456 courtesy of the Royal BC Museum and Archives.

By 1900, sustaining fisheries with hatcheries had become a powerful idea internationally. Although early fisheries managers knew little about the life cycle of Pacific salmon, the DMF was operating hatcheries on the Great Lakes and in the St. Lawrence River by the 1870s. Its first salmon hatchery on the Fraser was built in 1884; seven more followed over the next fifty years. Canners built a few others, mostly in the final years before World War I. Hatcheries had become popular in the lower Columbia River basin of the US a little earlier because they appeared to guarantee an endless supply of fish, thereby ensuring economic progress while easing conflicts over the resource. The allure for Canadian fisheries managers was that it was easier to manage hatcheries than to control the fishing industry. The BC Board of Trade also believed in the virtues of hatcheries. In fact, it attributed a particularly large catch on the Fraser in 1897 to fish raised in a hatchery established there in 1884. And it demanded that Ottawa spend more of its revenues from fisheries to build more hatcheries on the Fraser and other BC rivers.

Disaster struck the Strait's salmon fishery in 1913. A mishap during railway construction at Hells Gate in the Fraser Canyon blocked the river channel through which millions of Sockeye and Pink salmon normally migrated on the way to their spawning beds, vastly reducing the number of salmon returning to the river to spawn in future years. The Hells Gate slide helped create greater awareness of the pressing need for sound stewardship of this resource among fisheries scientists in particular. The fishers themselves adapted by moving their boats to other river mouths and adopting ever more efficient technologies.

The changing geography of salmon fishing in the interwar years

The early development of the commercial salmon-fishing industry on the Strait closely mirrored the path taken by the forestry industry, a pattern that continued during the interwar years. As salmon became depleted—particularly at the Fraser mouth—and other stocks around the inland sea where fishing had previously been concentrated began to decrease, larger gas-powered fishing boats and other new technologies made it easier for fishers to move to new fishing grounds beyond the Strait. At the same time, firms seeking economies of scale centralised their fish processing at larger facilities. Government efforts to manage the fisheries were outpaced, as usual, by technological improvements.

The only people with a long-standing tradition of fishing on the Strait were Indigenous fishers, and their traditions had been virtually regulated out of existence by the 1920s. Yet a distinctive fishing culture—a combination of intense individuality and solidarity among people facing the dangers of the work—had emerged in the settler fishery. Writer Frederick Marsh would later muse about the Strait's fishermen, who, "like loggers, live their lives wrestling with natural forces… [but are] often even more individualistic because their work is more lonely." Describing the sea and the wind, Marsh wrote: "They impress men's souls, not with any easy optimism, but with a sense of underlying mystery and even terror."[8]

Francis John Barrow's summer cruises in the 1930s took him among thousands of these commercial fishers (see photograph page 145), and he documented them and

the canneries in action. He found fishers of different ethnic groups, each given to their own particular fishing methods, types of fish, fishing grounds and organisations representing them. Indigenous and Japanese Canadian fishers, for example, gillnetted for the canneries around the Strait, catching mostly Sockeye, Pink and Chum. Japanese Canadians dominated this niche at the Fraser mouth. In contrast, white fishers trolled for Spring and Coho around the Strait. And both whites and Indigenous fishers resented competition from Japanese Canadian boats in the local salmon (and herring) fisheries as well as competition from Japan's national fishery in international markets. During World War II, political agitation and increasing resentment culminated in the government removing the Japanese Canadian fishers and selling their boats very cheaply. They, like Indigenous people who fished for food, made particularly convenient targets when fishing was bad.

Salmon fishing and canning remained the lucrative heart of the Strait's commercial fishery, and the canneries were thriving again by the mid-1920s. They had largely recovered from the shock of the Hells Gate slide, thanks to abundant salmon runs on other rivers and higher prices for fish in international markets. In 1928, two local fish-packing plants merged to form British Columbia Packers Ltd., which dominated the fishing industry along the West Coast of Canada for decades. Export markets for canned salmon remained good through the 1920s, but the economic downturn of the 1930s and Japanese competition in the British market forced the company into receivership and the closure of many of its plants. By 1939, however, BC Packers had rebounded on the strength of its exports to many other countries.

Fishing boats at Galiano Island in the 1930s: Thousands of diesel- or gas-powered boats plied the Strait, supplying the canneries, the fresh fish market and the workers' own families.

Image B-07318 courtesy of the Royal BC Museum and Archives.

Canneries began to concentrate more around the mouths of the Fraser and Skeena rivers in the interwar years, but the overall number of canneries on the coast began to decline, from ninety in 1917 to thirty-six in 1928. This number held steady through the 1930s but fell to twenty-seven by the late 1940s. There was no decline in canning capacity, however. By 1939 the remaining fish plants were considerably more mechanised and packed four times as much fish as they had a generation earlier. Fishing boats, too, were faster and larger, and were powered by gas and equipped with on-board refrigeration technology. Instead of the small gillnetters that had earlier landed most fish, more of the catch was being taken by larger seine boats. This new equipment allowed more fishers to fish in more locations, including the mouths of the Strait's many spawning rivers. They then moored their boats in dispersed home ports after selling their catch. Fish buyers often followed them to the fishing grounds and then returned with their purchases to canneries at the Fraser mouth.

This new geography of the fishing industry was enabled by evolving technology, but it was also made necessary by changes in supply and demand. Sockeye catches on the Fraser before the 1913 slide had averaged around 9 million fish per year, whereas the average from 1914 to 1949 was just 2.4 million. In 1913, the overall catch of Sockeye and Pink at the Fraser mouth had been 29 million fish. In the next big years of 1917 and 1921, due to the Hells Gate slide, these numbers fell to less than 7 million and 2 million fish, respectively. Up to 1913, the industry had produced between a million and 1.4 million cases of tinned salmon in big years, of which 50 to 80 percent had been Fraser Sockeye. In 1925, which ought to have been a big year, only about 30,000 cases (or less than 2 percent) of the coast's overall pack of 1.7 million cases contained Fraser Sockeye. In 1936, a relatively big year for Fraser River Sockeye, about 170,000 of almost 1.9 million cases contained Fraser Sockeye. However, this number was still less than 10 percent of the total BC pack. It would take decades, and much international negotiation and regulation, for the Fraser Sockeye runs to approach earlier levels.

Despite the sudden decline in Fraser Sockeye stocks, global demand for salmon continued to grow through and after World War I, and the local industry responded by rapidly expanding catches of other salmon. To keep the catch growing, fishing for Pink, Coho, Chinook and Chum—as well as other fish species—increased on other reaches of the Strait and beyond. And this diversification meant, among other things, a longer fishing season. Continued growth in the salmon catch reflected the broader trend on North America's west coast, where the annual pack expanded from 2,000 to 10 million cases between 1870 and 1920.

Norman Safarik spent his life processing fish in Vancouver, and his memoirs provide rich detail about salmon trolling in the 1920s and '30s, the period he called the "salad days" of fishing on the Strait. Up to 1,500 trollers, mostly boats 10 or 11 metres long, operated on the inland sea by the mid-1930s. They fished most reaches of the Strait, even trolling in Vancouver Harbour when the weather kept them from going farther offshore. From May through January, they fished for Coho and Spring salmon; in August and September, for Pink. For processors such as Safarik, Coho were the most prized fish because of their firm, bright red meat. Coho spawned in the innumerable little streams spilling into all parts of the Strait and fed on the rich populations of herring and shrimp.

By the interwar period, both salmon fishing and processing on the Strait were heavily regulated. Ottawa governed the fishery and exports, but Victoria still regulated fish processing and commerce within the province. The federal government tried to influence the distribution of canneries on the coast but lost its right to license canneries in 1929 when the Privy Council in London ruled that the province alone had jurisdiction over the canneries. Meanwhile, twelve government boats cruised the Canadian side of the border by 1915, alert to depredations of US-based boats taking "Canadian" salmon. Yet the fish migrating to the Fraser were not inclined to respect the border. Concerns about depletion of migratory stocks, particularly Sockeye, finally resulted in a treaty between Canada and the US, and a new international governing body to oversee the fishery. Formed in 1937, the International Pacific Salmon Fisheries Commission (IPSFC) was tasked with controlling the Sockeye fishery, its goal being to divide the catch between Canadian and US fishers in a way that would ensure enough escapement of spawning fish to restore stocks to their earlier abundance. The very long negotiations that had led to the creation of this commission also helped to finally abolish Washington state's stationary salmon traps in 1935.

William Sloan, the head of a provincial fisheries commission looking into the salmon fishery, delivered an eloquent warning about the dangers of overfishing. His 1919 report called for a shift to more efficient fisheries management, inspired by conservationist principles: "We have overdone the thing," said Sloan. "We have drawn, and are drawing, too heavily upon our supply of salmon [and what]…we need is a complete and radical change of policy." He went on to call for government to "step in and take over our salmon fisheries and administer them for the benefit of the people as a whole." The West Coast salmon fisheries, Sloan said, "will last for all time if they are properly handled." Foreshadowing later messages from fisheries biologists and advocates like Haig-Brown, Sloan insisted that depleted runs could be restored as long as enough fish were allowed to reach the spawning beds. On the other hand, he warned, this rich fishery would "entirely disappear if left to corporate and individual control [only]…to satisfy the short sighted greed of a small minority."[9]

Despite Sloan's concerns, salmon harvesting expanded rapidly beyond the Fraser mouth through the 1920s and 1930s, when thousands of fishermen around the sea were utterly dependent on commercial and subsistence fishing to sustain their families. Then came World War II, when the canneries operated "at a fever pitch" to supply guaranteed markets. Whatever conservation had been achieved was relaxed, and "virtually every catchable salmon" was pursued and canned. What was bad for conservation was good for the canneries (Sloan's "greedy minority"). They would not only contribute to the war effort but also re-establish their share of the British market lost earlier to the Japanese.

Fisheries research activities around the inland sea during the interwar years

A federal fisheries research centre was set up in Nanaimo in the 1870s, as the federal Department of Marine and Fisheries began to establish a modest presence on the West Coast, but until 1924 it had only one full-time scientist—the director. In those early years, most of the scientific research was carried out in the summer months by visiting scholars; however, by 1932, the centre's year-round scientific staff had grown to eleven. Almost from the moment of their arrival, federal fisheries authorities had proposed artificial propagation of salmon as a means to both increase stocks and "smooth out" the huge variations in Sockeye populations returning to the Fraser River. Yet early in the twentieth century, some Canadian fishery experts and their counterparts in the American Pacific Northwest began to question the real impact of hatcheries. Despite their reservations, more and more salmon fry continued to be produced in hatcheries on the BC coast. By the time Canadian fisheries scientists finally concluded that these hatcheries were having little effect on the size of salmon runs, fry production had reached over two billion annually, mostly Sockeye and mostly in the Fraser Basin.

Salmon catches were being maintained, most scientists now believed, not because the stocks were being artificially regenerated but because more fishers were covering a larger area and catching species such as Chum and Pink that had previously been considered less desirable. Similar patterns would emerge in many parts of the world later in the century. Many people in the fishing industry suggested that the solution to stock depletion was not to build more hatcheries but—as Sloan had suggested in 1919—to allow enough wild fish to escape the fishery and reach spawning beds, where they could reproduce and keep up future population levels. Others viewed this "depletionist" narrative as alarmist, feeling that it ignored the improvements that had been achieved. They argued that this pessimism did not allow for what the optimists euphemistically described as "the readjustment" after 1913. That is, if one made allowances for the huge reduction in catches on the Fraser since the Hells Gate slide and recognised that innovative approaches had ensured that catches increased elsewhere, then things didn't look too bad. A federal report on the Strait's fisheries published in 1940, perhaps aiming for a compromise, suggested the truth lay somewhere between these two views. As in the forest sector, conservation concerns took a back seat to the need to pull out all the stops in support of the war effort during World War II. The debate over the best way forward would heat up again in the post-war years.

Salmon on the Strait after 1945: familiar challenges, great plans and aquaculture

Fishing intensified rapidly around the world after 1945, and this trend was reflected on the Strait. Over the whole BC coast, the marine fishery employed close to 20,000 people in boats and processing plants into the 1960s, and the industry remained important for many of the province's coastal communities. In the early 1960s, fishers in BC were landing an average of nearly 300,000 tons a year, worth almost $40 million, or a third of Canada's total commercial fishery earnings. Salmon accounted for two-thirds of this BC catch by value, herring and halibut most of the rest. Of these species, only halibut was not being fished commercially on the Strait. Yet by the early 1970s, the fishing industry on the inland sea, as elsewhere on the West Coast, had come to be viewed in Ottawa and Victoria as a marginal "problem sector" in need of "rationalisation."

Trends in salmon fishing on the inland sea were broadly similar to global ones. Maintaining yields was requiring ever more technology and capital. Between 1945 and 1955, equipment investments per fisherman tripled as fishers invested in innovations such as mechanised drums to draw in nets and sonar to locate fish, both of which increased the risk of overfishing. Similarly, rapid marine transport and brine refrigeration technology adopted after World War II made it feasible to freeze fish for later canning, which sped up the centralisation and closure of fish plants and changed the nature of fish processing. Yet regulations on the Strait, especially before the 1960s, did not do enough to respond to these innovations, which increased the range, mobility and efficiency of the salmon fleet and changed its composition. With fish stocks declining in many places around the Strait, many small-scale fishers were forced out and quit fishing because they found themselves ever less able to compete with the larger boats carrying more sophisticated gear and ranging over more of the inland sea—and increasingly, beyond it.

Changing technologies affected the canneries too. Some of the bigger ones began to invest in large-scale cold-storage facilities that allowed them to extend their processing seasons. And they began to concentrate again, as they had in the nineteenth century, around the mouth of the Fraser: by 1970, 40 percent of Canada's West Coast canneries were located there. By setting up near Vancouver, they could better cope with seasonal peaks and dips in the demand for labour; the Lower Mainland's available and flexible workforce allowed them to operate more efficiently than smaller canneries elsewhere on the Strait. Writing in the 1950s, Haig-Brown had correctly predicted the disappearance of the coast's many isolated canneries. Between 1920 and 1970, the total number of canneries on the whole BC coast fell from over sixty to fifteen. One result was that, while the number of canneries located on the Strait declined from fourteen to seven, this lower number now represented almost 50 percent of Canada's West Coast canneries.

The coastal fleet congregated around the canneries, but though most boats were now registered at Lower Mainland ports, far less commercial fishing took place at the Fraser mouth. Almost three-quarters of the 5,500 vessels fishing the BC coast in the early 1970s operated out of ports on the Strait, most of them in Greater Vancouver. The wholesale value of the salmon caught along the coast in that period ranged from $100 million to $220 million each year, yet the average annual value of the catch on the Strait was barely $30 million. The adjacent North Vancouver Island/Mid Coast–Queen Charlotte Islands region, with less than 15 percent of the coast's registered fish boats, accounted for over half its catch.

As it had through most of the century, the Strait's salmon harvest varied greatly from year to year after World War II, both in size and value. For example, catches in the four seasons from 1968 through 1971 ranged between 26,000 and over 59,000 tons, their values from $15 million to over $44 million. The following year, the *Vancouver Sun* reported the annual salmon pack was down nearly 30 percent on the year before.[10] The debate about this resembled the one over the once vast Columbia River fishery. The participants were the same—the different types of fishers, the fish processors, the citizens' groups and the officials from various levels of government—and they demonstrated the same selective memory and propensity to blame others rather than share responsibility for effectively managing the resource. Their tactics, as in the Columbia fishery, included making scapegoats and caricatures of their opponents and marginalising the weaker ones. On the Columbia, geographer Jay Taylor concluded in *Making Salmon*, "Complexity and contingency evaporated through deliberate acts of amnesia. Political myopia infected every group in the debate." The same could be said of the dialogue about salmon fishing on the Strait after 1945.

No evidence or expert opinion could change the minds of resource economists in the 1960s and '70s who identified overfishing as the overwhelming cause of most declining salmon stocks. Commercial fishermen, for their part, focused on causes other than overfishing, which few of them saw as a major problem. Fishers felt that placing increasing restrictions on their fishing was a way of "blaming the victim" for declining salmon stocks. Geoff Meggs, an outspoken advocate for commercial fishermen, suggested in his book *Salmon* that the main problem in the 1980s salmon fishery was its ongoing domination by a processing industry that dictated fishery policy. The salmon, said Meggs, were BC's "canary in the mine," indicators of a dangerous situation in coastal waters. Despite "overwhelming evidence that salmon runs are in crisis because of environmental destruction," the "corporate conservationists," he said, continued to insist the main problem was commercial fishers' overfishing. And so on. About the only thing the different players agreed on was the enormous potential value of salmon fishing. In one of his last articles, Haig-Brown claimed that a "fully rehabilitated" Fraser River could yield catches of 22 to 33 million salmon every second year.[11] Unfortunately, their complex life cycle made such "rehabilitation" challenging and created endless opportunities for key stakeholders to blame each other for the fishery's decline.

Salmon science, "enhancement" and hatcheries

Fisheries science gained prestige after World War II as a result of the International Pacific Salmon Fisheries Commission's (IPSFC) success in rebuilding the Fraser Sockeye and Pink runs that had earlier been devastated by the Hells Gate slide. Fisheries biologists were increasingly at odds with resource economists, however, over the best ways to manage salmon stocks. IPSFC scientists were aware of the challenges of rehabilitation. Spawning Fraser Sockeye had to run a gauntlet of fishing fleets—in the Strait of Juan de Fuca, in Puget Sound and again around the Fraser mouth. Each fleet had the capacity, if uncontrolled, to catch virtually every returning fish, so local fisheries scientists were understandably proud of this stock's slow recovery in the 1940s and '50s. They had carried out research to support innovative "fish ladders" at Hells Gate and elsewhere, removed obstructions, ensured improved pollution control at new pulp mills built on the Upper Fraser, brought a number of vestigial salmon runs back from the edge of extinction and created many effective spawning channels and incubation ponds.

These and other "salmon enhancement" activities were designed, in one way or another, to expand salmon populations and increase the number of fish that could survive in spawning streams and then reach the sea, grow to adulthood and be available to commercial or sport fishers before the survivors returned to spawn. During the early post-war decades, salmon enhancement shared the good reputation of fisheries science in general. Haig-Brown, writing in the 1950s, described how salmon populations on tributaries of the Fraser—such as the Stuart, Bowron and Horsefly rivers—that had seen their spawns almost wiped out after 1913 were now growing rapidly. The Quesnel River spawn increased from a thousand fish in 1941 to

600,000 in 1953, with 2 million predicted for 1957. Sockeye returns to the Adams River were expected to reach 18 million fish by 1958, yielding 8 million for the commercial fishery. Haig-Brown was convinced that "the work of the Commission would restore the Fraser runs to their former abundance [and that] with…effective construction measures and the elimination of watershed abuses, the Fraser salmon runs will become greater than they ever were in recorded time."[12]

In addition to carefully engineered and protected watersheds and hatcheries, restoring depleted Fraser River stocks also involved elaborate controls. Instead of fishing on the Strait being allowed most months of the year, commercial fishers were restricted to fewer months, and within these months fishing was closed for certain periods each week. Net use was increasingly regulated and certain areas, mostly close to the mouth of spawning rivers, were closed to fishing altogether. Government officials had flexibility in applying these provisions, depending on the estimated size of the spawning population, and could close a fishery entirely if necessary to allow enough fish to reach the spawning beds. Officials also attempted to control predatory seals and sea lions around the mouth of spawning rivers. All of these strategies were consistent with what UBC fisheries biologist Peter Larkin described as the "standard religion of Pacific salmon research and management," a creed of salmon husbandry formulated by the 1930s that persisted for four decades.[13] It called for research into salmon biology, implementation of catch regulations to ensure a "sustained yield" and enough protection of the environment to permit effective spawning. Hatcheries might be used, sparingly, to augment natural production and mitigate the effects of earlier flaws in regulation and protection.

In the late 1960s, however, salmon culture techniques that had been disparaged by federal fisheries authorities as ineffective in the mid-1930s—particularly the use of hatcheries to maintain stocks—became the object of renewed hope in the industry. Haig-Brown reminded biologists in 1965, "If you have a viable natural stock, don't write it off and say we can plant another; you just may not be able to."[14] He and many scientists still believed that hatcheries should be the solution only when all others had failed and that too much dependence on them to maintain stocks would likely create as many problems as it solved. Instead, he suggested that protection and improvement of spawning habitat—controlling stream flows and temperatures, improving spawning gravels and removing obstructions—would give far better results. Echoing Haig-Brown, Larkin called for salmon management "more closely identified with the perspective of the salmon."[15] Regulations, he suggested, should be based on salmon biology, not the demands of human convenience (and economists). New management approaches needed to be experimental and supported by long-term research. "Salmon enhancement" became the ascendant fisheries policy, and despite the misgivings of scientists and conservationists, hatcheries figured prominently in economists' new strategies for fisheries into the 1970s.

Carl Walters, a UBC fisheries scientist, pointed out that ecological studies else-where in the world had shown good initial results for hatchery-based enhancement followed by longer-term declines in the fish stocks, sometimes to levels below those at the start of the enhancement projects. He noted that hatcheries might initially increase the size of the fish population, but that this gain was often offset by fishers investing in more efficient gear and changing the timing and location of their fishing in the longer term to harvest this new, larger population. The systems within which these fisheries were conducted, warned Walters, were so complex that any enhancement activity had to be viewed as a huge experiment rather than industry and scientists pretending a level of understanding that didn't exist. In fact, these initiatives required decades of careful monitoring to determine their outcomes.[16]

This type of humility might be good science but it was neither familiar nor comfortable for resource economists, much less for politicians whose re-election might depend on guaranteeing improvements in fish catches. Scientists pointed to tremendous uncertainty surrounding a salmon's life in the open ocean, highlighting essentially unknown factors there that could affect population dynamics. In contrast, resource economists wanted to enhance fish stocks on some rivers so they could sacrifice them on others. Biologists suggested enhancement should focus on rivers where stocks were already reduced, cautioning against "throwing away" any spawning rivers since all were needed to ensure the health of the overall population. These views were particularly unwelcome, of course, among proponents of new hydroelectric dams in the Fraser River basin, such as BC Hydro chairman Gordon Shrum.

Scientists were not rejecting hatcheries and salmon enhancement outright, and even Haig-Brown conceded that in badly degraded watersheds, they might be a solution of last resort. But BC, he reiterated, should not be looking for last resorts. He described hatcheries as a "patent medicine panacea" that was especially inappropriate for keeping stocks high over long periods of time: they were expensive and polluting, and they bred diseases that could spread to wild stocks. They dangerously reduced genetic diversity in salmon populations. These drawbacks tended to get worse over time and they threatened to divert resources from better enhancement approaches. Achieving large, healthy salmon stocks required "doing it the hard way"—protecting and managing wild stocks, their spawning streams and the land around them. Here he ran up against fisheries authorities, who claimed they didn't know enough about stream rehabilitation to undertake it on a large scale. Haig-Brown countered that they had literally thousands of damaged streams to experiment with, and while they didn't know everything about restoring them, they knew enough to get started.

Provincial leaders, who depended heavily on forest industry revenues and were committed to dam construction, were more comfortable with the economists' talk of hatchery-based enhancement than the biologists' "excessive caution." Much science would eventually be applied to various enhancement strategies, but most of them were a messy mix of science, resource economics and politics.

Salmon governance, the Salmonid Enhancement Program & after

It was clear to many fisheries biologists that careful, flexible, multi-faceted and responsive fisheries policies were required to control the impacts of technological advances on fish stocks. Implementing such policies required political will, however. As in the past, such will was hard to come by, particularly across federal-provincial lines. While Ottawa controlled the salmon fishery, Victoria controlled land-based activities—including logging, farming, dam building, industrial and urban development—that had significant impacts on salmon habitat. Provincial fisheries authorities appreciated the need to protect salmon streams, but managers in most other sectors, especially the dominant forest sector, more or less ignored the issue.

Fish boats in Vancouver Harbour in 1948, before "rationalisation" of the coastal fishing fleet had occurred.

Image D-02639 courtesy of the Royal BC Museum and Archives.

It was in this challenging context that federal fisheries authorities began to pursue strategies aimed at "maximising economic returns" from the salmon fishery. By the late 1960s, identifying the "common property" nature of the fishery as one of its main problems, they limited access to it by reducing the number of commercial fishing licences available. Their goal was to force "inefficient" smaller operators (see photograph page 153)—many of them Indigenous fishers—out of the commercial fishery. As Geoff Meggs described it, resource economists were unfettered by any understanding of the salmon fishery's socio-cultural and biological complexities. To them it appeared to be "an enormous government and corporate effort to reap a relatively modest volume of fish"; the fishing industry accounted for 3.5 percent of the province's jobs but only 1.5 percent of its wealth.[17] From an economist's perspective, too many fishermen were going after too few fish. Their gear was increasingly costly and its efficiency was leading to ever-shorter fishing seasons. They were plagued by foreign competitors on the outside coast and competition from sport fishers on the Strait. Generous unemployment insurance and affordable fishing licences meant too many "marginal fishermen" were attracted to the fishery. These and many other factors, said the economists, were making it difficult to manage the fisheries "scientifically." For the economists, reducing the number of licences seemed the only logical response.

Peter Pearse, a resource economist whose advice helped guide the new licensing process, summarised the major ideas underlying the new strategy. First, the fishery ought to achieve the greatest possible sustained yield of fish from the most efficient possible use of labour and capital. Therefore, eliminating "inefficient" fishermen from the fleet would increase the "health" of the industry. Second, a complementary "salmon enhancement program" would ensure healthy stocks.[18] The economists' prescriptions initially seemed to have the desired effect. Stimulated by huge growth in demand from the Japanese, the coastal fishing industry saw record-high salmon prices, earnings and profits between 1973 and 1980. Yet by the 1980s, too many fishers were once again going after too few fish. Another Royal Commission warned that the coastal fishing fleet still had far more capacity than was needed to harvest the available fish.[19]

The 1970s marked the apogee of post-war government intervention in the economy. Victoria had begun to worry in the 1960s that the province was not involved enough in fisheries issues and called for enhanced provincial capacity for fisheries management. The result was a Marine Resources Branch established within the province's new Ministry of Environment in the 1970s, and subsequently a Memorandum of Understanding with federal counterparts in 1975 on a Salmonid Enhancement Program (SEP) that defined their respective roles with regard to marine fisheries on the sea. The SEP promoted the idea of expanding hatcheries on rivers around the Strait while also trying to better protect fish habitat and control pollution.

A federal-provincial agreement was a critical requirement for the SEP because it called for sweeping improvements in the way the province's coastal watersheds were managed. Federal planners recognised that the restrictions on forestry, mining and waste dumping called for in the SEP would mean direct costs to the province. They suggested these costs should be part of the province's contribution to the SEP. Provincial fisheries officials had limited control over such things, however, and Victoria did little to encourage other sectors to participate.

In the early 1970s, federal authorities called for massive expansion of their earlier successes in restoring salmon on the Fraser. They maintained that Sockeye catches there could be tripled and the Pink catch increased up to eight times. Resource economists proposed a seductive, flexible approach known as "no net loss," which allowed fish habitat to be destroyed in some salmon streams as long as it could be compensated by increased production through "enhancement" of other streams. The economists, though not the biologists, believed that hatcheries could ratchet up production as required in those compensatory streams. When Ottawa began its detailed planning of the SEP in the mid-1970s, the first five years of operations were expected to cost $150 million, and the total cost over a decade up to $300 million. Government officials predicted salmon production would double in the Strait and the Fraser watershed in ten years. Federal fisheries Minister Roméo LeBlanc said the SEP was "an exciting example of man's ability to enhance, rather than endanger, an invaluable natural resource." He explained that salmon catches on the West Coast had reached 360 million pounds a year early in the twentieth century but had fallen to half that amount as a result of "environmental damage and overfishing." Without the SEP, he maintained, salmon production of 145 million pounds a year would fall by 20 to 30 percent over the next two decades. But the "application of fish culture technology" (i.e., hatcheries) could reverse this trend, he said, and "increase production of salmonids by at least 190 million pounds annually."[20]

Ottawa recognised that the SEP would be challenging. However, Canada was said to have unique advantages over other countries that practised this technique, including its "high proportion of unspoiled natural streams, strong fishing and processing capacity...and a leadership role in the broad application of fish culture technology." The SEP would draw on diverse enhancement techniques, many of them "developed in Canada," including spawning channels, hatcheries, "fishways," stream modification, rearing ponds and incubation boxes. These would be combined with "new and promising techniques," such as lake and stream "enrichment." At the same time, officials discouraged salmon fishers and processors from making further capital investments, stating they already had the capacity to catch all the predicted increases in salmon. The government worried that fishers putting new money into fishing equipment would diminish the economic returns on the government's investment; it didn't speculate about the possible impacts on salmon stocks.[21]

The list of the SEP's prospective benefits was long, according to government authorities. By the end of the century, increased production was predicted to be worth close to $500 million (in 1976 dollars), up from less than $200 million in the mid-1970s. The program could create more than 4 million days of employment and opportunities for local and visiting anglers and tourists. Guides, marinas and other services were expected to benefit, as would many small communities. Tensions between commercial and recreational fishers would be reduced, particularly on the Strait, where recreational demand for salmon was concentrated. It was suggested that Indigenous people would have more fishing income, more food fish and more jobs in fishing and fish processing. The program would improve citizens' mental and physical health as the public got the opportunity to participate in the enhancement. Canada's balance of payments would improve, and welfare and unemployment insurance claims would decline. Advocates stopped short of promising a salmon-related cure for cancer, but they definitely painted a more encouraging picture than the biologists' gloomy "uncertainty" scenario. Peter Larkin called it "typically Canadian" and described it as "a creeping approach…[involving] a half-hearted commitment to science, a weak kneed approach to licence limitation, a blunt elbowed approach to international negotiations, a soft headed approach to subsidies and a long winded approach to planning." Instead, Larkin said, the industry needed "hyper modern, super efficient, technology rich fisheries" that could bring down world fish prices while increasing sales.[22]

In the end, the SEP was launched in 1977. Of the eleven hatcheries producing "sport fish"—Chinook and Coho—that were being developed or had been upgraded, nine were on the Strait or the Lower Fraser (see Figure 10, page 157). The following year, plans were made for four more salmon-rearing facilities on the Vancouver Island shore.[23] Much of the appeal of these SEP hatcheries was their potential to reduce the pressure for more effective conservation and governance, those "other measures" that Haig-Brown and many scientists insisted were far more effective than hatcheries. Concerns about the SEP's approach soon began to surface, however. There was concern about the possible negative effects of hatchery stocks on wild salmon populations. And, as federal fisheries Minister Roméo LeBlanc explained in 1978, they knew how many fish were entering the sea from rivers and they knew how many were being caught by commercial fishermen, but they didn't know much about all the other things happening to the salmon. As well, a long-standing international agreement on the Pacific salmon fishery had to be renegotiated with the Americans. And much of the critical fish habitat protection promised in the SEP depended on collaboration with less interested provincial and municipal governments.

Many federal fisheries officers also looked upon the Strait's rapidly expanding recreational fishery as a threat to commercial fishing interests. Sport fishers were taking an estimated two-thirds of Chinook salmon caught in the Strait. There were concerns as well that Indigenous people's "food fish" were finding their way onto commercial markets. The SEP had faded by the early 1980s but did not disappear. The dynamics of the salmon fishery, and Ottawa's inability to control them, continued to plague federal fisheries managers.

Other challenges: forestry, dams, ports, anglers

Many industries had a variety of destructive effects on the Strait's salmon. It had become recognised globally, for example, that logging damage to streams was among the most important causes of declining fish stocks. Logging had deforested virtually every watershed on the Strait at least once by the 1950s, leaving behind thousands of streams blocked by debris. As a result, countless smaller waterways dried up in summer and became torrents that destroyed spawning beds in winter. In larger streams, too, smaller summer flows had a reduced capacity to sustain juvenile salmon that had adapted to reproducing and spending their early lives in cool, oxygenated, sediment-free streams. By stripping away the vegetation, clogging streams and increasing sedimentation, logging greatly diminished the ability of adult salmon to spawn successfully and juveniles to survive at all.

Roderick Haig-Brown's work with the International Pacific Salmon Fisheries Commission focused on the Fraser, but he had spent decades watching the Strait's smaller streams be ravaged by mining, road building, logging and forest fires fuelled by logging waste. Having been a logger himself as a young man, Haig-Brown decried the "fifty years of notoriously destructive logging methods" that had eliminated thousands of salmon spawning runs. Yet he expressed optimism for the future. Logging methods, he said, were "not quite as destructive" as they had been before 1950, and many forests were regenerating. Where necessary, fisheries authorities could stimulate spawning on damaged streams with various grooming techniques and selective artificial regeneration. But he had no faith in authorities' "pious references… to multiple use" of forests.[24]

Haig-Brown's skepticism was well-founded; requests from federal fisheries authorities that Victoria properly manage the riparian forests surrounding salmon streams were almost never heeded. Following decades of damage, a report to the province's Marine Resources Branch in 1969 stated: "[The] relationship between streamside vegetation and salmonid stream ecology has been one of the most badly neglected areas of fisheries research in BC."[25] A note to the file in 1970 reported "precious few foresters" recognised that harmful effects of logging on fish could be mitigated by leaving bands of trees around streams undisturbed. Its author, R.G. McMynn, knew the forest industry of which he spoke, and it was a stunning observation a quarter-century after the Sloan Commission had recommended that foresters "leave strips" of intact forest around streams. McMynn, echoing Haig-Brown, hoped that BC's policies would begin to recognise the effects of logging. Two years later, the Fisheries Research Board noted that although almost no studies had looked at the impact of BC's logging practices on salmon, such studies were being launched.

Haig-Brown reported in 1973 that sport and commercial fishermen had been

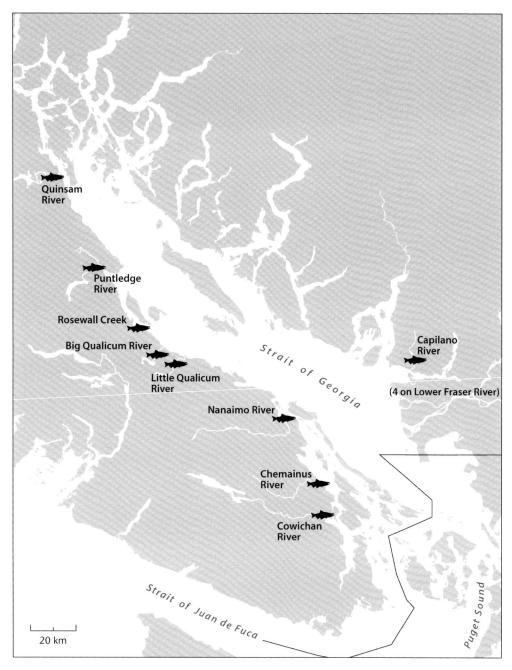

Figure 10: Salmon hatcheries developed, upgraded or planned around the Strait by the SEP, 1977.

"remarkably unsuccessful" during decades of trying to keep logging away from streams. He blamed "half hearted, ill-informed and totally inadequate co-operation" between provincial forestry and federal fishery authorities, between provincial departments, and between governments and loggers. Guardedly optimistic about new fisheries legislation to improve stream protection, he worried that Ottawa lacked the capacity to enforce it and that BC's foresters were not ready to make necessary changes. The only solution he saw was a radical shift in land-use planning, away from the "multiple-use" rhetoric that was contradicted by the province's policy of devoting entire watersheds to forest monocultures.[26]

BC's Pollution Control Board (PCB) had been established in the 1950s to address growing concerns about municipal sewage. The PCB slowly began to consider how best to control pollution created by the forest industry, particularly after it was called upon to do so in the province's Pollution Control Act of 1967 (chapter 5). An inquiry in 1970 then looked into how the industry might meet the requirements of this act, and by 1972 the PCB had issued "recommended guidelines and objectives for air pollution control, solid waste management and water, for different types of emissions, effluents and solid waste from a range of wood mills and pulp and paper mills."[27] There was no shortage of issues to address once the province was stirred to act. One of Peter Larkin's graduate students at UBC in the early 1950s had reported, for example, that a single sulphite pulp mill produced a liquid waste stream equivalent to that of a town of 450,000 people. Yet the provincial government consistently appeared to care far more about the financial health of the forestry sector than the marine fishery, and it seemed prepared to sacrifice the fishery for the short-term convenience of forestry. Besides, the commercial salmon fishery was a federal domain and the forest industry had become a far larger economic player with a great deal more clout in Victoria.

Developing BC's hydroelectricity generation capacity was also a higher priority than the salmon fishery. Dams' impacts on salmon were well known; they had been described repeatedly since the early 1960s. Dams delayed or prevented spawning and caused temperature fluctuations that affected both spawning fish and incubating eggs. Spillways and turbines killed migrating fish. In the 1950s, provincial and federal fisheries authorities had confronted the BC Power Commission about a dam on the Puntledge River. Provincial specialists worried the dam was damaging the river's migratory Steelhead, and federal authorities were concerned about spawning Chinook. Provincial biologists maintained: "The destruction of a large proportion of this resource through single-purpose river development for the sake of short term economics is not in the public interest." They estimated the dam did $30,000 damage a year to the Steelhead run alone,[28] yet the commission did nothing in the end to successfully mitigate the damage.

The biggest confrontation was on the Fraser. Demand for electricity and more effective control of spring flooding had risen rapidly after World War II. Geographer Matthew Evenden characterised the struggle that played out there over the next couple of decades as "Fish versus Power." C.H. Clay, a federal fisheries engineer who had worked on the construction of the Hells Gate fishways, and UBC's Peter Larkin both vigorously rejected another engineer's suggestion that fish protection and hatcheries could render hydro dams safe for salmon. Larkin asserted later that the province had done some of the best scientific research on interactions between fisheries and dams of anyone in the world and had concluded that the two could not easily coexist. He invoked the ire of BC Hydro chairman Gordon Shrum, who wanted to know why researchers would accept research funding if they couldn't solve such problems. Shrum was convinced that science *could* solve such problems and proposed a five-year "crash program" to do it. Haig-Brown declared that all the IPSFC's progress and potential for future improvement of the fishery would be "destroyed, wiped out forever, by one high dam on the river's main channel."[29] The Social Credit government clearly favoured power over fish, yet salmon's proponents eventually prevailed on the Fraser. This rare victory for the fish resulted from an effective coalition of supporters, from other factors that made investments on the Columbia and Peace River systems more attractive, and from advances in power transmission technologies.

A decade later, the rapid development of port facilities, particularly near the mouth of the Fraser and other rivers around the Strait, caused considerable debate over their potential effects on fish. The effects of dredging on the Fraser were far less ambiguous, however, and in the mid-1970s Environment Canada developed guidelines to control this practice, which disturbed gravel beds and killed virtually all juvenile salmon descending the river. The dredges, however, were still killing salmon and stirring controversy later in the decade.

Sport and commercial salmon fishers confronted one another on the Strait. The commercial fishery was most preoccupied with Sockeye travelling in large schools and living most of their lives in the open ocean, only passing through the Strait on their way to and from spawning rivers. The sport fishery was mostly concerned with Coho and Chinook, species that didn't move in large schools but did go after anglers' lures. Most local Chinook spent their entire adult lives in the Strait. The province estimated that by the early 1960s, sport fishers were landing 200,000 to 400,000 Chinook each year, about 1.5 percent of the total salmon catch on the BC coast. BC's saltwater anglers were estimated to be spending $19 million a year on their sport, the vast majority of it on the Strait.

Haig-Brown suggested in an interview with Imbert Orchard that angling on the inland sea had become "probably the most valuable tourist sport fishery in the world."[30] SEP planners—admittedly prone to hyperbole—estimated 250,000 saltwater anglers on the BC coast by the 1970s, most of them on the Strait. In towns up and down both shores of the inland sea, sport fishing had become a major form of recreation (chapter 6) and a significant element of local economies. The problem was that although commercial fishers caught mostly Sockeye, they also landed substantial numbers of Coho and Chinook. And by the 1960s there was no doubt that when commercial Coho and Chinook catches went up, the sport fishery declined and vice versa. Many felt that the economic return for the province from a Coho or Chinook caught by an angler was far greater than if the same fish were caught by a commercial troller and that the sport fishery should be given priority. An important part of the SEP's appeal for BC was its promised expansion of Coho and Chinook hatcheries. But the SEP did not reduce tensions between sport and commercial fishermen as much as its proponents had hoped it would.

Salmon farming

After a good decade in the 1970s, commercial salmon fishing declined again in the 1980s and both Ottawa and Victoria became very interested in salmon farming. It was a rare instance when both governments agreed—for the most part, at least—on the right way forward for the fishery. Salmon farming's emergence around the inland sea in the 1970s and '80s was a response to a series of factors, and it was much in tune with global changes. For federal officials frustrated by their inability to control BC's destructive logging practices or sign a new salmon treaty with the US, salmon farming was an attractive alternative. It was perhaps even a panacea that could replace hatcheries. Federal authorities already had a century of experience with fish culture and many were positively predisposed to it. For resource economists, fish farms were like hatcheries, only better. The government would not have to directly manage them, and their fish would not be at the mercy of careless loggers, miners, factories or towns. Provincial fishery officials, also frustrated by endless struggles to control the profligate loggers, welcomed this new way of stimulating fish production. As early as the mid-1960s, Victoria was corresponding with a Vancouver Island entrepreneur who aimed to combine oyster rafts with salmon farming.

The province knew there were challenges associated with salmon farming. It was costly in the 1970s compared with fishing wild stocks, though emerging technology involving open net cages suspended from rafts might change this. Raised in such pens, salmon often became a source of pollution, releasing vast quantities of contaminants—fish feces, food waste and the residue of antibiotics administered to the fish—into the surrounding water. And disease problems inevitably arose when salmon were raised in crowded pens. Ecologists warned of the dangers and instability of fish monocultures that tried to suppress complex ecological interactions in poorly understood environments. These concerns, like those about hatcheries earlier, failed to extinguish excitement about salmon farming's economic potential.

The province's new Marine Resources Branch elaborated on the promise of aquaculture on the Strait and in other protected BC waters that were already among the most productive in the North Pacific. Among its virtues, the Strait shared with Puget Sound (today's South Salish Sea) a sheltered location that was protected from fierce ocean storms. Powerful tidal flows would "provide a flushing…equivalent to immense rivers" to cope with the farms' waste. Research was looking into transforming this waste into fuel. Cheap sources of feed were available, and the expertise of the federal research station at Nanaimo would support fish farmers on the inland sea. In short, the Strait was well placed to join the "blue revolution," as aquaculture was being called. Proponents of salmon farming depicted an inevitable transition from marine *hunting* to marine *farming*, analogous to the Neolithic Revolution of a few thousand years earlier.

Despite some initial caution, the province's left-wing government of the day soon became an enthusiastic supporter of salmon aquaculture even before its economic viability had been demonstrated. Salmon farming was seen as the "wave of the future," and in 1974 the province financed a study looking at how the industry might develop. The report stated that BC's "unique marine geography" would allow the province to be a leader in fish farming by the end of the century and that the industry would be "environmentally safe" while helping to meet a growing demand for protein. Like the SEP, aquaculture was portrayed as a lifeline for struggling Indigenous communities. They and Premier Dave Barrett's trade union supporters were to be fully involved in new fish farming projects. One of the few threats facing marine aquaculture development in BC, according to the report, was large American corporations such as Union Carbide, whose growing interest in the technology might make it competition for local salmon farmers.[31]

Many federal specialists were equally enthusiastic about aquaculture's potential, though perhaps a little disoriented by BC's vigorous entry into Ottawa's maritime domain. They confirmed that oceanographic and coastal conditions in BC were as well suited to marine aquaculture as they were in Norway or Japan, where fish farming was already established. Few projects were under way in BC by the early 1970s, but federal authorities were receiving many inquiries from interested entrepreneurs.

Ottawa's specialists worried in private about their ability to provide the technical advice and regulatory authority they believed would be necessary to guide a rapid expansion of salmon farming. They felt they needed to develop greater capacity to prevent, diagnose and treat diseases. A pilot fish farm and breeding program would be required to increase growth rates and disease resistance among farmed fish and make their flesh a more attractive colour for consumers. They also needed a feedstock industry, ideally using local cannery waste. Federal specialists were also clear that fish farming ought to supplement the wild fishery, not replace it. Part of aquaculture's promise was to supply fresh fish to markets in those months when "natural supplies" were unavailable. The new industry would need to be "closely regulated to ensure continued high return from native stocks." This would involve developing new kinds of expertise from scratch or importing them from elsewhere. They called for a federal budget increase of a billion dollars to cover all required actions.[32]

Salmon farmers' early experiences on the Strait confirmed the federal worries, and involved a familiar pattern of federal-provincial squabbling. The Meneely family, described by local papers as "Canadian pioneers," had developed three operations off the Sechelt Peninsula by 1975. They farmed Coho and Chinook and complained of difficulties obtaining salmon eggs from federal hatcheries. To get expert help, Larry Meneely said, he had been obliged to hire biologists from the federal government's Nanaimo research station, who then failed to support him and didn't help him obtain eggs.[33] Victoria intervened on his behalf, alarmed that Ottawa seemed able to supply salmon eggs to Union Carbide, an American firm, but not to a local Canadian entrepreneur. The province began to wonder publicly whether federal authorities weren't trying to impede the development of BC's aquaculture industry.

The industry got established, however, with ten farms producing a little over 100 metric tons of fish by 1984. Four years later, 118 farms were producing 6,600 tons. Production increased fourfold in the next three years. And the theoretical questions of the 1970s—about feeding these crowded pens of rapidly growing fish and keeping them healthy—had become practical problems. Most answers were worked out by trial and error, with help from imported expertise and Atlantic salmon eggs. Publisher Howard White reported that seventy operations around Sechelt had "appeared like an overnight plankton bloom" only to be "quickly washed away in a tide of bankruptcy."[34] Salmon prices fell precipitously in the late 1980s, a devastating blow to many fragile start-up farms (and to fishers of wild salmon). The industry would become concentrated in the hands of a few large foreign enterprises, as the province had earlier worried it might, though these were mostly Norwegian, not American.

As it had in the late nineteenth century, much salmon harvesting on the Strait had rapidly become almost unrecognisable compared with earlier technologies. Although Ottawa and Victoria supported salmon farming, it alarmed many in the "wild fishing" community and the public at large. Concerns about salmon farming on the Strait then became more muted as most early farms closed and newer ones were established mainly on or beyond the sea's northern boundary, farther away from the Strait's largest settlements.

Oyster harvesting, 1850s–1980s

A number of other stories could illustrate the rapid changes and growing conflicts that characterised humans' relations with the Strait's marine life after colonisation—oysters, herring and whales all come to mind. But space is limited, so we will consider only the first. Oysters were mostly gathered by Indigenous people until the 1880s, when settlers began to commercially harvest the Strait's relatively modest population of native oysters, *Ostrea lurida*. As an experiment, they introduced exotic oyster species, which were better suited to commercial cultivation, just before World War I. Atlantic oysters, *Crassostrea virginica*, thrived only in Boundary Bay, which sustained a local oyster industry through the first half of the twentieth century. Larger Japanese or Pacific oysters, *Crassostrea gigas*, were seeded into Ladysmith Harbour in 1912. But it was only in 1926, when twenty cases of seed oysters imported from Japan were put out in Ladysmith and Esquimalt harbours, that they began to be cultivated in any quantity. Pacific oysters were introduced to a few other places around the Strait by the 1930s, including Pender Harbour, Comox Harbour, Baynes Sound and Cortes Island.

The first significant natural spawn of Pacific oysters occurred on the Strait in 1932, in Ladysmith Harbour. In 1942, the Strait's warmer northern reaches were heavily seeded with what most people on the Strait came to consider "wild oysters," the seeds of Pacific oysters bred naturally in local BC waters. This seed supply would partially compensate for the lack of imported oyster seed, as trade with Japan was suspended during World War II. In fact, the large natural spawn, or "set," in 1942 and another in 1958 had naturally spread these exotic oysters far beyond the beaches originally seeded by oyster farmers. And in the late 1940s, entrepreneurs began to sell local seed oysters, or "spat," when they discovered that they could induce oysters to spawn regularly in the reliably warm summer waters of Pendrell Sound on East Redonda Island at the far north end of the Strait. So, while seed imports from Japan continued for almost two decades after the war, dependence on this source began to decline.

Early oyster farming had few of the inherent disadvantages of later salmon farming. As oysters are filter feeders that extract nitrogen, phosphorus, carbon and suspended solids from the water column, they can actually improve water quality. A single adult oyster can filter over 200 litres of water a day. A larger problem, from an ecological perspective, was that the Strait's growing population of larger, highly adaptable Pacific oysters threatened the less prolific native oysters. As in other places around the world, native oysters were in decline around the Strait by 1950.

After World War II, commercial oystering expanded, on the Strait's northern beaches in particular. The water there was mostly cleaner, the infrequent natural breeding more vigorous and Pendrell Sound's seed oysters were nearby. Cortes Island was an important oyster producer by the 1970s, shipping to specialty markets around the world and experimenting with more intensive production on the island's protected inlets and harbours. While oysters were farmed on seeded beaches, "wild" Pacific oysters were also being harvested from the foreshores of Cortes and smaller islands nearby, which had been colonised during the great set of 1958 in particular. This natural bounty was fortuitous in the early 1970s, as traditional oyster producers, including those in France, Portugal and Japan, were facing growing problems with pollution and disease. By the mid-1970s, Cortes Island oystermen had to compete with harvesters coming from Baynes Sound to take wild oysters from choice beach sites on nearby islands. Comox Harbour had also become an important oyster-producing area. The province issued Denman Island's first commercial oyster lease in 1944, and thirty years later islanders were celebrating Victoria Day with oyster-shucking contests. Oyster farming had become a significant part of the local culture.

The 1942 and 1958 spawns of Pacific oysters also brought these large bivalves to many beaches in front of reserves. Some Indigenous people considered these plump oysters unhealthy compared with native species, whereas others adapted to a new source of income. Despite concerns about pollution and competition from other pickers, the Chemainus people on Vancouver Island began to harvest the Pacific oysters showing up on their beaches after 1958. The Comox people farther up-island purchased their first oyster lease in the late 1960s. A decade later, the Sliammon on the northern Sunshine Coast began to invest in oyster culture. For the most part, though, commercial oyster harvesting remained overwhelmingly based in settler communities around the sea, not Indigenous ones.

Unlike other fisheries on the Strait, Victoria rather than Ottawa oversaw oystering in the post-war years. In the mid-1960s, with the industry growing steadily, confusion emerged over the two governments' responsibilities for managing, inspecting and researching the oyster industry. The province's Commercial Fisheries Branch began to administer a system of permits governing oyster harvesting from "vacant Crown lands" (meaning the foreshore between low- and high-tide lines) by commercial and recreational pickers in 1966. Prior to this time, there had been no restrictions on commercial or private harvesting of oysters on public beaches. Under the new system, recreational pickers were limited to 45 kilograms of oysters in the shell, or 4.5 litres of shucked oysters per person. Commercial pickers required a monthly permit issued by the Commercial Fisheries Branch that allowed harvesting in specific areas, for a royalty payment of a dollar per ton of shellfish. Provincial fishery authorities, however, began to receive complaints from irate citizens who felt that the commercial harvesters, who were averaging 1,000 to 1,500 tons of wild oysters a year, were increasingly taking more than their fair share. Francis Dickie of Heriot Bay on Quadra Island voiced these feelings of injustice in a 1968 letter to Victoria describing activity around the oyster bed extending south from his beach:

> For 30 years the people living along its waterfront adjoining and nearby have con-served carefully the needed supply…Imagine my astonishment the other day to see a crew of six men "looting" it…I was astounded to be told by one he had a LICENCE…It is incredible that the Department, before granting such licence, never sent a biologist and the local Warden to thoroughly examine this small bed, to examine its size and what could economically be taken…You personally know how for years I have written many articles stressing the need for conservation published in the *Colonist*, *Vancouver Sun*, *Maclean's*, *Winnipeg Free Press*, *Rod & Gun*…And now, at my very door, this unbelievable [thing] is happening. It may be too late.[35]

Dickie went on to suggest that the government's biologists ought to come see for themselves, then cancel the man's permit and post a permanent notice stating the bed was closed except for "moderate use" by local residents.

By the late 1960s, many British Columbians had come to see such "moderate use" of exotic oysters as the settlers' birthright. Growing numbers of people in places such as Savary Island and Gabriola Island, and their legislators, complained bitterly about commercial pickers decimating diminishing stocks of wild oysters on their favourite beaches. Relations between commercial harvesters and the oyster-gathering public deteriorated as the Strait's rapidly growing fleet of pleasure boaters and other recreationists continued to take wild oysters from beaches. By 1973, the province was obliged to further reduce the allowable harvest by recreational users to a maximum of twenty-five oysters, or a litre of shucked oysters, per person per day.[36] Indigenous people were also growing incensed by commercial pickers harvesting wild oysters from the foreshore in front of reserves. The commercial pickers believed it was their right to pick as many as they could manage because these oysters were simply "escapes" from their seeded beach farms, akin to stray cattle.[37]

Starting in the early 1970s, commercial oyster farms on public beaches, mostly on Cortes Island and in Baynes Sound and Ladysmith Harbour, began to be governed by renewable ten-year provincial licences. Victoria was increasingly dissatisfied with the industry's performance. Influenced by resource economists, government analysis of problems and prospective solutions for oystering resembled contemporary

Pacific oysters seeded on a Denman Island beach. This was the old style of oyster farming, now being eclipsed by more plastic-intensive oyster culture from rafts.

Howard Macdonald Stewart photo

prescriptions for salmon. Almost all oyster production was still done on the beach by small, independent, labour-intensive operations, and the government alleged that all these small, marginal producers made the industry "uneconomic." It estimated that a more mechanised industry that grew oysters in cages suspended from rafts in the sea could produce ten times as many. Raft culture, it claimed, could generate more than 22,000 kilograms of oyster meat per hectare per year, which compared very favourably with land-based meat or grain production. Farmed oysters, it suggested, might even be an answer to the global famines that many were anticipating in the 1970s.

Provincial managers worried about the challenges of growing pollution from diverse land- and sea-based sources, conflict with waterfront landowners and various types of "encroachment" by other beach users. One of the greatest challenges was ensuring that oyster producers, once they had begun the transition to raft-based production, had access to the sheltered sites needed for this new system. It was estimated that at least 600 hectares of coastal waters were suitable for raft culture on the Strait in the early 1970s, but the competition for such sites was becoming intense. The forest industry was already accustomed to using beaches for storing logs, and Victoria's oyster managers worried that the rapid growth in boating and waterfront recreation

Oyster rafts in Gorge Harbour, Cortes Island.

Howard Macdonald Stewart photo

might further diminish their chances for expanding and intensifying commercial oystering. They had seen the negative effects of resorts and marinas on those small areas of Ladysmith Harbour still available for oystering. New marine parks in places such as Desolation Sound might further block expansion of oyster rafts.

The health of the oyster industry provided a rough indicator of water quality on different parts of the Strait; oysters thrived where pollution was minimal and were driven out of areas exposed to municipal and industrial waste (chapter 5). Many oyster producers considered this growing pollution a more serious problem than any need to "rationalise" their industry. Pulp mills built on the western shore of the Strait in the 1950s, for example, threatened nearby oyster harvesting. Domestic sewage pollution was also becoming widespread. Oyster farming in Boundary Bay had accounted for over half of the Strait's oyster production into the 1950s, yet by the early 1960s it had ceased due to domestic waste flowing into the bay from the Nicomekl and Serpentine Rivers. More than 80 hectares of beach on Ladysmith Harbour were also declared contaminated by 1965. Only one of Ladysmith's twenty-eight leases remained active, and it had to treat its oysters in a "depuration plant" to render them marketable.

Before this closure, Ladysmith had accounted for almost a quarter of the province's oyster production. Pollution affecting the harbour originated from diverse sources and was difficult to manage. Much of the harbour was still closed to oystering in the early 1970s when the Commercial Fisheries Branch suggested that growing oysters there could be compatible with the forest industry but not with municipal waste. The shellfish ban might eventually be lifted, it said, if the town "made good on its promise" to build a secondary sewage treatment plant.[38] It didn't. At Comox, only 4 hectares of the original 80 devoted to leases in the harbour were still being used for shellfish production in the early 1970s. Initially, these businesses had to transport their oysters south to Baynes Sound to be "decontaminated" in cleaner waters before harvest but within twenty years, the industry had shifted to Baynes Sound, where almost 100 oyster leases employed 200 people. Even these leases faced occasional summer closures due to household pollution.

From "teeming with life" to "coping with challenges"

Compared with what it had been in 1849, the Strait's abundant marine life—the marine resource mine—was much diminished by the 1980s. Many animals not discussed here, such as whales, groundfish and herring, had declined dramatically in response to rates of harvesting that their populations could not sustain. The changes in salmon and oyster populations discussed in this chapter were more complex because they were subjected not only to intense pressure from harvesting but to the indirect effects of diverse land-based activities, including growing marine pollution. As a result, salmon and oyster populations declined in some places and recovered in others, changing dramatically in the process. Their future seemed ever more likely to involve cultivation of exotic varieties—such as Atlantic salmon and Pacific oysters—that were better suited than native ones to the techniques of aquaculture.

These changes diminished fears of loss among some, who were reassured that salmon and shellfish production could continue more or less undiminished. But the same changes stoked the fears of others, who worried about the effects of these new technologies and non-native species on beleaguered native species and on the Strait's recreational values. Indigenous people, having resisted prolonged colonial efforts to separate them from the sea life that had sustained their ancestors, began to assume more influence over marine harvesting technologies such as salmon farming and oyster culturing, but these technologies were far removed from what had been used by their ancestors. Indigenous people had developed sophisticated methods for trapping wild fish in estuaries and rivers and cultivating shellfish on protected beaches. These technologies did not leave behind the vast volumes of sea-floor effluent associated with salmon farms or the copious plastic waste shed by modern oyster-farming techniques.

Conflicts between industrial harvesters of marine resources and other stakeholders, recreationists in particular, increased after the 1980s, while those with municipal polluters continued. In contrast, the industry's disagreements with industrial polluters diminished as traditional fishing on the Strait declined and aquaculture itself became a significant source of pollution.

THE STRAIT AS WASTE DUMP | 5

MIXING STORIES OF navigation, colonisation and capitalist development (chapters 1 to 4) with tales of health, disease and recreation (chapters 5 and 6) complicates the history of places like the Strait of Georgia. But it also makes for a history in which we can more easily see ourselves. Considering issues of politics and economics together with those of public health, safety and well-being helps us understand the Strait's many diverse roles, the complex interactions among them and how they have evolved over time. Around 1950, opposition to the use of the Strait as a waste dump began to grow tremendously as a result of the increase in the volume of waste being dumped, the rapid growth of recreation on the Strait and ongoing fears about threats to fish. Many more people began to scrutinise what was

being dumped, how and where it was being dumped and the effects it was having on the sea and the people and animals that interacted with it. The relationships between waste dumpers and commercial fishers and, especially, between waste dumpers and sea-based recreationists began to change. Suddenly, waste dumpers feared losing their lucrative right to consign increasingly complex waste streams to the waters of the inland sea. Like the others, this story has its roots in the late nineteenth century and is still unfolding today.

The origins of waste dumping, 1849 to World War II

The Strait's traditional Indigenous settlements were relatively small and spread out enough that their impact on the quality of sea water would have been insignificant except on a very local scale. And the Strait's role as a waste dump aroused little interest during the early years of colonisation. Most British settlers would have been aware of London's epic struggle with the disposal of human waste and industrial effluent in the 1850s, the decade of that city's Great Stink. But in the Strait's new settler towns, the sea could be counted on to absorb waste with no ill effects, in a way that rivers like the Thames in London could not. Settlers' laws in those decades reflected an approach adopted elsewhere in North America: they focused on ensuring access to fresh water for irrigation, industry and municipal water supplies—but not on water quality. Like Indigenous societies before them, settlers worried only about marine pollution as a potential threat to fish. In fact,

Pages 168-169: Freighters in English Bay, waiting to dock in the port of Vancouver. Waste spilled accidentally or intentionally from ships has been a contentious issue.

David Nunuk photo

Canada's Fisheries Act of 1868 authorised Ottawa to protect fish habitat from waste dumping. The new federal Department of Marine and Fisheries was looking into a few cases of harmful dumping of industrial waste in the older provinces by the 1870s, but it had not yet started doing so on the West Coast.

By the 1890s the inland sea had become a valuable waste dump for the Strait's largest settler towns and for resource industries. At the same time, Western scientists and engineers had generally accepted there was a link between water polluted by sewage and the spread of diseases such as cholera and typhoid, and this idea was a driving force behind improving urban sewage systems to protect municipal drinking water supplies. Having access to more water in these municipal systems had led people to use more of it, which soon overwhelmed the capacities of cesspools and septic tanks and increased the danger of surface water contamination. A sewage collection system therefore came to be seen as a sign of a progressive community, and the sea was a great boon to the civil engineers tasked with disposing of this liquid waste. Sewers in towns along the shore could be built to discharge into the sea, where currents dispersed their contents.

Like most North American cities, larger towns along the Strait had built sewer systems by 1914, and most of them, guided by city planners and engineers, dumped their sewage untreated into adjacent waterways. Often this meant the inland sea or near the mouths of rivers feeding into it. This marine sewage disposal was not contentious.

At the time, Vancouver had far fewer problems with water-borne contagious diseases than eastern Canadian cities of similar or larger size. In part this was because the city was newer and less congested, but it was also because the Strait and the Lower Fraser, which surrounded the city, offered inexpensive and effective waste disposal options. Vancouver's first sewers were built in 1890 and discharged into Burrard Inlet, False Creek and English Bay, where it was suggested their nutrient loads might enhance local fisheries. The city grew rapidly, however, and twenty-five years later a new sewerage plan was needed. R.E. Lea from Montreal spent two years studying Vancouver's sewage and drainage challenges and options. In 1913, he recommended new sewage outfalls along the south shores of English Bay, Burrard Inlet and the North Arm of the Fraser. Lea also suggested the city construct separate sewage and drainage water removal systems so it could treat its sewage in the future. The city built the new outfalls recommended by Lea but decided against the more expensive separate systems.

A similar debate over systems separating municipal sewer lines from storm drains was taking place in many North American cities during this period. Towns on the Strait—and most larger North American cities at the time—opted for the simpler and cheaper combined systems. The idea was that rainwater coming into the system from the storm drains could absorb and disperse any waste consigned to it by the sewage system. By 1916, Vancouver's investments in its combined sewers dwarfed those of other towns on the Strait: $4.5 million for 320 kilometres of sewer lines (see Table 3, page 173).

Industrial waste from canneries, sawmills and pulp and paper mills was different from sewage. For one thing, it was more likely to be recognised as a wasted resource. But the sea provided the same low-cost waste disposal option regardless. Mines

Table 3: Municipal sewers around the Strait by 1916[1]

Town	Length of sewers laid by 1916	Investment in sewers by 1916
Vancouver	320 km	$4,500,000
New Westminster	80 km	$400,000
Nanaimo	16 km	$200,000
Ladysmith	16 km	$65,000
Powell River	Town sewers installed during the construction of the Powell River townsite, 1910–12; details not available at provincial health department.	

mostly left their waste materials on land, but they generated toxic drainage that quickly reached the sea via surface streams and groundwater.

Occasional concerns about industrial waste from fishers or recreationists were mostly about waste from canneries starting in the late 1880s, when their operations on the Lower Fraser and Burrard Inlet were expanding rapidly. A decade later, with canneries converting their waste into fertiliser, glue and fish oil, the Board of Trade announced the problem was on its way to being solved. Yet it recurred early in the twentieth century. Writer Geoff Meggs described the situation in 1901: "The river was polluted with the carcasses of hundreds of thousands of fish and the offal from several million more…[while Vancouver suffered] the stench of rotting salmon carried by the tides onto English Bay beaches."[2] The year 1901 was a "big year" for Fraser River Sockeye, and the canneries simply couldn't process all the fish delivered to them. Rotting salmon flesh accumulated on Vancouver's beaches again in the summer of the next big year, 1905. As a result, the provincial medical health officer instructed Burrard Inlet canneries to dump their fish offal at least 5 kilometres offshore. And federal officers were tasked with controlling "excessive" dumping of fish waste at the Fraser mouth if it was deemed likely to damage a commercially important fishery.

Farther from Vancouver, other kinds of industrial pollution were viewed as a necessary part of progress. A complaint registered by locals on Howe Sound in 1912, not long after the pulp mill opened at Port Mellon, declared that the new mill was poisoning shellfish. The fisheries inspector demanded that the mill fix the problem, but the owners maintained that their waste stream was already sufficiently diluted and the fisheries department subsequently withdrew its complaint. No similar grievances were recorded at the vast new complex up the shore at Powell River (see photographs page 174 and page 175). For the time being at least, industrial dumping in the sea, if it was considered at all, was seen as a minor inconvenience.

The expansion of waste dumping in the interwar years

As more towns on the Strait built new sewer systems and others upgraded existing ones, the volume of waste being dumped into the Strait expanded, but still its role as a waste dump went mostly uncontested. The practical rule of thumb was to get your drinking water as far upstream as possible on a creek or river and protect your source. Then you

would dump your sewage as far downstream as possible, ideally directly into the sea below the low-tide line, so the currents would disperse and dilute it.

Local outbreaks of typhoid in 1919 further stimulated improvements in sewerage and water systems. A letter to Victoria's chief sanitary inspector from a Parksville resident attributed the outbreak of typhoid there to wells contaminated by septic tanks. The issue was "increasingly vital," said the writer, because "this settlement is now attracting a big holiday public."[3] Through the next two decades, authorities in Nanaimo focused on the threat of typhoid from contaminated drinking water even though city maps showed swimming beaches adjacent to sewage outfalls with "heavy bacterial growth with positive faecal contamination."[4]

In Powell River, typhoid first broke out the year after the town had been constructed. Its "excellent sewers" spilled into the sea in front of town just below the low-tide line. As long as people swam in Powell Lake, above the townsite, there was no problem. But when they swam at the town's ocean beaches, it was a different story. The polluted beaches were officially discounted as a cause when an epidemic of acute gastroenteritis broke out in the 1930s; however, health authorities took the opportunity to advise the town to either extend its sewers farther into the sea or install a primary treatment plant.

Ironically, most towns around the sea didn't worry much about the impact of sewage on their marine recreation, though they were increasingly concerned about contamination of their water supply, particularly by human waste created by recreational water users. People were encouraged to avoid lakes and rivers that supplied drinking water and to seek recreation only in the sea, especially in summer, when the supply of fresh water was lowest and most vulnerable to contamination.

In Vancouver, engineers had designed the sewer system with marine outfalls located directly on the Strait to maximise sewage dilution and dispersion. Controversy arose just after World War I over sewage dumping on the grounds of the Jericho Golf Club, near Spanish Banks on the south shore of English Bay. But the most serious and persistent problems were on False Creek. The city's government had disregarded earlier recommendations to stop dumping sewage into this tidal basin in the middle of the city, and by 1927 sixteen sewage outfalls were spilling into False Creek. The result was chronic problems with pollution at the city's most popular swimming

beach at English Bay. By the early 1940s, raw sewage from some 600 hectares of the city core was still being dumped into False Creek despite an outbreak of typhoid in the 1930s that was caused by this very sewage.

As in eastern North America in earlier years, resource industries that grew up around the Strait during the interwar years were often located where fresh water was available. For example, the Strait's first pulp and paper mills used prodigious quantities of fresh water to carry away the waste they produced at each stage of manufacturing. These mills generated over 350,000 litres of wastewater containing everything from wood fibres to residual chemicals for each ton of pulp produced. Writing about the biggest new plant on the coast in 1934, summer cruiser Francis John Barrow noted, "A new evil smell every hundred yards or so from the large paper works…We left Powell River without regret."[5] Yet the Strait's pulp and paper mills operated for sixty years before federal authorities made any sustained effort to curtail their waste dumping practices.

The Strait's mines also operated in a regulatory vacuum. Provincial and federal authorities sometimes attempted to persuade miners to respect certain waste management norms, but the results of these sporadic efforts mostly depended on voluntary compliance by industry. The province's Department of Health intervened regarding water management at Britannia in the 1920s, but its concern was only to ensure the town's water supply was drawn from streams high enough to avoid being contaminated by mine waste. The government was not otherwise concerned with controlling that waste—or its effects on the sea.

Fish processors were also subject to very modest government control. Early in the 1940s, the province began receiving complaints about a rendering plant operated by BC Packers at Deep Bay, south of Courtenay. The secretary of the local Liberal Party association wrote to the provincial Minister of Health in 1941 describing "terrible fumes and smells…[that] travel all over the district" in the warmer months. Every resident in his district, he said, would sign a petition against the plant. The local MP's letter to the Commissioner of Fisheries in Victoria described a smell "one hundred times worse" than a pulp mill. It was causing nearby residents to vomit and ruining local tourism. A petition signed by ninety neighbours demanded that something be done to end the unbearable stench. In mid-1941, the Chief Sanitary Inspector informed the Provincial Health Officer that these "odour nuisances" were being produced mostly by exhaust gases from the rendering plant. Scows of rotting dogfish and offal waiting to be off-loaded at Deep Bay were also foul, he admitted, but "not considered serious enough to cause complaints at any great distance." The inspector recommended BC Packers do something only about the exhaust odours. The Chief Sanitary Inspector then met with executives at BC Packers, who told him that their plant was part of the war effort, responding to "the urgent request of the Dominion Government," but they agreed that it might be possible to reduce the odour. By late 1941, despite cooler weather, the Chief Sanitary Inspector reported "no lessening of the odour nuisances in the surrounding area [and]…the company has made no attempt to abate the nuisance."

Complaints about the odour from the Deep Bay plant continued through 1942; locals were still vomiting and were forced to stay indoors with their windows and doors shut. Citizens near Nanaimo also complained about a scow load of rotting dogfish apparently destined for Deep Bay but left on their shore for a month. By 1943, the "vile stench" had spread and people downwind were getting sick as far away as Qualicum Bay. Still, the government continued to favour BC Packers. After *three years* of this intense olfactory assault, a letter to Victoria from BC Packers' general manager admitted, "I cannot say that we have met with a great deal of success" in controlling the odours at Deep Bay. Spraying formaldehyde on the carcasses hadn't worked as well as they had hoped. Another approach, involving treatment of the rotting fish with sulphuric acid and chlorine, had proven more effective, he said. But it was too expensive to use very often and so would be used only during "the peak of production." He welcomed any other suggestions the health officials might have.

In another letter to a fisheries official, the BC Packers executive admitted that controlling the smell would require more investment than his company was prepared to make. He reminded the official that the plant's fish meal and oil were a vital contribution to the war effort. And he insisted that BC Packers was a good corporate citizen that had spent thousands of dollars to improve both its manufacturing processes and employees' living conditions. He concluded that the company had explored "all the known means of endeavouring to overcome this odour, some of which is inherent in the nature of the fish itself." These odours were part and parcel of living beside meatpacking plants, gasworks and pulp mills and, inevitably, were "offensive to some people." Even in San Francisco and Monterey, he pointed out, "the smell of cooking fish is very noticeable and offensive to some." He didn't mention whether such odours were ever a problem in Vancouver's tony Shaughnessy neighbourhood, where he lived.[6]

Such casual dismissal of public complaints was destined to grow more difficult in the future. The sheer volume and increasing variety of waste being dumped into the Strait was on a collision course with the evolving sensibilities of an expanding and ever more affluent population living around it. Progressively fewer people living around the Strait would depend on its resource industries for their livelihoods, while more would enjoy its recreational possibilities. In other words, most people would begin to expect different things from the sea.

The emergence of serious opposition to waste dumping after 1945

Rapid industrialisation and urbanisation in many parts of the world after 1945 led to dramatic physical, biological and chemical changes in the Earth's aquatic environments. And these changes increasingly affected people's understanding of, and interactions with, this water. Rather than thinking of their biophysical environment as simply being affected by human activities, many people began to see it as affecting them. It was an emerging world view in which humans were an influential component of broader "ecosystems." For example, rather than focusing exclusively on biological agents of disease, public health specialists and the public in general became increasingly aware of other environmental sources of disease such as agricultural pesticide residues in food and water, and radioactive contamination resulting from the atmospheric testing of nuclear weapons. Around the Strait, the focus began to shift in the 1970s and '80s to include not only micro-organisms bred in sewage and the vast streams of waste fibre from mills but also things like the complex organic pollutants escaping from pulp mill waste that, like pesticide residues, could accumulate in microscopic quantities in the tissue of marine organisms and humans, with serious health effects for both.

The degradation of the world's seas and large lakes was one of the most disturbing post-war trends. Although generally less damaged than freshwater environments, coastal zones such as the Strait of Georgia were worse off than open oceans. Many of them were surpassing their capacity to safely "assimilate" waste, threatening the engineers' time-honoured "solution to pollution by dilution." By 1970, many Mediterranean and Caribbean beaches and a growing number farther north were experiencing regular late-summer algal blooms. Enclosed seas were particularly prone to eutrophication, a condition caused by the accumulation of nutrients derived from human waste and the runoff from farmers' fields; these nutrients in turn spurred luxuriant growth of aquatic vegetation that reduced the amount of dissolved oxygen in the water and killed fish. In industrialised areas, meanwhile, people were increasingly aware that dangerous chemicals and metals spilling from factories, mills and mines were being absorbed by fish and shellfish, and then by the humans who consumed them.

The Great Lakes and the Atlantic coast of the US seemed to be in crisis by the mid-1960s. Cleveland's Cuyahoga River spilled bacteria into Lake Erie at up to 1,200 times the level deemed safe for swimmers, and only three beaches on the lake's south shore were still swimmable. Boston, the lower Hudson River and Chesapeake Bay all faced deepening, high-profile ecological crises. All three were coastal areas with complex physical and human geographies similar to those of Vancouver, the Lower Fraser River and the Strait. By the early 1960s most New Yorkers viewed their portion of the Hudson River as an open sewer and avoided eating fish from it or even walking beside its stinking banks. Public health officials agreed and had closed 250 kilometres of the river's most popular recreation areas to swimmers, all the way from New York City to Albany.

Local critics were quick to compare the declining state of the Strait with such degradation elsewhere. Speaking before a crowd at English Bay, Roderick Haig-

Brown declared: "The Baltic Sea is polluted, the Mediterranean is polluted, the Strait of Georgia can be polluted." And he urged those listening: "We can do our part by keeping our waters clean and productive."[7] In a manuscript entitled *Pollution for Profit*, he noted ominously that it would cost a billion dollars to clean up the Hudson; the Potomac, another billion; and that both were warnings to people living on the Strait. The pollution of Ladysmith and Vancouver harbours, or the Fraser mouth, did not stay in those places, he stressed. Instead, the Strait's counter-clockwise currents carried the Lower Mainland's growing pollution north to the Discovery Islands and then along the eastern shore of Vancouver Island. To illustrate this point he told the story of a woman who had jumped off the Pattullo Bridge on the Lower Fraser whose body later washed ashore on Quadra Island.[8]

Many local governments and industries contested these growing calls to reduce municipal and industrial pollution in the Strait. Of course, they aimed to avoid the cost of constructing more elaborate waste disposal systems. But why such resistance to changing to more environmentally benign approaches? Linda Nash, in *Inescapable Ecologies*, has suggested North American culture was "built on, and absolutely dependent on, a sharply alienating, intensely managerial relationship with nature." Besides, even if engineers, accountants and the leaders they advised might be willing to change their business-as-usual approaches, their options were limited by previous design decisions. For example, towns with combined municipal sewage systems that wanted to improve their sewage treatment by separating the storm drains from the sewage pipes faced enormous challenges. But perhaps a greater challenge was the idea that the best solutions were "efficient" ones. Using the Strait as a dump for the steadily growing waste stream was an "efficient engineering solution" because sewage outfalls into the sea were easy to build, and it was an "economically efficient solution" because the marine waste dump was inexpensive to use and manage.

Pollution's changing significance

Much early debate over liquid effluent resulted from changing views of the significance of this pollution. Local scientists and engineers were accustomed to gauging the significance of different waste streams by measuring various parameters of water quality and determining how much waste could be absorbed into the sea without harming commercially important fish, particularly salmon. Haig-Brown, NGOs and other critics began suggesting the significance of different waste streams needed to be judged over larger areas, longer time frames and more affected organisms, including people. An increasing number of writers around the Strait, from Malcolm Lowry and Earle Birney on Burrard Inlet to M. Wylie Blanchet in Desolation Sound and Jack Hodgins on Vancouver Island, were also sympathetic to this ecological world view. Governments, however, were slow to catch up.

In the years after World War II, the province was responsible for controlling the pollution of streams flowing into the Strait. As in a lot of other places in those years, many departments were involved and each of them acted independently. For example, the Provincial Health Officer was responsible for administering the Health Act and overseeing sewer construction. The Fish and Game Branch was responsible for protecting freshwater fish. Although these departments were often dealing with the same polluters, because of their piecemeal approach none of them exercised much actual control. Growing sewage pollution problems in the sea off Vancouver, however, finally highlighted the need for more effective pollution control. And as a result, Victoria created the Pollution Control Board (PCB) in 1956.

Ottawa was responsible for controlling marine pollution. Its Fisheries Act prohibited activities detrimental to marine fish populations, including the dumping of organic materials such as sawdust, pulp mill fibre or canneries' offal in quantities that could reduce water oxygen levels enough to kill fish. It also outlawed the dumping of toxins including mining and smelting wastes, pulp mill liquors and oil products. Such control was seldom exercised during the 1950s. The worsening municipal pollution off Vancouver, however, did mobilise federal authorities.

The 1953 Rawn Report analyzed the feasibility of Vancouver's prospective sewage projects. Like a study carried out forty years earlier, the Rawn Report was unable to accurately predict the complex tides and currents in the sea around Vancouver or anticipate episodic pollution of beaches by nearby sewage outfalls. To better predict this behaviour and the Strait's resulting capacity to assimilate waste, federal scientists and oceanographer Michael Waldichuk began a decade of detailed studies in Burrard Inlet and the open Strait in 1957.

By far the largest influence in changing public perceptions about the Strait, though, was Roderick Haig-Brown, who emerged as a powerful voice against pollution. Addressing a regional gathering of the tourist industry in Spokane in 1967, Haig-Brown declared that all forms of pollution were "use of public property for private profit" and were often a waste of valuable materials. He estimated that even the newer generation of sulphate pulp mills wasted a half to two-thirds of the raw material they used. And he called for taxes on their wasteful, polluting operations "to stimulate much more aggressive examination of ways to put this enormous waste to good use." These mills, he said, should be obliged to return their organic wastes to the forests. Domestic sewage should also be applied to the forests rather than fouling aquatic environments. Haig-Brown spoke of "bills now due and overdue" after a century of rapid, ruthless resource exploitation that had polluted local waters with devastating effects on recreation, fisheries and aesthetics. The Strait and Puget Sound, he told his followers, were overtaxed "finite resources" in need of proper management and protection and whose capacities as "cesspools" were limited.[9] Two years later, he stated that BC was "within sight of destroying or seriously damaging some of our finest assets, before we have had the time or the intelligence to put them to intensive use." These assets included the Lower Fraser and the Strait of Georgia. What was needed, he declared, was a "sharp change of thinking."

The province, said Haig-Brown, was doing "just about nothing." In his opinion, Victoria was wondering, "How much pollution can we get by with?" instead of how to better control it. At the same time, he singled out municipalities as the greatest polluters but conceded that industry was "not far behind" and was sometimes worse because of "the toxic nature of their effluents." To compensate for the province's "gross neglect," Haig-Brown called on Ottawa to take the lead in controlling pollution on the Strait, though he recognised that the federal government could have little impact without provincial cooperation. Joint federal-provincial action was unlikely, he cautioned, "without the strongest public pressure, relentlessly maintained." And he urged academics and the environmental movement to fill this niche. If all these players made the right moves, he concluded, "within a decade it should be possible to control all pollutions to rigid minimums and put most of the waste to constructive use."[10]

The engineers' dilution approach to the Lower Mainland's sewage flows had attracted increased scrutiny as pollution built up in the Fraser estuary and occasionally spilled over onto Vancouver beaches. And this clear discrepancy between what the public was being told—that marine pollution was being controlled effectively—and what they could plainly see—that their beaches were frequently closed because of high coliform bacteria counts—stimulated protests, cast doubt on "expert judgements" and generated much media attention. By the end of the 1960s, a report from Nanaimo's Fisheries Research Board (FRB) station finally challenged conventional wisdom about the Strait's longer-term capacity to assimilate waste based on new evidence that currents on the sea floor, where the waste was coming to rest, were far slower than surface currents. Many observers in the late 1960s and early 1970s had come to believe that industrial pollution was the greatest threat to the West Coast fishery. For this reason, the most important rationale for controlling industrial pollution throughout this period was to reduce harm to fish, particularly economically valuable fish. In contrast, the main rationale for controlling sewage pollution was to stop transmitting seaborne bacteria to humans.

The provincial government was on the defensive. Its loosely organised Pollution Control Board had been reformed twice, in 1963 and 1965, and a new Pollution Control Act was passed in 1967. Three ministries—Lands, Forests and Water Resources; Health; and Municipal Affairs—had been made jointly responsible for overseeing the PCB. In 1969, the PCB's senior minister, Ray Williston, who was Minister of Lands, Forests and Water Resources, issued a statement assuring the public that untreated sewage discharge to enclosed or confined bodies of salt water was prohibited wherever there was doubt about the "adequacy of the tidal flushing effect." He stated that discharge of untreated sewage in fresh water was also prohibited and forbidden in any designated recreational body of water or on beaches "regardless of the flushing or assimilative capacity of salt water bodies." Williston further assured citizens that the Ministry of Health would protect them by upholding its standards for all waters being used for waste dumping. The PCB, he said, would ensure that any party receiving a permit to dump liquid waste would respect "prescribed effluent standards."[11]

Three months later, UBC scientist and rising politician Patrick McGeer sent a brief to Vancouver's city council questioning the competence of the PCB and the Greater Vancouver Sewerage & Drainage District (GVS&DD) in ensuring the safety of the city's beaches. The PCB recommended a maximum of 1,000 coliform bacteria per 100 millilitres of sea water at Vancouver's beaches, yet the American Public Health Association and the Conference of State Sanitary Engineers suggested this level was the boundary between "poor" and "very poor" water quality. And the World Health Organization recommended a limit of 200 to 500 coliform bacteria per 100 millilitres in "developed countries." McGeer challenged the PCB's assumption that bacteria didn't survive in salt water. In fact, he reported, Vancouver beach water contained only a third to two-thirds as much salt as the open sea, and bacteria thrived in such brackish environments. Furthermore, the beaches received a plume of water sweeping up from the Fraser mouth, and year-round coliform levels in this plume near the Iona sewage plant's outfall averaged 24,000 bacteria per 100 millilitres. He explained that the GVS&DD readings were taken in deep water whereas the city's, which had yielded coliform counts three times higher, were taken from the surface and shoreline water, where people actually swam.[12]

McGeer and Williston agreed that improved pollution control standards would likely impose financial and technical difficulties on local governments and industries. Williston pointed out that the public had "often been reluctant to provide the necessary funds or give pollution control their proper position of priority in planning fund allocation." McGeer reminded Vancouver's leaders that the right level of pollution control was a judgement call that required distinguishing between what was "ecologically necessary" to protect humans and what was merely "desirable" but might not be affordable. Thomas Berger, a Vancouver lawyer and leader of the province's opposition New Democratic Party (NDP), was less inclined to compromise. He declared that pollution control in the province was a myth and that pollution was out of control.[13]

Industries and municipalities continued to claim their right to pollute and pushed back against demands for new standards, even as marine pollution peaked on the Strait's public and political agendas in the early 1970s. Municipal governments pointed out they could not meet higher standards without substantial new investments to modify their existing combined sewage and storm sewers. After heavy precipitation, they said, storm runoff overwhelmed the new sewage treatment plants and currently the only "economically viable" response was to discharge the whole combined stream untreated. The PCB accepted this explanation and amended its new, stricter policy early in the 1970s to allow these "exceptional" releases of untreated sewage.[14] Once again, opposition politicians were more confrontational. Harry Rankin, the lone communist on Vancouver's city council, published a manifesto entitled *Pollution— Suicide or Survival*, in which he excoriated the province and municipalities for the current situation. "The standards and tests established…are so inadequate as to be almost ridiculous. They have been deliberately designed to allow the pollution producing industries to carry on without fear of interference," he wrote. "Government officials and the PCB are assiduously spreading the propaganda smokescreen that society as a whole is responsible for pollution and not industry." Furthermore, he said, "The PCB refuses to require industry to prove that its effluents won't cause undue harm; instead it requires anyone who objects to prove that the effluent is causing damage."[15]

Rankin scorned the provincial Minister of Recreation and Conservation, Ken Kiernan, who had recently joked: "We are polluting the atmosphere every time we breathe" and accused individuals and groups seeking pollution control of "emotionalism" and "a loss of perspective." It was, said Rankin, like saying that "if we want pollution controls, we must give up spending money on roads, schools, and hospitals, close down our industries and go back to living…on deer and salmon."[16] Instead, Rankin maintained that the way to control sewage pollution had been "known for a very long time…[but] it costs money to do" and that in the absence of provincial leadership or adequate municipal responses, it was up to Ottawa to solve the problem. "The federal government can, and should, offer both leadership and a significant measure of subsidy. Federal standards should be high and specific," he declared, yet Ottawa was simply "going through the motions of taking a stand against water pollution [despite] the new Canada Water Act." That legislation "is so full of loopholes that it cannot be taken seriously…[It] does not set out firm standards as to just what polluted water is, nor does it project any specific ways in which polluted water can and should be cleaned up." The result, Rankin felt, was that "industries can pay fines and keep on polluting." And furthermore, he charged, there is "no provision to help municipalities…to build sewage treatment plants, aside from some vague promises about loans."[17]

Perhaps not surprisingly, Rankin found the union movement's growing concern about pollution "one of the most heartening developments." Maritime pollution was so serious, he said, that the United Fishermen and Allied Workers Union (UFAW), led by another old communist, was worried about the fishing industry's survival. Rankin claimed the UFAW Union under Homer Stevens had been "sparking" campaigns "to save our waters" for many years.[18] Rankin was partisan and didn't have to negotiate or compromise, of course, but there was much truth to his criticisms.

An NDP government elected in 1972 promised to "change the system." Its newly appointed Minister of Lands, Forests and Natural Resources, Bob Williams, promised to use "economic disincentives" to discourage polluters.[19] Several non-governmental organisations, especially the Scientific Pollution and Environmental Control Society (SPEC), kept the pressure on the new government. Roderick Haig-Brown was eloquent, opinionated and well informed, but SPEC had affiliates in most major towns around the Strait by 1972 and was becoming good at capturing headlines. In 1970 it had targeted MacMillan Bloedel, at the time the owner of large pulp and paper mills in Nanaimo and Powell River. SPEC had depicted the forest industry giant as *Tyrannosaurus rex*, "the king of polluters," and made headlines with an abortive stink-bomb attack on a Vancouver meeting of the Council of Forest Industries—to remind the industry of the stink of pulp mills. To raise awareness about the Strait-wide impacts of the Lower Mainland's sewage, SPEC dropped floating bottles near sewage outlets at the Fraser mouth and later recovered them near Comox and on the Strait's southern islands. In April of 1973 it urged the new government to designate Howe Sound as a recreation area protected from further industrial or port development. That same year it called on an intergovernmental panel on oil spills to tighten shipping controls on the Strait. And a year later it urged the provincial government to ensure secondary sewage treatment at Annacis Island on the Lower Fraser, to protect the "$600 million salmon fishing industry." In 1975, the PCB upheld SPEC's appeal to halt plans to discharge sewage into Ganges Harbour on Saltspring Island.

By the late 1970s, the first wave of environmental concern about the Strait had passed. Public and media attention had shifted first to the oil crisis of 1973 and then to the economic downturn that followed.[20] Although SPEC remained active into the 1980s—conducting a tour of the Lower Fraser in 1981 to highlight its "filth and pollution" and protesting the disposal of industrial sediments from the floor of False Creek into the Strait two years later—its membership dwindled. Marine pollution again became mostly the domain of experts.

Many local government experts did remain focused on water quality issues in the 1980s out of concern that they might affect marine recreation. B.F. Talbot, the Greater Vancouver Regional District's senior assistant engineer, responded to concerns about high coliform counts raised by the Eagle Harbour Yacht Club in 1985. The bacteria counts in the waters off West Vancouver were high in late spring and early summer. Citing Department of Fisheries and Oceans research, Talbot explained that "slippery" fresh water from the (polluted) Fraser's peak flows was riding over heavier salt water and sweeping north to Eagle Harbour.[20] The spring freshet, it seemed, was flushing the bacteria out of the Fraser and into the Strait.

As Vancouver hosted hundreds of thousands of visitors for Expo 86, city staff sought advice about how to monitor beach water quality from staff in other coastal cities around the Pacific. They wanted to know: Did their counterparts in San Diego and Sydney have jurisdiction over recreational water-quality monitoring? If so, what parameters did they consider significant enough to measure, when and how frequently? How did they decide when beaches had to be closed? Did they have separate storm and sewage systems or problematic combined sewers, like Vancouver's? Over a thirty-year period, the "significance" of marine pollution in the Strait had shifted from the purely scientific to the ecological, and these changing interpretations continued to shape what the public saw as dangerous pollution and how it should be addressed. However they were defined, progress on the issues remained slow and difficult.

Oil drilling and pollution on the Strait

Stories about oil spills on the Strait were infrequent before World War II, although spills of various petroleum products appeared to have become relatively common by the interwar years, when shippers and industry took little care to avoid them. Hamilton Mack Laing, for example, complained to a colleague in Ottawa in 1928 about "our latest water bird disaster" after loggers at Deep Bay south of Courtenay accidentally dumped more than 2,000 gallons of crude oil into the bay. The result was 40 miles of shore littered with oily and dying birds or, as he put it, "thousands of birds cashed in." Why, Mack Laing asked, could federal regulations convict a hunter for shooting "scooter out of season" but not nab a logging company for killing thousands of them?[22] It was a good question, and such impunity diminished after 1945 as the public and different governments grew more concerned about drilling for oil around the Strait, shipping oil across it and spilling oil into it.

Oil exploration had taken place sporadically around the Strait without noticeable public concern since 1902, when the *Colonist* newspaper described an "oil expert's" favourable report on oil prospects in North Vancouver. Canadian Collieries drilled unsuccessfully for oil on Saturna Island in 1958.[23] A decade later, as advances in offshore drilling technology raised the possibility of drilling for valuable new deposits of oil on the floor of the Strait, a jurisdictional dispute flared between Victoria and Ottawa over who owned the mineral rights under the water. Ottawa claimed that it held the rights because it governed maritime space. The province maintained that it held the rights to the near-shore waters because these were enclosed by provincial land and therefore an extension of it. Victoria pointed to precedents such as grants that had been made by the colonial government to seabed off Nanaimo and then a succession of grants made by the province to sea floor at other locations around the inland sea.

The conflict was reminiscent of earlier struggles over cannery licensing, as both Ottawa and Victoria claimed jurisdiction over offshore minerals and both issued permits for undersea seismic exploration on the Strait in the early 1960s. In 1967, the Supreme Court of Canada ruled that Ottawa was solely responsible for subsurface minerals below the low-tide line, but the province did not accept this ruling and continued to issue permits. As late as 1970, the Vancouver Parks Board was still petitioning Victoria to cancel provincial oil-drilling permits that threatened Vancouver's beaches. Alderman Harry Rankin challenged assurances from both the provincial and federal governments that drilling would be allowed only where they could guarantee no associated pollution. He argued, correctly, that no one could give such guarantees and that they would be "as worthless as they are meaningless."[24]

When West Vancouver's Jack Davis was appointed the federal Minister of Fisheries, he stated there would be no oil and gas drilling on the inland sea. The Strait, he maintained, was "obviously a priceless asset from a recreational point of view and…a funnel through which a hundred million dollar fishery moves." A press release from his office that year announced: "The combination of property and recreational values in the Strait of Georgia is so great that its possible contamination with oil could not be countenanced."[25] SPEC and the Sierra Club of BC applauded Davis's stand and joined the City of Vancouver in calling for the province to revoke all drilling permits. In a letter to Frank Richter, the province's Minister of Mines, SPEC claimed oil drilling represented a "great and immediate" threat to Greater Vancouver and adjacent islands, insisting "the health and well-being of our people must take top priority over any other consideration."[26] Ottawa prevailed and no drilling occurred, even as the federal-provincial jurisdictional dispute over the Strait's seabed simmered through the 1970s.

Various petroleum products had long been shipped across the Strait. Spills had already been occurring before World War II and they continued afterwards as industry expanded. For example, the provincial Fish and Wildlife Branch received complaints about vessels continually spilling oil and pumping oily bilge into the seas off Cowichan and Maple bays in 1946. Duncan's Chamber of Commerce worried this oil was killing ducks, fouling beaches and fishing grounds, reducing real-estate prices and damaging budding shoreline tourist camps. Although the province was trying harder to control the pollution of streams by the late 1940s, it could do little about such marine spills because they fell under federal jurisdiction.

Marine oil spills on the Strait began to receive broader attention by the mid-1950s as Canada prepared to sign the International Convention for the Prevention of Pollution of the Sea by Oil and incorporate its statutes into the Canada Shipping Act. Initially, local attention focused on oil products spilled or dumped during the operation of vessels, especially in ports. A federal Ministry of Transport (MoT) report in 1955 confirmed that Vancouver-area oil refineries had the necessary shore facilities to deal with "oily residues" from vessels arriving at Vancouver and New Westminster, and no new facilities were needed. Ship owners, however, complained the new system made it difficult and "exceedingly expensive" to dispose of their oily residues and they looked to the National Harbours Board (NHB) for a solution. The NHB didn't find one, and ships continued to dump oil and oily waste around the Strait. The MoT's Marine Regulations officer complained to the Coastwise Operators Association in 1960 that waste oil from their ships was drifting ashore, fouling beach and fishing gear, and killing thousands of seabirds each year. He sent the association a copy of the federal Oil Pollution Prevention Regulations, which were meant to control oil discharges from ships, and "earnestly requested" its members' compliance. Four years later, the ministry again consulted ship and towboat operators about extending the federal prohibition on dumping marine oil to include light diesel fuel.[27]

Although concerns about ships dumping oil products remained, new worries surfaced about more substantial spills from tankers transporting large volumes of crude oil. Until 1954, this unrefined petroleum had been imported by rail and ship from California to refineries in the Lower Mainland.[28] Then the Trans Mountain Pipeline began to carry crude from Alberta's new oil fields, and for the next decade, limited amounts of this oil were shipped out from the Strait.

Oil shippers on the Strait sailed into a perfect storm in the late 1960s, however. Vividly illustrated stories of oil spills on the postcard coasts of Cornwall, Brittany and southern California were fresh in the public's mind as plans were being developed to ship crude from new oil fields in Alaska to the southeast corner of the Strait, just inside Washington. In anticipation of increased traffic on the Strait, the US Department of Commerce and the US Coast Guard commissioned a study to help identify "promising techniques" for controlling and preventing damage from oil spills. Puget Sound and the Strait were considered together and described as joint components of "an immense salt water inland estuary" displaying "combined and interrelated characteristics of a bay, estuary and coastal region."[29]

The study deemed the existing impacts of sewage and industrial effluent to be "highly localised" and to present "no immediate danger to the ecological balance" of either the Strait or Puget Sound. Large oil spills were potentially more dangerous, however, as oil would not be easily absorbed into the salt water and would break down slowly even under "satisfactory" conditions, which might not be present after a spill. The Strait and the Sound, the study concluded, were unique in several ways. First, the prevailing pattern of currents, tides and winds meant that oil spilled in Puget Sound could spread across the Strait, exposing the shores of countless inlets, fjords and islands to damage. The region was a critical rest stop for migratory birds, and its many coastal marshlands would be especially vulnerable. Finally, commercial fisheries would also be severely damaged by oil spills in certain seasons. To complicate matters further, these waters were governed by two countries and further managed by many local and regional authorities.

Public fears about tanker spills continued to grow on the Canadian shores of the Strait into the early 1970s. Tales of possible "American pollution" flowing into Canada were especially compelling during the Vietnam War years, when anti-American sentiment was high even as some of the most eloquent critics of the Strait's expanded tanker traffic were American. In the US, Friends of the Earth maintained that a collision, sinking or grounding involving oil tankers in these waters was a "statistical certainty…just a matter of time." They cited recent research from the Woods Hole Oceanographic Institution suggesting the impacts of an oil spill on marine organisms could be far greater than once assumed, and might be permanent.

Haig-Brown, for example, described the location of the Cherry Point refinery, amid sensitive shoreline habitats near Blaine, Washington, as "totally inept" and representing a "fantastic hazard" to the Strait. In June 1972 before an assembly of small boats on English Bay, he announced: "Crude oil has spilled massively." He was referring to a spill of about fifty barrels at Cherry Point. The mayor of Surrey (and future provincial premier) Bill Vander Zalm upped the ante, pointing out that it could just as easily have been 500 or 5,000 barrels. The inept response to this spill infuriated environmentalists and demonstrated that authorities had "no experience, no knowledge, no plan" for dealing with any spill.[30] As oil from the Cherry Point spill began to wash up on Canadian beaches, a local environmental newsletter described it as White Rock's "baptism in oil" and pointed out that the damage would have been far worse in winter, when the beaches hosted thousands of birds. Furthermore, the article continued, not without some hyperbole, there was "now every reason to believe that the Cherry Point refinery was located where it is precisely because of advantages expected from allowing spills to wash into Canadian waters." To help "fight the tankers," readers were asked to send donations to the Canadian Wildlife Federation.[31]

The following month, Victoria signed a memorandum with Washington state committing both governments to "work toward a joint monitoring and inspection program" and "plans of actions to cope with oil spills and exchanges of information and mutual aid." As geographer William Ross in Victoria noted at the time, "a perception of crisis" had emerged following media coverage of oil spills elsewhere and of the very minor ones on the US shore of the Strait, and it was this fear that had led to the agreement. Ross declared, "Existing institutions are still either so powerless that they are unable to reduce the impact of international oil pollution or they lack the specific jurisdiction to do so"; only public opinion around the Strait had forced BC to enter into talks with the mostly uninterested officials in Washington state, where oil industry expansion was still the priority. Regardless, these modest steps—which Ross characterised as cosmetic—marked a high point in regional recognition of marine oil pollution as an international problem. British Columbia subsequently developed its own plans for a disaster fund to pay for activities related to a potential transboundary oil spill, but it remained to be seen, concluded Ross, whether upcoming United Nations conferences on the environment and the Law of the Sea might help bring in the required "new order."[32] (They did not.)

Local capacity to manage "all-Canadian" oil spills was discussed through the 1970s, with concern focused on the increasing but still modest volumes of crude being shipped out of Vancouver, the issue of waste oil spilled from ships and, in particular, the movement of petroleum products along the coast. By 1971, an impressive body of mostly federal laws governed marine pollution by petroleum products (see Table 4, page 187), yet correspondence from this period suggests that authorities were a long way from effectively controlling how ships handled spills on the inland sea.

Crude oil exports through Burrard Inlet were sporadic before 1970, but they increased as it became more profitable to move Alberta crude to California by sea. A report for Environment Canada estimated the total port capacity for shipping oil at around 13 million barrels a year in 1971 and suggested that it was likely to rise to 30 million barrels annually by 1985. Such exports of crude oil that left the port for a single destination were relatively easy to monitor compared with the movements of refined petroleum products around the coast, which were dispatched to many diverse users of these products.

Table 4: Laws governing oil spills on the Strait to 1971[33]

Date	Law
1868	Federal Fisheries Act, amended 11 times by 1970
1886	Federal Navigable Water Protection Act
1917	Federal Migratory Birds Convention Act
1956	Canadian government's acceptance of the International Convention for the Prevention of Pollution of the Sea by Oil (1954, London Conference) and incorporation into the Canada Shipping Act
1965	Second London Conference amends the 1954 Convention in 1962; in 1965 Canada accepts the amended convention and incorporates it into the Canada Shipping Act
1967	Provincial Pollution Control Act
1969	Amendments to the anti-pollution sections of the Canada Shipping Act
1971	Further amendment of the Canada Shipping Act to reflect International Convention on the Establishment of an International Fund for Oil Pollution Damage

Once crude oil had been refined into various end products such as gasoline and kerosene, it became potentially more threatening to marine life because of the greater toxicity of many of these refined products. By 1970, coastal shippers of petroleum products were obliged to meet federal MoT standards for their ships' hulls, machinery and navigational equipment. The next year, as public worry about oil spills continued to grow, the MoT requested advance notice of all marine shipments of "oils as cargo" on the West Coast. Vancouver's harbourmaster, R.E. Holland, complained the same year that vessels were still deliberately or inadvertently spilling various oil products and oily residues into the sea off Vancouver. He reported that ships' masters and engineers continued to plead ignorance of local regulations, and he requested that the Vancouver Chamber of Shipping "once again advise all Agencies of the seriousness of these offences and stress the importance of advising the vessels prior to their arrival in Vancouver."[34] After small spills in Vancouver Harbour and Nanoose Bay near Nanaimo during the movement of oil between ships and shore, Victoria amended its Petroleum and Natural Gas Act and Pipelines Act in 1972 to allow the province to intervene when necessary to control damage from such spills. The legislation didn't address the causes of these spills.

In 1973, the *Vancouver Sun* reported that "BC's worst spill," 450 tons (around 3,000 barrels) of bunker oil, "the filthiest of them all," had quickly spread across 90 kilometres of coastline after an Irish freighter ran aground in Blackfish Sound.[35] Although this spill had occurred north of the Strait, Melda Buchanan, an environmental activist in Comox, wrote to Ottawa to find out what the federal government was doing to prevent such accidents from occurring on the inland sea. Jack Davis, Canada's first Minister of Environment, assured her that accident prevention was the prime objective of his government's oil pollution control policy. The federal government had clean-up equipment in Victoria and Vancouver and "joint contingency plans" with US authorities to deal with an "international event." Ottawa, Davis told her, was "pursuing the best possible means of protecting our coastal waters from oil damage."[36] His reply, in fact, failed to address most of Buchanan's concerns.

William Ross accused British Columbia of "refusing to recognise responsibility for its own shores and waters." He speculated the province might be trying not to duplicate federal efforts or that it might be avoiding the significant costs necessary to prevent oil pollution. He also wondered if Victoria might be attempting to force the federal government to reconsider its ban on offshore oil drilling in the Strait. Whatever the case, the province's mostly hands-off approach made it difficult to implement a comprehensive plan to control oil pollution in coastal areas. A letter from M.L. Richardson, director of the Chamber of Shipping of BC, to the regional director of the federal MoT, H.O. Buchanan, not long after the spill on Blackfish Sound spoke of "complete confusion amongst the Shipping Agents and Operators in BC as to the procedures to be followed in the event of an oil spill." This confusion existed, he said, because they had no specific instructions from the MoT or any other government agency. The prompt reply? If there was confusion, "It is not the sole fault of the MoT." The Oil Pollution Prevention Regulations, wrote the federal representative, had been in force for many years.[37]

In fact, no major oil spill occurred on the Strait in this period, and the public began to lose interest in the topic as its priorities shifted. Had governments needed to respond to such an event at the time, their actions would certainly have been poorly coordinated and would have fallen far short of what was needed to prevent severe ecological damage. Until they slipped from people's minds, fears of loss along the shoreline had been amply justified.

Forest industry pollution and pulp mills on the Strait

In the post-war era, log storage and pulp and paper production were the forest industry's biggest sources of marine pollution. Once trees were harvested, the logs were assembled in booms and floated to the mills to be processed. So much wood was being cut at some times of year that the mills couldn't keep up, and log booms might sit on the water for weeks in inlets and bays, especially around Vancouver. By the mid-1970s, almost 2 million cubic metres of timber was in "water storage" each year, waiting to be processed in Lower Mainland sawmills. Forty percent of Howe Sound's foreshore, an area of almost 10 square kilometres, was devoted to log booming.

The biggest problem was that the bark shed from the endless abrasion of boomed logs accumulated on the sea floor. Fish and other aquatic animals depend on dissolved oxygen in water to live. In a healthy system, this oxygen is put into the system when marine plants photosynthesise and stream flows bring in new oxygen. Quantities of bark accumulating and breaking down, however, caused a very high biochemical oxygen demand (BOD)—it used up oxygen in sea water. The bacteria that decompose this sort of organic material rely on oxygen to do their job, which meant less oxygen was available for fish and other marine animals. The booms also reduced the light available for photosynthesis performed by bottom-dwelling marine vegetation. Finally, as all the bark—plus wood chips, sawdust and wood waste spilled from barges or stripped from logs by shoreline mills—became waterlogged and sank to the bottom, not only did it destroy marine habitat but it poisoned bottom-feeding organisms that ingested this woody material. Combined with dredging, mining and overfishing, these effects had contributed to a much-reduced salmon spawn on the Squamish River and eliminated Howe Sound's once vast herring spawns.[38]

Most efforts to control forest industry pollution around the Strait in this period focused on pulp and paper production. The industry had expanded rapidly in the 1950s, and new mills were built at Crofton, Nanaimo and Campbell River on Vancouver Island. Despite growing scientific knowledge about pulp mill pollution, federal authorities mostly chose to regulate along the coast using a "research and negotiation" strategy. Into the 1970s, federal officials were constrained by limited authority and information, and by generally uncooperative provincial and local governments. Ottawa attempted to work with the industry on strategies for protecting fish from mill pollution without actually enforcing laws that prohibited the discharge of effluent known to be dangerous to fish.[39]

A post-war research program at the federal government's Pacific Biological Station in Nanaimo focused on pulp mill effluent. Its investigations aimed to determine coastal waters' ability to "assimilate" pulp and paper mill waste without harming valuable fish species. It originated from earlier research by oceanographer J.P. Tully on the Alberni Canal on the west coast of Vancouver Island. Tully had concluded that the extremely high BOD associated with a sulphite pulp mill's effluent would cause unacceptable damage to the marine environment found at the head of the canal; the proposed development in Alberni would have to be a kraft mill. Federal researchers on the other side of the Island continued to work with the pulp and paper industry, now expanding around the Strait. Michael Waldichuk began carrying out oceanographic surveys near sites where new mills were proposed or existing ones proposed to expand. He documented what he judged to be the effectiveness of the physical dispersion of pulp mill effluent in different oceanographic contexts. Waldichuk concluded that mills with significant tidal flushing, such as existed off Powell River and Nanaimo (see photograph page 190), resulted in relatively little pollution. He developed a system for classifying different coastal bodies of water according to their oceanographic features and their capacity to "assimilate" industrial waste.

Other federal research looked at the impact of Vancouver Island's newer kraft pulp mills on oysters. Waldichuk suggested in the mid-1950s that oystering around Crofton would be little affected by the new mill, as long as effluent was dispersed out into the narrow channel between Crofton and Saltspring Island. However, after the mill was built in 1957, local oystermen protested that its waste was damaging their production. An unpublished 1964 report from Nanaimo's Fisheries Research Station agreed with them. Yet two years later, the province's Pollution Control Board approved the Crofton mill's expansion and the mill's owners bought some of the local oyster leases. Apparently reaching their own conclusions based on the Crofton experience, the provincial Marine Resources Branch noted in 1969, "Oyster culture is not compatible with pulp and paper activities."[40] In 1973, the province's Inspector of Fisheries would confirm that the Crofton mill had in fact damaged twelve local oyster leases and "compromised" 80 hectares of foreshore. By then, the local oyster industry had disappeared.

Through most of the 1960s, however, there appeared to be little concern about pulp mills' effects on oysters, or anything else, on most parts of the sea. It was generally

The Harmac mill, seen here in 1957, helped fill the gap left by Nanaimo's defunct coal mines. In the 1950s and 1960s, Michael Waldichuk concluded that flushing Harmac's effluent into Northumberland Channel was an effective strategy.

understood that a town such as Crofton should absorb pollution in exchange for prosperity, that the pulp mills' sulphurous atmosphere was "the smell of money." The only reference to water quality in a 1967 history of Port Mellon, for example, concerns "dirt" residues taken into the mill's machinery after heavy rains that had overloaded the filtering capacities of its freshwater intakes. A history of Powell River from the same period similarly makes no mention of the mill's prodigious pollution. It does mention, however, the province's first concerted effort to raise money for cancer research, an initiative launched in 1946 under the leadership of Powell River Paper Company chairman Harold S. Foley. The company's resident manager, R.M. Cooper, led a local cancer fundraising initiative four years later. By this time it had become quietly acknowledged that Powell River had a high cancer rate, though the company only confronted the issue of carcinogenic complex organic compounds in its waste stream in the late 1980s.[41]

By the late 1960s, the public had become less tolerant of pulp mill pollution. And though the PCB had extended its jurisdiction to include industrial pollution control in 1965, its apparent inability to control pulp mills and other polluters made it an easy political target. Haig-Brown told Imbert Orchard in 1969 that the Strait's growing and "entirely unnecessary" pulp mill pollution was "killing all local life." The effluent from pulp mills, he explained, was largely made up of chemically complex solids that were hard to manage. The standards meant to control this pollution were "extremely lax," though he saw "some indication" that they were tightening. And he recognised that newer kraft mills were less damaging than the older sulphite mills because of the lower BOD in their waste stream.[42] Yet this waste was still copious, and much of it

190

still accumulated on limited expanses of sea bottom, where it destroyed everything. Even worse, some of this waste could be dispersed over a larger area when disturbed, causing its "evil influence" to spread farther.[43]

An article in the *Georgia Straight* newspaper in 1970 cited SPEC's alarming statistics from Eastern Canada and new federal fisheries research on the Strait. The Ontario Water Resources Commission had recently called the pulp and paper industry the "greatest pollution problem" in North America. In BC the industry produced more liquid waste than any other economic activity, even more than municipal sewage plants. A kraft mill producing a thousand tons of pulp a day (about 20 percent less than was being produced at Nanaimo) discharged 270 million litres of liquid effluent per day. This generated BOD equivalent to the sewage of a city of 200,000 people and was highly toxic to fish. Of BC's seventeen "major mills," the six on the Strait accounted for 40 percent of effluent province-wide. The Powell River and Nanaimo mills alone generated close to half of this effluent (see Table 5, page 191). These figures were alarming, but qualitative differences between the effluents of different mills were also important.[44]

Table 5: Volume of effluent per day from coastal pulp mills, 1970[45]

Mill (industrial process)	Effluent (million gallons/day)
Powell River (sulphite)	75
Harmac–Nanaimo (kraft)	72
Elk Falls–Campbell River (kraft)	56
Crofton (kraft)	54
Port Mellon (sulphite)	32
Woodfibre (sulphite)	31
Four new mills in the Upper Fraser watershed	140
Total effluent from BC's 17 major pulp & paper mills	811

A few people living in pulp mill towns had begun speaking out by 1970. In the isolated company town of Powell River, a courageous local teacher named Colin Palmer prepared a public brief for the town's new Anti-Pollution Association. Palmer stated that the paper mill, now the largest in the world, consumed more than twice as much water as New York City and dumped 50 million gallons of untreated effluent daily into Malaspina Strait (a conservative estimate compared with SPEC's figures in Table 5, page 191). The sea, Palmer said, was stained brown for fifteen kilometres. Black liquors and solid debris being dumped into it perpetually marred local beaches. SPEC's Cowichan branch took on the mill at Crofton the same summer, accusing it of "careless dumping of pulp chips, belching sulphurous smoke visible from thirty miles away" and of dumping 50 million gallons of effluent daily into the sea. Vancouver's Harry Rankin explained that the problem lay with a provincial government that was unwilling to spend money on pollution control or force industries to install pollution control equipment. The large pulp and paper producers were "foreign owned," he said, and told the government what to do. They were not interested in investments that might diminish their profits. The result was that the PCB, rather than protecting the public from pollution, was instead protecting polluting industries from public criticism.[46]

The Strait's dirty mills achieved international notoriety. French oceanographer Jacques Cousteau visited Vancouver in October 1970 and announced that the United Nations Food and Agriculture Organisation (FAO) had put the Strait of Georgia on its list of "notoriously contaminated areas." Pulp and paper mills "dump an incredible amount of very toxic material into the water and are among the worst polluters in the world," he said. If the Strait was not set aside as a marine park, Cousteau warned, there would be no life left in it by 1990.[47]

Such views on the mills' impacts were not uncontested. Dr. Timothy Parsons, a biologist at Nanaimo's Fisheries Research Station, declared the Strait was *not* polluted and denounced both Cousteau and the FAO. Charles Keenan, former chief of the province's PCB and a "water management consultant," presented a brief entitled "Dollars and Common Sense" to a PCB inquiry the same summer that Cousteau visited. Keenan explained that his views were based on his "many years of close association with government and industry." He insisted that the province's existing industrial pollution legislation was "excellent and workable" and that people simply needed to learn to coexist with pulp mills. Pollution was a problem and always would be, but the situation was hardly the "environmental disaster" that "pressure groups" and the press were depicting. Keenan criticised "voluntary and…ad hoc pressure groups" for "meddling in affairs of which they had no expert knowledge," suggesting that these groups did more harm than good.[48] The "dollars" in Keenan's title were important. While the new mills in the interior of the province had been designed to reduce the quantity and toxicity of their effluent, the older mills on the Strait had not, and retrofitting them to reduce these problems would be costly.

Political pressure for change was growing, however. Federal politician Jack Davis, an engineer himself, declared he was "on the side of the conservationist—on the side of life itself." He promised in 1970 that Ottawa would end the pulp and paper industry's aquatic pollution within ten years. The provincial government, almost twenty years in power and losing favour with the electorate, also confirmed it would "get tough" with the pulp and paper industry at last. Even older coastal mills, it said, would be obliged to adopt some form of effluent treatment.[49]

The provincial and federal governments did introduce new effluent standards over the next few years, which led to prolonged negotiations with each mill. To ensure no mill would have to close if it couldn't afford to meet the higher standards in the short term, individual "compliance schedules" were set out based on the age of the mill, its location and its prospective upgrading costs. Writing a decade later, Charles Keenan described baffling jurisdictional overlaps and duplications in the complex new regulations. The result of what he called the "environmental anarchy" unleashed in those years was confusion and conflict over ostensibly province-wide or national standards.[50] Yet the mills, slowly and unevenly, complied with the new provincial and federal standards. Responding to indications that zinc in pulp mill effluent accumulated in oysters near the Strait's mills, the industry, together with Victoria and Ottawa, began to monitor metal levels in shellfish in 1973. A 1980 study of the Port Mellon mill (see photograph page 193) confirmed that its effluent, even diluted by the sea, was highly toxic to fish and was killing juvenile salmon up to 350 metres from the mill's waste outfalls.

Despite these gains, government research on the Strait's pulp mill pollution continued to overlook some of the most ecologically damaging dimensions of mill waste. As early as the late 1960s, Haig-Brown and others had suggested people ought to be looking for more "subtle, insidious and ruinously accumulative…effects of pollution."[51] Some federal fisheries reports in these years recognised that the techniques scientists used to evaluate effluent toxicity were not permitting them to make accurate forecasts of its effects and that more research was needed into the biological effects of pollution, such as had begun elsewhere in North America.

New evidence was emerging about the longer-term effects of highly toxic substances present in relatively small quantities in different types of industrial, municipal and agricultural effluent. After widely reported incidents such as the flushing of hundreds of tons of toxic sediments down the Hudson River towards New York City in 1973, the public learned that complex organic compounds (such as polychlorinated biphenyls, or PCBs) don't just sicken or kill fish but also accumulate in their tissues and can cause birth defects and cancers in people who eat them. By the late 1970s, local research led by the Westwater Research Centre at UBC focused on heavy metals (such as mercury), pesticides (such as DDT) and other complex organic compounds in the highly polluted waters of the Fraser River estuary. From their research and many other studies around North America it was clear by the 1980s that PCBs, dioxins and furans, which all fall into the category of highly toxic "persistent organic pollutants," were present at dangerous levels in pulp mill effluent. Veteran oceanographer Michael Waldichuk came to recognise the need for longer-term ecological studies into the effects of the Strait's pulp mill waste.

In 1987 the US Environmental Protection Agency (EPA) released studies demonstrating that dioxins were a by-product of pulp bleaching. Present in very small amounts that were hard to detect and apparently ubiquitous in the pulp mills'

The Port Mellon pulp mill (seen here in 1968), the oldest on the Strait, first opened in 1908. It was a good place to make a living but a dangerous one for young salmon.

Image NA-23710 courtesy of the Royal BC Museum and Archives.

effluent, these forms of pollution persisted and accumulated in the environment for decades. Not long after the EPA study, the Canadian Wildlife Service announced it had found dioxins in a great blue heron colony near the Crofton mill. The mill's owner, BC Forest Products, insisted there was no need to worry about dioxins because they were present in the effluent only in very tiny quantities. The *Vancouver Sun* meanwhile described dioxins as "the most poisonous contaminant created by man." Crofton mill workers didn't trust the company and did their own sampling. And when federal scientists began looking for dioxins and furans in the marine environment the following year, they found high levels in prawns, shrimp and crabs around the older mills at Port Mellon and Woodfibre, and the commercial crab fishery on Howe Sound was closed. At this point, the Canadian pulp and paper industry was congratulating itself for its success in reducing the *quantity* of effluent it was dumping. The focus, however, had shifted to the chemical *quality* of this organic waste. And this new understanding undermined the strategy of using the "assimilative capacity" of tides and currents to disperse industrial waste, though the approach continued to prevail for domestic sewage.

Pulp mills on the Strait had been remarkably slow to reduce the quantity of their effluent, and most had done little to change its quality. With few exceptions, total levels of BOD and suspended solids (small particles that remain suspended in water) in the waste streams of most of the mills on both shores changed little between 1980 and 1990—and some went up (see Table 6, page 195). By 1989, only Powell River among the mills on the Strait had started even primary effluent treatment, in which heavier solid materials are allowed to settle out of wastewater, while lighter materials like oil, grease and light solids are allowed to float to the surface, then all are physically removed from the wastewater. Meanwhile, studies had begun to show "significantly above average" rates of mortality from cancer and other diseases among pulp and paper mill workers in other regions of North America and Europe.[52] And this scare over the long-term effects of complex organic pollutants encouraged more companies to treat their primary effluent as a way to bring down the levels of dioxins and furans they were dumping (see Table 7, page 195).

In 1990, Environment Canada reported that BC's pulp mills were "ahead of the nation" in reducing their pollution and eliminating dioxins. However, others pointed out that dioxin contamination from BC's mills was still among the worst in the world. The province promised tough new pollution regulations for pulp mills, requiring that their discharges of complex organics be reduced to 1.5 kilograms per metric ton of pulp produced by 1994. All coastal mills agreed to this limit except MacMillan Bloedel's Powell River plant, which pleaded that financial difficulties impeded it from making a firm commitment to effluent reduction. As Powell River's plant was the province's single largest source of complex organic pollutants, the government rejected this plea. Soon, the mill reported dramatic reductions in the amount of toxins it was releasing into the marine environment (see Table 5, page 191, and Table 6, page 195).

The public, however, was not fully reassured by the mills' relatively quick response to these new threats. Calling the persistent nature of the toxins a "creeping Chernobyl," journalist Stephen Hume described an interview with Cortes Island oyster farmer Grant Webb in 1991. The Powell River mill 30 kilometres to the

Table 6: Rates of effluent discharge at pulp mills on the Strait, 1980–91[53]

Mill location	BOD5 1980 (tons /day)	BOD5 1990 (tons/ day)	TSS 1980 (tons/ day)	TSS 1990 (tons/ day)	AOX 1989 (tons/ day)	AOX 1991 (tons/ day)
Crofton	53.4	46.3	22.7	18.1	14.4	3.4
Campbell R.	41.1	51.4	21.3	32.5	13.4	2.6
Nanaimo	20.6	24.1	13.0	10.3	8.2	2.5
Port Mellon	13.8	9.7	10.5	5.8	3.1	0.8
Powell River	28.9	30.3	29.1	14.3	28.8	1.8
Woodfibre	20.8	19.2	44.0	3.1	2.5	1.2

BOD5 = Biochemical oxygen demand occurring in wastewater during a five-day period, used as a measure of the organic content of wastewater.
TSS = Total suspended solids in wastewater.
AOX = absorbable organic halogen compounds, which include persistent organic pollutants such as PCBs, dioxins and furans.

Table 7: Dates of initiation of primary & secondary effluent treatment at pulp mills on the Strait[54]

Mill location	Start of operations	Location of effluent discharge	Date of initiation, primary treatment	Date of initiation, secondary treatment
Crofton	1957	Stuart Channel	1992	1992
Elk Falls	1952	Discovery Passage	1992	1992
Harmac	1950	Northumberland Channel	1993	1993
Port Mellon	1908	Thornborough Channel, Howe Sound	1990	1990
Powell River	1911	Malaspina Strait	1978	1992
Woodfibre	1912	Upper Howe Sound	1992	1992

south of Webb's oyster farm had been spewing dioxins into the Strait for eighty years. The newer Campbell River mill, about 40 kilometres to the west of his beach, recently claimed to have reduced its use of chlorine (a key source of complex organic pollutants) by 70 percent. Webb lamented, "Now they're poisoning us by a third instead of by a full dose." His dismay over this invisible pollution, Hume noted, was destroying "his belief in the pristine quality of life that brought him…to Cortes Island in the first place."[55]

Mining pollution on the Strait

The mining industry was a relatively minor player on most stretches of the sea by the 1960s and was virtually unregulated. However, mining waste became a more high-profile issue there in the late 1960s and early '70s, with locally important mines at Britannia on the Mainland, Gillies Bay on Texada Island and Campbell River on Vancouver Island feeling the heat. An early SPEC campaign attacked plans to dump more than 2 million gallons of effluent from the Gillies Bay iron mine into the Strait. In 1970, Roderick Haig-Brown and Harry Rankin (strange bedfellows indeed) criticised the Buttle Lake copper mine on Vancouver Island. Rankin declared that miners were "pouring their poisonous tailings into our waters, destroying marine life."[56] These tailings had been linked to high levels of heavy metals in local salmon and trout by 1971 and were the subject of ongoing studies for the next twenty years while the mine continued to operate. The Britannia mine closed for good in 1974, but its toxic legacy lives on even today, despite millions of dollars being spent on remediation.

Regulations introduced in the early 1970s required changes in the way miners extracted and transformed their ores, but no one was happy with the province's regulations. The miners resented the restrictions on their ability to dump tailings in the fast and easy ways they were used to. Critics of the new regulations viewed them as largely cynical gestures with minimal substance that failed to stem the flow of toxic substances from mine waste.[57] The province was under some pressure to respond to these criticisms but—as with the Strait's pulp mills—Victoria was reluctant to impose significant new costs on industry.

In 1973, the Deputy Minister of the Department of Recreation and Conservation complained that the Pollution Control Board's accepted levels of water-borne metals, cyanide and fluoride that were lethal to salmon. He also charged that the PCB's guidelines made no reference to potential problems caused by sediment from mine tailings, which could contaminate freshwater and marine environments. According to other government agencies, the PCB ignored the context in which it was permitting pollution; it also disregarded the possible cumulative effects, the relative sensitivity and dilution capacity of each "receiving environment," and the interests of competing resource users. The cumulative effects from multiple polluters on industrialised shorelines such as Howe Sound and Discovery Passage made it difficult to effectively control individual contributions from mines and other polluters in such areas.

Municipal sewage dumping outside the Lower Mainland

Larger cities such as Vancouver and Nanaimo had built sewer systems before World War I, but many smaller communities still relied on wells to obtain their drinking water and septic fields to manage their human waste. Early in the post-war period, Vancouver Island communities from the Cowichan Valley north, and those on adjacent islands, began to experience growing problems with septic tanks contaminating their drinking water. This problem was especially acute in summer, when tourists, campers and cottagers all used wells and septic tanks. Industrialist H.R. MacMillan contacted the Central Vancouver Island Health Unit in 1948, worried about sewage contamination of the well water at his Qualicum Beach summer home. Chief Health Inspector C.R. Stonehouse replied that the health unit was promoting the sterilisation of contaminated well water with chlorine. In an internal memo he said he hoped that his staff might be able to use the opportunity to convince MacMillan to reduce the water pollution from his mills too.[58]

Where sewers replaced troublesome septic fields in smaller towns, they succeeded in solving local contamination. For example, Parksville approved a municipal sewage system in 1963 to alleviate septic tank pollution of its beaches. The plan was to collect and dump the town's sewage, untreated, from outlets 2,400 metres offshore and 240 metres deep. Qualicum still depended on septic fields into the 1970s, but it opted for sewers after pollution warnings were posted on its beaches in 1973. That town's sewers were connected to Parksville's deep-water outlets, and one local history credits the new sewers with stimulating rapid population growth in both towns. Where sewers had been built earlier, however, they were beginning to create new problems. Disposing of untreated sewage in the sea had often been seen as a good solution, but this practice was becoming less acceptable by the late 1960s. For example, sewage discharged from an air force base had polluted public beaches in nearby Comox. In Comox Harbour, there were concerns about the impact of sewage on the local shellfish industry.

The PCB ruled in 1967 that all new municipal sewage outlets would have to provide at least primary treatment before discharging the sewage, and existing outlets would need to ensure at least this level of wastewater treatment within eight years. The PCB then set provincial standards for municipal waste treatment and introduced a permit system for all discharge points in 1971. These new regulations were creating new headaches for smaller communities like Comox. A 1975 report from the province's new Environment and Land Use Committee (ELUC) mostly muddied the waters in the Comox Harbour case. Water quality in the harbour, it said, was "similar to other coastal waters" (which were in fact of diverse quality) but *might* be of concern to growers and consumers of shellfish and to swimmers. Theoretically, at least, there was a danger of people contracting hepatitis and other diseases, though to the committee's knowledge no definite cases had arisen "as a result of exposure to the waters of Comox Bay to date, either through eating shellfish or from direct recreational use of the waters." The report did confirm, however, that coliform counts in the harbour exceeded the acceptable limits for safe shellfish harvesting. By then, much of the harvesting of oysters and clams had shifted to nearby Baynes Sound.

The ELUC report on Comox Harbour was slightly more coherent about possible responses to the situation. The committee opposed secondary sewage treatment (that is, treating the effluent to remove dissolved and suspended organic compounds through biological processes, following primary treatment) because this process would "only reproduce artificially and expensively what the Strait of Georgia has proved to do naturally and cheaply." Furthermore, stated the report, treatment had "little effect on…chemicals originating from agricultural and other land use, and which may or may not adversely affect the marine environment." A more promising option, the committee said, might be land-based sewage disposal, but it would have to do more research. In any case, noted the report, minimal water-quality standards for the marine environment were needed and the community should be committed to maintaining these standards.[59]

The Comox Valley's population grew steadily into the early 1980s, when public pressure mounted to end sewage contamination in the harbour, on nearby beaches and in Baynes Sound. In a report to the PCB, the engineers overseeing construction of the district's new sewage treatment system explained which options they had considered, what they had decided and why. It was written in the familiar style in which "experts" justify decisions already made while trying to create the impression of objectively analysing the pros and cons of each option, before selecting the one that is the specialty of the experts. The land-disposal approach, they claimed in this case, would require too much land and too much money to operate. Instead they proposed, once again, a long outfall pipe sending sewage deep beneath the Strait several kilometres north of town after a "partial primary" treatment. Their proposed design, they said, would protect the oyster beds of Baynes Sound because waste from the new outfall would reach those waters only after being swept back and forth by three or four tides, ensuring enough "mixing and biological die away" that "the water would be unrecognisable as having a sewage content."[60]

Proponents of the new Comox facility recognised that local citizens would probably not trust their proposed government monitoring programs, or government enforcement of pollution standards for their waters. They blamed such public skepticism on "notable examples" of poorly managed industrial pollution and the fact that "many treatment plants around the province have exceeded permit limits." They also noted a "general concern that the total accumulative [*sic*] effect of all discharges into the Strait of Georgia would eventually destroy the marine environment." Responding to concerns that "no local monitoring could assess the long term effect of wastewater discharges on the Strait of Georgia as a whole," they suggested that a centrally operated government lab monitor water quality around the Strait, with each individual polluter contributing to its operation.[61] Their modest suggestions were not pursued.

Marine sewage disposal around Vancouver

In the late 1940s, Vancouver's engineering staff still subscribed to R.E. Lea's proposition that water sweeping north and east from the Fraser River had a beneficial effect on water quality in Burrard Inlet. They focused on lowering the pollution in False Creek by dumping more of the city's waste into the North Arm of the Fraser. Yet, with numerous outfalls dumping raw sewage into the North Arm, high tides had begun to regularly push raw sewage and industrial waste up the river, while low tides carried filthy river water into English Bay. The province's Attorney General, Robert Bonner, described the Lower Fraser in 1958 as "an open sewer draining the whole valley."[62] Some sixty sewer outfalls discharged raw sewage into the river or onto the urban shoreline farther north. Between Fraser River water, the still fetid waters of False Creek and various other outlets (see Figure 11, page 200), the city's swimming beaches were under assault.[63]

An American civil engineer named A.M. Rawn had been engaged earlier in the decade to help solve these problems. A former general manager of the Los Angeles County Sanitation District and chairman of the California State Water Board, Rawn believed in the extraordinary value of marine disposal of municipal effluent; it was "a picture of such great allure as to capture the imagination of the dullest," he claimed. In a paper delivered to the First International Conference on Waste Disposal in the Marine Environment in 1959, Rawn summarised the philosophy that guided his work: "The great economy inherent in the discharge of urban sewage and industrial wastes into near shore water for final disposal is apparent to all who will investigate. [The ocean's] vast area and volume, its oxygen laden waters, its lack of potability or usefulness for domestic and most industrial purposes, present an unlimited and most attractive reservoir for waste assimilation." Moreover, he continued, this sea disposal option allowed engineers "to relegate the entire job of secondary sewage treatment to a few holes in the end of a submarine pipe and the final disposal of effluent to the mass of water into which the fluid is jetted…without material cost or maintenance and none for operation."[64] While chemical treatments might be important in fresh water with limited assimilative capacity, the "indiscriminate application of secondary treatment to ocean discharges," he said, was "improper." Rawn did recognise, however, that ocean dumping could well have negative effects on marine ecosystems over the longer term; they would have to wait and see.

To resolve Vancouver's increasingly intolerable situation, federal oceanographers, the Hydrographic Service of Canada and UBC's Oceanographic Institute all supported Rawn during a year-long survey of tidal flows and weather patterns in the Fraser estuary and adjacent Strait, as well as in English Bay and Burrard Inlet. Rawn's 1953 report confirmed that the future of Vancouver's beaches was at stake: "Unless corrective measures are taken to bring about more proper disposal of sewage, the conclusion is inescapable that the degree of contamination will increase as the volume of sewage flow increases until large areas of the beaches will no longer be safe or even decent to use."[65] In fact, Vancouver's situation was not so unusual. In the 1950s, over 5 million Canadians lived in towns facing similar sewage pollution problems. Only about fifty of the 300 municipalities surveyed by the Canada Mortgage and Housing Corporation in 1957 were treating their sewage, and most of those fifty carried out only primary treatment.

A key objective of Rawn's strategy was to protect swimming beaches because people belonging to local groups such as the Lower Kitsilano Ratepayers' Association and the Vancouver Parent-Teacher Association were worried about their families' health and had begun holding protests. The President of the BC Physical Fitness Association expressed his resentment to the *Province* newspaper in 1957. "In our health conscious age," he wrote, "pressure to have our sea fouling sewage system improved has to come from private citizens…who, it seems, are to be 'fobbed off' by glib statements to the effect that the city health authorities have been 'aware of the situation' for years…Who is responsible for community health and sanitation? If ever Vancouver needed a strong hand to direct its health and fitness policy, it is certainly now." Echoing the public sentiment, he continued: "Our present sewage system is still little more than a vast outdoor sea lavatory…Unfortunately, our children and tourists have to bathe in [and swallow] this sewage soup called seawater."[66]

Rawn's plan was relatively simple: stop all direct flows of sewage into English Bay and divert them south while gathering the sewage already being dumped in the Fraser into a single collection system to deliver it to Iona Island, where the Fraser's North Arm reaches the Strait. There it could be dumped into the sea after primary treatment. Another primary treatment plant was proposed at the mouth of the Capilano River, on Burrard Inlet's north shore. Rawn's strategy involved identifying some shores—particularly English Bay—as places to be protected for recreation,

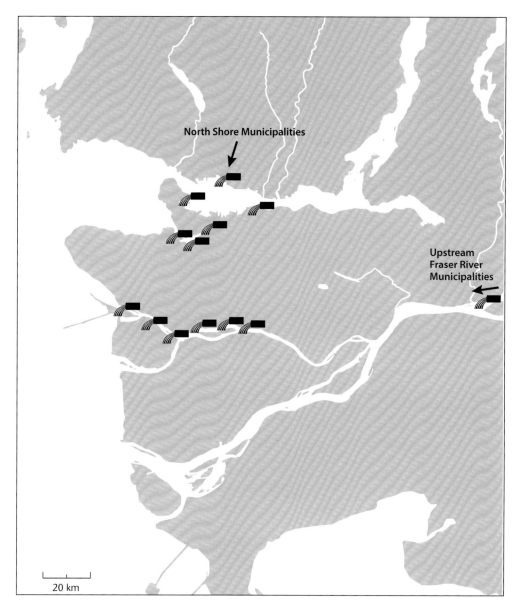

Figure 11: Main sources of sewage pollution on Vancouver beaches, 1958[67]

whereas others—especially off the mouth of the Fraser and Capilano Rivers—would be designated waste dumps.

Rawn's recommendations were not implemented quickly, and public frustration grew as local and provincial governments appeared to be doing nothing in the midst of a deepening crisis. When authorities closed city beaches during the hot summer of 1958, the *Vancouver Sun* said that the Rawn plan, and the province's recent creation of the PCB, were like "setting up a fire alarm system, then doing nothing when the fire broke out."[68] The reality was that not all local governments wanted to incur the costs involved in Rawn's recommendations. Richmond opposed the plan, fearing its shore would bear much of the pollution resulting from the primary treatment plant to be built on Iona Island. The PCB, which had been established to break the logjam, approved the Rawn plan, but Richmond appealed the decision. When the beaches shut down due to sewage pollution, Vancouver's mayor, Frederick Hume, implored

Premier W.A.C. Bennett to give an early go-ahead for the Iona Island treatment plant. Bennett replied that they were still considering Richmond's appeal and had asked the BC Research Council's Dr. Gordon Shrum to carry out further studies.

Finally, after spending $20 million, the Greater Vancouver Sewerage & Drainage District (GVS&DD) claimed in 1965 that it had reduced the "noxious load" pouring into English Bay by half a billion gallons a year, or 750,000 pounds of "solids," and the appearance of bathing water had "greatly improved" as a result. Coliform levels at the beaches didn't go down significantly, however. The GVS&DD explained that storm sewers on English Bay and False Creek were still dumping raw sewage during heavy rainfalls. As well, a growing number of boats were dumping their own waste into False Creek and the bay. Most important, the GVS&DD surmised that increasingly polluted water from the Fraser was sweeping into English Bay.

The head of the GVS&DD confirmed: "The major battle…removing sewage discharged directly into English Bay, is behind us. The program now…calls for the construction of a large trunk sewer to intercept all sewage originating on Vancouver's south slope which discharges to the North Arm of the Fraser River. This will be carried to the treatment plant." Furthermore, he said, "The effect of this development will be carefully weighed and assessed and the Sewerage District will then proceed in the elimination of outfalls from its member municipalities upstream as the need arises."[69] Simply put, the GVS&DD would implement this approach, then see what further adjustments were needed as its impacts became better understood.

As early as 1958, critics of Rawn's plan pointed out that the enclosed Strait of Georgia did not have the assimilative capacity of southern California's open ocean. R.W. Pillsbury, an assistant professor of biology at UBC, described the Strait as "a fairly large lake of sea water with extremely narrow inlets and outlets two hundred miles apart." He pointed to findings of limited exchange between the surface waters of the Strait and the open Pacific. Effluent from Rawn's proposed Iona Island treatment plant, Pillsbury suggested, was unlikely to go far from Vancouver's beaches.[70] Yet a decade later, G.H. Bonham, the city's health officer, denied that there were any health risks for swimmers, except those foolish enough to swim near sewage outfalls. As the situation at Vancouver beaches remained ambiguous and as pollution in the Lower Fraser became ever more severe, public awareness and concern about all forms of pollution soared. And these concerns, stimulated by critical voices outside government, ushered in new standards even as new concerns emerged.

Officials in Vancouver were once again on the defensive. They reported that most of the city's beaches were safe for swimming early in the summer of 1969. English Bay (see photograph page 202) and Spanish Banks continued to meet their standard of 1,000 coliforms per 100 millilitres of sea water, though the south shore of Burrard Inlet, False Creek and the North Arm of the Fraser all exceeded that level. Two weeks later, politician and medical researcher Patrick McGeer criticised city health officials for failing to post warnings at "grossly contaminated" beaches on the Fraser and at Wreck Beach near the mouth of the North Arm. McGeer reported he had "posted" Wreck Beach personally after his spot check found coliform counts of 15,000 per 100 millilitres.

The city had also failed to post warnings on the beach at Lumberman's Arch in Stanley Park, which lay a few hundred metres from the Brockton Point sewage

In 1975, English Bay beach was apparently safe for swimming, as most Vancouver sewage was being discharged into the Strait off the mouth of the Fraser River.

Image I-21622 courtesy of the Royal BC Museum and Archives.

outfall. That drain still wasn't linked to the Iona system, and it discharged most of the raw sewage from downtown Vancouver. Although highly publicised reports spoke of human feces fouling log booms and fishermen's nets on the Lower Fraser River, False Creek remained the biggest concern. It was an open sewer in the heart of the city, adjacent to its most popular swimming beaches, with coliform counts of up to 100,000 per 100 millilitres. Such levels revived old fears of typhoid—nineteen cases had in fact been reported in the city in recent years, including three fatalities. All were traced to people eating crabs caught, rinsed or cooked in False Creek water.

Local citizens' groups, especially in Kitsilano, had been among the first to speak out about polluted beaches in the 1950s. A decade later, SPEC, which was based in Kitsilano and was supported by young UBC biologists, drew attention not only to the untreated human waste pouring into the sea off Vancouver, but also to local industries using municipal sewers to dispose of their waste. Dealing with these isolated industrial "point sources" was relatively easy; the bigger issue was how to address the lingering problem of the city's combined sewers. To eliminate the contaminated "first flush" meant separating the storm sewers from the sanitary sewers, which would be costly for the city, its builders and its citizens. By 1970, however, the city required that all new building construction and new subdivisions construct separate sewers, and that old sewer lines being updated be replaced by separate sewers. The new lines were still being tied into combined trunk sewers, but the long-term plan was to replace those with separate lines too.

In fact, the city and the neighbouring municipalities made significant progress in controlling sewage discharges over the next few years. The PCB had already announced in 1968 that all future sewage outlets on the Fraser River below Hope would require no less than primary treatment and chlorination. On the Middle and

202

North Arms of the Lower Fraser, effluent from all future sewage outlets would require secondary treatment and chlorination, as would organic industrial effluent. By 1975, all existing sewage discharges into the Lower Fraser would also require secondary treatment, which the newly opened Annacis Island Sewage Treatment Plant would provide. Vancouver's sewage was also being treated by then, though only primary treatment, at the Iona Island plant at the mouth of the river.

Despite these improvements, sewage pollution in English Bay and Burrard Inlet was *still* a problem. Seagoing vessels could discharge their waste directly into the water, and because marine waterways were a federal responsibility and Ottawa had no specific legislation to address the issue, no one enforced any pollution control on these vessels. Vancouver's health officer had raised the issue with his federal counterparts in 1972, and they had suggested he speak with the National Harbours Board. City officials also encouraged the province to adopt uniform regulations for effluent from shoreline marinas, but the province declined on the grounds that it did not have enough staff to enforce such legislation. The following year, the city's health department complained about "the potentially dangerous situation with respect to pollution of Vancouver harbour from pleasure crafts and live-a-boards." It noted that the number of vessels "had increased dramatically over the last few years and will increase even more [with] the proposed marinas in the False Creek area."[71] The province had enacted regulations that prohibited boats from discharging their waste on the lakes in BC's interior, but no such legislation existed along the coast.

Although the city had spent fifteen years and many millions of dollars to upgrade its sewer system and improve the quality of local sea water, fecal coliform counts in English Bay were higher than normal during the summer of 1986, partly because of increased boat traffic resulting from Expo 86 (see photograph page 205). The city had done everything it could, said its engineers, to control discharges from docked vessels but could do nothing about boats moored offshore. Ottawa still did not require holding tanks on vessels in Canadian waters, and most ships still discharged untreated sewage directly into the sea.

Ottawa said it was considering measures for various classes of vessels. New amendments to the Canada Shipping Act would give each province the power to decide which local waters could be protected from vessels' sewage discharge. Other regulations would require tour and charter boats to install holding tanks for their waste, but issues related to pleasure craft had to be resolved first. Finally, regulations might be introduced to govern waste dumping by ocean-going freighters and cruise ships, such as those that moored in English Bay and Burrard Inlet. Because of the international ramifications, however, progress on these latter regulations was expected to be slow.

False Creek and the Fraser mouth remained the focus for most concerns about the Lower Mainland's marine environment into the 1980s. A *Vancouver Sun* article in 1980 described a massive fish kill on Sturgeon Bank, at the mouth of the Fraser, which was attributed to severe oxygen depletion in the water due to sewage. Less than a year later, Vancouver's new Iona Island Wastewater Treatment Plant was judged to be in violation of the province's Pollution Control Act. The city and the province had agreed that a "deep sea outfall" was needed to better disperse the plant's growing effluent stream, which was not only killing fish but also *still* polluting Vancouver's beaches. However, the new plan was based, once again, on dispersing the sewage into the Strait after primary treatment rather than building a costlier secondary treatment facility.

The plan went ahead despite objections from SPEC that the proposed $50 million project to extend the pipe 8 kilometres into the Strait offered no guarantees that lightly treated sewage would not drift back to the shores of English Bay and did nothing to correct the main sewage disposal problems—"industrial and household toxic chemicals washed into the system and the lack of effective treatment plants."[72] A brief prepared in 1985 by an umbrella group known as the Fraser River Coalition had pointed out that California and Oregon were experiencing "grave problems" from sewage dumping in the Pacific and that the seas off Point Grey didn't have nearly the flushing powers of the open ocean. The group had encouraged the city to aim for the best solution instead of the cheapest one and suggested that it adopt primary, secondary and tertiary sewage treatment to remove toxic chemicals being disposed of in the municipal sewage system. Ultimately, the city was concerned about the cost of secondary treatment and possible malfunctions that might be caused by peak flows more than four times greater than average that would come through the city's remaining combined sewers during heavy rains and spill untreated sewage at the river mouth. Ken Hall, a UBC civil engineer who had studied the effects of pollution at the river mouth, declared the city was deceiving itself with its 8-kilometre pipeline and solving one problem by creating others down the line.

Every summer in the 1980s, the city's health department received a steady stream of computer printouts detailing various water quality measurements at the city's most popular beaches. The summer of Expo 86, health officers confirmed water quality was good at the city's most popular beaches, far better than it had been in the late 1960s and early 1970s, and safe to swim in according to federal and provincial standards, except for Sunset Beach at the mouth of False Creek. The former industrial lands farther into the basin were being transformed into high-density housing and were also the site of the world's fair.

Although no public beaches existed on False Creek, the inlet's redevelopment, which had begun in the 1970s, was already leading to "incidents of swimming, windsurfing, zodiac football, etc. in spite of the medical health officer's declaration that the water was unfit for swimming."[73] City officials realised they faced two distinct challenges in controlling pollution there. The first, water pollution from domestic sewage, was diminishing as a result of the city's new sewers. The second, "bottom sediment pollution," could be resolved only with expensive dredging. Especially in the east basin of False Creek, toxic sediments—mostly from previous sawmilling operations—had essentially killed the sea bottom, which meant that it could no longer recover naturally. For the time being, children in particular were discouraged from participating in water sports there and everyone was advised to avoid contact with the intertidal zone or the sea bottom below the low-tide line.

By the 1980s, the sewage system the city had inherited from Rawn in the 1950s, one that depended on the power of marine dilution, had changed very little. Each successive strategy had simply moved the sewage a little farther into the inland sea, a little farther away from Vancouver's beaches, with as little treatment as the city could get away with.

Once a waste dump, always a waste dump

Although political action on pollution control took place only slowly after World War II, public and scientific perspectives reflected a more dramatic global shift. Instead of viewing the Strait as a vast uncontrolled marine waste dump, people began to see it as a "vulnerable marine ecosystem" that provided economically valuable fish habitat and precious recreational space. Growing evidence of the damage being wrought by pollution in aquatic environments was convincing people that the steadily growing volumes of industrial and domestic waste ought to be better managed.

By the 1980s, environmental managers had begun touting the "precautionary principle": the idea that decisions made in the present should not risk future harm to people or the environment. Yet this principle was seldom put into practice with decisions regarding the Strait, where the governments and engineers responsible for designing and operating waste disposal systems remained focused on short-term, "cost-effective" solutions to current problems. For them, the Strait was, and remains, the perfect low-cost waste receptacle.

Expo Centre was raised above a False Creek that was far cleaner than it had been before. At the time of Expo 86, Vancouver was aiming to transcend its dependence on natural resources but still needed to dredge toxic industrial waste from the basin.

Image I-21684 courtesy of the Royal BC Museum and Archives.

RECREATION ON THE RESTORATIVE STRAIT | 6

RECREATION ON AND BY the sea was firmly established in European culture by the time settlers began arriving on the Strait. The world's first yacht club was started at Cork in Ireland in 1720, North America's first in New York City in 1844, and the Strait would have a couple before 1900. The settlers introduced competitive rowing as well. Events that had begun as races among rowers ferrying passengers on rivers had become popular sport by the mid-nineteenth century both in Britain and eastern North America, and the Strait also proved well suited to rowing races by the late nineteenth century. Settlers brought the concept of a "sea cure" as well—bathing and other pastimes associated with cleansing, healing and rejuvenating the body that were often prescribed by Britain's eighteenth-century

physicians. Whereas England's coastal dwellers had once turned their backs on the sea whenever they weren't working on it, by 1800 they understood it to be a font of physical, intellectual, social and cultural well-being and designed their seaside residences to take advantage of the views.

Visitors from growing cities regularly took the air on seaside promenades; children played on beaches at Brighton on England's south coast and at other resorts springing up along the coastline of northwestern Europe. British Romantic poets, such as Samuel Taylor Coleridge, Percy Bysshe Shelley, John Keats and Lord Byron, further extolled the power of the sea and its shores to stir the soul and induce visions, epiphanies and physical liberation, and to nourish and restore the body and soul. For those living in the smoky squalor of rapidly growing European and eastern North American cities, the curative properties of "sea air" were becoming even more important than those of sea water. The Strait appeared to many new arrivals to offer both of these in seemingly unlimited quantities.

The beginnings of settler recreation on the Strait, 1849–World War I

Recreation on the Strait was not often talked about in the first decades of colonisation, yet the inland sea was recognised early on as a good place for newcomers to restore themselves. The Great Britain Emigration Commission confirmed in 1859 that "no fevers or epidemics of any kind are known among the white populations" of Vancouver Island. An 1866 article in the *Colonist*—

perhaps aimed at drumming up business for the steamships now advertising in the newspaper—encouraged readers to cruise along Vancouver Island's eastern shore. Such trips "for the sake of the scenery alone, would amply repay those having leisure [time off] from business."[1] Those from the comfortable classes of Anglo-American society in Victoria began holidaying in the Comox Valley by the 1880s, attracted by its wealth of game and fish. And navigating the capricious tides and winds that had earlier drowned so many gold miners (chapter 1) became another kind of summer adventure for a privileged few who could now ply these waters with their own pleasure boats.

For settlers wanting to start over and make themselves anew far from the traditional Eurasian centres of civilisation, the Strait offered a chance for "re-creation." African-American settlers arriving on Saltspring Island in the late 1850s, for example, declared their determination "to seek an asylum in the land of strangers" so that they might "repose…under the genial laws of the Queen of the Christian Isles"[2] rather than those of an oppressive American federation. People coming from afar could appreciate the spectacular coastal scenery and the opportunities for recreation, and by the 1870s, ship owners had become concerned about their sailors jumping ship to join the good life on Vancouver Island. When the Royal Navy's HMS *Tribune* put into a broad sand beach on Hornby Island, its crew leaped ashore to play polo, dig for clams and swim in the clear water. The captain and another Englishman later married local Indigenous women and pre-empted land around the *Tribune*'s bay.

Into the 1880s, though, settlers' journals and letters from the Strait mainly talk of the hard work of fishing, logging, mining and farming. Many remarked on the good fishing and hunting but even these were still work for most people—a way to feed the family or earn a living. By the early twentieth century, however, those who prospered had begun to find time for outdoor leisure and recreation. For example, the diaries of the Pidcock family from the Comox Valley and Quadra Island began to talk less of the logs they'd hauled to the shore or the hundreds of salmon they'd caught and more about tennis, skating and angling in their spare time, which seemed to be increasing. Other families increasingly took advantage of opportunities to savour the sea's mild climate and exquisite scenery.

The Strait's largest southern islands—Saltspring, North and South Pender, Galiano, Mayne and Saturna—had been settled by 1900, mostly by middle- and upper-class Britons who valued their combination of fine weather and scenery, good fishing and hunting, and proximity to new settler towns. Adventurer Warburton Pike created a "gentleman's estate" on his Saturna Island property, which soon became a gathering place for well-heeled young Englishmen "equally at home with rifle, oyster fork or champagne glass."[3] Even islanders of more modest means led lives of relative leisure; their elders in fact worried the lives of these young people might be *too* easy, failing to prepare young men, in particular, for life off the islands.

Land on these southern islands soon became valuable. Perhaps inspired by Captain Horatio Robertson, an "old China hand" who'd bought Moresby Island in 1888 and populated it with family and household servants who had accompanied him from China, others began to see the southern islands' potential for genteel retirement. A notice in the *Colonist* in 1893, for example, asked $2,000 for a mile and a half of beach property on Galiano. Obtained through pre-emption and "improved" through clearing some forest and building some fences a few years earlier, this land boasted "a splendid view of the pass and the Gulf of Georgia."[4] A Seattle buyer posted an ad in 1903 seeking an island for sale in the southern Strait of Georgia. The damper islands farther north had mostly been pre-empted by settlers who were now farming, fishing, logging and mining, rather than seeking recreation, but even Denman and Cortes Islands had a few bush gentry before World War I.

The *Colonist* reported that farms were selling well in the southern islands by 1907. "Artisans" were buying some of them, but most buyers were "well to do people with a knowledge of farming."[5] Wealthy retirees arrived with fortunes from the Yukon gold rush. Max Enke from Belgium brought in twenty Belgian labourers to work his 320-hectare estate on Galiano. The newspaper also regularly praised the "beautiful islands of the Gulf of Georgia…famed throughout the length and breadth of North America as rivalling the Thousand Islands of the St. Lawrence."[6] And a series of articles by early BC writer Captain Clive Phillips-Wooley, a distant relative of Clive of India, confirmed that despite problems finding suitable help, the islands were thriving and already boasted "some of the most beautiful homes in the province." He noted the good steamship connections to the capital and the new Saanich railway, the twice-weekly mail service and the recent advent of gas-powered motor launches, which all contributed to the quality of island life. Telephone connections were also expected soon.

A couple of years after his effusive articles began to appear, the *Colonist* announced that Phillips-Wooley's own 250-hectare estate on Piers Island, at the north end of the Saanich Peninsula, was for sale. It was described as "a regular sun trap," with pheasants and grouse, salmon and clams: "a rare opportunity for one who is fond of fishing, shooting or boating." The following year the paper announced that this land—"one of the most desirable tracts…in the Strait of Georgia"—had been sold.[7]

Nearby D'Arcy Island, also located at the north end of the Saanich Peninsula, was populated involuntarily. It served as a leper colony for the City of Victoria starting in 1891. Victoria was then the landing port for immigrants from Asia, and when a handful of newly arrived Chinese were discovered to have leprosy, they were quarantined and then confined to D'Arcy Island indefinitely "to prevent the spread of this loathsome disease among the Asiatic population and its possible transmission to the whites."[8] Quisisana Sanitorium was built in 1909 on the shores of Saanich Inlet and catered to more fortunate unfortunates including "post-operative cases, and those requiring change, rest and outdoor recreation [but not] tubercular or mental cases."[9]

As the Strait became more populated, some people chose to live away from the madding crowd. Early in the twentieth century, creative entrepreneurs described the Mainland shore north of Howe Sound—an area so isolated by impassable fjords that it resembled an archipelago—as the "Sunshine Coast," another place to restore oneself. Oral historian Imbert Orchard spoke of a family that sold its house in Ladysmith shortly before World War I and moved to the wilds of Jervis Inlet to restore the father's failed health. Others chose to buy summer cottages. A particularly North American "rest cure," the first cottages were typically near the Strait's largest towns—on Indian Arm, Howe Sound, Saanich Inlet and Gabriola Island—but accessible only by water. Many were built on the same shores where Indigenous people had until recently harvested clams, camas and fish every summer for centuries.

Boating on North Vancouver's Seymour Creek circa 1890; this was also a prime angling site. Note the mix of rowboats, canoes and sailboats.

Image A-03311 courtesy of the Royal BC Museum and Archives.

Along with recreational property came recreational activities, especially boating on the sea. Although many people used rowboats in their everyday work, these boats were also used for recreation (see photograph page 212). Workers on Burrard Inlet staged the first formal rowing races there in 1882,[10] and within a decade the Burrard Inlet Rowing Club was formed. Club rowing races became major sporting events in the decade that followed, with the winners taking home hundreds of dollars in prizes. Recreational sailing was already popular around Vancouver by the mid-1880s; sailing races were being organised and heavily bet on during the summer the City of Vancouver was founded, in 1886. Victoria's first yacht club was founded in 1882; Nanaimo's and Vancouver's followed in 1897. By 1900, sailing yachts regularly explored the hidden corners of the inland sea, and races were staged from Vancouver to the north end of the Strait and back.

Alexander MacLaren, a local lumberman and founding member of the Vancouver Yacht Club, launched a 21-metre, 21-ton racing schooner made from local Douglas fir and yellow cedar. The *Maple Leaf*, as it was called, was a wonder of West Coast shipbuilding equipped with an auxiliary diesel motor and electricity. Others explored the inland sea in powerboats: the *Colonist* reported that Mrs. Joan Dunsmuir, widow of Vancouver Island magnate Robert Dunsmuir, was touring on the steam tug *Lorne* in the summer of 1906, a cruise that took her to "many of the beauty spots of the archipelago of the Gulf of Georgia."[11]

Recreational fishing and hunting also became more widespread around the Strait. Early Campbell River settler Frederick Nunn, still living on his pre-empted land,

boasted of the splendid salmon fishing nearby in his letters to family in England. Victoria's merchants worried that the Strait's magnificent sport fishing—far better than in New Brunswick's famed salmon rivers, they insisted—was not being properly advertised. By the 1910s, federal fisheries authorities were under pressure to eliminate commercial fishing in Cowichan Bay, Saanich Inlet and other places that had become popular angling sites. Before the Powell River mill was built in 1912, hunting was so good on the Malaspina Peninsula that it seldom took visiting hunters more than an hour to kill a deer. However, officials in Victoria were already receiving complaints about overhunting, and Indigenous hunters were often identified as the culprits. By 1908, the province had commissioned a fast motor launch to help game wardens patrol hunting on the islands, and the *Colonist* encouraged it to appoint additional officers to help with the task.[12]

Improving land transportation helped make the Strait a tourist destination. Railways carried locals and visitors to the best swimming beaches, where picnicking and camping became popular. A Canadian Pacific Railway employee working on the northern extension of the Esquimalt & Nanaimo (E&N) Railway on Vancouver Island was so impressed by the beach at Qualicum that he had the area subdivided into a number of 8-hectare lots. A few miles away, the Rath family developed a picnic site near Parksville that later became a favourite commercial campground. And summer camps began to emerge all around Howe Sound, organised for city children and designed to encourage healthy living by the sea while promoting Christian values.

Parks were becoming attractive places to escape the stresses of town life. Vancouver's Stanley Park was established in 1887, the first substantial public park on the Strait. Although it mimicked the pastoral model of parks created in larger cities, Stanley Park was nonetheless defined by the sea around it. The park's sandy beaches and rocky cliffs became as much a draw as its flowers and trees. The city soon expanded its shoreline park space at Hastings Park on Burrard Inlet and around English Bay (see photograph page 213, left), but Stanley Park remained Vancouver's principal recreation area and "tourist destination." By 1913, when automobiles were

Above left: Young women enjoying the waters of English Bay, circa 1900, when it was already a popular recreation site.
Image B-04127 courtesy of the Royal BC Museum and Archives.

Above: The Port Augusta Hotel in Comox in the 1900s. It was opened as a trading post in the 1880s by J.B. Holmes, a former Hudson's Bay Company clerk. By 1900 his customers were from coastal steamers and navy ships. His daughter married a sportsman who had come to fish and hunt.
Image E-00408 courtesy of the Royal BC Museum and Archives.

finally allowed to enter, the park was receiving 50,000 visits a week at a time when Vancouver's population was not much over 100,000. Elsewhere on the Strait, James and Moresby islands, south of Saltspring, were sold to a local politician and a "wealthy Englishman,"[13] respectively, in 1906, to be converted into private game parks.

Surprisingly from a contemporary perspective, travellers were drawn not only to the spectacular coastal beauty and the fishing and hunting but also to the raw power of the Strait's frenetic extractive industries (chapters 3 and 4). Tours of the inland sea advertised it as "one of the most delightful parts of the world…in the sense of natural beauty, wildness and healthfulness" while including visits to logging sites and the bustling mining town of Vananda on Texada Island. The *Colonist* described Nanaimo as "the Black Diamond City" for its role at the centre of the Strait's booming coal industry but also as "a beautiful summer resort…overlooking the picturesque Gulf of Georgia."[14] The journalists suggested that these contrasts enhanced the appeal of the Strait's working towns.

Travellers needed places to stay, and they were offered shelter in a growing collection of hotels (see photographs page 213, right, and page 214) around the Strait. For decades, Mayne Island had been a convenient place to stop for a drink and perhaps to camp overnight when travelling between the Mainland and Vancouver Island. In the 1890s it boasted the Point Comfort hotel, which promised respite:

The Wigwam Inn on Indian Arm, seen here around 1914, did a brisk business with steamship passengers from Vancouver. It became a Royal Vancouver Yacht Club outstation in 1985.

Image G-07263 courtesy of the Royal BC Museum and Archives.

The Right Place for Spending a Summer Holiday Pleasantly and Well—Scenery, Accommodation, Hunting, Fishing—Everything to Make Visitors Happy…Greatly needed in the Province of British Columbia heretofore has been some comfortable and quiet resort where the business man in search of needed rest from his many cares, could, without being too far removed from his office, find pleasant means of recuperation. The tourist too, wearied with long journeys, often sighs for some picturesque spot where the bustle and roar of civilisation are left behind and its comforts alone remain…a virtual sportsman's paradise…fishing…hunting…white sand beach…with a wharf being built so passing steamers can stop at the hotel on every trip…[15]

Elsewhere, Parksville's Seaview Hotel opened next to the beach in the late 1880s and Comox had three hotels near the dock by the 1890s. The Thulin brothers operated a hotel at Lund, north of Powell River, by the early 1890s and they opened another in Campbell River a few years later, announcing: "Sportsmen will find…the best HUNTING and FISHING."[16] Bowen Island's Howe Sound Hotel, its first tourist establishment, opened just south of Hood Point in 1895 and catered to an eclectic mix of loggers, boaters and "wealthy foreigners." By the following decade, the Cates family had opened the Hotel Monaco on Bowen, offering meals, lodging and their own private park complete with a lagoon, Japanese tea garden, dance pavilion and telephone link to the city.

In the heady days before World War I, all these new parks, cottages, camping beaches, excursion boats and hotels attested to the Strait as a place to restore oneself, escape the pressures of work and regain one's health. In a short story by T.L. Grahame published in the *Colonist* in 1903, a man from Toronto, employed in Vancouver and vacationing on the shore of what he calls "Gabriano Island," waxes lyrical about the sea:

It was a gorgeous riot of colour indescribable, making all the waters over by Howe Sound like autumn peaches on autumn leaves of maple…I stood there breathing my fill of that exquisite panorama. The Gulf lay like a vast mirror of beryl, the young sunbeams flashing joyously from its vast expanse…Texada's purple sierra sharply cut the tender azure of the northern skyline…The air was of that indescribably delicious freshness which comes when sea and mountain mingle their fresh breaths. So there I was, in Nature's very temple, exulting in form and colour and feeling…unashamed to cry in the ecstasy of the moment.[17]

The charmed vacationer then dives in, only to be enveloped in the tentacles of a giant Pacific octopus. Assuring us that he is a big, strong and virtuous Briton, the man also admits to being scared to death. In his tale, then, is the mix of joy and fear that is common to so many views of the Strait. One might see his underwater monster as the threat of losing the Strait as a restorative recreational space, a narrative that would become far more familiar after 1945.

Recreation in the interwar years

Recreation continued to evolve despite—and partly because of—the grave challenges of the interwar years. More than ever the inland sea offered diversion, now from the grim reality of the wars and the Depression, and a sanctuary from the cities and the industries of the Strait and beyond. And there were now many ways to get to and around the inland sea. The E&N Railway, for example, ran up the coast of Vancouver

Island all the way to Courtenay by 1914, stimulating a diverse mix of recreation and tourism there. The Pacific Great Eastern Railway (PGE) hadn't yet overcome the challenging cliffs of Howe Sound, but by 1920 it extended south from the interior of BC to the head of the sound at Squamish and north from Vancouver Harbour to the mouth of the sound at Horseshoe Bay. Both lines supported growing recreation on the water in between. New highways first supplemented and then increasingly replaced the railways (chapter 1). The PGE ended its service from North Vancouver to the beaches of Whytecliff and Horseshoe Bay in the late 1920s, for example, when buses took their place. From these shoreline communities, excursion boats took visitors on day trips to neighbouring Bowen Island. Others crossed the Strait from Vancouver to Newcastle Island near Nanaimo or up Burrard Inlet into Indian Arm. Recreational automobile traffic to the North Shore later increased when the Lions Gate Bridge was built across the First Narrows in 1937. Drivers could now easily reach a Union Steamship Company (USC) resort at Whytecliff, rent cottages there or take a passenger ferry over to Bowen Island.

Steamship companies like USC helped develop tourism on Savary, Hornby and Cortes Islands, corners of the northern Strait until then seldom visited by settlers, except to log. USC also promoted its hotels and guest cottages on the Sechelt Peninsula, which in the 1930s it began to call the Gulf Coast Riviera. Although people complained in private about the forest fire–induced haze over the Strait in summer and the stench of pulp mills, fish plants and sewage outfalls, not much conflict arose between recreational and industrial activities. And little was said about the aesthetic impacts of rampant deforestation of the shoreline around the sea. Complaints and silences about such things were remarkably similar in the otherwise very different diaries of the Pidcock family of Courtenay and Quathiaski Cove, and Francis John Barrow of Victoria. The pressures of global conflict and a deep economic malaise weighed more heavily on many people's minds than deforestation or the smell of rotten eggs.

Prosperous locals with the means to travel the inland sea found "their" Strait was increasingly being enjoyed by well-heeled fellow travellers, especially rich Americans. For example, Barrow and his partner spent their summers through the 1930s on extended cruises around the northern Strait and beyond, searching for petroglyphs, filming life and work on the sea, and thoroughly enjoying themselves. The Barrows, like writer M. Wylie Blanchet, who recorded her family's summer wanderings around the sea in a small cruiser in the same decade, viewed wealthy American boaters as unwelcome intruders threatening their idyllic summer sea. In fact more people were beginning to join them on the sea (see photograph page 217), though not that many were American. Vancouver's yacht club thrived in these years; the club's move to a new dock on English Bay in 1927 was followed by years of growth. More club members operated powerboats than sailboats, while many larger sailing craft began to carry auxiliary motors; these changes eased access to all corners of the Strait.

The Strait's fame spread among the international elite, and the inland sea came to be known across much of the English-speaking world. Beaches at the mouth of the Englishman and Qualicum Rivers on Vancouver Island were particularly favoured. After the railway arrived there in 1914, Qualicum Beach became a resort town. Monied celebrities from the King of Siam to writer Edgar Rice Burroughs to actors

The Cowichan Bay Regatta of 1920: Pleasure-boating and salmon fishing were among the favourite pursuits of the area's many remittance men.

Image A-07244 courtesy of the Royal BC Museum and Archives.

Errol Flynn and Shirley Temple stayed at the Qualicum Beach Hotel. The Hornby Island Lodge and the Royal Savary Hotel opened during the interwar years, as did another exclusive lodge on the Twin Islands off Cortes in 1939. Qualicum also began to nurture a colony of genteel retirees, and by 1943 a quarter of its population was over the age of fifty-five. In nearby Parksville, Matthew Beattie sought "a tranquil retirement retreat" after a lucrative career in the Far East. He built the Newbie Lodge in 1920 on land purchased from his father-in-law, a settler named Gibbs. The Beatties' gracious home then became a social hub for the area's remittance men, retired soldiers and colonial administrators. The Beatties lost their fortune and their dream home after the Wall Street collapse of 1929.

The islands, too, were popular with retirees. In 1920 General "One Arm" Sutton, a well-heeled British retiree from a life in China, bought Portland Island at the south end of Saltspring Island. An American named Fred Lewis established his domain over nearby Coal Island in the 1930s, "with a fleet of boats, a modern machine shop, wharves, roads, houses and a productive farm." By the 1940s, a visitor characterised the southern islands as being "without visible means of support," a place where "the main industry was undoubtedly the cashing of pension cheques and dividends."[18] A North Pender resident in those years suggested the place be renamed Pensioner Island. By most accounts, the islands were "fine places to live but poor places to make a living."[19]

For many people, both prosperous and of more modest means, the Strait was a refuge to restore themselves and, in some cases, to start again. Barrow described numerous encounters with often eccentric and always intensely individualistic folk in hidden corners of the northern sea. Many were also deeply wounded, and the seclusion of these places and their reputation for a healthy lifestyle drew those escaping the strife-ridden world beyond. For example, a Captain Waard and his family attracted much attention when they crossed the Pacific from Shanghai to Victoria in a small junk in the early 1920s; explaining their need to escape the chaos in China, they settled on Galiano.

217

The provincial government, again animated by a myth of agricultural settlement, also made land available at Merville, north of Courtenay, for soldiers returning from World War I. The aim was to give veterans a chance to work in a healthy environment and restore themselves after the nightmares of the Western Front, but the land in these "soldier settlements" was poor. Most farms were soon abandoned, though veterans could make a living fishing and lumbering.[20] Writer Hubert Evans, a recovering veteran, published a short autobiographical novel in 1927 entitled *The New Front Line* that described what it was like to wash ashore on the Strait at that time.

For those seeking spiritual restoration, the Strait offered many options. In *Quadra Island*, Jeanette Taylor describes Read Island in the interwar years as "a haven for people seeking religious and personal freedom." By the 1920s the island, located east of Quadra Island in the northern Strait, had hosted "so many different kinds of religion…that it was hard to find a suitable day for community celebrations." The Hamilton family, meanwhile, chose Saltspring Island for its "Spiritualist Camp" in 1940, because it offered a "peaceful, restful detachment from materialism."[21] Among the more colourful characters was Edward Wilson—better known as Brother XII— and his Aquarian Foundation. The English-born accountant from Victoria had spent much time exploring the shores of the inland sea in small boats and contemplating world religions. In 1920 he founded a spiritual community at Cedar-by-the-Sea near Nanaimo, on a beach that had once been a meeting place for the Cowichan people.

As Brother XII, Wilson declared himself Earth's representative of a supernatural order known as Chila that encompassed eleven other domains floating in the "Outer World." Together with his partner, Madame Zee, Brother XII created a syncretic cult based on elements of ancient Egyptian religion, Buddhism, astrology and theosophy that promised "a wondrous land," "a place by the sea…[with] trees around it" where followers could eliminate greed and evil from the world. It would also, Brother XII explained, "usher in a new dispensation, a new sub-race to make way for the return of the Messenger…around 1975."[22] The Aquarian Foundation's doctrine of impending doom and reincarnation was implausibly appealing to many people at the time; it had attracted eight thousand followers worldwide by 1927, many of them rich Americans disenchanted with the materialism of their age.

As the contributions poured in, Brother XII and Madame Zee converted the money into gold bars in Nanaimo. But accusations of financial misbehaviour in 1929 forced the pair to move their operation to nearby De Courcy Island, where a visitor to their island home remembered years later "the exquisite loveliness of the ceremonial scene: In the centre of a clearing, lit by the moon a huge fire…Near this was a sort of rock altar behind which Brother XII stood in long blue robes embroidered in gold… against background sounds of the sea breaking upon the rocky shore."[23] Hounded by further criminal charges, however, Brother XII and Madame Zee disappeared in 1933 and were never seen again on the Strait.

Not all religious groups around the inland sea were attracted by religious freedom or spiritual growth, though. In the early 1930s, over 600 Doukhobors from the BC interior who had been convicted of parading naked were imprisoned by the federal government on Piers Island, the erstwhile "sun trap" of Clive Phillips-Wooley. A barbed-wire fence divided the island, with female prisoners on one side and male prisoners on the other. Although this experiment in penal isolation lasted only two years, the idea of rehabilitating the sect on the Strait reappeared again briefly in the late 1950s (chapter 1).

The idea of recreation on the Strait was firmly established by the 1930s. Instead of seeing tourism simply as a means of promoting the province's resource industries, Victoria—as many people and companies around the sea already did—began to see it as an important economic activity in its own right. As primary resource wealth shrank in small shoreline communities, many of them pursued seasonal tourism. In Sechelt, for example, the summer hotel business thrived around the docks. The Union Steamship Company and other resort owners provided visitors to Bowen Island and Sechelt with their choice of a hotel room or a cottage, and on Bowen, the USC also offered tennis courts, picnicking grounds, a putting green, a lawn bowling green, hiking trails, horses and ponies for riding, and outdoor concerts.

Privately owned summer cottages spread farther around the Strait. Savary Island became one of the coast's more popular summer colonies in the 1920s with hundreds of cottages lining its white sand beaches. The local real-estate agent greeted visitors at the USC dock dressed in a grass skirt and lei. A summer colony of schoolteachers grew up in the mid-1920s on Texada's Gillies Bay, while Keats Island hosted a collection of Baptist cottages. More sedate cottaging developed by Qualicum's broad beach, where two provincial lieutenant governors, the mayor of Vancouver, four judges and forestry magnate H.R. MacMillan all had summer homes by the 1930s. Cottages also continued to proliferate closer to cities, at Crescent Beach, Point Roberts and White Rock on the Mainland (see photograph page 219), and on the Saanich Peninsula and at Maple Bay on Vancouver Island. These places could easily be reached by train and, increasingly, automobile.

The less well-off had excursion boats. Publisher Howard White has written about

In the 1920s, many families had summer cottages at Crescent Beach, which was easily accessible by train or automobile from Vancouver.

Image F-06149 courtesy of the Royal BC Museum and Archives.

RECREATION ON THE RESTORATIVE STRAIT

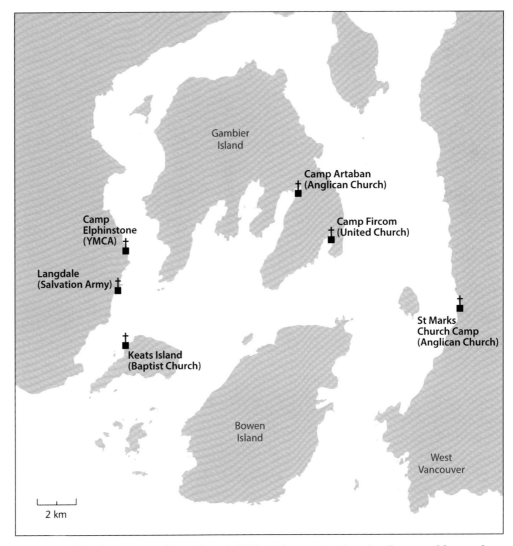

Gambier
Island

Camp Artaban
† (Anglican Church)

Camp Fircom
† (United Church)

Camp
Elphinstone
(YMCA) †

Langdale
(Salvation Army) †

St Marks
Church Camp
(Anglican Church)

Keats Island
(Baptist Church)

Bowen
Island

West
Vancouver

2 km

Figure 12: Church camps on Howe Sound, 1930; in the coming decades they would spread up the Sechelt Peninsula.

the town of Sechelt in those years, swamped by factory and office workers pouring off these boats.[24] The USC's *Lady Alexandra* carried up to 1,400 passengers on picnic and dancing tours to Bowen Island.[25] The CPR's Princess ships offered cruises to a lively dance pavilion on Nanaimo's Newcastle Island. Earlier mined for coal then quarried for sandstone, the island had become a vast recreation site accommodating up to twelve thousand people at a time. The ships moored there became floating weekend hotels. So popular were these events that locals raced to the island early to beat the crowds arriving from Vancouver, and everyone danced far into the night.[26] By 1931, the CPR also offered weekend trips aboard its steamships from Vancouver to Jervis Inlet, Powell River, Princess Louisa Inlet, Knight Inlet and the San Juan and Gulf Islands. And it ran "holiday excursions" linking Victoria, Seattle and Vancouver as well as various "cruises" between New Westminster and Nanaimo, Nanaimo and Bellingham, and many other combinations.[27]

Although tourist hotels, cottages and excursion boats were spreading around the Strait, these were also difficult years for many, especially after 1929. Francis John

Barrow spoke of visiting a poor family on Cortes Island in 1933: "They said they had a very hard time last winter…They have not bought any clothes for five years but Mrs Roark showed us cushions she had made out of gunny sacks…We bought two pillow slips she had made out of flour sacks."[28] Poorer families living in the city could apply for a subsidised place for their children in new church camps. The shores of Howe Sound hosted many of them, aiming to combine healthy summer fun with a good dose of spiritual instruction (see Figure 12, page 220, and photograph page 221).

Parks offered more affordable access to the Strait. In 1911, Victoria had established Strathcona Provincial Park inland on central Vancouver Island, the first park in a provincial system it intended to grow. New parks were established at Englishman River Falls and Little Qualicum Falls near Parksville in 1940. However, like their predecessor, neither of these places was actually on the shores of the Strait. Initially they were used as campgrounds for unemployed young men rather than for recreation. Citizens in the Comox Valley pushed for a major park located on the seashore, proposing a stretch of beach near Oyster River south of Campbell River. Their initial goal was a national park, but their appeals stressing the area's spectacular sport fishing and freedom from pests of all kinds seemed more designed to engender envy than gain support in Ottawa.

Just before the start of World War II, Elma Pearse appealed to the province's lieutenant governor, Eric Hamber. She emphasised the need for a park at Oyster River for the province's children and noted that the sandy beach was "better than Qualicum…a children's paradise." She underscored the fact that it was also the "last large piece of sandy beach left on the east side of Vancouver Island [not yet privately owned]."[29] And she pointed out that Canada had numerous national parks in the mountains, but few by the sea and none at all on the Strait. In the end, Ottawa declined to develop a national park at Oyster River, in part because with four national parks—including most of the "mountain parks" Pearse had mentioned—the province already had more than its fair share.

Members of the Crescent Beach Girls'
Relay Swimming Club in the 1920s:
swimming was the principal form
of recreation at beach parks, and
competitive swimming in the sea was
popular.

Image I-82377 courtesy of the Royal BC Museum
and Archives.

Although neither the federal government nor the province had yet designated parks along the Strait, municipal parks by the sea were becoming more numerous and were heavily used. Nanaimo's Newcastle Island Park received tens of thousands of visitors annually in the 1930s and Vancouver's Stanley Park remained the flagship of that city's growing park system. In 1917, alarmed over shoreline erosion around the park, the city began to build a corniche, or "seawall" promenade, around the periphery. Two years later, the main road through the park began experiencing its first weekend traffic jams.

English Bay was the city's most crowded beach, and the Vancouver Parks Board was gradually gaining control over the waterfront around it. The Parks Board vigorously opposed plans to expropriate Squamish reserve land for new construction south of the Burrard Bridge, and the city eventually developed parks there instead. It also inherited more beach park at Locarno and Spanish Banks on the south side of Burrard Inlet when Vancouver absorbed the Municipality of Point Grey in 1929. Mostly these urban beach parks were used for swimming (see photograph page 222), and to meet growing demand a new concrete bathhouse replaced the original wooden one on English Bay. North America's largest saltwater swimming pool opened at Kitsilano Beach in 1930. Other forms of recreation blossomed on the beaches as well. For example, the annual English Bay Carnival started in 1937, evolving into the Vancouver Sea Festival.

Until World War II, Indigenous people remained largely absent from the stories about these recreation spots and from the recreation that took place there. In a 1944 report, the Vancouver Parks Board mentioned an Indigenous past in its parks for the first time. It explained that archaeologists excavating the Great Fraser Midden, a Musqueam village and burial site unearthed earlier in the city's Marpole neighbourhood, had revealed that Indigenous people inhabited the coast of BC perhaps as much as three thousand years ago. "For numberless generations," stated the report, "tribes of these Indians made homes at Snauq and Eyalmu on the southern shore of English Bay, as well as at Whoi Whoi, where Lumberman's Arch now stands, in Stanley Park." Then, explained the Parks Board rather disingenuously, as the city grew up and became "too noisy for Indians," they looked for somewhere else to live.[30]

This kind of growing awareness was also reflected in the use of Indigenous motifs in promotional material aimed at tourists. Summer adventurers such as Francis John Barrow sought out petroglyphs, "Indian graveyards" and coffins suspended in trees by certain Indigenous groups. But these were beyond the recreational experience of most people. Increasingly, as such sites around the Strait were exhausted of their artifacts, the searchers had to move farther north. Some Indian reserves leased low-cost waterfront land to settlers for cottages. But relations with Indigenous people were still uneasy, especially among recreational anglers, who grew more upset about what they considered "Indians' wasteful fishing practices" and the effect they believed these were having on dwindling stocks of Chinook and Coho salmon (chapters 2 and 4).

Fishing had become one of the most important recreational activities on the inland sea, and visitors to the province were attracted by the Strait's reputation for salmon fishing. A cadre of nature writers with substantial national and international readerships, including Hamilton Mack Laing in Comox, Francis Dickey on Quadra Island and Roderick Haig-Brown in Campbell River, published widely in those years and extolled the virtues of hunting and fishing, especially, around the Strait. The USC's tourist brochures, first published during World War I, also spread the word. "North by West in the Sunlight" described tours "to give knowledge to the outside world regarding the beauties, grandeurs and sport potentialities of the coast of BC." "Fin, Feather and Fur on the British Columbia Coast" spoke to a war-weary population and offered "a much-needed vacation" before informing readers of the USC's network of coastal resorts.[31] By World War II, the province was also throwing its weight behind tourism and its promotions helped draw an estimated 1.7 million American tourists during the war years, most of them to the shores of the Strait.

As tourism grew, so did a community of wildlife conservationists, especially on the western shore of the Strait. Attracted by the Comox Valley's gentle climate, beauty and profusion of wildlife, artist Allan Brooks moved to the area and persuaded his hunting companions and fellow birdwatchers Ronald Macdonald Stewart and Hamilton Mack Laing to join him in this "very birdy place." Stewart arrived first, in 1908, initially working as a farmer and later as a game warden. He became Mack Laing's mentor in the woods when the latter settled on Comox Harbour in the early 1920s after studying art at Brooklyn's Pratt Institute. Brooks was a successful artist, and his wildlife paintings appeared in *National Geographic* and other international publications in the 1930s. He also illustrated American author Aldo Leopold's *Game Management*. The fourth member of the group, another birder neighbour on the beach, was a lawyer and one-time mayor of Courtenay named Theed Pearse. Pearse and his wife, Elma, became outspoken supporters of local conservation issues, and

Comox writer Hamilton Mack Laing with a 65-pound Chinook salmon, around 1925. Mack Laing and his friends fished a "Tyee pond" near to where huge Indigenous fish traps had earlier been constructed. Haig-Brown described such fish as "powerful advertising for the province."

Photo from author's private collection.

the couple's well-preserved forest land at the mouth of Black Creek eventually became the site of Miracle Beach Provincial Park.

Mack Laing (see photograph page 224) published hundreds of articles over several decades, becoming the best known of the Comox group and its unofficial spokesman. His writing revealed a complex relationship with the natural world. "Yes," he wrote at one point, "I am dippy over trees—beautiful, useful, wonderful creations."[32] He and Stewart also devoted much of their lives to bird collecting. Both men collected thousands of specimens, which sometimes led to conflict with neighbour and birdwatcher Theed Pearse, who believed wildlife ought to be left intact in its natural setting; Brooks, however, was happy to use the collectors' specimens as models for his paintings. In fact, Mack Laing saw himself unequivocally as a part of nature and made no attempt to be impartial about his fellow creatures. As well as shooting thousands of birds for his collection, he regularly killed deer, raccoons and rodents that threatened his well-being. He harboured a visceral hatred for species that preyed on animals he loved to hunt, fish or observe. He had an especially jaundiced view of the "blackfish" (Orca), which fed on so much marine life in the Strait. Bald eagles and domestic cats he considered "bird killers" and shot them on sight.[33]

None of the Comox Valley naturalists were wealthy, but they lived rich lives close to nature in a place they had chosen. Despite doctrinal differences with the American philosopher Henry David Thoreau, Mack Laing saw himself as a "back-to-the-lander" and his Baybrook farm on Comox Harbour as his Walden. He bemoaned the contemporary youth he saw "streaming headlong into the yawning gape of that vast monster we call the Industrial Machine."[34] Ultimately his writings laid the groundwork for a younger generation, including Francis Dickey and Haig-Brown, who lived a few miles farther north along the shore.

Recreation on the Strait offered sanctuary from the grim realities of war and economic collapse that dominated much of this period. Things were about to change dramatically, and recreation on the Strait would become more important still.

The flowering of recreation on the inland sea after World War II

Recreation became firmly established as an important part of the Strait's culture and economy during the post-war decades as incomes rose, technologies evolved and people found themselves with more leisure time. However, the elaborate network of dance cruises, dance pavilions, seashore hotels and cottages linked by steamships that had grown up around the Strait by 1940 was soon to disappear as highways, automobiles and ferries proliferated. Local historian Barry Broadfoot suggested that when Bowen Island reached peak popularity right after the war, it was probably "the most used resort in Canada other than Toronto's Centre Islands." In 1946, the USC recorded over 100,000 round trips between Vancouver and its Bowen Island playground, mostly in summer. It was a remarkable number given that Vancouver had a population of 365,000.

In 1947, the USC was still heavily advertising its Bowen property, describing it as "a pleasure garden" and "a wonder of scenic charm" on "the happy isle." Yet mass recreation on the island was declining rapidly and this decline would prove terminal. The USC took its Bowen-bound ships out of service in the early 1950s, closed its hotel for good in 1957 and sold off its cottages, many of which were barged to other locations on the Mainland coast. "The idea of a boat ride, a picnic basket on the lawn and splashing in the ocean," Broadfoot concluded, had become "just a little passé."[35] Post-war citizens travelling in cars on a rapidly growing highway network now had a broader range of recreational opportunities to choose from.

As ferries were increasingly used to move cars, more sedate forms of sea travel on local ships almost disappeared. By the mid-1950s all the landings from Williamsons, Hopkins and Gibsons to Vananda and Powell River could be reached from the Lower Mainland by car and ferry. No longer did people have to wait for the USC's scheduled rounds to reach these places along the Mainland shore. They could still sail on one of the CPR's luxurious Princess ferries from downtown Vancouver to downtown Nanaimo, but fewer people did and this service also disappeared by the mid-1970s.

For the most part, the types of recreational activities in vogue before and during the war continued afterwards, though often with far more participation. Sea kayaking became popular in the 1970s and windsurfing a decade later, but both were variations on older themes rather than entirely new pastimes. Scuba diving was more novel; in the 1950s the first recreational divers started exploring the depths with new artificial breathing apparatuses in clear, protected waters like Howe Sound. Undersea diving was relatively complex, physically demanding and expensive, and the sport was limited to a small number of practitioners. However, their new perspective on the marine environment and growing awareness of the underwater world helped not only to stimulate the development of marine parks but also to bring attention to pollution below the water's surface. The renowned French undersea explorer Jacques Cousteau, for example, robustly condemned the Strait's pulp mills in the early 1970s (chapter 5). By the end of that decade, the Underwater Archaeological Society of British Columbia had identified a number of "underwater heritage sites" in need of "conservation and development." The many shipwrecks littering the sea floor, vestiges of earlier marine transport disasters (chapter 1), were being billed as repositories of the Strait's settler culture *and* novel recreation sites. Among the sites designated were the SS *Zephyr*, lost off Mayne Island in 1872; the SS *Chehalis*, sunk off Brockton Point in Vancouver in 1906; the SS *Iroquois*, wrecked near Sidney in 1911 (already a provincial heritage site) and the SS *Capilano*, lost off Savary Island in 1915.

The post-war era also brought efforts to convert some of the Strait's more polluted shoreline industrial sites into a series of parks and residential neighbourhoods. Parks Board commissioner Joseph Malkin envisioned a twenty-five-year project converting Vancouver's False Creek into a single marine park with public marinas, a seawall, a bird sanctuary and a rowing course. He proposed dredging the basin and making it safe for swimming by rerouting its many sewage outfalls. In the early 1970s the city embarked on a more modest version of Malkin's vision. False Creek's seawall, constructed between 1973 and 1988, gave the city a seaside promenade stretching over 25 kilometres. New marinas, parks and residential developments replaced old industries, though water quality remained a problem and the city still advised against "unnecessary" contact with it.[36]

Perhaps the biggest change during the post-war era was the rising tensions that such tremendous growth in recreation had created. Industries in particular found themselves increasingly at odds with those using the inland sea for pleasure. By the early 1970s, the Strait was being described as a "veritable Pandora's box of diversified recreational opportunity."[37] Yet again, conflicting visions and people's fears of losing "their" Strait were surfacing.

Recreation and conflicts on the water

Recreational boating (see photographs page 226 and page 228) grew very rapidly after World War II. In 1949, for example, the Vancouver Parks Board reported receipts of $4,394.75 from the rental of 564 rowboats and 2,838 dories powered by inboard motors—over three times the earnings in 1945. Another 300 inboard-powered dories were available for rent on the North Shore, where 500 more were privately owned. The introduction of these small inboard-powered boats was leading to rapid growth in the rental business. The North Shore Boat Rental Association boasted in 1948 that its members were giving "the average working man a chance to fish at a cost which is not prohibitive." At the same time, it complained of Ottawa's attempts to impose new safety standards on these "glorified rowboats," most of which were around 4 metres long and powered by a motor under 2 horsepower with a maximum speed of 8 kilometres per hour. As long as renters heeded warnings to avoid the dangerous tidal rips at First Narrows on Burrard Inlet, they were generally okay. Three boaters didn't and drowned there in 1948.[38]

Vancouver Harbour in 1953: The rapid expansion of the Strait's pleasure craft fleet had begun, and docking facilities close to the city would soon be at a premium.

Image I-27914 courtesy of the Royal BC Museum and Archives.

By 1966, an estimated 72,000 pleasure craft were operating around the Strait, more than 50,000 of them in Greater Vancouver. Overall numbers were projected to increase to over 100,000 by 1976. A later survey estimated that the number had reached 88,000 in 1973, which suggested the earlier projection was accurate. The same study found that 17.4 percent of households around the Strait owned one or more pleasure boats, though numbers varied greatly among communities, with the lowest rates of ownership in Vancouver and Victoria and the highest on the Mainland north of Howe Sound (see Table 8, page 227).

Table 8: Household ownership of recreational boats around the Strait, 1973[39]

Community	Percentage of households with one or more pleasure boats, 1973
Greater Vancouver (excluding Delta, Surrey, White Rock)	12.5
Victoria	17.1
Powell River area (including Texada, Lasqueti, Harwood and Savary Islands)	45.1
Sechelt area	41.5
Gibsons area	40.2
Campbell River region (including Quadra Island)	40.7
Comox Valley (including Denman and Hornby Islands)	36.3
Parksville	32.8
Ladysmith	31.3
Duncan–Gulf Islands	32.4
Average in all communities surveyed on the Strait	17.4

As the fleet of small craft grew, the proportion of motorised craft also increased. In 1966, a little over 60 percent of these boats were powered by inboard or outboard motors, about 6 percent by sail and the rest—about a third—by either oar or paddle. Another survey seven years later found that powerboats had risen to over 70 percent, sailboats to 10 percent, and human-powered craft accounted for less than 20 percent of the fleet. People indicated they would continue shifting to gas- or diesel-powered craft; over 90 percent of the boats they planned to buy that year would be motorised.

Also growing rapidly was the number of larger pleasure craft requiring a "wet berth" and moorage space. The sheltered waters of English Bay, Burrard Inlet and Saanich Inlet were the most popular boating sites, and all saw big increases in the facilities offered at adjacent marinas throughout these decades. In 1971 an estimated 13,000 small-craft berths were available around the Strait, most near Vancouver and Victoria. Projections by the mid-1970s suggested that 7,000 more berths would be needed by 1980 around Vancouver alone. Ottawa responded with plans to reduce commercial fishing wharves and other shore facilities in False Creek in order to add hundreds of new berths for pleasure craft to the 1,700 that already existed in the

The annual bathtub race across the Strait, seen here in 1969, its first year, was invented by Frank Ney (front left), a swashbuckling Nanaimo politician. Ney also developed Hornby Island's Galleon Beach subdivision.

Image I-21965 courtesy of the Royal BC Museum and Archives.

basin. The province, once again more ambivalent about marine issues, reserved a few patches of shoreline for small-boat moorage. By the 1970s, though, Victoria was developing a network of provincial marine parks largely for the use of boaters. Yacht clubs on the Strait, meanwhile, offered their members urban docks as well as safe moorage at a growing network of outstations around the inland sea. The boom in boating would continue into the 1980s, though it would not grow at the rate projected earlier.

Many of the new boats carried sport fishermen, as interest in saltwater angling on the Strait also grew dramatically. Haig-Brown vigorously promoted this expanding sport fishery, declaring it an important component of the tourist industry and defending its claim to a greater share of the Strait's salmon. He confirmed, "A lot of people want to spend money on going fishing," adding, "It represents a consumer's choice and a consumer's demand...with the additional advantage that it also contributes to the physical health, the mental well-being and the spiritual character of the nation."[40] In 1969 Haig-Brown announced that the Strait's sport fishery was probably the most valuable in the world, though he was short on hard numbers. Geographer Mary Barker estimated in a 1974 report for the federal government that Canadian sport fishers on the Strait were now spending 800,000 "recreation days" (a recreation day being one day spent on a recreational activity by one individual) to land over 750,000 Coho, Chinook and Pink salmon each year.

Recreation and conflicts on private and public lands

The network of children's summer camps that had earlier been concentrated around Howe Sound expanded after the wars, spreading along the Sechelt Peninsula in particular. In *Sunshine Coast*, Howard White would later describe the peninsula as "infested with summer camps" run by a range of NGOs, including the Boy Scouts, the Girl Guides "and every church in the phone book." Similarly, recreational cottaging boomed after World War II, mostly north of Vancouver and in the southern islands, as people around Vancouver and Victoria especially sought to get out of the city. Even the province's long-serving leader, W.A.C. Bennett, had a getaway on Saltspring Island by the 1960s.

By the mid-1970s, soaring prices reflected strong demand for shoreline recreational property around the Strait. In some places, like Tsawwassen and Departure Bay, recreational properties were replaced by suburbs and permanent homes. On islands near cities, including Bowen, Gabriola and Saltspring, the distinction between suburb and recreational property became fuzzier as ferry services improved. In 1963 an innovative developer even began running full-page ads in Calgary and Edmonton newspapers offering to reimburse the airfare of people who bought at least one cottage property on North Pender Island. Summer camps and cottages remained popular escapes into the 1980s, when recreational land prices slowed their vertiginous rise. Although many islanders now depended on the influx of "summer people" to keep the local economy afloat, many were also happy to see them leave at the end of August.

Promises of mild weather, a relaxed lifestyle and healthful recreation attracted growing numbers not just to visit but to live on the post-war Strait. On what writer Frederick Marsh christened the Leisure Islands of the southern Strait, people sought simpler lives surrounded by beauty and supported by art-loving communities that tolerated eccentricity. Except for a few tiny Indian reserves, these were very white communities. As Marsh described in the late 1940s, they were places for "the carpenter with tools and a little money, the small farmer, the amateur gardener, the fisherman, the business man with stomach ulcers, the pensioner, the lover of earth and sea who had found a distraught world too much for him." It was, he said, "an earthly heaven entirely surrounded by sea" where "a man and his family can be close to all that grows and walks and swims and flies." A Saltspring Islander explained to Marsh, "Most of us here believe there is still such a thing as an art of living…people need to relax, to stand off and look at themselves too. What is life without fun?"[41]

Many island forests and farmsteads were already being subdivided for sale by the end of the 1940s, mostly as retirement or recreational properties. This subdividing had become controversial by the 1960s, yet throughout these decades the southern islands retained much of their idyllic, sometimes sybaritic character. They remained a destination for seekers of a "better lifestyle"—for a few days or a few years or the rest of their lives—and provided the freedom to pursue interests outside the mainstream. Many writers and journalists, from Jean Howarth and David Conover to Bill Deverell, Audrey Thomas, Jane Rule and Bill Richardson, took up residence and explored the quirky, unconventional personalities of their islands.

Islands farther north—a little wetter, colder and more isolated—were still more sparsely populated in the first post-war decades and more devoted to the Strait's resource industries. They also began to change dramatically in the 1960s and '70s as they too became destinations for the escapees, artists and retirees already common in the southern islands. They were joined by a new wave of back-to-the-landers, urban middle-class young people in search of alternative lifestyles, whose influx signalled a cultural revolution on a number of islands until then mostly home to farmers,

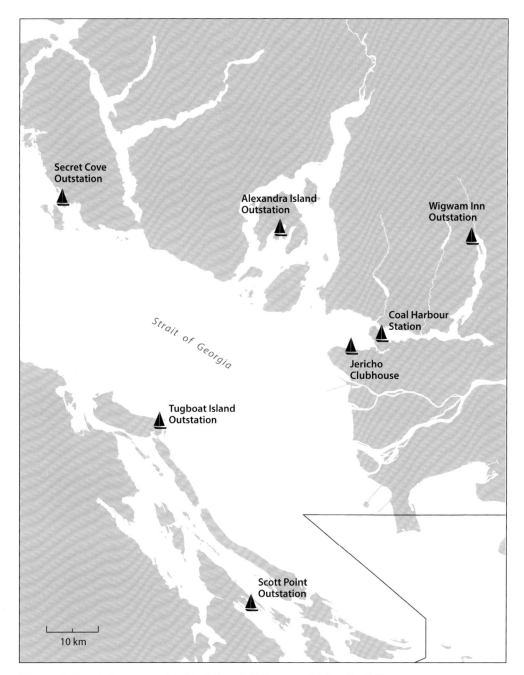

Figure 13: Royal Vancouver Yacht Club outstations on the Strait, 1985.

loggers and fishermen—aging settlers who planned to finance their retirement by subdividing family lands. Writer Des Kennedy described the newcomers arriving on Denman Island, which had a population of around 250 in the 1970s: "We were a pretty bizarre looking bunch...The men had wild hair and big beards and they arrived en masse, in the span of a few years." Up until that point, he noted, "There was nobody like that here and then all of a sudden there were several hundred of us."[42]

Kennedy and others questioned the way Denman's old-timers did things. Writing in the newcomers' "alternative newspaper" after a discussion about the role of tree worship in ancient belief systems, he wondered: "Do we need to cut all those trees down? Do our roads always need to be wider and wider? Do we have to batter and push and slash at everything living around us until we've destroyed it all? Perhaps no tree-spirit will descend and smite us for needlessly destroying living things; but if we destroy the tree of life, the tree of the knowledge of good and evil, then we shall have destroyed the chance of ever becoming any better than we are now; and that, perhaps, is the worst punishment of all."[43] To the newly arrived, swimming nude and smoking marijuana were exalted expressions of freedom, whereas the old-timers' practices—cutting down trees, hunting the plentiful island deer and speculating on real estate—were misguided acts that were hurting the planet and perpetuating economic greed.

These differences between old-timers and newcomers, and contentious issues such as limits on the subdivision of land, were more factious on some islands than others. Read, Lasqueti and other more isolated islands were often more open to newcomers than those closer to mainstream society, such as Quadra, Denman and Texada. In 1974, some issues appeared at least partially resolved when the Islands Trust was established with a mandate to protect the islands' natural beauty and bucolic lifestyle (see Islands Trust section page 244). This federation of island planning authorities encompassed most of the larger southern islands. It extended no farther north than Denman and Hornby, yet even big northern islands like Texada, Quadra and Cortes, outside the ambit of the Trust, were increasingly recognised for their unique lifestyles.

The islands' invasion by back-to-the-landers was part of an established tradition of people seeking new lives—restoration or re-creation on the Strait. Broken men fleeing the killing fields had sought out isolated bays and islands to retreat to and heal after both world wars. Others sought escape and restoration in religious colonies and organised spiritual retreats more reputable than Brother XII's experiment. The Cold Mountain Institute on Cortes Island, reincarnated later as the Hollyhock Retreat, specialised in restoring short-term visitors with Gestalt therapy.

The rapid expansion of tourism

After World War II, building on foundations established before 1945, the province had begun to view tourism as a key sector, a means of "economic diversification" that created jobs, generated government revenues and drove development on a par with the Strait's resource industries. And the decline of those industries seemed to be looming. The BC Government Tourist Bureau ranked tourism one of the province's key industries as early as 1950, and by the early 1970s, it had become the province's third-largest source of revenue. Tourists, most of them from the western US and Canada's prairies, had become valuable commodities whose spending was vigorously stimulated and carefully monitored by the province.

Victoria recognised that tourism on Vancouver Island, on the islands in the Strait, and on the Mainland north of Howe Sound all depended overwhelmingly upon tourists travelling in cars, which needed ferries. The province was increasingly committed to improving car ferry services (chapter 1) but it faced a dilemma: the need for infrastructure to move and accommodate these tourists came in summer, when ferries, tourist lodgings and campgrounds were typically overtaxed. Most were then chronically underused during the other nine months of the year. A study for the province's inter-ministerial Environment and Land Use Committee in the mid-

1970s recommended promoting tourism that didn't require automobiles, noting that the 20 percent of out-of-province tourists who travelled without cars typically spent almost three times more money than the average tourist.[44] Yet this was an era when car dealers were prominent in most provincial governments and the idea of promoting tourism without cars was not vigorously pursued, while car ferry service would continue to expand to meet the growing demand.

As early as the 1950s, Haig-Brown had called on the province to make sure the recreational needs of local populations would continue to come first, despite the heady growth of tourism. Already communities had been debating the role that tourism should play, how to encourage it and what kinds of tourism to encourage. Parksville and Qualicum became an interesting contrast in these years. Both towns were recreational destinations and neither had strong resource industries compared with neighbouring towns. After the 1950s, despite the continued importance of the tourist industry, Qualicum didn't seek visitors as aggressively as Parksville did. Parksville's stock of hotel and motel rooms grew by almost 150 percent between 1959 and 1988 whereas Qualicum's declined by over 10 percent. Qualicum increasingly shifted its focus to meeting the needs of incoming retirees—by 1982, most of the population was full-time residents, almost half of them over 55 years old—rather than the seasonal peak demands of tourists (see Table 9, page 232). Yet Parksville also attracted growing numbers of retired newcomers, and both towns would continue to grow during the challenging years of the 1980s.

Table 9: Tourist accommodation units in Parksville and Qualicum, 1957–88[45]

Year	Parksville	Qualicum
1957–58	136	296
1959–60	188	325
1967–68	186	245
1969–70	192	230
1977–78	326	304
1979–80	335	264
1985–86	397	304
1987–88	354	258

Local needs sometimes had to come second in order to meet the demands of paying guests, but the situation on the Strait was hardly unique. By the 1970s authorities in a growing number of wealthy coastal regions with booming tourist industries, such as those along the north shore of the Mediterranean, were struggling to mediate among the competing demands of tourists, seasonal homeowners and full-time residents along their shorelines.

A growing network of parks

Rapid post-war growth in demand for recreational space encouraged provincial, municipal and federal authorities to expand their park systems around the Strait.

Although Miracle Beach, seen here in 1955, was earlier rejected as a national park, local pressure caused it to become a provincial park in 1950.
Image I-29967 courtesy of the Royal BC Museum and Archives.

The province was the largest player, though not a particularly enthusiastic one before the 1960s. By then, options for creating new parks by the sea were much diminished by the soaring price of land. When Haig-Brown described the 1950s and early '60s as "a bad time...an open season on parks," he was mostly referring to provincial parks. These, he said, had lost "much good ground...both literally and figuratively, in spite of the protests of those who saw and understood the steadily increasing recreational needs."[46] The provincial park system as a whole had acquired over 44,000 square kilometres of land between 1911 and 1948 but then shrank significantly to about 25,000 square kilometres by 1961 because the interests of resource industries—particularly forestry and mining—were usually put ahead of the park system. At the time, the concept of parks as instruments for wilderness preservation was devalued, while parks close to population centres were more likely to be recognised as valuable economic assets. Attendance at provincial parks, meanwhile, increased from a little over 100,000 visits in 1948 to an estimated 3.5 million visits in 1960.

The province's cavalier treatment of Strathcona Park in the late 1940s and '50s and Haig-Brown's unsuccessful struggle to protect it had marked his coming out as a budding environmentalist and strident critic of the Social Credit government's policies on industrial development and protected area management. In what Haig-Brown described as "industrial vandalism," the British Columbia Power Commission had "sacrificed" part of the park to "supply cheap electricity to pulp mills—power whose cheapness has been handsomely subsidized by reckless disregard for the recreational and other uses of the watershed." The dam built across the Campbell River between Upper Campbell Lake and the sea was part of a hydroelectric project and, according to Haig-Brown, "a simple matter of selfish, short-sighted and badly planned resource use, an incompetent decision based on totally inadequate information, tolerated by a public that has been deliberately misled."[47] When a new Ministry of Recreation and Conservation was created in 1957, partly in response to Haig-Brown's vociferous criticism, it assessed potential park sites around the sea in terms of their ability to cope with the expected increases in ferry- and highway-borne visitors and the demands of boaters.

In the early years after World War II, there was growing concern that most citizens were being excluded from seashore recreation as more and more waterfront land fell into private hands. The province's Social Credit government favoured slow and cautious expansion of shoreline parks—especially small parks near towns (like Miracle Beach Provincial Park, see photograph page 233) and those acquired as gifts. Fillongley Provincial Park opened on the east side of Denman Island in 1954 on land bequeathed to the province by its settler owner, George Beadnell. Similar parks opened near Heriot Bay on Quadra Island in the 1950s and on Hornby (Helliwell Park) in the '60s, following the deaths of their previous owners. Farther south, the province presented Portland Island to England's Princess Margaret in the 1950s to commemorate her visit and then lobbied to get it back; it was returned and gazetted as Princess Margaret Provincial Park in 1967. The Parks Branch established another shoreline park on Quadra Island's Waiatt Bay (Octopus Islands Marine Park) in 1974 through a more complicated deal that saw Robert Filberg, owner of the Comox Valley Logging and Railway Company, cede almost 2.5 kilometres of waterfront in exchange for land on adjacent Read Island.

Earlier warnings to expand the park system while land was still relatively affordable had been ignored, so provincial authorities were obliged to trade or beg for waterfront property. Their parkland acquisition budgets were tiny compared to the soaring costs of this land. Unless people could be found to donate land, park establishment was slow and unsteady because most desirable sites around the Strait were unaffordable. Speculators, meanwhile, looked repeatedly to the government to acquire waterfront properties they couldn't sell; the province was often interested and monitored different pieces of shoreline around the Strait for years but seldom had the resources to acquire them. The province spent years in the late 1960s and into the '70s, for example, trying to engineer a complicated deal to secure waterfront parkland north of Heriot Bay. Government officials approached private owners in the US and Toronto, as well as the provincial Ministry of Forests. The Toronto owner, a prominent banker, eventually agreed to trade for land elsewhere. The Ministry of Forests was willing to trade, but only for choice forest land inside Strathcona Park. The Americans, based in Oregon and Idaho, declined. They were skeptical of the province's ability to offer them equivalent properties elsewhere, insisting they had spent a long time finding this ideal Quadra Island waterfront. Eventually the Parks Branch decided the area, though perfect for a park, was more trouble than it was worth. A 1965 attempt to secure Pym Island near Sidney by petitioning its owner, Seattle aviation magnate William Boeing, was equally unsuccessful.

Meanwhile local landowners, appealing to the rising anti-American sentiment of the time, desperately lobbied the province's Parks Branch to buy waterfront land to prevent it from falling into the hands of "rich Americans." By the 1970s, this narrative of wealthy Americans buying up the best shoreline and cutting off local access to the sea was widespread and clearly a concern for at least some officials in Victoria. Whether American-owned or not, affordable waterfront land *was* increasingly hard to come by. A 1970 study determined that the price of shoreline property in the southern islands had increased by 300 percent between 1950 and 1970. Only about 10 kilometres, or 3 percent, of that shoreline land was still publicly owned in some form; most of the rest was privately owned recreational property.

Many local governments also campaigned for the province to open new parks in their areas, as these public recreational lands had come to be considered important economic assets. The Powell River Chamber of Commerce, for example, lobbied the province in 1967 for a provincial park on Hernando Island. Powell River's business community was concerned about rumours that the island's aristocratic German owners might be preparing to subdivide and sell off the island. In their proposal to Victoria, the merchants signalled their disapproval of the kind of "commercial development" that had taken place on nearby Savary Island. Yet their vision for a park on Hernando sounded like a high-latitude Club Med. The island, they claimed, had "unlimited potential for development over the next century for all kinds of recreation, served by both sea and air traffic. Sandy beaches second to none in the Province surround much of the island and sheltered anchorages make public marine development ideal. As a Provincial Holiday Resort, developed over the years, one can easily envisage camping areas, golf courses and other recreational facilities, tourist accommodation of all kinds, an aerodrome, ferry connection(s) and many other attractions." The province pleaded that it was unable to consider the proposal because of previous commitments to acquire bits of land at Porpoise Bay, Smuggler Cove and Pender Harbour on the Lower Sunshine Coast that would consume all available funds.[48] By 1964, Victoria had shifted its criteria for selecting new park land, embracing the concept of "nature conservancy zones" to preserve areas representative of the province's "bio-geo-climatic zones" rather than assessing parks from a strictly economic perspective.

When Premier Bennett appointed Kenneth Kiernan his new Minister of Recreation and Conservation in 1963, one of Kiernan's first initiatives was to open previously protected parks to mining and logging. Haig-Brown was not impressed; while doing "substantial damage" to the park system, said Haig-Brown, the new minister was making no improvements to its management, opting instead to make "aggressive use of his department…as an advertising agency to attract more and more tourists to less and less value." Even Haig-Brown had to concede, however, that the province had responded to growing public pressure by establishing many smaller, "strategically placed" seaside parks, camping and picnicking grounds around the Strait of Georgia by the late 1960s.[49] By 1974, through a combination of donations, complicated trades and outright purchase of small parcels, the province had gazetted a total of thirty shoreline parks around the inland sea.

One of the province's most important recreation initiatives on the Strait in the 1960s and '70s was a new system of marine parks catering primarily to recreational boaters. The first marine park was established in 1959 at Montague Harbour on Galiano Island, and another in 1961 when Nanaimo ceded Newcastle Island to the province. By the late 1960s, Victoria committed to systematically developing a chain of marine parks to meet the needs of an estimated 75,000 Canadian and 10,000 American pleasure craft then plying the Strait in summer. As with the Strait's terrestrial parks, the lack of suitable shoreline in the public domain and the prohibitively high cost of acquiring private land made establishing new marine parks difficult. Yet by 1973 the province had established a dozen marine parks around the Strait and was proposing five more (see Figure 14, page 237).

Through the rest of the 1970s and into the '80s provincial authorities continued to spend much time looking on, frustrated, as attractive prospective park sites around the Strait became increasingly unaffordable. They did consummate a few plans for marine parks in places such as Desolation Sound, Jervis Inlet and Indian Arm, where land prices were less inflated due to a lack of road access. Acquisition of the land, however, was seldom rapid. The need to establish one or more marine parks in Indian Arm was identified as an "urgent priority" for the province in 1974. The tiny Twin Islands and nearby Raccoon Island were gazetted as provincial marine parks seven years later.

The chronic inability to acquire land was not the only problem related to under-funding. An ongoing shortage of resources meant that many parks were managed less well than their neighbours expected. To many, it looked as though Victoria had put the cart before the horse, adding numerous parks to its system and improving road and ferry services to them before it had the capacity to manage them. Discontent spilled over on Saltspring Island in 1967, when local residents discovered a new provincial campsite at Beddis Bay and complained to Minister Kiernan that "their" beloved beach had been changed from "amateur to professional status" and was attracting unwanted visitors. They suggested the province post a sign at the site: "No hippies, no harpies, no boat launchers—and particularly, no sharpies."[50] Others worried about fires and vandalism in the province's recently acquired and undeveloped parks, particularly on the islands. In the early 1970s, a new ferry connection and several new parks were attracting growing crowds to Cortes Island, where locals began to complain that they felt like "bears in cages," to be viewed by visitors passing through.[51]

An aging couple on Hornby Island who identified as socialists began to negotiate a deal with Victoria's new social democratic government after 1972. They aimed to live out their lives on 7 of their 17 waterfront acres, giving the rest to the province for a park. The deal fell through when the prospective donors backed out. The couple had spent a summer camping on their beach, where they had witnessed the devastation wrought by members of the public who dumped garbage, carved their names into petroglyphs and carted away sea anemones. Victoria assured the couple that if their land became a park, then the Parks Branch could help with posters and other "public education" but admitted it wasn't able to exercise any real control, even in other parkland it had already acquired on Hornby.

Many of the Strait's cities and towns established their own waterfront parks in the first few decades after World War II. In the 1960s and '70s Vancouver embarked on an ambitious program of shoreline park expansion, partly in response to a mid-1960s study that suggested public beach frontage in Greater Vancouver (see photograph page 239) had fallen from 100 feet per thousand people in 1941 to 70 feet per thousand in 1965 and might be in precipitous decline. The authors recommended a target of 88 feet per thousand people, which would require 20 more miles of public waterfront. In response, Vancouver acquired or developed new parkland at Jericho, Locarno and Spanish Banks Beaches and Vanier and New Brighton Parks by 1980. This acquisition of new shoreline recreation space would later slow to a crawl as land prices climbed in the latter decades of the century, but the city improved citizens' access to the shore in other ways. The 10-kilometre seaside promenade around Stanley Park was finally completed in 1980. In 1985 the city established Fraser River Park, its first park on the Lower Fraser, and then its first municipal marina, on former

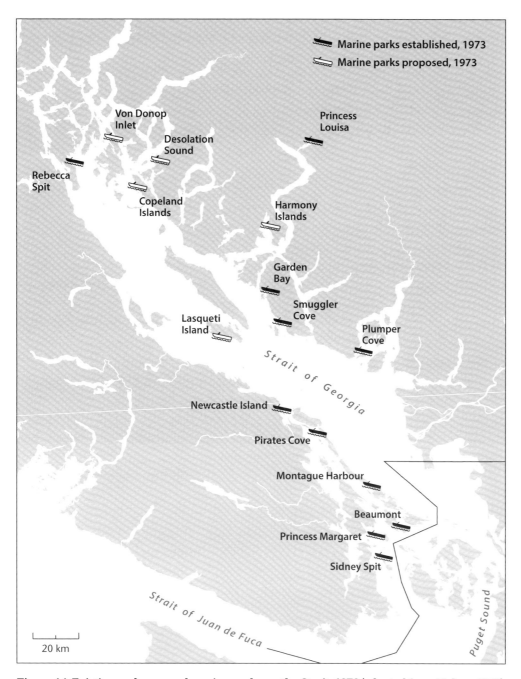

Figure 14: Existing and proposed marine parks on the Strait, 1973 (adapted from Nelson 1973).

Kitsilano Indian Reserve land at the mouth of False Creek, in 1988. Elsewhere, Hamilton Mack Laing bequeathed his 2-hectare property on Comox Harbour for the creation of a municipal park in the early 1980s.

The only level of government not involved in creating parks around the Strait was the one in Ottawa. After rejecting the idea of a national park on the Strait in the 1930s, the federal government was open to the idea again by the late 1960s, though it recognised the process would be complicated. Jean Chrétien, then minister of Indian Affairs and Northern Development, was interested in a federal park on Hernando Island but reminded local proponents that any land would have to be acquired by the province and then transferred to federal jurisdiction. A lively controversy broke out on the southern Strait a couple of years later when David Anderson, Liberal MP for Esquimalt–Saanich, began to talk of a land trust on the southern Strait. Anderson explained the idea to a constituent in early 1971:

> The suggestion regarding preserving the large [and largely uninhabited] tracts of land and the as yet unbuilt-up coastline is very sound. There is absolutely no need…to turn the islands into a park in the traditional sense…no need to remove houses and cottages and try to turn the islands back to what they were before settlement began. What is needed is to preserve the character of the islands, not only for the present residents but for the inevitable influx of visitors and residents who will be going to the area in the years to come…a private non-profit body to be known as the Coastal Trust or some such name to administer, to acquire land by gift or purchase…[T]he time has come to think about present trends and where they are leading us…more and more Americans are turning to Canada for land. We know this will increase, particularly when their Islands Trust is established (in the adjacent San Juan Islands)…we can expect the number of boats to double every seven years.[52]

Anderson was *not* talking about a national park, and the province would go on to form the Islands Trust (see below) several years later, which in many ways resembled the model he had in mind. Nonetheless Anderson *was* a federal politician, and initially his suggestion was widely perceived as a hint that Ottawa was about to launch a vast expropriation of private lands across the southern islands. Many reacted badly to the rumour. Tommy Douglas, former head of the federal NDP, was drawn into the debate to defend the private property rights of constituents in his Nanaimo–Cowichan–The Islands riding against the spectre of a federal takeover of their island properties. Those who read Anderson's proposal carefully mostly agreed with his ideas about the need for some kind of "trust." But fears of a park persisted. An editorial in Saltspring Island's *Driftwood* newspaper at the end of 1971 declared:

> Mr. David Anderson…has made a remarkable proposal for the establishment of a national park…The operator of a business is well aware that the implementation of the Anderson plan will leave him penniless and without recourse to a court of law. A number of property owners are reported to have already abandoned plans for home construction here for fear of losing their homes after working on them and spending their life savings…As a park devoid of people, devoid of homes, populated by tent dwelling refugees from Esquimalt–Saanich [Anderson's riding], without ferries, accessible largely to the wealthier elements of United States coastal cruising traffic, the Gulf Islands would yet be a scenic wonderland, though reserved for the wealthy and the eccentric.[53]

Buzz Brown, a retired provincial tax assessor turned director of Salt Spring Lands Ltd., dismissed claims by Anderson and others about the threat of foreign takeover, estimating that at most 5 percent of Gulf Island properties were held by Americans. On Saturna, the island closest to the US, Americans owned only 31 out of 410 properties. On North Pender, then the focus of the most intense real-estate development on the southern islands, Americans held barely 2 percent of the almost 1,900 properties. The real problem, said Brown, was people trying to protect the southern islands as an "exclusive and undeveloped reserve" for people from Greater Vancouver and Victoria.[54]

Vancouver's English Bay beach in 1947: Its recreation value would drive much of the local debate about marine sewage pollution over the next four decades.

Image I-27944 courtesy of the Royal BC Museum and Archives.

Jack Davis, then federal Minister of Fisheries and Forestry, tried to reassure voters that Anderson, his fellow Liberal, did *not* intend to turn the islands into a national park. Davis reminded them, as Chrétien had, that any national park would depend on the province acquiring the land and handing it over to Ottawa, adding, "Can you really imagine Premier Bennett doing this in the 1970s?" Davis, though, was enthusiastic about converting stretches of the sea around the islands into a national underwater or marine park. "All land below the low water mark," he pointed out, "already belongs to the people of Canada and so it is not a question of expropriation… or of transfer of provincial land to the Federal Government."[55]

Davis pursued this idea of a federal marine park as vigorously as he had his earlier initiatives. Many areas on the Strait, he said, had become more valuable for achieving "social" goals than economic ones and needed to be preserved for their aesthetic qualities and "peculiar" ecological character. In 1971 he appointed a task force to study the feasibility of a marine park, proposing to link it with a marine "water quality management area." After Jacques Cousteau endorsed the idea of an underwater marine park on the Strait the same year, the task force declared that the waters around Gabriola Reef, Plumper Sound and Victoria's Race Rocks all met the standard for a national marine park. Haig-Brown commended this "bold idea" of a Strait of Georgia national marine park, marvelling that a concept that "could scarcely have been seriously considered a few years ago" was now almost certain to become a reality.[56]

The province, though, responded to the idea of a federal marine park in the Strait with the familiar mix of truculence and paranoia so often seen in its relations with

Ottawa. Provincial authorities were particularly sensitive about federal initiatives aimed at stopping oil drilling and reducing marine pollution on the inland sea. From Victoria's perspective, Ottawa's proposals ignored the province's progress in developing its own system of marine parks and improving its Pollution Control Board. The feds, said the provincial government, were failing once again to demonstrate what Victoria considered the required "knowledge or sensitivity on just how province and federal must work together" and choosing instead to flex their muscles and exclude the province from important consultations.

Senior officials in Victoria worried that the public awareness generated by pronouncements from Davis and others threatened to make the province look bad. A better strategy, Kiernan's office suggested in 1971, would be "to upstage the federal proposal" by calling instead for the creation of an International Quality Marine Management Region. This region would encompass all of the islands and the adjacent shores of both the Strait of Georgia and Puget Sound, under the guidance of an international commission. Such an approach would help refocus federal attention on issues for which its mandate was more clearly defined and hopefully put an end to its meddling in the province's inland sea. Apparently the strategy worked: the US National Park Service and Parks Canada jointly developed a plan for an international marine park the following year. The project was vast and complicated and went nowhere.[57]

A decade later in 1983, the federal Minister of the Environment and the provincial Minister of Lands, Parks and Housing both responded to a Nanaimo citizen inquiring about the status of plans for a Gulf Island marine park. Ottawa indicated that federal-provincial plans were progressing, with new policies proposed for identification, selection and management of protected areas and new discussions on these policies scheduled for a few months from then. When Victoria replied to the same inquiry a month later, it made no reference to any such federal-provincial discussions. Instead, the province emphasised its own extensive marine park system and plans to continue improving it. BC, wrote Victoria, had "no current plans for such a national marine park."[58]

Clashes between recreation users and other stakeholders on the Strait

The increasing ease of movement around the Strait by sea and land improved access to recreational opportunities while threatening to diminish them in other ways. As ferry terminals grew bigger, especially on the major routes between Vancouver and Vancouver Island, conflicts increased. Most wharves and marinas near the Strait's larger settlements suffered from growing congestion, but this situation was most acute where pleasure boats shared harbour space not only with commercial fishing boats but with ever-larger ferries arriving and departing all day long. By the mid-1970s, collisions between ferries and smaller craft had come to be expected every summer around the busy Horseshoe Bay terminal. The provincial ferry fleet was also blamed for degrading recreational values by delivering too many visitors to places that could earlier be reached by only a few. An irate Saltspring Islander complained to the Minister of Recreation and Conservation in late 1967: "I suppose it can be partly blamed on summer TV commercials…sponsored by our own Government… which say, more or less, — 'Want to enjoy an old fashioned picnic? Then why not go to the Gulf Islands by Ferry for a picnic'; …AND THEY ALL END UP ON OUR BEACH! Have you ever seen the size of the beach?"[59]

Comparable struggles arose between proponents of more efficient road networks and opponents who strove, among other things, to protect valued recreational land along the shore. A plan tabled in the early 1960s in Vancouver called for an eight-lane highway along the beach at English Bay, from Prospect Point to the Burrard Bridge. Later in the decade a proposed second crossing of the First Narrows called for a bridge landing at Brockton Point and a highway along the shore of Coal Harbour connecting it to the city. Both were successfully resisted, as proposals in the 1950s and '60s to establish a small-aircraft runway on the beach at Spanish Banks had been. A similar attempt in the Comox Valley to convert recreational beach into a commercial landing strip was successfully blocked two decades later.

Much shoreline recreation inevitably took place on sites that were earlier used by Indigenous people, whose lives had mostly been lived by the shore. The provincial and municipal parks proliferating at various shoreline sites often contributed to the degradation of Indigenous heritage resources in these places. The City of Vancouver, for example, had long sought control over land still officially owned by the Squamish band at Kitsilano Point and finally absorbed it into its growing shoreline park system in 1967, when the federal government granted Vancouver a 99-year lease there for a dollar a year. The province's first marine park was on Montague Harbour, a sheltered bay on Galiano Island popular with recreational sailors that was also the site of a half-dozen clamshell middens built up over thousands of years of Indigenous occupation. Sandy Island Marine Park at the northern entrance to Baynes Sound was established in 1966 on territory claimed by the nearby Comox people and three other Indigenous groups. The Comox maintained that, before they were suddenly pre-empted in the late nineteenth century, the island and its foreshore had been used for centuries for shellfish harvesting, hunting and ceremonies. A park master plan prepared in 1987 called for protection of any remaining "archaeological resources" from further disruption, though by then few artifacts were left.

The same was true of much Indigenous heritage at other shoreline sites around the Strait. In the mid-1970s a survey by the Provincial Archaeologist of eight hundred known archaeological sites around the islands of the southern Strait and Howe Sound found under 10 percent of them still intact. Most had been disturbed after the 1870s, while the worst damage was caused by the construction of permanent and summer homes. Ferry landings, wharves and marinas had also taken a great toll.

Clashes between recreation and the Strait's resource industries became more frequent after 1945 not only because of the rapid growth in marine recreation but also because the recreation and tourism sector gained clout as an economic sector in its own right. Haig-Brown wrote in 1955 that the province's primary resource industries typically caricatured recreation advocates as "sentimental, unrealistic and anachronistic" and saw recreation resources as "inevitable sacrifices to progress." Although demands from "consumers of recreation" were becoming impossible to ignore after World War II, defenders of recreation values still had to fight, he said, because "the pressure of other resource users will always work against the sportsman." To successfully resist threats from pollution, encroachments into parks, loss of access to recreation space and "all the other dangers of increasing civilization," they would have to demonstrate the socio-economic and moral values of recreation.[60]

Cottagers who lived around Quadra Island's Gowlland Harbour eventually stopped the spread of log booms in "their bay" despite the powerful economic influence of the forestry industry (chapter 3). They were able to prove that small-boat owners and swimmers—recreationists—had equal, if not more important, socio-economic and moral value. Similar events were playing out elsewhere around the Strait by the 1960s. The established right of logging companies to use sheltered bays for log-boom storage was being undermined in many places by economic and moral arguments for recreation, not to mention the growing property value of recreational land along the shore.

Likewise, as mentioned earlier, recreational fishers were attracting growing support for their claims to a share of the Strait's dwindling catch of Coho and Chinook salmon, especially from provincial and local governments that sought to boost the economic returns from this sport fishery. Reduced numbers of salmon available for the tens of thousands of saltwater anglers around the Strait, though hard to quantify, could now be counted as real economic damage inflicted by reckless logging in coastal watersheds, commercial fishermen taking "more than their share" or hydro dams blocking access to spawning beds. When BC Hydro contemplated expanding its Comox Lake dam, Haig-Brown testified in 1962 to the "severe damage" that had been done to salmon runs downstream on the Puntledge River. Overall, he claimed, the Strait's sport salmon fishery was "one of the greatest on the continent" and the large Chinook bred on the Puntledge were "powerful advertising for the province." Tens of thousands of salmon were still being taken by the sport fishery around Comox each year and it could not afford further damage from ill-conceived dam expansion.[61]

By the late 1950s the Strait's sport fishers had a substantial claim on its salmon. Along the whole BC coast, commercial trollers—those who used hook and line instead of nets to catch fish for a living—were still taking six million salmon a year, around twenty times the number taken by recreational anglers. But in the Strait, sport fishers were taking fully a third of all salmon caught there by hook and line; both their share of these fish and the money they spent to catch them were expected to grow rapidly. Economists demonstrated that each of the several hundred thousand Coho or Spring salmon that anglers caught in the Strait every year generated far higher returns to the local economy per fish than those same fish hooked by commercial trollers or gillnetters. In Washington state, the sport salmon fishery was worth an estimated $70 million at the time versus only $20 million for the commercial fishery.

As the value of the sport fishery increased in the 1960s, so did pressure to manage the Strait's salmon in its interest. In 1969, Howe Sound was closed to all fishing except the sport fishing of salmon, and Haig-Brown suggested it might be time to take the same approach for the whole Strait. The Fraser River Sockeye run would still sustain a commercial fishery; those fish didn't often take an angler's lure anyway. But Coho and Chinook were by then so important to the sport fisheries in most major towns on both sides of the sea that Haig-Brown claimed they might simply be too valuable to leave to the commercial fleet. A report prepared for Victoria's Environment and Land Use Committee in 1975 supported his claim, indicating that closing the Strait to commercial fishing of Chinook and Coho salmon might not significantly reduce commercial fishermen's returns and could greatly enhance "recreational returns from the resource."[62]

However, federal authorities ensured that the commercial fisheries remained open for all salmon species on the Strait and, as predicted, competition between sport and commercial fishers grew more intense. Sport fishers began to call for "social justice," complaining that they received far less value for their licence fees than their commercial competitors and would still only be assigned a tiny portion—700,000 of 24 million—of the extra salmon predicted by the Salmonid Enhancement Program (chapter 4). Sport fishers didn't often contemplate the possibility that they might also be contributing significantly to the depletion of the Strait's Coho and Chinook stocks.

The idea that various types of pollution might be turning the inland sea—prized as a place for healthy recreation and restoration—into a dirty, unhealthy place was particularly galling for many shore dwellers in the post-war era. Around Vancouver especially, swimmers—or their parents—were at the forefront of growing public outrage over the expanding sewage stream flowing into False Creek, English Bay, Burrard Inlet and the Fraser mouth. Civil engineers designing improvements to Vancouver's sewage management infrastructure starting in the early 1950s had to figure out how to minimise this pollution of local beaches (chapter 5).

A new source of marine pollution that remained largely unresolved throughout this period was the waste discharged by boats operating on the Strait. Worries about human waste being discharged from pleasure craft were becoming common where these small boats congregated, especially in summer. Later, in 1984–85, the Islands Trust office in Victoria tried, unsuccessfully, to mobilise federal, provincial and City of Vancouver support for measures to improve the regulation of waste dumping from small craft. City health officials advised the mayor of Vancouver, Mike Harcourt, that while the Trust's concerns were laudable, the problem was far less serious than unresolved problems with land-based sewage discharges into the sea around Vancouver. For the Islands Trust, however, this sort of conflict among different forms of recreation was its reason for being.

Haig-Brown had warned that many other places in North America, including Ontario, New York and California, had "woken up" after World War II to find their outdoor recreation resources badly degraded, especially near the largest population centres, where they needed them the most. He insisted the solution to these challenges was long-term planning that recognised the public's right to outdoor recreation space. He expected that a provincial ministry devoted to recreation in general and parks in particular would fulfill this role, and he lobbied vigorously for it. But the careful husbandry of the province's recreational lands did not materialise in the way Haig-Brown had envisioned, and by the late 1960s he was thoroughly disillusioned. He believed that residents of BC and similarly wealthy places in the world were heading towards ever greater economic security and leisure time, and that they sought lives with high-quality outdoor recreational opportunities and a world where environmental damage was minimal. In the absence of the careful planning that Haig-Brown called for, threats to high-quality recreational opportunities and environmental quality on the Strait grew rapidly. Conflicts among tourists, residents, cottage owners, boaters and others, "all of whom want[ed] a piece of the beach pie,"[63] would not go away, he said, but they could be anticipated and managed. In the 1970s, an innovative and controversial response emerged.

The Islands Trust era

As Frederick Marsh moved around the Strait's southern islands in the late 1940s, taking careful note of the islands' inhabitants and their lifestyles, old settler families with large parcels of pre-empted land were already discussing plans to subdivide them. By then, the islands had grown distinct from most Mainland and Vancouver Island communities. Islanders shared a strong sense of their own uniqueness and their islands' value as refuges from the excesses of modern life. However, much of the island settlers' earlier work—logging, fishing, boat building, mining and quarrying—had become less viable after World War II. Farming continued, particularly production of specialty products such as seeds, bulbs and flowers. But service industries, mostly tourism and real-estate development, had become the largest economic sector on most of the larger islands south of Nanaimo by the late 1960s, and many residents had begun to worry about an erosion of island character resulting from rapid population growth.

In the early 1970s, in the wake of improved car ferry service and the subdivision of ever more old farms into small building lots, fear was widespread that the islands were destined to become crowded exurban wastelands with substandard services and no water. Three thousand new island lots were developed between 1959 and 1968— one-third of them on Saltspring alone. In 1969, Victoria announced a temporary freeze on further subdivision of island lands and decreed that all future lots would have to be at least 4 hectares in size. But local governments accepted another 1,900

applications for development *before* this freeze came into effect in 1970. Victoria subsequently came under considerable pressure from developers to end the freeze and from island residents to make it permanent.

One of the most disturbing new developments, for those who wished to preserve the islands' character, was the one built around North Pender Island's Dead Cow Swamp, which was renamed Magic Lake. The development, called Magic Lake Estates, was the largest in the Capital Regional District and one of the largest in the province: it consisted of 1,400 lots on 480 hectares, on an island with 700 full-time residents. Almost all the lots were sold in 1971, and the developers' optimistic public pronouncements about Magic Lake as the wave of the future confirmed many islanders' worst fears. James King, one of Magic Lake's principal owners, told the *Vancouver Sun* there was "no way they are going to hold the islands down—the population pressure is right there…I know a lot of people who, if there was a commuter [ferry] service put in, would live there now."[64] Another developer, Cy Porter, predicted in 1971 that Mayne Island's population would grow from 250 to 10,000 in the next five years and could well reach 50,000. He forecast 15,000 to 20,000 for North Pender.

Gabriola Islanders managed to block "speculators' plans" for a subdivision of 550 properties in 1972. A resident explained: "I am constantly aware of truth here…so close to the earth, and to the ocean, you are continually reminded about reality…Very often people who live in the plastic city dimly realise that they're missing out on reality

This tiny islet off Gabriola Island was now one of the 250 islands in the Strait included in the Islands Trust area.

David Nunuk photo

245

and so they go out trying to buy it. In places like this, where the land is unspoiled and the air is free. But they don't leave it the way they found it—they immediately begin cutting down trees and putting up supermarkets."[65] Gabriola Islanders had other reasons to oppose new developments. The water and sewerage systems serving the island's 1,000 residents (4,000 in summer) were already substandard and the impact of the threatened "instant suburbia" promised to be disastrous. Other islands, from Saltspring and Galiano to Bowen and Hornby, faced their own threats from rapid, unmanageable growth of summer and year-round populations.

The idea of special status for the islands was discussed—and widely misunderstood—as early as 1970. A committee of provincial legislators toured the islands in 1973 and expressed "distress and alarm" about the effects of speculation and poor planning. They declared the islands too important to the people of Canada for their fate to be left to developers and speculators; they recommended the creation of an Islands Trust—an approach adapted from the British model of land trust to oversee the land-use planning—and the new NDP government supported the idea. The Islands Trust Act of 1974 encompassed roughly 5,000 square kilometres; 250 islands accounted for 15 percent of this area and the rest was open water, including stretches of Howe Sound, Haro Strait and Baynes Sound. Most residents in the Trust area lived on thirteen of the largest islands (see Figure 15, page 247). Some larger, more populated islands with significant ongoing industrial activities or Indigenous populations, including Kuper (now Penelakut), Quadra, Cortes and Texada, were conspicuously absent from the initiative. Citizens on each of the largest Trust islands elected two trustees for four-year terms to oversee land-use planning, which was to be the Trust's principal tool in carrying out its mandate "to preserve and protect the islands' unique amenities and environment." Each island would otherwise remain subject to municipal, provincial and federal regulations.

Paradoxically, the Islands Trust was the product of an emotional crusade to protect the recreational value of the Strait's islands from the influx of too many urban refugees, yet the islands it was charged with looking after were to be protected for the benefit of the province as a whole, especially the growing urban populations nearby. In other words, to preserve the islands' unique character, neighbouring city dwellers would need to be made welcome but discouraged from visiting too frequently or staying too long. The situation was similar to the one that had created Stanley Park almost a century earlier. Then, proponents had seen the park as a necessary counterpoint to city growth; defenders of the Trust argued that the islands met a need for balance in harried urban lives. Unlike Stanley Park's original Indigenous residents, however, the islands' roughly 10,000 inhabitants would be allowed to remain and new residents to move there, albeit at a more modest pace than during the decade leading up to the Trust's creation.

Although Liberal MP David Anderson had earlier spoken of a trust based on the British model, Hilary Brown, the first head of the Islands Trust, also saw it following in the footsteps of innovative North American approaches. Its goal, as with similar initiatives in Ontario, California and New York, would be to reject the "premise of greed" that American ecologist Garrett Hardin declared was the cause of the "tragedy of the commons." Tragedy was bound to strike, Hardin said, when "common property" resources were degraded by populations that had grown too large to steward them

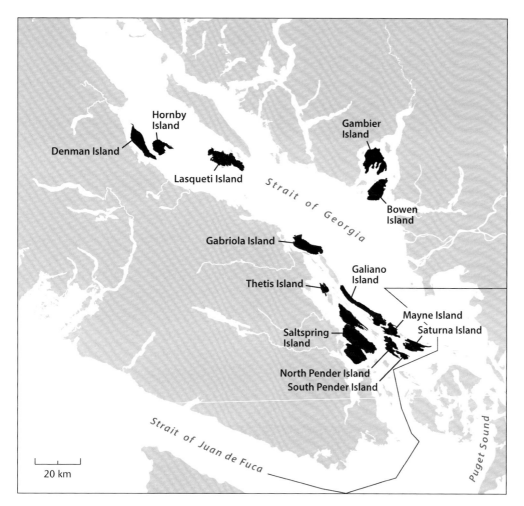

Figure 15: The large islands in the new Islands Trust, 1974.

effectively using their traditional approaches.[66] Hardin's ideas would later be hotly contested by more accomplished analysts such as Nobel Prize winner Elinor Ostrom, but his "tragedy of the commons" idea captured the public imagination and was widely invoked in the 1970s.

Under Hilary Brown from Hornby Island, the new Trust formulated an ambitious policy agenda. Its 1975 policy document explained the rationale behind the Islands Trust initiative, where it hoped to go and how it would get there. But to many the Trust still looked like a park by another name. The islands were described as "a resource of national importance but of finite size." The core objectives included "provision of a varied recreational opportunity and experience" and "retention of native flora and fauna and both unique and typical island scenery." And the document noted that further reserves would be created within the Trust area to protect the "most fragile ecosystems."

Furthermore, this initial policy statement used language that foreshadowed the 1990s debates about how to make development more "sustainable." It called for "patterns of land use which will allow needed and reasonable development in the present but which will...[allow future] generations [the] opportunity to make their own choices and decisions." One of the Trust's primary concerns would be the welfare of the island's existing and future populations, even as it ensured the islands developed in a way that was "in sympathy with the landscape and which makes the most of each site's natural characteristics."[67] Islands Trust policy overall promoted careful planning and zoning regulations that would allow local island communities rather than off-island development companies (which were presumed to be more susceptible to the "premise of greed") to determine the character of their communities. The Trust would "encourage types of development that will maintain the essentially rural nature of the islands."

As concern grew in the 1960s and early 1970s over the rate at which the relatively limited farmland around the sea was being developed for suburban and recreational building sites, Dave Barrett's NDP government was pushed to establish the Agricultural Land Reserve (ALR). To protect this agricultural land, areas designated as part of the ALR could not be readily converted to residential or other use. The Islands Trust also embraced the concept of the ALR not for reasons of food security but in pursuit of its goal of preserving the islands' rural character. It rushed to protect moribund island farms—to the dismay of many owners, who had hoped to cash in on the real-estate boom and secure their retirement. On the Trust islands, at least, farming had gone from being an instrument of Indigenous dispossession to a modest source of livelihood to a means of protecting "valued rural character," all in three or four generations.

The Islands Trust viewed forest as being even better than open farmland, but it nonetheless recognised the key role that logging still played on many islands. Its policy called for logging practices that recognised the special character of the islands, done "on a scale appropriate to the island concerned." In other words, a type of "boutique logging" that was entirely foreign to the industry at the time. Moving logs to water and gathering them in booms was to be "carried out in a manner that is the least damaging to the environment and in areas that will not conflict with other shoreline uses."[68] Sawmilling was to be restricted to small mills supplying mostly local markets. Pollution would be strictly controlled and mills screened from public view.

Likewise, rather than seeing most other extractive industries as opportunities, the Islands Trust perceived them as threats and sought to control them even more tightly. For example, quarrying sand and aggregate from beaches was no longer allowed, as the recreational and aesthetic values and the ecological role of all island beaches were deemed more important. For similar reasons, the entire Trust area, land and sea, was to be closed to all oil and gas drilling. Infrastructure improvements, too, were subject to stricter standards, to minimise the threats they might pose to the islands' "unique and fragile" natural areas. For instance, though island residents had earlier welcomed their roadways, the Trust engaged in a prolonged struggle with the provincial Department of Highways, whose "urban road standards" resulted in "excessive tree clearing and unsightly cuts and fills which destroy the pastoral nature of the islands." The Trust also took aim at increased automobile traffic, fed by expanding ferry service, which was deemed to be "contributing to the destruction of the islands;" it lobbied BC Ferries to improve foot passenger services.[69]

Protecting the islands as recreational space was central to the Trust's mandate. But recreational activities also needed to be carefully managed on Trust islands. A 1975 study conducted together with the Nature Conservancy identified the Strait of Georgia–Puget Sound region, with the Trust islands in the middle, as North America's most important outdoor recreation area. The Trust committed to safeguarding the recreational resources in its care with a "well planned and integrated recreational system" that addressed the needs of both residents and a diverse range of visitors and promoted recreation with the smallest negative effects on the islands. It aimed to increase public access to shoreline but also to prevent the overuse or abuse of beaches. Furthermore, marine activities, from swimming and scuba diving to kayaking and other forms of boating, as well as wilderness parks, hiking and horse-riding trails, and bicycle paths were all to be promoted. Scenic drives and automobile-based campgrounds, however, were discouraged; some recreational needs were more equal than others.

The Trust didn't underestimate the challenge of its commitment to enhanced recreational opportunities for (almost) all. By the mid-1970s, land access to the shore was "virtually non-existent" on many islands. Although the importance of recreation and environmental protection were now recognised, less than 4 percent of the land on Trust islands was dedicated to these purposes. Many island residents began to look upon visitors from off-island as an inconvenience or worse, synonymous with enhanced fire risk, garbage and crowded ferries. Trust policy sometimes seemed to suggest that potential residents might have to be screened in the future. Artists and craftspeople, as well as other small-business owners who catered to local markets and created local jobs, were to be encouraged. The elderly occupied a special place in many island communities, and home nursing, elder housing and community care facilities were to be given priority. Larger-scale enterprises in general were judged to be at odds with the islands' character.

Predictably, the Trust's sweeping utopian vision encountered resistance from various quarters on and off the islands. It did little to improve the often rocky relations between certain islands and other actors that predated the Trust. Provincial ministries of highways and forests, for example, pursued their established policies. Private forestry companies continued to control much of the islands' forests, and developers still harboured ambitious schemes. Most Trust islands remained under the jurisdiction of adjacent regional district governments that were often sympathetic to the salutary effects of land development on their tax base.

The key instrument for delivering the Trust's vision was the Official Community Plan (OCP) to be prepared by each large island, and the first OCPs developed under the Trust were contentious, especially on islands close to large towns. In 1975 the description given by Victoria's *Monday Magazine* of the process on Saltspring was a little tongue-in-cheek: "Islanders found themselves so much in agreement with one another concerning the details of their future development that it took only seven years [that is, far longer than usual] to produce an official community plan."[70] Whereas locally elected Trust officials on Saltspring had considerable control over land-use decisions determining the island's tax base, the Capital Regional District remained responsible for delivering services to island residents and these had to be paid for with their land taxes. If islanders wanted an industry-free and recreation-intensive island without subdivisions, they would have to accept the combination of higher land taxes and fewer services that went with it.

Reality did not always match the goals of the Trust. The number of residents on Saltspring continued to rise significantly into the 1980s, and the population on Bowen doubled in that decade. In 1978, Denman passed into law its first OCP, which identified preserving the island's rural environment as its highest priority. Two years later, the community was locked in a protracted struggle with the provincial government authority that had approved a new land development in contravention of the island's OCP. The island prevailed in court, establishing a legal precedent that limited but didn't eliminate Victoria's right to ignore local island bylaws.

The province's NDP government was defeated in the 1975 election by Bill Bennett's Social Credit, who had close ties with the development industry and shared few of the values expressed in the policies of the Islands Trust. Bennett's government was ready to repeal the Islands Trust Act in 1982 and hand the islands back to the sole jurisdiction of their respective regional districts. Bill Vander Zalm, Bennett's Minister of Municipal Affairs, suggested the Trust was no longer necessary since all the major islands had prepared an OCP under its guidance. Public opinion was powerfully opposed to dissolving the Islands Trust, however, and the government backed down. The *Vancouver Sun* suggested Vander Zalm and his advisers were "naive in the extreme to think that remote control by regional districts could effectively protect the islands from the predations of greedy developers." In fact, various islands' trustees confirmed that developers still exerted tremendous pressure through regional districts. In the absence of the Trust, the *Sun* said, the islands were destined to become "Coney Islands in the Strait."[71]

The Strait's many bald eagles were, and still are, an attraction for tourists, even if Mack Laing in Comox didn't approve of them.

Dean van't Schip photo

The Islands Trust experiment had clearly helped protect recreational and other values that many on the Strait wanted preserved. But its vision of rural communities in pristine environments where artisans and old folks enjoyed a high-quality lifestyle and harried urban folk came to regenerate was regularly contested. Denman Island's Des Kennedy summed up the Trust islands' situation by the mid-1980s: it was not perfect and certainly not the utopia envisioned a decade earlier. The province's Minister of Municipal Affairs, William Ritchie, appeared more committed to opening up the islands to rapid development than to respecting the Trust's mandate to "preserve and protect." Other provincial agencies continued to contravene local Trust policies. Most significantly, island populations continued to grow rapidly.

In the latter half of the 1970s, the total number of people living on the islands went from 9,500 to 12,700. By 1983, 5,200 permanent homes and 4,500 summer cottages existed on the islands. Another 10,000 properties were zoned for development; most of these were under a hectare and many were already on the market. Despite a steep downturn in the economy and the real-estate market, the Trust was still approving subdivisions, for an average of 600 new lots each year. The official land-use plans in place for the thirteen big islands could now accommodate an aggregate population of up to 70,000 people. Opinion was divided: many islanders were deeply disturbed by the continuing growth, while others found Trust planning policies unacceptably restrictive.

Despite the broken dreams, said Kennedy, the islands remained a "magical heritage" and their lifestyle a magnet "to rich, to poor, to dreamers and tinkerers, artists, farmers, fisherfolk, retired executives and a cast of characters as eccentric and hospitable as you'll find anywhere."[72] Their future, and that of recreation on the Strait more generally, remained uncertain. The Islands Trust would remain in place into the twenty-first century and succeed in maintaining a bucolic, park-like atmosphere in most parts of most Trust islands. Some places, like Ganges on Saltspring Island—unquestionably the least bucolic corner of the islands—remained hotly contested, as provincial governments and property developers continually pushed to escape the control of the Islands Trust.

The Strait as refuge and recreation space

Settlers early recognised the Strait as a valuable place for recreation and restoration. The more "their Strait" was transformed from barrier to highway—by steamships, ferries and diverse small craft—the more recreational opportunities it offered. Beaches that had previously given Indigenous people places to live beside the sea and its resources became the sites of cherished shoreline parks or high-priced real estate.

Conflict in this space was inevitable. The resource industries on the Strait's waters and along its shores helped generate the higher personal incomes that made recreation on the Strait affordable to growing numbers of people. Yet these same industries would eventually stand accused of turning prized retreats or recreation spots into industrial wastelands or of taking too many salmon. In many cases, waste dumped into the sea by rapidly growing towns was literally washing up against recreational users of the Strait.

By the 1960s recreational users were increasingly competing with one another for the same patches of sea and shore. Those who valued motorised pursuits ran afoul of those who preferred to sail, paddle, swim or dive. Those whose recreational pursuits changed the land or the plants and animals that occupied it—hunting, fishing and cottaging, for example—were at odds with those whose preferred recreation called for preservation and minimum impact—birdwatching, kayaking, camping and so on. These types of tensions have continued into the twenty-first century, not least on the Islands Trust islands.

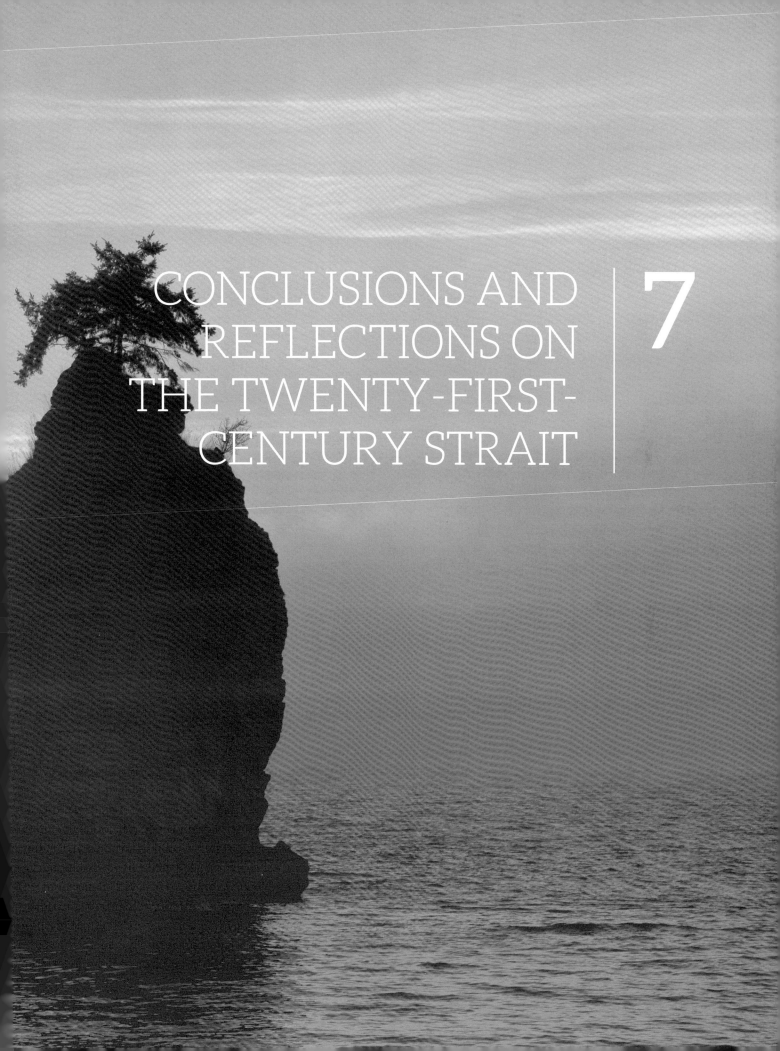

CONCLUSIONS AND REFLECTIONS ON THE TWENTY-FIRST-CENTURY STRAIT | **7**

BOOKS LIKE THIS ONE speak of the past, but they are firmly rooted in the present and concerned about the future. I have looked at issues, and relationships between them, that are not usually considered together in histories of British Columbia. Yet to really understand the Strait of Georgia as a highway or a barrier, an empty or a stolen space, a resource mine, a waste dump or a recreational space, we need to know the other four stories and how all five relate to one another. We also need to come to terms with these five stories and their complicated interactions if we want to begin to grasp what has happened here, in the heart of modern British Columbia, since the onset of colonisation. A better understanding of the Strait's past can be a valuable asset for the many people who hope we will better manage our relationship with the rest of nature here in the future.

If we aim to do a better job of controlling the effects of technologies in the future, then we need to understand how the ways we have fished, harvested our forests, produced our paper, disposed of our wastes, opened new parks, and so on have so consistently outrun our capacity to properly control the effects of these activities. If we aim to redress past injustices done to the Strait's Indigenous people and to cooperate with First Nations effectively in managing this shared space and resources in the future, then we must be able to see the Indigenous experience in relation to the laws and technologies introduced by settlers and all that has followed in their wake since the mid-nineteenth century. If we wish to protect the immense recreational values of the region, then we need to be familiar with the historical experiences and narratives upon which others base their own long-standing, competing claims to the future use of this space. Above all, I hope this book helps people around the Strait to better know it, and their evolving place on it.

Each of these stories about the North Salish Sea involves people who worried about various threats to "their" Strait from other people who saw this place differently. These perceived dangers evolved steadily and shifted in various ways for the many stakeholders around the sea. Early European navigators simply feared for their lives when facing the Strait's many treacherous, uncharted hazards. On the Indigenous people's sea, the overwhelming threat of colonial dispossession loomed large and mostly got worse over time. On the settlers' industrialised sea, assorted resource extractors threatened each other's livelihoods

Pages 252-253: Siwash Rock and seawall on the western tip of Stanley Park. The 10-kilometre seawall promenade around the park's perimeter, started in 1917 and completed in 1980, has become a major recreation resource for residents and visitors alike.

David Nunuk photo

in various ways. On the post-war recreational sea, ship owners, resource industries, polluters, and recreationists with competing claims to access and ownership clashed with one another and with environmental activists. Much fear of loss that appears throughout these chapters is closely related to what one might call "the law of the jungle"—the strongest prevail and the others get out of their way. Many of the actors involved expected to control events, and expected others to get out of their way or face the consequences. At one time or another, land-hungry settlers and their governments, miners, canners, fishers, lumbermen, ship or port authorities and recreationists variously seized, devastated, exhausted or fouled space or resources that were either shared with or owned by others. That is to say, most people's fears of loss were very rational—and still are today.

All the stories in the preceding chapters wrap up in the 1980s, a decade that saw BC's deepest economic downturn since the 1930s but also witnessed the stunning economic reforms of Deng Xiaoping in China and years of heady economic success in Japan. The Strait's role as Canada's portal to vast Asian markets, a dream the Canadian federation had held since it was created, was evolving rapidly. And this combination of economic challenges and opportunities helped suppress, once again, the push for more effective conservation of the Strait's resources. The highly urbanised population on the sea's shores in the 1980s was firmly attached to the Strait as a recreation space and highly dependent on it as a waste dump. At the same time, Indigenous people were slowly beginning to exercise some influence over the Strait and its resources again, after a very dark century.

The 2010s: *Plus ça change...*

Skip ahead about thirty years and roughly two-thirds of BC's total population (now approaching 5 million) *still* lives near the Strait; they represent about a third of Western Canada's population and 10 percent of Canada's. Most live in Greater Vancouver, which remains among the fastest-growing places in the province and the country. Like the residents who preceded them between the 1850s and 1980s, people living around the Strait today value it for widely varying reasons. The five stories recounted in this book have continued into the new century, as familiar stakeholders—Indigenous people, commodity exporters, resource miners, waste dumpers and recreationists—continue to look for the best ways to use the marine highway, compete for the right to use its shoreline and marine space, clash over primary industries like aquaculture and try to cope with persistent flaws in governance. Many of their concerns are familiar; other struggles emerging around the Strait involve the same stakeholders facing new sorts of challenges. Brand-new stories are unfolding as local Indigenous claims to traditional lands and resources and global climate change both gather momentum, as the influence of the Chinese economy looms ever larger, and as global fisheries continue to collapse at an alarming rate. These contemporary influences are intertwined with older ones in fascinating ways.

The people living on this rich littoral, and those farther away who claim the right to use it, remain anxious about the threats that others pose to "their Strait." As the global community becomes ever more tightly bound, all of us face diverse opportunities and challenges that are often difficult to understand. The histories sketched in this book aim to help us with this task.

We're still overfishing

Tony Pitcher of UBC's Department of Zoology and Fisheries Centre noted in 2005 that fish scientists were no longer debating whether the global fisheries crisis is real; it is the confirmed result of more than a century of overfishing by ever more efficient industrial fleets. The same year, Boris Worm and his colleagues at Dalhousie University estimated that two-thirds of the world's fisheries exploited since 1950 had collapsed. Fisheries managers across the globe had consistently mismanaged the resource for the benefit of large industrial interests at the expense of small fisheries-dependent communities. The Strait of Georgia is still one of Canada's most productive marine ecosystems, but its fish stocks, along with those of the rest of the world's seas, have been dramatically depleted.

As in the past, disagreement and uncertainty exist about the nature and extent of this overfishing. Stocks of resident salmon, mostly Coho and Chinook, appear to be the most severely depleted, their numbers down to perhaps 10 percent of what they were in 1900. Journalist Stephen Hume reported extreme cases in 2002: Coho runs in the Seymour River had fallen from around 14,000 in the early 1980s to fewer than 500, the Coho spawn in Black Creek on the east side of Vancouver Island had fallen from close to 8,000 in 1975 to fewer than 150. Populations of transient salmon, such as Sockeye and Pink, have fared better, but their numbers are perhaps half of what they were a century ago. Many varieties of bottom fish—those that feed on the sea floor, such as cod and halibut—have been nearly wiped out after decades of overfishing.

The status of resident herring and transient Sockeye populations has been the

Recreational boats at the Discovery Harbour Marina in Campbell River. There's often a waiting list for moorage as more and more people retire in the area.
Boomer Jerritt photo

subject of the most acrimonious debates. According to Indigenous and settler histories and recent archaeological research, herring were once exceptionally abundant in the Strait. Many beaches around the inland sea were thick with spawned herring, and the Strait supported much larger populations of fish, birds and marine mammals than it does now. Herring were an important food fish for humans in pre-colonial times, especially on the northern Strait, and they have been the focus of a commercial fishery since the onset of colonisation. Populations of herring on the Strait have fluctuated greatly, largely in response to fishing pressures but also industrial pollution. Federal fisheries authorities closed the herring fishery completely in the late 1960s as herring stocks around the Strait collapsed under heavy pressure from industrial fishing for the purposes of oil, fertilisers and animal feed. It was reopened a few years later and became the focus of a very lucrative business supplying herring roe to new markets in Japan. The roe fishery remains significant on the coast, still overseen by Fisheries and Oceans Canada. At the turn of the millennium, some observers celebrated the largest herring populations on the Strait since 1950, and herring have now begun to spawn again at once heavily polluted sites, including in False Creek and Howe Sound, where they had not been seen for decades. Not surprisingly, however, disagreements have broken out over what this means about the health of the herring population and how it should be fished.

Such competing views are the result, at least in part, of what UBC's Daniel Pauly has described as a "shifting baseline."[1] On the one hand, proponents of the herring fishery point to increasing numbers of herring as proof that fish populations have recovered and are robust and well managed. Other biologists, fishers and conservationists blame the alarming decline in the Strait's resident salmon and other fish species on the earlier collapse of local herring populations and have called for a multi-year moratorium on all commercial herring harvests in the Strait to permit herring and other fish stocks to recover. They maintain that those who proclaim "the biggest catch in fifty years" are comparing today's numbers with baseline populations in the 1950s that were already far below earlier maximums. It is like extolling (as many have) the near miraculous economic growth rates in places like Mozambique and Rwanda in recent years without acknowledging the baseline of devastation from which these places were recovering.

The dramatic changes in the number of Sockeye salmon returning to the Fraser River from year to year stimulated some of the earliest rumblings about conservation on the inland sea over a century ago; they remain a source of uncertainty and debate among fish scientists, fishers and the public today. For several years prior to 2010, the numbers of Fraser River Sockeye returning to spawn reached lows that hadn't been seen since the catastrophic Hells Gate slide of 1913. In 2009, when federal fisheries authorities were expecting a return of 10 million Sockeye, only 1.5 million arrived. Many scientists, conservationists and other observers attributed this collapse to the influence of farmed Atlantic salmon (chapter 4). Farmed fish had begun to escape from their pens and were said to be competing with indigenous Pacific Sockeye for diminishing resources in the sea and on spawning beds. Salmon farms were also blamed for spreading parasites like sea lice and new diseases such as infectious hematopoietic necrosis (IHN), which had started to afflict wild salmon populations. Then, confounding most experts, more than 25 million Sockeye returned to the

Fraser in 2010. It was the highest return since 1913. In 2016, 2.2 million fish were expected but less than a third of this number arrived, stimulating yet another round of debate over the collapse of the stock, the role of fish farms in this collapse and the effectiveness of hatcheries.

It is not surprising, then, that there is still little agreement about how to ensure sustainable fish harvesting on the Strait in the future. Some observers insist that aquaculture will never be able to replace the earlier productivity of the wild fisheries; they call for large cuts to the industrial fishery, large marine protected areas and widespread rehabilitation of salmon spawning streams to halt the decline in the Strait's fish populations. Others, as in the past, see industrial-scale fish breeding as the answer. Despite the daunting ecological impacts of fish farms, they call for a progressive move to aquaculture of various kinds as the only way to maintain high rates of biological productivity and provide enough fish to meet the needs of both commercial and sport fishing on the Strait. All parties agree, however, that the overall production of the Strait's fisheries falls far short of past levels and is far from meeting the demands of commercial and recreational fishers.

Indigenous people are re-emerging

Indigenous people never disappeared from the Strait and never stopped resisting their dispossession there, despite over a century of government policies aimed at marginalising and assimilating them. The Constitution Act of 1982, under which the federal government affirmed Indigenous rights, was a critical turning point. Much ferment has since arisen in relations between the Strait's Indigenous people and the majority white settler population. Subsequent legal decisions have confirmed the existence of Indigenous rights to lands and resources that were never formally ceded to the Crown, as well as the potential validity of Indigenous oral histories for establishing claims to these lands and resources. An ambitious program of treaty negotiations between First Nations, Victoria and Ottawa has yielded modest results to date. The government in Victoria in particular seems eager to achieve lasting settlements with Indigenous people. The province's First Nations can now block much local resource and infrastructure development by using the courts to uphold their claims that such development interferes with the extensive "unceded traditional territories" that lie beyond the tiny patches of land earlier assigned to them by Victoria.

While the Canadian Constitution now enshrines and protects Aboriginal rights, it does not define them in detail. One result of this is that Victoria and the small, scattered First Nations with whom it is negotiating around the inland sea must commission archaeological and historical studies to confirm where and how Indigenous people used to live and harvest resources in pre-colonial times. And because several First Nations often have overlapping claims to the same territories and resources, especially fisheries resources, it can be difficult to reach final agreements. Yet the province can't walk away from the table; it is obliged to reach negotiated treaty settlements if it wants to remove the legal uncertainties that constrain local and regional development wherever land claims are unresolved. Nor can Victoria return much of the land Indigenous people claim as traditional territory because most of it is now occupied or used by voters who would never countenance its expropriation.

One of the few ways out of the impasse, at least from Victoria's perspective, is to offer "softer" resources such as lands in parks or the Agricultural Land Reserve, or "common property" fisheries resources. Non-Indigenous fishers have become increasingly resentful of Indigenous claims to fisheries resources and of changes to Fisheries and Oceans Canada regulations that allow some salmon caught by Indigenous food fishers to be sold commercially. Indeed, Indigenous fishers may benefit as some non-Indigenous fishers leave the industry, much as happened when Japanese Canadian fishers were abruptly forced out of the industry in the early 1940s. The difference is that Indigenous people would inherit a fishery much diminished in size.

As with Indigenous repossession of the fisheries, conflict has sometimes arisen between groups devoted to conservation and environmental stewardship and local First Nations keen to acquire land and resources to help their members overcome chronic poverty. For example, valued recreation space on Tree Island (Sandy Islets) between Comox and Denman Island, currently managed as a provincial marine park and part of the Gulf Islands National Park Reserve, has long been part of the dispossession process and could be among the objects of repossession under the ongoing treaty negotiations. The province's willingness to sacrifice conservation values to achieve treaties is evident in a recent agreement with the Tsawwassen First Nation. This agreement involved the transfer of almost 400 hectares of land that had been reserved for agricultural purposes to the Tsawwassen people for development without constraint. In return, the First Nation relinquished its claim to adjacent land along the shore, allowing the province and Ottawa to proceed with their ambitious plans to expand port facilities.

Arriving at such arrangements in the context of broader treaty negotiations is challenging and time-consuming, and details are seldom shared with the public until a deal is closed. It is reasonable to assume that similar arrangements will emerge in various places around the Strait in the coming years—possibly on Howe Sound, for example. Such complicated bargains are paving the way for federal, provincial and municipal governments to build new infrastructure for resource and industrial development while making important concessions to Indigenous negotiators, who are seeking new opportunities for their own communities.

Aquaculture is established but changing

Proponents of salmon and shellfish farming, like the backers of hatcheries in the past, continue to extol their ability to deliver spectacular biological and economic results while downplaying their limitations, particularly their ecological effects and other public concerns.

By the end of the twentieth century, as farmed salmon production began to exceed the wild fishery on the BC coast, salmon farmers had moved north and mostly abandoned all but the northernmost passages into the Strait of Georgia. These farms now raise Atlantic salmon (*Salmo salar*), which are better able than Pacific salmon species to live in high densities in confined pens. Although Atlantic salmon themselves are less prone to outbreaks of disease, they are hardly immune to it, and they have repeatedly been linked with parasites and diseases spreading to wild Pacific salmon as they pass near salmon farms during their migrations towards spawning grounds around the Strait.

Independent scientists such as Alexandra Morton, an eloquent and widely trusted opponent of current methods of salmon farming, have repeatedly challenged the industry and its government backers over the impacts of salmon farms on the health of wild salmon and marine mammal populations. Even Ottawa's Auditor General has questioned whether Fisheries and Oceans Canada is capable of fulfilling its mandate to protect the wild salmon fishery while also supporting the salmon-farming industry. Federal government reluctance to share information about its scientific research on salmon pathology has drawn sharp criticism from the national and international scientific communities, though this situation has improved recently. Despite the fact that most salmon farming in BC is now controlled by a handful of Norwegian firms, the provincial government still remains a steadfast supporter of salmon-farming, seeing the industry as a valuable complement to the wild salmon fishery.

Publicists for the aquaculture industry and its government supporters are inclined to wrap salmon farmers in a cloak of sanctity, as efficient producers of protein in a protein-deficient world, and leaders in an inevitable transition from "fish hunting" to "fish farming." They imply that pond-farmed carp raised on farm waste in the Yangtze basin in China and Atlantic salmon raised on fish meal in open pens along the BC coast have similarly benign ecological impacts. Meanwhile, detractors demonise salmon farmers as wasting resources by using unconscionable volumes of the oceans' smaller fish to feed expensive, drug-riddled salmon bound not for famine-relief operations but for supermarkets and restaurants. Fish farms, say the critics, damage the marine environment in ways that are poorly understood, threatening to undermine the health of the wild fishery and the broader marine environment by propagating dangerous diseases—all for the profit of a few large foreign-owned corporations, and very much at the expense of wild salmon stocks and the thousands of small, independent fishers who depend on them to earn a living.

As with earlier debates about salmon around the sea, a baffling number of factors other than fish farms may be affecting the health of the Strait's wild salmon populations. These include warmer temperatures in spawning streams reducing survival rates among returning salmon, growing numbers of "run of the river" hydroelectric producers around the Strait closing off spawning streams, and hard-to-understand changes in the North Pacific Ocean. Such uncertainty, however—much like the uncertainty that allowed the tobacco industry to keep its critics at bay for decades—helps salmon farmers avoid making the adjustments called for by their critics, such as confining their salmon to fully enclosed pens in order to minimise pollution of the marine environment. In any case, because salmon farms are physically concentrated outside the inland sea, they are less of an issue to people living around its shores.

In contrast, ambitious plans to expand shellfish aquaculture on the Strait may give this issue a higher profile in the coming years. Baynes Sound, between Denman Island and Vancouver Island, remains the centre of BC's shellfish aquaculture industry, producing more than half of the province's output of close to 4,000 tons of shellfish annually. Tension is growing between these producers and their local critics. Opponents on Denman Island urge respect for the Islands Trust's mandate to "preserve and protect" their island's natural environment, including adjacent coastal waters, rather than continually expanding the shellfish aquaculture industry

Oyster skiff heads off to catch the morning tide in the Comox Valley.

Boomer Jerritt photo

in the sound. The growing conflict between shellfish growers and islanders bears some resemblance to American historian Richard White's story of loggers versus environmentalists in the western US in the 1990s. Both are classic divides between people for whom nature is mostly a place to work and others who see it mainly as a place for recreation. But critics of current practices in BC's shellfish industry also stress the need to protect the long-term resilience, productivity and biological diversity of the local marine environment, not just its recreation values.

Shellfish farmers are more inclined than even salmon farmers to extol the benign nature of their business; theirs, they say, is "a protein source that takes nothing from the planet other than phytoplankton."[2] Like many on the coast, shellfish farmers aim to prosper by supplying new markets across the Pacific, and the markets there for geoduck clams are particularly promising. The annual value of geoduck landings on the BC coast rose from virtually zero in 1970 to more than $50 million in 2012: much of this is wild stock harvested from the Strait of Georgia. The K'ómoks First Nation has announced ambitious plans to cultivate these large bivalves in the sandy sea bottom off Denman Island. Perhaps as part of its treaty settlement with Victoria, it aims to secure control over hundreds of hectares of suitable seabed, predicting that its geoduck harvests will equal the entire province's current production. If, as some observers suggest, shellfish cultivation on the Strait is destined to grow into a billion-dollar export industry, geoduck could well be one of its most lucrative commodities and Indigenous people could play a significant role in its production.

Proponents of an expanded shellfish industry depict it in much the same way that Victoria's policy-makers viewed salmon farming in the 1970s—as an ecologically benign industry run by a large number of small-scale, independent local operators. If recent developments on Baynes Sound are any indication, the industry is more likely to follow the actual path of the salmon farmers: many disturbing questions about their possible ecological impacts remain unanswered while production is increasingly controlled by a few large foreign interests with local partners, including First Nations.

Critics of shellfish aquaculture, like those who question salmon farming technology, decry its damage to the marine environment. They say that growers and the government staff who work with them drive their vehicles onto beaches, risking damage to the sensitive foreshore habitat of other species of vertebrates and invertebrates such as spawning herring, sand lance and other forage fish critical for sustaining the sea's larger fish and mammals. Shellfish growers working the beaches during the winter's nighttime low tides keep neighbours awake with their noise and lights. Growing fleets of rafts, from which the molluscs are suspended in plastic containers, spread farther across Baynes Sound each year. Tons of plastic materials lost from these shellfish operations litter surrounding beaches. Many sand beaches are now draped in "predator nets," which are intended to protect clams from burrowing predators but threaten a variety of fish, marine birds and mammals, including swimmers, who can become entangled in them. All this in a rich estuary that has been recognised as an "ecologically and biologically sensitive area."

The prospect of expanded geoduck cultivation is particularly offensive to local residents. Experiments have already begun with plastic pipes 15 centimetres in diameter being sunk into the sandy substrate of an intertidal zone on the Baynes Sound shore of Denman Island. These pipes protect the juvenile geoduck seeded inside them. They are covered with the same predator nets used on other beaches to prevent damage to the clams during the seven years it takes them to mature. These nets can break loose during storms, entangling other animals. To harvest the geoduck, shellfish farmers use high-pressure hoses that transform their sandbar habitat into an amorphous slurry that is uninhabitable for many other species. Questions remain unanswered about the ecological consequences of mobilising PCBs and other toxins that were deposited within these sediments decades earlier.

The Strait of Georgia as a whole is an important source of the various persistent organic pollutants that accumulate to dangerous levels in the flesh of marine mammals, increasingly through ingestion of microplastic debris. Baynes Sound has become a repository of large amounts of this toxic plastic waste. Denman Islanders already collect tons of mostly plastic refuse left on their beaches each year by the shellfish industry. They stage high-profile waste-gathering events intended, among other things, to encourage the shellfish growers to reduce their waste stream. The soaring volumes of microplastics suspended in the marine environment may represent a serious threat to the very shellfish industry that could itself be a source of this material. Evidence suggests their oysters and other bivalves are already ingesting and accumulating these tiny plastic particles. For their part, the dedicated stewards of the island's shores—like the American environmentalists Richard White wrote about in the 1990s—may be perceived as being so rigid in their protection of the marine environment that they risk being left out of discussions among local and provincial decision-makers. This would be a great loss for all involved. Yet, if these stewards are seen as being unable or unwilling to consider the local importance of the shellfish industry, they will likely be seen as impediments, rather than participants, in any agreement between the provincial government and the K'ómoks First Nation, which is understandably impatient to regain a century and a half of lost ground.

By the 1980s, farming on the Strait had evolved from an instrument of colonial dispossession to a means of protecting the "valued rural character" of the Islands Trust islands. In the early twenty-first century, new techniques of farming the sea have become powerful and controversial instruments for Indigenous people to repossess their rights to marine space and resources. Scenarios like the one unfolding around Denman Island could well be seen in other places around the Strait in the coming decades.

Recreation continues to increase in importance

Howe Sound became a valued recreation space during the twentieth century because of its clear waters, secluded beaches and good fishing as well as its proximity to Vancouver. In 1969, it was closed to all but recreational salmon fishing and a few years later Scientific Pollution and Environmental Control Society (SPEC), an

environmental NGO, called for the entire sound to be designated a recreational area and protected from any further industrial development. Since then, this vision has been mostly fulfilled. Most of the sound's older, resource-based activities such as logging and mining have stopped. Instead, tourism and recreation, and a real-estate market that benefits from its close association with them, have become the backbone of the local economy. The change has been gradual yet dramatic, and it remains contested today.

The giant copper mine at Britannia on the eastern shore of the sound closed for good in the 1970s to become a mining museum and, occasionally, a movie set. The aging pulp mill on the sound's western shore at Woodfibre shut down in 2006. Between them, these sites have left a legacy of heavy metals, PCBs, dioxins and furans in the sound itself, while the province continues a costly long-term program to contain the acid drainage from Britannia. Although another old pulp mill still operates at Port Mellon, it was refitted in the 1990s to reduce its impact on the marine environment. And marine life does appear to be returning. A few Pink salmon were reported to be spawning in Britannia Creek in 2012, for the first time in eighty years. With the help of volunteers sealing off pilings that had been soaked in toxic creosote, herring have begun to spawn again in the Squamish Estuary. Dolphins and larger whales, long absent from the sound,

Campbell River is a transportation hub and sport-fishing destination on the Strait's northern entrance. Its pulp mill has closed but it is still the site of the Strait's last coal mine.

Boomer Jerritt photo

Beaches like this one near Parksville are still a major tourist attraction.

iStock.com/EmilyNorton

have started to visit the area again. Provincial and local governments have invested hundreds of millions of dollars to stimulate tourism along the Sea-to-Sky Corridor. As a result, the sound is now closely associated with recreation: from windsurfing and kitesurfing at Squamish Spit and scuba diving at Porteau Cove to salmon fishing, sea kayaking, and sailing around the islands. One even sees the occasional cruise ship there, taking the long way up the coast.

In recent years, talk of developing the abandoned pulp mill site at Woodfibre as a liquefied natural gas (LNG) storage and export facility has alarmed those who view the sound as a "restored natural space" and a valuable place for recreation. And a gravel quarry has been proposed for a site farther south. As with Baynes Sound, these kinds of ongoing friction between recreation and resource development still exist in many places around the Strait, dividing communities and challenging all levels of government.

Marine pollution and oil spills are still an issue

The volume of municipal sewage being dumped into the Strait every day increased by almost two-thirds between 1983 and 1999 as towns on all shores grew and continued to expand their sewage treatment facilities. Although much of this sewage is now subjected to secondary treatment, more than half of the Strait's coastline was closed to shellfish harvesting by the early twenty-first century, mostly due to sewage pollution. On the other hand, much progress has been made in reducing

persistent organic pollutants in industrial effluent, and concern today has shifted to polybrominated diphenyl ethers (PBDEs). These fire-retardant chemicals have been very widely used in recent years in the production of a huge number of products we use daily, such as electrical appliances, consumer electronics, plastics and textiles; PBDEs are now ubiquitous in the tissues of both marine animals and humans.

In 2008, the three federal port authorities created early in the twentieth century to govern Lower Mainland ports were consolidated to create a single entity named Port Metro Vancouver. By 2011, Port Metro Vancouver was handling 122.5 million tons of cargo, almost 80 percent of it international trade, mostly exports of raw or semi-processed natural resources. Port authorities estimated (somehow) that their activities generated close to 130,000 jobs across the country that year, $6.1 billion in wages and $10.5 billion in GDP.

As in the early 1970s the most contentious pollution issue on the Strait today is the possibility of a major oil spill. Petroleum products currently make up a modest portion of the overall volume of exports and the number of ships moving through Vancouver. China's demand for imported hydrocarbons continues to grow, however, and producers of heavy oil from the tar sands in northern Alberta, some now Chinese-owned, are anxious to improve their access to this market. One way is to increase the volume of this heavy oil exported through the port of Vancouver.

Widespread concern exists today, as it did in the 1970s, that our governments are poorly prepared for an oil spill. Pollution control strategies on the Strait have

False Creek has been transformed in recent decades, from an open sewer to a vibrant waterfront. People are still advised to wash their hands and shower after contact with its water however, especially the eastern basin where high levels of PCBs and heavy metals are still found in sediments.
David Nunuk photo

variously aimed to reduce the volume and toxicity of pollutants, to concentrate pollutants in one place, or to disperse them beneath the surface of the sea from a fixed point. An oil spill on the Strait, by definition, could not be carefully planned or easily controlled. Adding to the uncertainty is the fact that no one is quite sure how diluted bitumen, or "dilbit"—a diluted heavy-oil product currently being delivered to the coast and carried in tankers plying the Strait—will behave when it is spilled into the marine environment. Industry experts have said they expect it to behave like lighter crude oil, but a spill of dilbit into Michigan's Kalamazoo River, where much of the oil settled on the stream bottom, suggests otherwise. Studies are being carried out around the Strait, but it is still too early to draw many conclusions.

One well-respected early study of the possible effects of a major oil spill on the Strait (and Puget Sound) pointed out that hundreds of kilometres of shoreline along inlets, bays and islands would be exposed to damage, as well as large populations of migratory birds, ecologically important coastal marshlands and still significant commercial fisheries. Among the places possibly affected would be the Gulf Islands National Park Reserve and a significant number of the province's marine and land-based parks, which now touch virtually all shorelines of the inland sea from Indian Arm to the Octopus Islands. More recent studies by pipeline-project backers have focused less on the negative effects of a spill and more on the statistical probability of one occurring and on local capacities for responding to such a disaster.

Kinder Morgan, a Texas company, owns the Trans Mountain Pipeline which already moves crude oil and refined products from Alberta to Burrard Inlet. It has proposed a major expansion of that line that would increase oil shipments through the Strait by up to 500 percent, using more than 400 tankers a year. The company's study concluded that the likelihood of a major spill occurring is very low: once every 460 years (about the same likelihood as a major earthquake occurring). This falls, they say, to about once every 2,300 years if suitable "mitigation measures" and safeguards are in place. Opponents point to their own evidence, which suggests the chance of an oil spill occurring is far higher than the estimates generated by Kinder Morgan's consultants, and there is not enough local capacity to effectively mitigate this risk. A demonstration in 2013 designed to show local spill-response capacities backfired when the flagship of the oil clean-up fleet ran aground on its way to a press conference. Committed to ensuring a "world class" capacity to respond to coastal oil spills, the provincial Liberal government led by Christy Clark commissioned its own study, which further confirmed the current state of unpreparedness.

Clearly, the Strait will remain the focus of considerable political struggle over oil shipments in the coming years. Residents of its shoreline communities for the most part are determined to defend treasured recreational resources and coastal ecosystems, while many in the rest of the province and Western Canada in general remain convinced of their right to use the Strait as a highway to world markets.

Governance is changing on the Strait

When the federal government created its Department of the Environment in 1971 and appointed Jack Davis as its first minister, it signalled a commitment to carefully managing how natural resources were used as well as the impacts of human activities on the environment. The new agency's capacity to manage the marine environment of

the inland sea increased, albeit slowly and unevenly, in the decades that followed. After 2006 it shrank rapidly during nearly a decade of radical cuts to federal government capacities under Stephen Harper. In 2012, this government passed the Jobs, Growth and Long-term Prosperity Act (better known as Bill C-38), an extraordinarily wide-reaching "omnibus bill" disguised as a federal budget that greatly reduced Ottawa's involvement in marine protection. Provincial governments, including the one in Victoria, suddenly became responsible for overseeing the environmental impact assessments of new infrastructure projects, a role that many of them had little or no demonstrated capacity to do.

This reduction in federal oversight was only the most high-profile change among many that diminished the federal role in protecting and managing the environment while expanding Ottawa's support for resource development and infrastructure projects such as pipeline construction. The Fisheries and Oceans Canada department, like Environment Canada, shrivelled under the Harper government. It passed legislation reducing the protection of fish habitat while cutting budgets for environmental monitoring and restoration in the Gulf Islands National Park Reserve and muzzling federal fish scientists. At the same time, the Harper government "streamlined" the environmental review process for resource development and infrastructure projects by exempting 3,000 of them from review by the Canadian Environmental Assessment Agency. Independent scientists and community groups strongly criticised the government for failing to pursue its mandate to ensure the long-term viability of marine resources and habitats. Reversing the effects of extreme and wide-reaching measures introduced under Harper will take time. A new federal government elected in late 2015 has stated its commitment to improving environmental governance while, like the Harper government, supporting the controversial expansion of the Kinder Morgan pipeline.

Meanwhile, as in the 1970s, the government in Victoria, at least until very recently, has remained preoccupied with "dollars and sense" issues on the Strait (chapter 5); it was aligned with the Harper government's vision of future prosperity based on

Orcas in the southern Strait, with Mount Baker in the background. A large increase in heavy-oil shipments to the south coast from northern Alberta would result in a great expansion of oil tanker traffic. This in turn would threaten the survival of this species in the southern Strait.

Jens Benninghofen/AllCanadaPhotos.com on behalf of Alamy

hydrocarbon exports. But whereas the Harper government was partial to heavy-oil exports (as Ottawa continues to be), the province focused on exporting liquefied natural gas, while sharing Harper's commitment to shrinking the machinery of government. The provincial Auditor General's report for 2011 stated that Victoria's Environmental Assessment Office had become virtually a rubber stamp for industry, rejecting only one out of 219 development proposals submitted in the previous fifteen years, while failing to carry out monitoring needed to ensure that these approved projects met their legal obligations for environmental management. The province's approach to environmental assessment reflected a commitment to allowing industry to self-regulate whenever possible. Many citizens and local governments around the inland sea question whether this approach will be sufficient to prevent accelerating environmental degradation or respond to major accidents such as oil spills.

Local governments around the Strait are generally far more concerned than their senior counterparts about local damage resulting from industries' self-regulated activities. But these lower levels of government mostly lack the capacity and legal authority to challenge initiatives favoured by Victoria and Ottawa. The larger and most vulnerable players among them, such as Vancouver, Burnaby, North Vancouver and other shoreline municipalities, will pursue whatever political means they have at their disposal to oppose the federally approved pipeline expansion project that would dramatically increase the movement of diluted bitumen through Burrard Inlet. Most First Nations, municipal and regional governments lack the technical capacity, and the defined legal authority, to participate effectively in environmental management on the Strait. But Indigenous people in particular wield considerable influence as a result of their unresolved land claims and could play a decisive role in future disputes with the province and Ottawa.

Some analysts have proposed provincial legislation that would create an integrated coastal zone management (ICZM) process. This process could involve all levels of government as well as a range of specialists and key stakeholder groups that would address and, hopefully, resolve emerging conflicts about and threats of environmental degradation on the Strait. This approach would allow more local influence over decisions about the Strait, decisions that are currently dominated by a distant federal government more often influenced by powerful industries and their lobbyists than by local interests. Echoing the sorts of reservations expressed last century by Roderick Haig-Brown, contemporary critics are skeptical that an ICZM approach can deliver the promised results. Such an approach has often proven to be a smokescreen that allows dominant players to continue to exert control over shared space and resources. Nonetheless, on a Strait threatened by large new projects with unknown and potentially disastrous consequences, even an imperfect ICZM process would be a marked improvement over the current free-for-all in which local interests are consistently steamrollered by powerful forces with deep pockets and the governments they influence.

Ferry service is declining

The Strait may no longer be the highway it was in the days when settlers travelled from town to town by steamship, but it is still a vital link for hundreds of thousands of people who live and work on Vancouver Island, the Mainland north of Howe

Sound and the Strait's larger islands. BC Ferries became semi-privatised in 2003 when the erstwhile provincial Crown corporation started operating as an independently managed company. Since then, the provincial government has progressively "eliminated subsidies" for what was earlier considered an essential public service. Fares on the larger ferries connecting the Lower Mainland and Vancouver Island have been increasing several times faster than the rate of inflation, and on the smaller routes fares have risen almost twice as fast again. As a result, ridership on BC Ferries plummeted, its costs soared and its "losses"—which were earlier considered the cost of operating a necessary public service—continued. Vehicle traffic in 2012 reached its lowest level in thirteen years, passenger traffic, the lowest in twenty-one years. Meanwhile, BC Ferries' many managers were receiving a variety of bonuses.

BC Ferries' inability to deliver service while managing costs has been predictably damaging for communities that depend on the ferries to help them move people and goods around Strait. It has been particularly hard on communities that depend on seasonal tourism and recreation for economic survival. For example, journalist Stephen Hume reported that the "tourist dependent Gulf Islands" had lost a total of 2.7 million visitor trips since the privatised BC Ferries began reducing service and raising fares. He also blamed poor ferry service for a decline of more than $1.6 billion in the value of residential properties on the islands between 2010 and 2013 alone.[3] Further cuts in service and fare hikes far beyond the rate of inflation were introduced early in 2014. A large number of people—roughly 20 percent of BC's population and most people who live on the Strait outside of Vancouver—are affected by these continuous blows. They can only hope that the province will eventually recognise the essential nature of their marine links and begin, once again, to reinforce rather than undermine them.

The climate is changing

Among the few truly new issues that have arisen around the sea in recent decades are those related to accelerating climate change. Sea temperature rises have been recorded all along the BC coast over the past fifty years, while the biggest increase—of 1.5°C—has been recorded in the Strait of Georgia. This warming trend is expected to continue, causing some marine species to thrive while others move north to cooler waters, or perish. Pink salmon, for example, are the smallest and most thermally tolerant of the indigenous salmon species, and it appears they will be the best adapted to deal with such rapid temperature changes. Other salmon may prove vulnerable to these rising temperatures.

Sea levels are rising in many places around the Strait and along the rest of the coast. The effects are likely to be relatively modest along many rocky shorelines but far more dramatic in low-lying areas, such as coastal estuaries and the alluvial plains behind them. Most of these low-lying areas are rich habitat for a wide variety of animal species, and a great deal of the region's agricultural, industrial and port activities occupy this land as well. Moreover, a boom in residential development in the Lower Mainland is making much of this low-lying land ever more densely populated. Andrew Yan, a local urban planner, has estimated that the City of Vancouver, with its over 50 kilometres of shoreline, will be obliged to spend more than $500 million on dikes and seawalls in the twenty-first century, and billions more to purchase the land for these structures, just to keep pace with rising sea levels. Damage to shoreline real estate and infrastructure is predicted to cost a further $25 billion.[4]

And the inland sea is becoming more acidic. Up to a third of the carbon dioxide released into the atmosphere globally is absorbed by the world's oceans, where it produces carbonic acid that in turn enhances the oceans' acidity. As with rising sea temperatures, acidification may be more extreme on the Strait than in the open Pacific, though scientists are still debating this point. Regardless, acidity levels are likely to broadly follow those of the open ocean, where the average pH has already declined from 8.2 to 8.1 in recent decades and is expected to fall to 7.8 or below over the rest of the century. It is more difficult for marine species to adapt to this kind of trend because they cannot escape it by moving. Even an individual species that is not very sensitive to acidity will be affected by the deaths of other species that are further down the food chain—zooplankton, for example. Shellfish farmers on the Strait have already begun to suffer from diebacks of those bivalves, such as scallops, that are most sensitive to increasing acidity.

Responses to these trends by governments in Victoria and Ottawa have resulted in a kind of cognitive dissonance. On the one hand, they have now acknowledged that climate change exists and have committed to reducing the greenhouse gas emissions that are one of its leading causes. BC has a Climate Action Plan, while Canada has signed the Paris Agreement on Climate Change and has worked with the provinces to find ways to meet our commitments under the agreement. On the other hand, both governments have remained determined to increase the production and export of hydrocarbons, mostly heavy oil from the tar sands and gas from hydraulic fracking processes that generate much fugitive methane. These are the same fossil fuels that create greenhouse gases when burned, gases whose generation both governments insist, meanwhile, that they are determined to dramatically reduce.

The great majority of the world's climate scientists have concluded that most of our hydrocarbons should be left in the ground if we are to avoid runaway climate change by the end of the century. The hydrocarbon industry and the politicians who are beholden to it remain anxious to extract and sell the stuff as quickly as possible. That is to say, they are displaying the same kind of short-sighted, profit-seeking, chronic *imediatismo* that has characterised so much of our resource industry around the inland sea over the past two centuries. This approach will contribute to disruptive environmental changes of the sort already starting to appear on the Strait. Such local changes, as dramatic as they may be, will be a drop in the global bucket. Climate change will inevitably affect the Strait to some degree for many years to come, irrespective of whatever policies we adopt locally now or in the future. And our losses may prove relatively modest on a global scale—think of the hundreds of millions whose lives will be disrupted in the coastal plains, agricultural regions and fast-growing cities of Africa and Asia. But climate change will directly and significantly affect the people who live around the inland sea. *How much* climate change will directly affect us, including influencing where and how people will be able to live and work on the Strait, will depend in large part on the policies of our governments, and those of our global partners, today and in the decades ahead. Our governments know this already; they need to start acting like they know it.

What does the Strait's history mean for today's policy-makers?

The five portraits of the Strait in this book were inspired not just by a love of this place and a desire to understand and explain it, but also by my experiences in many other beautiful and resource-rich places. Since the 1970s, I have often found myself working with clever, capable people whose home regions have been plagued by human folly. Think, for example, of the Aral and Caspian seas, until recently rich and vital marine ecosystems abounding with life that are now largely toxic cesspools, ruined due to decades of abuse by industrial agriculture and the oil industry. Of the beautiful eastern Congo, so rich in people and land and valuable minerals yet now a chaotic, violence-prone mess of shattered communities and broken infrastructure after a few generations of external manipulation and chronically bad government. Of Haiti in the heart of the Caribbean, like BC a rainy and mountainous place—the rich and fertile treasure chest of the French Empire barely two centuries ago, it is now eroded to the nubs, the poorest country in the western hemisphere. Are there lessons for us in these places? All of them could and should be much better places to live. All are, or were, resource-rich; all are, or were, prized spaces where local factions backed by powerful outside interests pursued their competing claims to these lands and their riches, at the expense of most people living there.

The North Salish Sea has finally come into its own as a gateway to a powerful East Asian economy that is itself finally realising the ambitions of its citizens and the long-standing expectations of its European and North American trading partners. Not only has the Strait become a portal for this trade, it also serves as a "resource mine" for these pan-Pacific economies, just as it had been for the US and, earlier, the British Empire. It has become a place between the world's two dominant powers—the US and China—with strong ties to both. With BC's exports evenly split between these two countries, the province now occupies a position well known to Kazakhstanis and Congolese: being relatively weak and dependent compared to powerful external interests. These comparisons will seem outlandish to many. Such suggestions always do, until you experience a faraway place and see its obvious flaws, then return home to discover local versions of these same shortcomings. Consider, for example, our crumbling provincial (and, until recently at least, federal) civil service; our often short-sighted or venal political leaders; our traditions of squandering valuable shared resources, of bullying and even outright theft of public property by dominant individuals and corporations, and so on. These five stories of the evolving relationships between the Strait, its resources and its people offer many disturbing examples of similar failings in our own past. As competition for space and resources intensifies around the Strait in the twenty-first century, the threat of future transgressions against our common interest will also intensify. Those of us who wish to prevent them will need to act vigorously and take a stand against them.

This vision of the Strait's past and present, and its future prospects, will seem unjustifiably pessimistic to many. In response, I cite one of Haiti's choicer proverbs: "A paranoid is someone who understands the situation." Many of our political leaders have hitched their wagons to the hydrocarbon industry—the twenty-first century's tobacco industry, on steroids—with its inherently corrupting influences.

The administrators—our provincial and federal civil services—are still repositories of much valuable expertise but their ranks have been decimated and their effectiveness hobbled by debilitating cuts and repeated "streamlining" over the course of decades. And though Canada's resource base is still vast by global standards—faint praise, perhaps—around the inland sea we have rapidly squandered an immense wealth of renewable resources. Now some leaders are telling us that our future wealth and happiness depend on using the Strait to facilitate the fastest possible extraction and export of non-renewable resources whose use threatens global stability. What comes after that?

Taken together, these five stories confirm what we already know, and what those who make decisions affecting today's Strait should know: it is a highly valued, complex and contested space whose management is remarkably challenging and is certain to grow more challenging in the future. Effective stewardship of this space will be impossible if we continue to treat it with benign neglect, "streamline" our regulation of it and allow the industries that use it to mostly self-regulate. Companies may make the right decisions for their shareholders, in the very short term at least, but they cannot reliably manage how the Strait's diverse resources are shared with the millions of BC residents who also have high stakes in this valued space. If we intend to pass this precious sea and its shores on to future generations with its inherent richness and diversity somewhat intact, we must carefully guide the wide range of public- and private-sector interests whose actions affect it. Getting these players—especially from the private sector and the federal, First Nations, provincial, regional and municipal governments—to work together effectively will almost certainly require some sort of coastal zone management framework. This is the best available option, despite the recognised flaws of such an approach.

To make such a management approach work effectively around the North Salish Sea will take time and effort. It will inevitably need to be improved through trial and error, determining what can take root in this unique context and what can't. Approaches and attitudes imported from outside the region—ways of doing things that have worked in other places—will not succeed here unless they can be carefully adapted to our local needs and capacities, our constraints and opportunities. Many of our American neighbours living around the different lobes of the Salish Sea are deeply committed to assuring its future well-being, and we need to include them in our new approaches. But we cannot let inevitably complex negotiations with partners in the US become an excuse for inaction in our own backyard.

To paraphrase George Orwell, everyone's home is special, but ours is more special than most. Whether we've had the good fortune to be born near the North Salish Sea or the good sense to move here, we know that we live in an extraordinary corner of the world. And by most measures, we are among the world's most privileged people. We have no excuse for squandering this place, ruining it for our children and their children, in our rush to satisfy short-term needs or fulfill the shifting priorities of industries or governments that are demonstrably *not* acting in the best interests of our local or global communities. It is our duty to begin treating this place with the care it deserves. We need to learn from our past successes and failures, then re-dream our future here and make it happen.

NOTES

Sources frequently cited have been identified using the following abbreviations:

BCA = British Columbia Archives

CVA = City of Vancouver Archives

DMF = Department of Marine and Fisheries (now Fisheries and Oceans Canada)

SPEC = Scientific Pollution and Environmental Control Society

TBC = The *British Colonist* newspaper, later known as The *Daily British Colonist*, The *Daily Colonist*

UBCLSC = University of British Columbia Library, Rare Books and Special Collections

Preface

1 K.T. Carlson, ed., *A Stó:lo Coast Salish Historical Atlas* (Vancouver: Douglas and McIntyre, 2001), 27.

Introduction

1 "Timberline," MS-0364 box 4, folder 1, Imbert Orchard Papers, "People in Landscape, series I (Gulf of Georgia)," BCA.

2 Peter Puget, *A log of the proceedings of* HMS *Discovery, January 4, 1791 to January 14, 1793*, Public Records Office (London), Group: Admiralty: 61, cited in Doreen Armitage, *Around the Sound: A History of Howe Sound-Whistler* (Madeira Park, BC: Harbour Publishing, 1997), 30.

3 Government of Canada, *Census of Canada, 1880–81* (Canada Census and Statistics Office, Volume 1. Ottawa: Mac-Lean Rogers, 1882); Government of Canada, *Census of Canada, 1890–91* (Ottawa: S.E. Dawson, 1893); Government of Canada, *Fourth Census of Canada, 1901* (Ottawa: S.E. Dawson, 1902); Government of Canada, *Fifth Census of Canada, 1911* (Canada Census and Statistics Office, Volume 1. Ottawa: C.H. Parmelee, 1912); Government of Canada, *Sixth Census of Canada, 1921* (Ottawa: F.A. Ackland, 1924); Government of Canada, *Eighth Census of Canada, 1941* (Ottawa: Edmond Cloutier, 1950); Government of Canada, *1961 Census of Canada* (Ottawa: Dominion Bureau of Statistics, 1962); Statistics Canada, *1981 Census of Canada* (Ottawa: Ministry of Supply and Services, 1982).

4 The permanently populated islands represented in the Trust were Saltspring, North and South Pender, Galiano, Mayne, Saturna, Thetis, Gabriola, Lasqueti, Denman, Hornby, Bowen and Gambier.

1. The Sea as Barrier, the Sea as Highway

1 R.L. Stevenson, "The English Admirals," *Cornhill* 38 (July 1878), 36, cited in Cynthia F. Behrman, *Victorian Myths of the Sea* (Athens, OH: Ohio University Press, 1977), 25–26.

2 E.A. Freeman, "Latest Theories on the Origin of the English," *Contemporary Review* 57 (January 1890), 45, cited in Behrman, *Victorian Myths*, 27.

3 Herbert Hayens, *Ye Mariners of England: A Boy's Book of the Navy* (London: Nelson, 1901), 10, cited in Behrman, *Victorian Myths*, 27.

4 "Log of Wm Lomas from Liverpool to Victoria" in 1862, MS-1236 Lomas Family, William Henry Lomas Fonds, BCA.

5 "Extracts from Commissioner Nugent's Report," *TBC*, 23 April 1859, 1.

6 "A holiday journey—along the east coast and the adjacent islands," *TBC*, 13 July 1881, 2.

7 "New Pilot Regulations," *TBC*, 24 Oct 1869, 3.

8 "The Ball at Government House," *TBC*, 13 December 1866, 3.

9 Martin Robin, *The Rush for Spoils: The Company Province, 1871–1933* (Toronto: McClelland and Stewart, 1972), 57.

10 "The Western Terminus," *TBC*, 26 September 1877, 2.

11 Stephen Kern, *The Culture of Time and Space 1880–1918* (Cambridge, Mass: Harvard University Press, 1983), 17.

12 "The Mission to England," *TBC*, 4 March 1882, 2.

13 "Victoria as Timber Shipping Center," *TBC*, 12 June 1910, 25.

14 "Lower Fraser," *TBC*, 27 July 1873, 3.

15 Most advertised in the *Colonist*, see examples of their posted schedules: *TBC*, 30 July 1888, 3; "Union Steamship Company" *TBC*, 20 November 1898, 3.

16 "Trade Competition," *TBC*, 7 Feb 1902, 4.

17 "Victoria the Beautiful," *TBC*, 16 June 1907, 17.

18 "Through to Yale," *TBC*, 13 January 1883, 2–3.

19 "A Missing Yacht," *TBC*, 11 Sept 1884, 2.

20 "Tidal Survey To Benefit Shipping," *TBC*, 10 June 1909, 2; "Collecting data For Tide Tables," *TBC*, 29 April 1910, 1.

21 "An Imperial Frontier," *TBC*, 5 September 1909, 5.

22 Stubbs, "Indian History Recounted by Matriarch," unpaginated clipping from *Comox District Free Press*, 30 October 1952, MS-0436, volume 98, Scrapbook "Comox Valley" II, A.F. Buckham Personal and Professional Papers, Alexander Buckham Fonds, BCA; "Found," *TBC*, 10 July 1896, 2.

23 R.S. Mackie, *Island Timber: A Social History of the Comox Logging Company, Vancouver Island* (Victoria: Sono Nis Press, 2000), 234.

24 William D. Hudson, *Railway and Harbour Report, Vancouver, B.C., to Vancouver Town Planning Commission* (Vancouver: Harland Bartholomew and Associates, September 1927), 9, file PD 631, CVA.

25 Hudson, *Railway and Harbour Report*, 16–18, 25.

26 Letter from Dickie to Harold Brown, Esq., General Manager, Union Steamship Co., Vancouver, BC, 21 June 1939, MS-0006, box 1, Francis Joseph Dickie Papers, BCA.

27 Doreen Armitage, *Around the Sound: A History of Howe Sound-Whistler* (Madeira Park, BC: Harbour Publishing, 1997), 139.

28 T. McCarthy, *Auto Mania: Cars, Consumers and the Environment* (New Haven, CT: Yale University Press, 2007), 41.

29 "Toktie Logs: Sept 16 1939, Sept 4 1941," MS-1636, Diaries, John Barrow Fonds, BCA.

30 Update by the Women's Institute, 8, MS-0436, volume 106, A.F. Buckham Personal and Professional Papers, Alexander Buckham Fonds, BCA.

31 H.L. Cadieux and G. Griffiths, *Dogwood Fleet: The Story of the British Columbia Ferry Authority from 1958* (Nanaimo: Cadieux and Griffith, 1967), 10.

32 Briefing notes for the Minister, 22 December 1975, MS-1246, Box 1, Folder 4, Hilary Brown Papers, Islands Trust Fonds, BCA.

33 "Leisure Island Laughter" manuscript, MS-1176, Frederick Marsh 1888–1951, Frederick Marsh Fonds, 31, 128, BCA.

34 "Roads," Briefing notes for the Minister, 22 December 1975, MS-1246 Box 1, Folder 4, Hilary Brown Papers, Islands Trust Fonds, BCA.

35 Letter dated 30 July 1976 from Kenneth McEwan, Port Manager, North Fraser Harbour Commission to B.E. Marr, Deputy Minister, Dept. of Environment, Victoria. Re: Fraser River Estuary Study, Originals, GR-1002, box 8, BC Environment & Land Use Committee, Administrative Records, BCA.

36 Ports and Harbours, GVRD Lower Mainland Environmental Issues File, submission from BC Environmental Council, 1974, Originals, GR-1002, Box 28, Administrative Records, BCA.

37 Ports and Harbours, Minister of Environment, Canada, press release, 16 March 1979, Originals, GR-1002, Box 28, Administrative Records, BCA.

38 "Ripple Rock Area Probed by Ships—Mighty Blast Believed to Have Ended Menace," *Vancouver Sun*, Saturday 5 April 1958: 1–3, File 567-E-6-5, CVA.

39 Ports and Harbours: Potential Port Industrial Sites SE Vancouver Island file: Ted Burns and Rob Falls, *A Survey of Possible Coastal Industrial Sites on Southeast Vancouver Island from an Ecological Viewpoint.* Confidential and unpublished report prepared for the Fish and Wildlife Branch, Ministry of Recreation and Conservation, Province of BC, November 1977, Originals, GR-1002 box 28, Administrative Records, BCA.

40 "Leisure Island Laughter" manuscript, 439.

2. Empty Land or Stolen Land? The Colonial Strait

1 Letter to Colonial Office from Dundas, Adam, GR-0328 Great Britain, Colonial Office Correspondence, BCA.

2 Sean Miller, *An Environmental History of Latin America* (New York: Cambridge University Press, 2007), 112.

3 Douglas C. Harris, Landing Native Fisheries: Indian Reserves and Fishing Rights in British Columbia, 1849–1925 (Vancouver: University of British Columbia Press, 2008), 9.

4 John Weaver, *The Great Land Rush and the Making of the Modern World* (Montreal: McGill University Press, 2003), 87.

5 Ibid, 176.

6 Letter from James Ed. Fitzgerald (*not* on behalf of HBC) 9 June 1849 to Colonial Office, BCA GR-0328 Great Britain. Colonial Office Correspondence, 22, BCA.

7 Letter from James Ed. Fitzgerald 9 June 1849 to Colonial Office, GR 0328 Great Britain. Colonial Office Correspondence, 38, BCA.

8 Richard S. Mackie, *The Wilderness Profound: Victorian Life on the Gulf of Georgia* (Victoria: Sono Nis Press, 1995), 52.

9 "People in Landscape" series I (Gulf of Georgia), MS 0364 Orchard - Box 4, File 1, 1, BCA.

10 Letter from Rear Admiral P. Hornby, dated 29 August 1849, Valparaiso, GR 0328 Great Britain Colonial Office Correspondence, 88, BCA.

11 *TBC*, 10 Aug 1859, 2.

12 E. Blanche, Norcross (ed.), *Nanaimo Retrospective: The First Century* (Nanaimo: Nanaimo Historical Society, 1979), 19.

13 Sproat's letters to the Minister of the Interior, Ottawa; in Camp, Skwawmish River, Howe Sound, BC, 17 November 1876, 6, RG 10 - T3967, Volume 11028, File SRR-1, UBCLSC.

14 "Will San Juan Be Occupied?" *TBC*, 15 June 1861, 2.

15 Sproat's letters to the Minister of the Interior, 12 December 1876, Comox, Vancouver Island, RG 10 - T3967, Volume 11028, File SRR-1, UBCLSC.

16 "Rumoured Butchery," *TBC*, 26 July 1877, 3.

17 Sproat's letters to the Minister of the Interior, Ottawa, 20 December 1876, 26; 7 January 1877, 4, RG 10 - T3967, Volume 11028, File SRR-1, Nanaimo, VI, UBCLSC.

18 Robert Cail, *Land, Man, and the Law: The Disposal of Crown Lands in BC, 1871–1913* (Vancouver: UBC Press, 1974), 71.

19 Ibid, 246.

20 Ibid, 177.

21 Ibid, 14, 182–3.

22 Sproat's letters to the Minister of the Interior; in Camp, Skwawmish River, Howe Sound, BC, 17 November 1876, 34–35, RG 10 - T3967, Volume 11028, File SRR-1, UBCLSC.

23 Report of the Government of BC on the subject of Indian Reserves, signed by Geo. A. Walkem, Attorney General, Victoria, 17 August 1875, RG 10 - T3967, Volume 11028, File SRR-3, UBCLSC.

24 Memo of the Dept. of the Interior, signed by David Laird, Minister of the Interior, Ottawa, 2 Nov 1874, 47, RG 10 - T3967, Volume 11028, File SRR-3, UBCLSC.

25 Great Britain Emigration Commission, *Vancouver's Island: Survey of the districts of Nanaimo and Cowichan Valley.* Reports by B.W. Pearse and Oliver Wells to accompany their surveys made under J.D. Pemberton, Colonial Surveyor (London: H M Stationary Office, 1859), 6–7, 14.

26 Sproat's letters to the Minister of the Interior, Nanaimo, 20 Dec 1876, 1–6, RG 10 - T3967, Volume 11028, File SRR-1, UBCLSC.

27 Precis of evidence from the hearings 1913, RG 10 - T3962, Volume 11024, File AH3A RC for IA in BC, Cowichan Agency, UBCLSC.

28 "Sketches from the life of Michael Manson," MS 0202 - Michael Manson, 11, BCA.

29 Certified copy of a report of a committee of the Privy Council approved by his Excellency the Governor General in Council on 7 July 1883, 216, RG 10 - C13914, Volume 1330, IA Cowichan Agency, Incoming Correspondence, 1882–84, UBCLSC.

30 Jean Barman, "Erasing Indigeneity in Vancouver: The unsettling of Kitsilano and Stanley Park" in Richard Mackie and Graeme Wynn, eds., *Home Truths* (Vancouver: UBC Press, 2012), 174.

31 Editorial in *Victoria Daily Times*, 19 April 1913, cited in Barman, "Erasing Indigeneity," 186.

32 Correspondence on 12 Jan 1916 by Secretary of Royal Commission on Indian Affairs in BC to Duncan Scott, Dept. of the Superintendent General of IA, 4, RG 10 - T3957, Volume 11020, File 517, UBCLSC.

33 Sixteen-page report on a conference with the Royal Commissioners by reps of the Dominion and Provincial Fisheries Department and DIA, 15, RG 10 - T3957, Volume 11020, File 517, UBCLSC.

34 Dianne Newell, *Tangled Webs of History: Indians and the Law in Canada's Pacific Coast Fisheries* (Toronto: University of Toronto Press, 1993), 89.

35 Correspondence of the Chief Inspector: Letter of 21 June 1913 from Chief Inspector, Dominion Fisheries, BC, DMF, New West, to McGregor Young, RG 10 - T3957, Volume 11020, File 517. UBCLSC.

36 Letter to the Attorney General of BC from Secretary of the RC on IA, 16 February 1914, and attached "Memorandum for the Commission re: hunting and game laws and relaxation of same for benefit of Indians," RG 10 - T3956, Volume 11020, File 516, UBCLSC.

37 Precis of evidence from the hearings 1913, 38–9, 89, RG 10 - T3962, Volume 11024, File AH3A. RC for IA in BC - Cowichan Agency, UBCLSC.

38 Ibid, 100–4.

39 Jeanette Taylor, *Tidal Passages: A History of the Discovery Islands* (Madeira Park, BC: Harbour Publishing, 2008), 115.

40 Letter to the Attorney General of BC from Secretary of the RC on IA, 16 February 1914 and attached "Memorandum for the Commission re: hunting and game laws and relaxation of same for benefit of Indians," RG 10 - T3956—Volume 11020 - File 516, UBCLSC.

41 MS-1176 - Frederick Marsh fonds, "Leisure Island Laughter," 543, BCA; MS-1636 - Francis John Barrow collection, BCA.

42 "Leisure Island Laughter" manuscript, MS 1176 - Frederick Marsh fonds, 38a, BCA.

43 Thomas King, *The Inconvenient Indian—A Curious Account of Native People in North America* (Toronto: Doubleday, 2012), 72.

44 Correspondence 1914–1943 re: Re: foreshore (riparian) rights and uses at various reserves, including Musqueam, Squamish, Sechelt, Klahoose bands and re: Municipality of N. Vancouver's attempt to take over Mission IR No 1 and remove Indians (1921), RG 10 - T 3954, File 987/31-7, UBCLSC.

45 Letter from Andrew Paull, Secretary, the Progressive Native Tribes of BC, 27 January 1937 to T.A. Crerar, MP, Supt. General of Indian Affairs, Ottawa, RG 10 - T 3953, File 978/ 31-2, UBCLSC.

46 Letter from J.E. Michaud, Minister of Fisheries, 21 May 1937, to CD Howe, Acting Minister, Dept. of Mines and Resources, RG 10 - T 3953, File 978/ 31-2, UBCLSC.

47 Supplementary to section 74–84, General Instructions to Indian Agents, Duncan C. Scott, Deputy Superintendent General, IA, DIA, Ottawa, 26 January 1916, RG 10 - T 3954, File 987/33-14 UBCLSC.

48 Ibid.

49 Ibid.

50 Correspondence about road through Malahat IR 11 of Saanich Indians and Mill Bay ferry terminus within the Malahat IR, 1924–1929: Letter of 23 July 1924 from Public Works Engineer Philip to Indian Commissioner Ditchburn, RG 10 - T3952, File 974/31, 4 -14 -11, UBCLSC.

51 Letter from Indian Agent Lomas, 1 August 1924, to Public Works Engineer; 28 May 1929 letter from Indian Commissioner Ditchburn to P. Philip, Deputy Min. and Public Works Engineer, Victoria, RG 10 - T3952, File 974/31, 4 -14 -11, UBCLSC.

52 BC's Centennial Committee, 1958. BC Official Centennial Record: 1858–1958: A century of progress (Vancouver: Evergreen Press). Cited in Arn Keeling, "The Effluent Society: Water Pollution and Environmental Politics in British Columbia, 1889–1980" (PhD thesis, Department of Geography, UBC, 2004), 288.

53 Indians of the Gulf, 3, MS-0364 Orchard - Box 4 File 2 #20 BCA.

54 To borrow the expression used by Shepherd Kretch in The Ecological Indian: Myth and History (New York: W.W. Norton, 2000).

55 Roadside panels were produced for the Department of Highways by the Archaeological Sites Advisory Board of BC, in Letter of 23 May 1978 from Bob Broadland, Chief, Heritage Administration Division, HCB, to J. Hendrickson, Victoria, re: Ministry of Highways, Spectralite Signs, MS-2009 Margaret Ormsby's records - BOX 3, File 7, File 3-2-15-11-4 Historic Markers: 1, BCA.

56 Memorandum dated 8 March 1976 from Provincial Archaeologist, Dept. of Provincial Secretary, Archaeological Sites Advisory Board of Brit. Columbia to Hilary Brown, Islands Trust, Ministry of Municipal Affairs, MS 1246 - Islands Trust Fonds 1974–76, Box 1, BCA.

57 Christine Cummins et al., Impact of the Salmonid Enhancement Program on Native People (Vancouver: Environment Canada, Fisheries and Marine, 1978), GR-1002, Box 37, File: SEP Native Program, 25, BCA.

3. Resource Mining by the Sea: Mining and Forestry

1 Roderick Haig-Brown, undated (but circa early 1960s), unpublished 44-page typed manuscript (draft chapter?) entitled The Pacific Northwest—Doubleday, 26, RHB papers, BN 58-1, UBCLSC.

2 Letter dated 28 May 1849 from James Douglas, Chief Factor, HBC at Fort Nisqually, Puget Sound, to J. Shepherd, GR-0328 Great Britain. Colonial Office Correspondence, 92–93: BCA.

3 Great Britain Emigration Commission. Vancouver's Island: Survey of the Districts of Nanaimo and Cowichan Valley. Reports by B.W. Pearse and Oliver Wells to accompany their surveys made under J.D. Pemberton, Colonial Surveyor. London: H M Stationary Office, 1859, 7.

4 "To Advertisers. To Agents." TBC, 27 Nov 1868, 2.

5 Cail, Land, Man, Law, 246–47.

6 "The last quarter century," handwritten, undated (1942 or 1943), unpaginated 11-page manuscript, RHB papers, BN 55-8, UBCLSC.

7 Ibid.

8 Ibid.

9 Ibid.

10 Ibid.

11 Ibid.

12 Elda Copley Mason, Lasqueti Island: History and Memory (Lantzville, BC: Byron Mason, 1991), 192.

13 "Leisure Island Laughter," 440, 457, 462, MS-1176 - Frederick Marsh fonds, BCA.

14 Extracted from the text of a 1967 MacMillan Bloedel brochure, cited in Richard Rajala, Clearcutting the Pacific Rain Forest: Production, Science and Regulation (Vancouver: UBC Press, 1998), 221.

15 "The Pacific Northwest," 44, RHB papers, BN 58-1, UBCLSC.

16 Letter to Superintendent of Lands, from a citizen in Heriot Bay, 8 August 1966, GR 1614 Parks and Outdoor Recreation Division, BOX 25, File 1.6.3.310, BCA.

4. Resource Mining in the Sea: Fish and Oysters

1 Callum Roberts, The Unnatural History of the Sea (Washington, DC: Island Press, 2007), 144.

2 Thomas Huxley, Inaugural Address to Fisheries Exhibition, London, 1883.

3 "Coffin on British Columbia," TBC, 5 June 1873, 2.

4 "Lower Fraser," TBC, 27 July 1873, 3.

5 Sproat's letters to the Minister of the Interior, Ottawa; in Camp, Skwawmish River, Howe Sound, BC, 17 Nov 1876, RG 10 - T3967, Volume 11028, File SRR-1, UBCLSC.

6 "Ships and Shipping," TBC, 2 August 1896, 3.

7 "Harvest of the Sea," TBC, 16 Jan 1898, 27; Newell, Pacific Salmon Canning, 242–3.

8 "Leisure Island Laughter," 124, MS-1176 - Frederick Marsh fonds, BCA.

9 Memorandum Respecting Salmon Fishery Regulations for the Province of BC, December 29, 1919, Memorandum from William Sloan, Commissioner of Fisheries, Province of British Columbia, to Hon. C.C. Ballantyne, Minister of Marine and Fisheries, Ottawa, GR-1118, BC Marine Resources Branch - Box 8 File 10, BCA.

10 The Vancouver Sun reported in an article on 23 Oct 1972 entitled "Salmon pack trailing 1971" that the total 1972 pack to mid-October was 1,049,850 cases compared to 1,401,121 in 1971, of which Coho was 82,860 compared with 215,189 cases the year before and Sockeye 312,304 compared with 567,831 in 1971.

11 R. Haig-Brown, "Moran Dam," 26, RHB papers, BN 146-5, UBCLSC.

12 R. Haig-Brown, "Canada's Pacific Salmon," 39, RHB papers, BN 137-3, UBCLSC; W.R. Hourston, "Roderick Haig-Brown," Waters: The Journal of the Vancouver Aquarium, 2, 3, (1977), 2, RHB papers, BN 146-7, UBCLSC.

13 Peter Larkin, "Maybe you can't get there from here: A foreshortened history of research in relation to management of Pacific Salmon," Journal of the Fisheries Research Board of Canada 36 (1978), 98–106.

14 Unpublished typed manuscript of address to Pacific Fishery Biologists, 26 March 1965, 4, RHB paper, BN 58-1, UBCLSC.

15 Peter Larkin, "Maybe you can't get there from here."

16 Carl Walters, Undated proposal in the file entitled *"Specific issues to be addressed with the model,"* GR-1002 BC ELUC Secretariat, Originals 1972–1980, Box 37, File: PAD (Program Assessment and Development) Group BCA. This problem of initial surges in hatchery populations followed by collapses is also seen in reservoirs created behind large dams.

17 Geoff Meggs, *Salmon: The Decline of the British Columbia Fishery* (Vancouver and Toronto: Douglas and McIntyre, 1991), 177.

18 Peter Pearse, Public Management and Mismanagement of Natural Resources in Canada, *Queen's Quarterly* 73 (1966) cited in: Nelson, *Seaspace*, 53.

19 G.A. Fraser, License Limitation in the BC Salmon Fishery. Technical Review Series No. PAC/T-77-13, Vancouver: Dept. of the Environment, Economic and Special Industry Services Directorate, Pacific Region, 1977, cited in Newell, *Tangled Webs*, 5–6, 50.

20 Environment Canada, *Major Development program to double BC Salmon output*. New Release from Information Branch of the Fisheries and Marine Service, Environment Canada, Ottawa, 24 March, 1975, GR-1002, BC ELUC Secretariat. Originals 1972–1980. Box 37 Salmonid Enhancement Program, General, BCA.

21 Ibid.

22 Norman Hacking, "Fisheries research program a farce?" *The Province*, 11 May, 1976: 16, GR-1002, BC ELUC Secretariat, Originals 1972–1980. BOX 37 Salmonid Enhancement Program, General, BCA.

23 Larry Still, "Government ready to get tough to protect salmon fishery," *Vancouver Sun*, 13 May 1978; B7, GR-1002 BC ELUC Secretariat, Originals 1972–1980, BOX 37, File #2, March 1977–August 1978, correspondence, BCA.

24 R. Haig-Brown, undated, "Some thoughts of paradise," 7, RHB papers, BN 138-5, UBCLSC.

25 Burns, J.E. 1969. "Some Notes on the Importance of Streamside Vegetation to Trout and Salmon in BC." Unbound 17 page report in file by J.E. Burns, Nanaimo, BC, 25 Nov 1969, 10, GR-1118, BC Marine Resources Branch - Box 12, BCA.

26 R. Haig-Brown, "Fish hatcheries: No substitute for stream protection," *BC Outdoors* (August 1973), 1621, RHB papers, BN 146-6, UBCLSC.

27 *Report on Pollution Control Objectives for the Forest Products Industry of BC as a result of a public enquiry held by the director of the Pollution Control Branch* (Victoria: Queen's Printer, September 1971), GR-1118: BC Marine Resources-Branch - Box 12, Department of Lands, Forests and Water Resources, Water Resources Service, 1972, BCA.

28 "Puntledge River pollution inquiry: A Submission to the Puntledge River Inquiry by BC Department of Recreation and Conservation, Fish and Game Branch, March 1962," GR-1027, op. cit. File 3; Puntledge River Inquiry Rebuttal by Department of Fisheries, Canada, 19 March 1962, 20-page unbound document, GR-1027, Originals, 1920–1977, Box 125, BCA.

29 R. Haig-Brown. "To the Small Boat Fleet Gathered in English Bay, Sunday, 11 June 1972." *BC Environment News* 1 (1972): 8, RHB papers, BN 146-5, UBCLSC.

30 R. Haig-Brown interview 1969 (Part of Imbert Orchard records), T0834: 0002 of Description Number AAAB0925, BCA.

31 Letter of 8 April 1974 from T.R. Andrews, Fisheries Biologist, BC govt. to Dr. T.R. Parsons, Institute of Oceanography, UBC, BCA, GR-1118: BC Marine Resources Branch, Box 5, File 12 BIO-04 Aquaculture - General 1974–1976; press release of 29 March 1974 from Honourable Gary V. Lauk, Minister of Industrial Development, Trade and Commerce, Ibid., File 13, "Mariculture," "Mariculture."

32 Confidential memo re: fish farming in Western Canada, dated 15 March 1974 from W.E. Johnson, Senior Director, Fisheries R and D, Pacific Region, to Management Committee, Fisheries and Marine Service, Dept. of the Environment, GR-1118, BC Marine Resources Branch, Box 5, BCA.

33 Moccasin Valley Mariculture (Meneely): Letter of 8 November 1973 from Jack Radford, Minister of Recreation and Conservation, Victoria, to Jack Davis, Minister of Dept. of Environment, Ottawa, GR-1118, Box 5, File 16, BCA; Leslie Yates, "Fish farm working despite difficulties," *The Peninsula Times*, Wednesday. 27 August 1975: 1.

34 Howard White, *The Sunshine Coast* (Madeira Park, BC: Harbour Publishing, 1996), 45.

35 Infractions and complaints (shellfish), GR-1118, BC Marine Resources Branch, Box 8, File 10, BCA.

36 SFP 01 Oyster regulations and policy, 1966–1975, GR-1118, Box 16, File 1, BCA; 22 Feb 1973 News Release from Office of Minister of Department of Recreation and Conservation, Bob Williams, GR-1118, op. cit.

37 Memo of 30 April 1970 from A.G. Karup, Inspector to R.G. McMynn, Director, Commercial Fisheries Branch re: Nelson and Hardy Island Closure, "Rolph Bremer," GR-1118, op. cit., File 2.

38 Memo of 19 October 1972 from Director of Commercial Fisheries Branch, R.G. McMynn, to Lloyd Brooks, Deputy Minister of Department of Recreation and Conservation re: Lot 250 Sibell Bay (Ladysmith Harbour), Box 23, File 1.6.2.144, GR 1614, BCA.

5. The Strait as Waste Dump

1 Government of Canada, *Water works and sewerage systems of Canada*, Commission of Conservation (Ottawa: Mortimer, 1916), TD 227 C35 1916, CVA.

2 Meggs, *Salmon*, 69.

3 Letter of 10 October 1919 from Miss Winifred Philpot, Parksville, BC to Chief Sanitary Inspector, Provincial Board of Health, Victoria, GR-0132: BC Dept. of Health and Welfare, Originals 1898–1957, Box 25, File 13: Water, BCA.

4   File 25, Water Nanaimo District, 1924–36, GR-0132, BCA. Correspondence through the 1920s and into the 1930s reveals much abiding concern about the threat of typhoid.

5   Toktie Logs: 9 July 1934, MS-1636 Francis John Barrow collection, BCA.

6   GR-0132: BC Dept of Health and Welfare. Originals, 1898–1957, Box 7, BCA: The exchange of letters between residents, the provincial health department and BC Packers executives starts in April 1941 and continues until August 1943.

7   R. Haig-Brown, "To the Small Boat Fleet Gathered in English Bay, Sunday, 11 June 1972," *BC Environment News* 1, 2 (July 1972), 7, RHB papers, BN 146-5, UBCLSC.

8   Handwritten 16-page untitled manuscript dated 1969, BN 55-8, UBCLSC; R. Haig-Brown interview 1969, Imbert Orchard records: T0834: 0002 of Description Number AAAB0925, BCA.

9   Handwritten 16-page manuscript of speech in Spokane to Pacific North West Tourism Association 18 April 1967, RHB papers, BN 55-6, UBCLSC.

10 R. Haig-Brown, *Pollution for Profit*. Handwritten manuscript, 1969, RHB papers, BN 55-8, UBCLSC.

11 Press release of the Pollution Control Board of BC, 14 March 1969, File 146 B 1 4, CVA.

12 In 1963, 1964 and 1965, the discrepancy between GVS&DD and the City of Vancouver average coliform readings at Kitsilano Beach was 230 versus 700, 430 versus 1,100 and 230 versus 790, respectively. McGeer meanwhile suggested a maximum acceptable count in beach water of 240 per 100 millilitres, in Patrick McGeer, "A Brief to the Mayor and Aldermen, City of Vancouver re: The Pollution of Vancouver Waters," 24 June 1969; and A. Goldie & C.J. Keenan, *Pollution and the Fraser* (Victoria: Pollution Control Board, 1968), cited in McGeer, "A Brief," all in File 19 G 4 2 C, CVA.

13 Press release for an address by Ray Williston, Minister of Lands, Forests and Water Resources, 23 October 1969, cited in McGeer, "A Brief"; Iain Hunter, "Berger calls Loffmark unhorsed pollution fighter," *Vancouver Sun*, 1 Feb 1969: 13.

14 Memorandum dated 29 April 1970 from Deputy Minister of Water Resources to Mr. F.S. McKinnon, Chairman, PCB, regarding storm overflow discharge from combined sewerage systems, GR-1118: BC Marine Resources Branch - Box 12, File 29, BCA.

15 Harry Rankin, *Pollution: Suicide or Survival* (Vancouver: Broadway Printers, 1970), 13–15, in File 46 A 2 19, CVA.

16 Ibid., 16.

17 Ibid., 16–17.

18 Ibid., 24.

19 News release, 1 November 1972, from Minister of Lands, Forests and Natural Resources, GR-1118: BC Marine Resources Branch - Box 12, File 29, BCA.

20 Gary Gallon, "SPEC's Roots," in twentieth anniversary edition of *Spectrum* (Winter 1989), 5–10, MSS 1556, SPEC Fonds, Box 729 D 6, File 4, CVA; J.W. Parlour, and S. Schatzow, "The mass media and public concern for environmental problems in Canada, 1960–1972," *International Journal of Environmental Studies* 13, 1 (1978), 9–17, cited in Arn Keeling, *The Effluent Society: Water Pollution and Environmental Politics in British Columbia, 1889–1980* (PhD thesis, Department of Geography, UBC, 2004), 320.

21 R.E. Thomson's 1981 "Oceanography of the BC Coast" and the DFO's 1983 "Current Atlas Juan de Fuca to Strait of Georgia," both cited thus in letter of 19 Dec 1985 from B.F. Talbot, Senior Assistant Engineer, GVRD, to J.R. Rawsthorne, Commodore, Eagle Harbour Yacht Club re: water quality in Eagle Harbour, File 243 D 6 5, CVA.

22 Richard S. Mackie, *Hamilton Mack Laing: Hunter-Naturalist* (Victoria: Sono Nis Press, 1985), 150.

23 "Testing For Oil" *TBC*, 15 October 1902, 1; Gulf Islands coal report: Buckham's summary of "bore holes" includes reference to the Saturna Island drilling, MS-0436, Alexander Buckham, Box 65, File 14, BCA.

24 Rankin, *Suicide or Survival*, 9.

25 Dept. of Fisheries, "Jack Davis forbids seismic exploration in Georgia Strait," press release of the Department of Fisheries, Pacific Region, Vancouver, cited in Nelson, *Seaspace*, 140.

26 CVA File 594 C 9 13, Undated copies of telegrams from Robin Harger, Vice President, SPEC, and Irving Stowe, Director, Sierra Club of BC, to Jack Davis and Frank Richer.

27 Anonymous report dated 21 June 1955 on "Pollution of the Sea by Oil" from the Department of Transport, File 567 E 6 10, Ottawa, CVA; Letter of 4 Oct 1956 from W.A. Sankey, Secretary of the Vancouver Chamber of Shipping to Capt. Johnson, Port Manager, National Harbours Board, Vancouver, File 567 E 6 11, CVA; Letter of 18 July 1960 from Alan Cumyn, Director, Marine Regulations, Dept. of Transport, to the Coastwise Operators Association of BC, Vancouver, File 567 E 6 11, CVA.

28 These were refineries of the sort that fuelled novelist Malcolm Lowry's nightmares on Burrard Inlet.

29 Battelle Memorial Institute and Pacific Northwest Laboratories, "Oil Spillage Study: Literature Search and Critical Evaluation for Selection of Promising Techniques to Control and Prevent Damage," report prepared for Department of Transportation and US Coast Guard, Clearinghouse for Federal Scientific and Technical Information (Washington: US Department of Commerce, 1967), cited in Ross, *Oil Pollution*, 60–61.

30 R. Haig-Brown, "Small Boat Fleet," "Pollution and fisheries. Some Broad Comments," notes for address to Fisheries Council of Canada—27th Annual Meeting, Quebec City, 10 May 1972, 8-page typewritten manuscript, RHB papers, BN 138-2, UBCLSC.

31 Colin Clark, "Oil Spill!" *BC Environment News* 1, 2 (July 1972), 9, RHB papers, BN 146-5, UBCLSC.

32 William Ross, *Oil pollution as an international problem; a study of Puget Sound and the Strait of Georgia*, Western Geographical Series No. 6 (Victoria: University of Victoria, Dept of Geography, 1973), 201–4, 228.

33 Adapted from Nelson, *Seaspace*.

34 Letter re: Oil Pollution, 15 Jan 1971, from R.E. Holland, Harbour Master, NHB Port of Vancouver to W. Sankey, Secretary, Vancouver Merchants Exchange, File 567 E 6 12, CVA.

35 Ron Rose, "Giant oil spill defies cleanup," *Vancouver Sun*, 26 January 1973:1.

36 Letter dated 15 March 1973 from Jack Davis, Minister of Environment to Melda Buchanan, Melda Buchanan Collection of the Comox Archive and Museum Society.

37 Ross, *Oil Pollution*, 209; letter of 9 March 1973 to H.O. Buchanan, Regional Director of Ministry of Transport, Vancouver, from M.L. Richardson, Director of Chamber of Shipping of BC re: Oil Spills; reply from Buchanan to Richardson on 15 March 1973, File 567 E 6 13, CVA.

38 Armitage, *Around the Sound,* 203; Nelson, *Seaspace*, 103–6.

39 Keeling, *Effluent Society*, 224.

40 Letter of 5 March 1969 re: Crofton Pulp and Paper from R.G. McMynn, Director, to W.R. Redel, Director of Lands, Department of Lands, Forests and Water Resources, Parks Branch, GR-1118, BOX 16 - File 6 SFL-05 BCFP, BCA.

41 The local RCMP detachment faced problems when officers refused assignment to their Powell River office, located adjacent to the mill, after high rates of cancer were remarked among staff. Two young local women, Ena (Clarke) Stewart and her best friend, devoted long-distance ocean swimmers, both died suddenly of liver cancer within a few months of each other in the late 1950s, after years of swimming near the mill. There were undoubtedly others.

42 The old sulphite mills were also being converted to kraft processes and would all be kraft mills by the 1980s.

43 R. Haig-Brown interview, 1969, Imbert Orchard records, T0834: 0002 of Description Number AAAB0925, BCA; *Pollution for Profit*, handwritten 16-page manuscript dated 1969, RHB papers, BN 55-8, UBCLSC.

44 SPEC Brief: "A big pulp mill spews as much waste as a city of 100,000," *Georgia Straight*, 19–26 August 1970; SPEC Fonds MSS 1556, Box 729, A2 file 6, CVA: Article cites the following report by R.E. McLaren and K.J. Jackson, "The Impact of Water Pollution on the Uses for Water—Fisheries," Canadian Fisheries Report 8–12, 1966.

45 Adapted from SPEC brief, "A big pulp mill."

46 Barry Broadfoot, "Pollution inquiry expert discounts pulp mill threats," *Vancouver Sun*, 21 August 1970:15, SPEC Fonds MSS 1556, Box 729, A2 file 6, CVA; "Angry group wages pollution battle," *The Province*, 3 Sept 1970, 27, SPEC Fonds, op. cit.; Rankin, *Suicide or Survival*, 13.

47 Alan Mettrick, "Georgia Strait isn't polluted," *Vancouver Sun*, 21 December 1970: 35.

48 Barry Broadfoot, "Pollution inquiry expert discounts pulp mill threats," *Vancouver Sun,* 21 August 1970: 15.

49 "Davis cites new legislation—Pulp water pollution end forecast." *Vancouver Sun*, 5 Oct 1970: 13; "Conform or close," *Canadian Pulp and Paper Industry Magazine* 23 (3 March 1970), cited in Keeling, *Effluent Society*, 249.

50 Charles J. Keenan, *Environmental Anarchy: The Insidious Destruction of Social Order: A Legacy of the Sixties* (Victoria: Cappis Press, 1984), 80–88, cited in: Keeling, "Effluent Society":250.

51 R. Haig-Brown, *Pollution for Profit*.

52 Stephen Hume, "Extreme view on pulp pollution gets some hefty support," *Vancouver Sun*, 4 June 1990.

53 Adapted from T.C. Lemprière, "Environmental impacts and economic costs: A study of pulp mill effluent in BC" (MSc. thesis, University of British Columbia, 1995).

54 Ibid.

55 Stephen Hume, "Shellfish farmers brace for a 'creeping Chernobyl,'" *Vancouver Sun*, 30 December 1991.

56 Rankin, *Suicide or Survival,* 5–6.

57 Their perception of cynicism was accurate. Working in the new field of environmental consulting in the early 1980s, I was with a firm that did many of the studies required by the province's mining industry to obtain permits in that decade. My boss imparted a simple strategy for ensuring clients' success with the regulatory agencies: "Look 'em in the eye and lie like a bastard."

58 Letter of 2 July 1948 from C.R. Stonehouse, Chief Inspector, to Central Vancouver Island Health Unit, Nanaimo, BC, re: Water sample—H.R. MacMillan, Summer Home, Qualicum Beach, GR-0132: BC Dept. of Health and Welfare Originals, 1898–1957- Box 26, Files 1, Water—Nanaimo—Central Vancouver Island Health Unit (1941–1952), BCA.

59 "Summary Report of Water Quality Evaluation of Comox Harbour and Associated Environs," ELUC Provincial Interagency Evaluation of Comox Harbour. March 1975 (unbound report), GR-1002, BCELUC Secretariat, Originals 1972–1980, Box 28, Ports and Harbours ELUC Secretariat, 1975, BCA.

60 Letter of 23 April 1981 from Associated Engineering to Chairman and Members of Pollution Control Board, Victoria re: Regional District of Comox Strathcona Pollution Control Permit, PE 5856, Summary and Rebuttal of Appeal Hearing Held at Comox, 7–9 April 1981, 8–16, "Save our Strait from Sewage" file, Melda Buchanan Collection of the Comox Archive and Museum Society.

61 Ibid.

62 "How's Pollution on the Fraser?" *Vancouver Province*, 2 October 1958, cited in Keeling, *Effluent Society*, 89.

63 Erwin Kreutzweiser, "City to Eliminate Polluted Beaches," *Vancouver News Herald*, 18 August 1949; "Controversy Rages over Beach Pollution," *Vancouver News Herald*, 19 August 1949; "City's Beaches Disease Free," *Vancouver News Herald*, 22 August 1949, all cited in Keeling, *Effluent Society,* 46, 66.

64 A.M. Rawn, 1960, "Fixed and changing values in ocean disposal of sewage and wastes," in E.A. Pearson, ed. *Proceedings of the First International Conference on Waste Disposal in the Marine Environment*, University of California–Berkeley, 22–25 July 1959, cited in Dolin, *Political Waters*, 58–59.

65 Letter of 17 May 1958 from Bruce Forrest of the Lower Kitsilano Ratepayers' Association to Premier W.A.C. Bennett re: appeal of the Municipality of Richmond pending on approval of the Iona Island primary treatment sewage plan, citing the 1953 Rawn Report, File 594 G 2 18, CVA.

66 Letter of 22 April 1957 from Harcourt Roy, President of BC Physical Fitness Association to the Editor, *Vancouver Province* re: Water Pollution, File 594 G 2 18, CVA.

67 "City beaches stay open—new talks due Monday," *Vancouver Province*, 1 August 1958, 1, File 36 A 7 109, CVA; "Must beaches be barricaded before the council acts?" Editorial, *Vancouver Sun*, 6 August 1958, 4, op. cit.

68 "City fumbling beach issue," Editorial, *Vancouver Sun*, 4 August 1958, 4, File 36 A 7 109, CVA.

69 Statement Regarding English Bay Water Quality by Commissioner of Greater Vancouver Sewerage and Drainage District, dated 17 September 1965, File 146 B 1 2, CVA.

70 "Some last, lingering doubts," Editorial, *Vancouver Province*, 23 October 1958, File 36 A 7 109, CVA.

71 City of Vancouver memo from City Clerk to Medical Health Officer re: Water Pollution in Vancouver Harbour, 1973, File 19 G 4 2, CVA.

72 "Water for Tomorrow—Time for Action" SPEC Fonds MSS 1556 Box 729 D 5, File 14, CVA.

73 Manager's Report to the Standing Committee on Finance and Administration, 31 October 1984, re: False Creek Water Quality—Improvement Options, File 239 E 6 5, CVA.

6. Recreation on the Restorative Strait

1 "From the East Coast," *TBC*, 9 July 1866, 3.

2 From an article in *BC Historical Quarterly* of April 1939 by Judge F.W. Howay; in Wolferstan, *Pacific Yachting*, 45.

3 BCA MS-1176 - Frederick Marsh fonds, "Leisure Islands," 480.

4 "For Sale," *TBC*, 13 May 1893, 1.

5 "Farm Land Selling in the Gulf Islands," *TBC*, 2 November 1907, 7.

6 "The Islands," *TBC*, 9 April 1907, 15.

7 "Are You Seeking an Investment?" *TBC*, 16 May 1909, 27; "News of the City—Pier Island sold," *TBC*, 7 June 1910, 6.

8 "The Island Of Death," *TBC*, 16 June 1895, 3.

9 "Quisisana," *TBC*, 20 May 1910, 11.

10 James P. Delgado, *Waterfront: The Illustrated Maritime Story of Greater Vancouver* (Vancouver: Vancouver Maritime Museum, 2005), 74.

11 "A Pleasure Trip," *TBC*, 15 July 1906, 3.

12 "Change in the Game Laws," *TBC*, 19 Feb 1908, 7.

13 "Buy Gulf Islands as Game Reserves" *TBC*, 22 December 1906, 1. This article reported that the Englishman G.L. Findlay was "struck with the climate and...the plenitude of the game."

14 "Travellers See the Whaler in Operation," *TBC*, 8 December 1907, 10; "Island's North End," *TBC*, 22 December 1907, 32; "The Black Diamond City," *TBC*, 5 April 1896, 11; "Take a trip on the Iroquois Sunday and you will be delighted," *TBC*, 12 August 1905, 5.

15 "Picturesques Pt. Comfort," *TBC*, 1 January 1893, 14.

16 "Willows," *TBC*, 29 June 1904, 6.

17 T.L. Grahame, "The Coward—The story of a fight," *TBC*, 2 August 1903, 9.

18 MS-0364 Orchard - Box 4, File 2, BCA.

19 "Leisure Island Laughter," 553.

20 Jeanette Taylor, *The Quadra Story: A History of Quadra Island* (Madeira Park, BC: Harbour Publishing, 2009), 169.

21 "Leisure Island Laughter," 331.

22 Ronald MacIsaac et al., *Brother XII: The Devil of Decourcy Island* (Victoria: Porcepic Books, 1989), 26.

23 "Leisure Island Laughter," 169–70.

24 White, *Sunshine Coast,* 44.

25 Gerald A. Rushton, *Whistle Up the Inlet: The Union Steamship Story* (Vancouver: J.J. Douglas, 1974), cited in City of Vancouver Archives, *Port Watch—A Retrospective Look at 100 Years of Ships and Shipping in Vancouver Harbour* (Vancouver: Vancouver City Archives, 1986), 46.

26 Norcross, *Nanaimo's Playground*; Richard S. Mackie, "The Newcastle Island Resort Pavilion" (unpublished manuscript prepared for the Heritage Conservation Branch, Victoria, BC, March 1983).

27 Mackie, "Newcastle Island," 34.

28 Toktie Logs, 9 July 1933, MS-1636, Francis John Barrow collection, BCA.

29 Letter from E.M. Pearse of 12 June 1939 to Lieutenant Governor of BC, Eric Hamber, Government House, Victoria, GR 1614, Parks and Outdoor Recreation Division (re: recreation land) Box 25, Oyster River Park Committee, BCA.

30 Board of Park Commissioners of the City of Vancouver, *The Parks of Vancouver, Canada* (Vancouver: City of Vancouver, 1944). The same introduction was used in Parks Board reports in 1946, 1954 and 1958.

31 CVA, Additional MS 75, vol. 5, cited in Mackie, "Newcastle Island," 14.

32 "Romance of Stump Ranching," MS-1900 Hamilton Laing fonds, Box 17, File 19, 20, BCA.

33 Much to my shock and the horror of his cat-loving neighbours.

34 MS-1900 Hamilton Laing fonds, Box 18, File 11, BCA.

35 "The old Union Steamship General Store building, Bowen Island, BC," unpublished brief prepared for the Provincial Heritage Advisory Board, Heritage Conservation Branch of the Ministry of Recreation and Conservation, by the Bowen Island Park and Store Use Society, April 1979, Volume II ("largely written by author and island resident Barry Broadfoot"), MS-2009 Margaret Ormsby's records, Box 6, File 3, Bowen Island Park and Store Use Society, BCA.

36 Richard Steele, *The First 100 Years: An Illustrated Celebration* (Vancouver: Vancouver Board of Parks and Recreation, 1988), 164–65, 264–66.

37 Nelson, *Seaspace*, 135.

38 Letter from T. Sewell, Secretary of the North Shore Boat Rental Association to T.M. Stephens, Divisional Supervisor, Steamship Inspection Service, Vancouver, 5 Feb 1948, 52 E 1 File 2 Boating—1945–1959, CVA; Letter from C. Smith, President of the North Shore Boat Rental Association to Chief Steamship Inspector, Vancouver, 27 October 1948, op. cit.

39 GR-1002 BC ELUC Secretariat, Originals 1972–1980, BOX 28, BCA: Ownership rates in Nanaimo-Gabriola, Squamish, North Shore, Delta/Surrey/White Rock were between 20 and 30 percent.

40 R. Haig-Brown, and S.B. Smith, foreword to *Distribution and Economics of the BC Sport Fishery—1954* (Victoria: BC Game Commission, 1955), BN 137, UBCLSC. This rapid post-war growth in saltwater angling is also noted, for example, in Newell, *Tangled Webs*; Qureshi, *Environmental Issues*; and Taylor, *The Quadra Story*.

41 "Leisure Island Laughter" manuscript: 2, 259.

42 Sharon Weaver, "First Encounters: 1970s Back-to-the-land Cape Breton, NS, and Denman, Hornby and Lasqueti Islands, BC," *Oral History Forum d'histoire orale* 30 (2010), 19.

43 Des Kennedy, Editorial, *The Denman Rag and Bone*, first issue, May 1974, cited in Weaver, *First Encounters*, 19.

44 BC Ferries Study, GR-1002, BC ELUC Secretariat, Originals 1972–1980. Box 11, BCA.

45 Brad Wylie, *Qualicum Beach: A History of Vancouver Island's Best Kept Secrets,* (Qualicum, BC: Qualicum Beach Historical and Museum Society, 1992), 72.

46 R. Haig-Brown, "Parks and the New Conscience," in *Park News: The Journal of the National and Provincial Parks Association of Canada* 8, 1 (January 1972), 3-4, RHB papers, BN 146-5, UBCLSC.

47 The Fight for Strathcona Park. Handwritten, undated, 9-page manuscript for address to Rod and Gun Club, RHB papers, BN 52-2, UBCLSC.

48 GR 1614 Parks and Outdoor Recreation, Box 26, File 1.6.3.535, BCA.

49 "Undermining the Park System; or Tear It Up. There Might Be a Buck around Somewhere," undated (but apparently mid-1960s) 8-page manuscript, RHB papers, BN 138-7, UBCLSC; R. Haig-Brown, "Resource Management in Canada: A Point of View," unpublished, typed, 33-page manuscript, undated but apparently 1966 or 1967 from context.

50 GR 1614, Box 22, File 1.6.1.351, BCA.

51 GR 1614, Box 26, File 1.6.3.540, BCA.

52 Undated letter from David Anderson to anonymous (name taped over in file) constituent, MS-2042 ANDERSON, David - File 5, BCA.

53 Editorial, *Gulf Islands Driftwood*, 17 December 1971, MS-2042, File 5, BCA.

54 "Gulf Islands US Owned? *Victoria Daily Times*, 21 June 1971: 17, MS-2014, File 5, BCA.

55 Letter dated 24 November 1970 from Jack Davis to Mr. T.W. Cross, Port Credit, Ontario, MS 2042, File 6, BCA.

56 R. Haig-Brown, "Parks and the New Conscience," *Park News—The Journal of the National and Provincial Parks Association of Canada* 8, 1 (January 1972): 3–4. RHB papers, BN 146-5, UBCLSC.

57 Letter of 21 June 1971 re: Strait of Georgia National Marine Park Proposal from Lloyd Brooks, Acting Deputy Minister, to the Hon. K. Kiernan, Minister of Recreation and Conservation, PB, Victoria, GR-1118: BC Marine Resources Branch, Box 8, File 8, BCA; Letter dated 23 February 1983, and from Federal Minister of Environment to an inquiry from a citizen in Nanaimo, GR 1614, Parks and Outdoor Recreation, Box 24, File 1.6.2.406, BCA.

58 Letters from Federal Minister of Environment, 23 Feb 1983, and from provincial Minister of Lands, Parks and Housing, 31 March 1983, to the same inquiry from a citizen in Nanaimo, GR 1614, Parks and Outdoor Recreation, Box 24, File 1.6.2.406, BCA.

59 GR 1614, Parks and Outdoor Recreation, Box 22, File 1.6.1.351, BCA.

60 R. Haig-Brown and S.B. Smith, foreword to *Distribution and Economics of the BC Sport Fishery—1954* (Victoria: BC Game Commission, 1955): 4, RHB papers, BN 137-3, UBCLSC.

61 "Statement for Puntledge River inquiry," handwritten 12-page manuscript dated 1962, RHB papers, BN 54-8, UBCLSC.

62 Underwood, McLellan and Associates, *Mid Coast North Vancouver Island—Mid Coast Queen Charlotte Islands Regional Study* (unpublished, preliminary draft report submitted to ELUC, Victoria, 10 March 1975), GR-1002 BC ELUC Secretariat, Originals 1972–1980, Box 7, BCA.

63 Lena Lencek and Gideon Bosker, *The Beach: The History of Paradise on Earth* (New York: Penguin, 1999), 273.

64 Jes Odam, "Gulf Islands at the crossroad: Water wonderland or just another suburb?" *Vancouver Sun*, 7 December 1971.

65 Kay Alsop, "With her back to the land," *The Province*, 31 Aug 1972.

66 Garret Hardin, "The Tragedy of the Commons," *Science* 162 (1968): 1243–48.

67 "The Policy of the Islands Trust" (Victoria: The Islands Trust, Parliament Buildings, 1975), 2–6, 13–14, MS-1246, Islands Trust Fonds 1974–76, Box 1, Islands Trust, BCA.

68 "The Policy of the Islands Trust," MS-1246, Islands Trust Fonds 1974–76, Box 1, Islands Trust, BCA; briefing notes for the Minister, 22 December 1975, op. cit.

69 Briefing notes for the Minister, 22 December 1975, MS-1246, Islands Trust Fonds 1974–76, Box 1, BCA.

70 Saltspring Island file: Doug Watters, "Are storm clouds clearing from Saltspring Island?" *Monday—Victoria's Magazine*, December 15–21, 1975: 10–11, MS-1246, Box 2, BCA.

71 "Crown jewels," Editorial, *Vancouver Sun*, 28 July 1982; "Ending Islands Trust would bring 'Coney Islands,'" *Vancouver Sun*, 27 July 1982.

72 Des Kennedy, "Whither the Gulf Islands? Nature's largesse spawns a B.C. dilemma," *Canadian Geographic*, 105, 5 (1985), 49.

7. Conclusions and Reflections on the Twenty-First-Century Strait

1 Daniel Pauly, "Anecdotes and shifting baseline syndrome of fisheries," *Trends in Ecology and Evolution* 10 (1995), 430.

2 Roberta Stevenson, "The View from My Desk," *Tidelines, BC Shellfish Growers Quarterly Newsletter* (Fall 2013), 2, accessed 2 June 2014, http://bcsga.ca/wp-content/uploads/2013/09/Tidelines_Fall_2013.pdf.

3 Stephen Hume, "Rising ferry fares, service cuts an 'economic' disaster," *Vancouver Sun*, 8 February 2014: D1; Hume, "Ferry cuts mean lost tourist dollars," *Vancouver Sun*, 1 March 2014: A9.

4 Daniel Wood, "The big chill of ocean warming," *The Georgia Straight*, 20–27 October 2011, 19–21; Kelly Sinoski, "Rising sea levels putting landmarks at risk," *Vancouver Sun*, 4 August 2012: A4.

Index

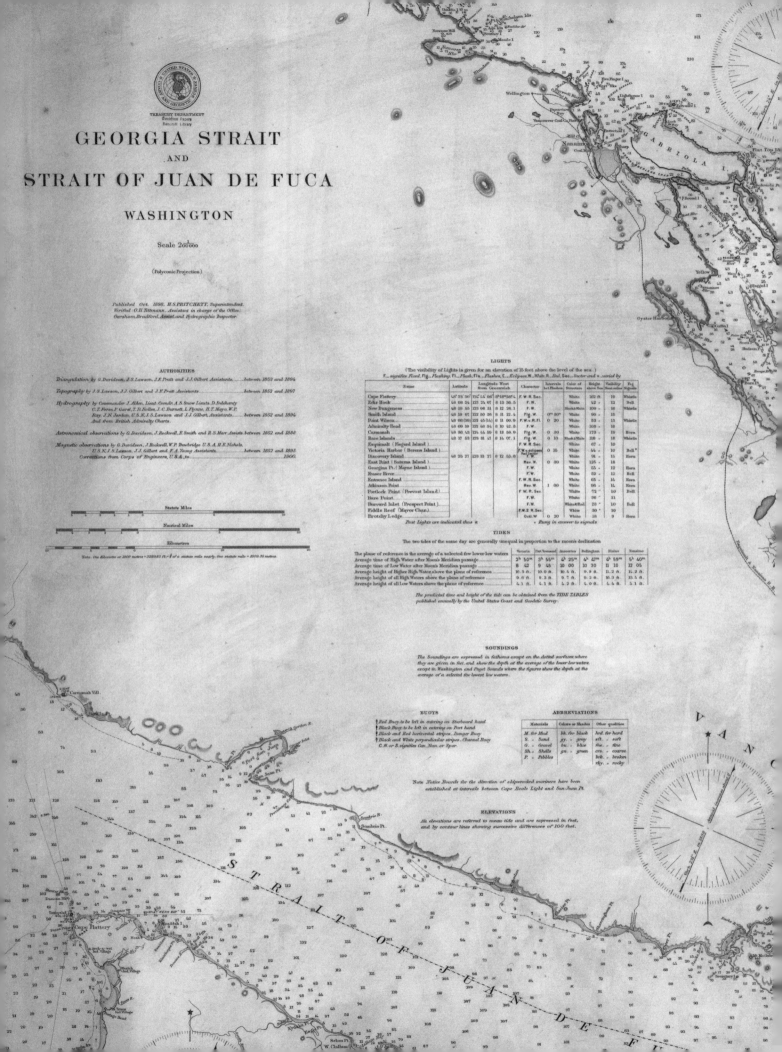